Ancestral Landscapes in
Human Evolution

Ancestral Landscapes in Human Evolution

CULTURE, CHILDREARING AND SOCIAL WELLBEING

Edited by

Darcia Narvaez

Kristin Valentino

Agustín Fuentes

James J. McKenna

and

Peter Gray

Patty, All the best in your vital work! Darcia N 2019

OXFORD
UNIVERSITY PRESS

OXFORD
UNIVERSITY PRESS

Oxford University Press is a department of the University of Oxford.
It furthers the University's objective of excellence in research, scholarship,
and education by publishing worldwide.

Oxford New York
Auckland Cape Town Dar es Salaam Hong Kong Karachi
Kuala Lumpur Madrid Melbourne Mexico City Nairobi
New Delhi Shanghai Taipei Toronto

With offices in
Argentina Austria Brazil Chile Czech Republic France Greece
Guatemala Hungary Italy Japan Poland Portugal Singapore
South Korea Switzerland Thailand Turkey Ukraine Vietnam

Oxford is a registered trademark of Oxford University Press
in the UK and certain other countries.

Published in the United States of America by
Oxford University Press
198 Madison Avenue, New York, NY 10016

Library of Congress Cataloging-in-Publication Data
Ancestral landscapes in human evolution: culture, childrearing and social wellbeing / edited by
Darcia Narvaez, Kristin Valentino, Agustín Fuentes, James J. McKenna, and Peter Gray.
pages cm
Includes index.
ISBN 978-0-19-996425-3
1. Parent and infant. 2. Primates—Behavior. 3. Psychology, Comparative.
4. Evolutionary psychology. 5. Child care. 6. Child rearing. 7. Child development.
I. Narvaez, Darcia.
BF720.P37A53 2014
155.6'46—dc23
2013033876

1 3 5 7 9 8 6 4 2
Printed in the United States of America
on acid-free paper

To the children of the world

{ CONTENTS }

SECTION V: **Child Flourishing**

{ PREFACE }

The impetus for this book was the symposium, *Human Evolution and Human Development*, held in October 2012 at the University of Notre Dame and co-sponsored by the Society for Research in Child Development and the University of Notre Dame's Henkels Lecture Series of the Institute for Scholarship in the Liberal Arts. Many of the presenters at the 2012 symposium agreed to write a chapter for this book. We also included chapters from speakers at the October 2010 symposium (Fry, Fuentes, Roughgarden, Suomi), also held at the University of Notre Dame and entitled, *Human Nature and Early Experience: Addressing the "Environment of Evolutionary Adaptedness."* We invited additional chapters and commentary contributions from other leaders in their respective fields. The result is an interdisciplinary glimpse at culture and early life experience through the prism of evolution, small-band hunter-gatherer society, and mammalian needs.

We thank all the contributors for sharing their insights presented in the various chapters of the book. We were pleased to obtain commentaries on most chapters, mostly from folks not present at the symposium. We thank all for their observations.

{ ACKNOWLEDGMENTS }

The five editors wish to acknowledge the Society for Research in Child Development (SRCD), Notre Dame's Institute for Scholarship in the Liberal Arts Henkels Lecture Series, the Center for Children and Families, and the Department of Psychology who supported the 2012 symposium, *Human Evolution and Human Development*, from which the book emerged.

{ ABOUT THE EDITORS }

Darcia Narvaez, Professor of Psychology at the University of Notre Dame, researches moral development through the life span. Her theories include how early life affects the neurobiology underpinning of moral functioning (triune ethics theory), how evolved parenting practices may foster optimal moral functioning and wellbeing (Evolved Developmental Niche), and how teachers can take steps to foster ethical capacities during regular instruction (integrative ethical education). She is widely published, and her authored and edited books have won several awards. Her forthcoming book is *The Neurobiology and Development of Human Morality*: Evolution, Culture and Wisdom. She is editor of the *Journal of Moral Education* and an active blogger at *Psychology Today* ("Moral Landscapes").

Kristin Valentino is an Assistant Professor of Psychology and the William J. Shaw Center for Children and Families Collegiate Chair at the University of Notre Dame. She earned her B.A. from Georgetown University and her Ph.D. from the University of Rochester. Valentino's research interests are in developmental psychopathology, where she studies how the integration of biological, psychological and environmental factors can inform our understanding of typical and atypical development. Her research focuses on at-risk populations; parent–child interactions; the development of memory, the self, and psychopathology; and the translation of developmental research into interventions for maltreated children and their families.

Agustín Fuentes is Professor of Anthropology at the University of Notre Dame. His current foci include cooperation and bonding in human evolution, ethnoprimatology and multispecies anthropology, evolutionary theory, and public perceptions of, and interdisciplinary approaches to, human nature(s). He is author or editor of 10 books, including *Evolution of Human Behavior, Centralizing Fieldwork: Critical Perspectives from Primatology, Biological and Social Anthropology*, and *Race, Monogamy, and Other Lies They Told You: Busting Myths About Human Nature*. His current research projects include the ethnoprimatology of Singapore, interdisciplinary approaches to understanding human nature(s), and an evaluation of the roles of cooperation, community, and niche construction in human evolution.

James J. McKenna is Rev. Edmund P. Joyce, C.S.C., Professor of Anthropology at the University of Notre Dame. He pioneered the first behavioral and electrophysiological studies documenting differences between mothers and infants sleeping together and apart and has become known worldwide for his work in promoting studies of breastfeeding and mother–infant co-sleeping. A biological anthropologist, he publishes mostly on primate development, infant sleep, breastfeeding, and sudden infant death syndrome, including five books, two of which are *Evolutionary Medicine* and *Evolution and Health* and a popular parenting book entitled *Sleeping With Baby: A Parents' Guide to Co-sleeping,* translated into seven languages. He won the prestigious Shannon Award (with Dr. Sarah Mosko) from the National Institutes of Child Health and Development for his SIDS research.

Peter Gray, Research Professor of Psychology at Boston College, has conducted and published research in neuroendocrinology, animal behavior, developmental psychology, anthropology, and education. He is author of *Psychology* (Worth Publishers, now in its sixth edition), an introductory textbook that views psychology from an evolutionary perspective. His recent research has focused on the role of play in human evolution and how children educate themselves through play. He authors a blog for *Psychology Today* entitled *Freedom to Learn* and is author of *Free to Learn: Why Unleashing the Instinct to Play Will Make Our Children Happier, More Self-Reliant, and Better Students for Life* (Basic Books, 2013).

{ CONTRIBUTORS }

Marc Bekoff, Ph.D.
Department of Ecology and
  Evolutionary Biology
University of Colorado—Boulder

Robyn Bluhm, Ph.D.
Department of Philosophy and
  Religious Studies
Old Dominion University

Frances A. Champagne, Ph.D.
Department of Psychology
Columbia University

Michelle Comas, M.A.
Department of Psychology
University of Notre Dame

Alyssa N. Crittenden, Ph.D.
Department of Anthropology
University of Nevada—Las Vegas

Amanda M. Dettmer, Ph.D.
Laboratory of Comparative Ethology
Eunice Kennedy Shriver National
  Institute of Child Health and
  Human Development
National Institutes of Health

Riane Eisler, J.D., honorary Ph.D.
Center for Partnership Studies
Pacific Grove, California and
  Washington D.C.

Karen L. Endicott, M.A.
Office of Communications, Thayer
  School of Engineering
Dartmouth College

Kirk M. Endicott, Ph.D.
Department of Anthropology
Dartmouth College

Steffen Foerster, Ph.D.
Department of Biology
Columbia University

Douglas P. Fry, Ph.D.
Department of Social Sciences
Åbo Akademi University, Finland
& Bureau of Applied Research in
  Anthropology
University of Arizona

Agustín Fuentes, Ph.D.
Department of Anthropology
University of Notre Dame

Tracy R. Gleason, Ph.D.
Department of Psychology
Wellesley College

Peter Gray, Ph.D.
Department of Psychology
Boston College

Eugene Halton, Ph.D.
Department of Sociology
University of Notre Dame

Barry S. Hewlett, Ph.D.
Department of Anthropology
Washington State
  University—Vancouver

Katie Hinde, Ph.D.
Department of Human Evolutionary
  Biology
Harvard University

Paula Ivey Henry, Ph.D.
Department of Social and Behavioral
  Sciences
Harvard University School of
  Public Health

Michael Jindra, Ph.D.
Department of Anthropology
University of Notre Dame

Kathleen Kendall-Tackett, Ph.D.
Department of Pediatrics, School
  of Medicine
Texas Tech University

Melvin Konner, Ph.D.
Department of Anthropology
Emory University

Ruth A. Lanius, M.D., Ph.D.
Department of Psychiatry
University of Western Ontario

Pierre Lienard, Ph.D.
Department of Anthropology
University of Nevada Las Vegas

Jonathan Marks, Ph.D.
Department of Anthropology
University of North
  Carolina—Charlotte

James J. McKenna, Ph.D.
Department of Anthropology
University of Notre Dame

Wendy Middlemiss, Ph.D.
Department of Educational
  Psychology
University of North Texas

Gilda Morelli, Ph.D.
Department of Psychology
Boston College

Darcia Narvaez, Ph.D.
Department of Psychology
University of Notre Dame

Eric E. Nelson, Ph.D.
Section on Development & Affective
  Neuroscience
National Institutes of Mental Health

Amy K. Nuttall, M.A.
Department of Psychology
University of Notre Dame

Joan Roughgarden, Ph.D.
Department of Biological Sciences
Stanford University

Jennifer W. Roulette, M.A.
Department of Anthropology
Washington State University

Zhiyuan Song, Ph.D.
Department of Biology
Stanford University

Stephen J. Suomi, Ph.D.
Laboratory of Comparative Ethology
Eunice Kennedy Shriver National
  Institute of Child Health and
  Human Development
National Institutes of Health

Kristin Valentino, Ph.D.
Department of Psychology
University of Notre Dame

Baselines for Human Mammalian Development

Children's Development in Light of Evolution and Culture

Darcia Narvaez, Peter Gray, James J. McKenna, Agustín Fuentes, and Kristin Valentino

"All child rearing is based on beliefs about what makes life
manageable, safe, and fertile for the spirit" so that "even with the
best, most rational, kindest advice from outside, child rearing will
likely always be so."
—(Bruner, 2000, p. xii)

Individual humans cannot grow up alone. Like all social mammals, humans need intensive caregiving in early life to survive, thrive, and disperse (Konner, 2010; Williams, 1966). Because child care takes a great deal of energy, mother–child dyads are necessarily aided by families and communities (Hrdy, 2009). Indeed, the contexts for raising children among all human societies include multiple layers of influence and support (Bronfenbrenner, 1979). Culture—socially transmitted and shared beliefs, understandings, and practices—is one of those influences.

Around the world, families and children are embedded in cultures and sub-cultures that support and encourage different approaches to childrearing. Some cultures encourage and others discourage physical closeness, based on potential psychological or physical outcomes; some consider babies to be in need of wooing into interdependence, whereas others consider them to be in need of strict discipline to learn independence (Deloache and Gottlieb, 2000; Doi, 1981; Georgas, Berry, van de Vijver, Kağitçibaşi, and Poortinga, 2006; Levine and Norman, 2001). Even within a particular society, the culture of child caregiving can change over time in terms of family constellation, community traditions, and everyday family pragmatics. Such variations in practices may challenge universalistic models like attachment theory, which affixes attachment labels to particular child behaviors that are matched to particular types of parental behavior (Bowlby, 1969, 1988; Main, 1995). But if some societies encourage psychological distance, demonstrating high levels of social detachment (avoidant attachment), one argue, as some do, that avoidant attachment is adaptive—which is contrary to the claims of attachment theory (Levine and Norman, 2001)?

The book delves into several issues. First, it probes the question of whether there is an optimal range of infant and childhood care and what that might look like. The beneficial or "expectable" range of care might to some degree be inferred from the common dimensions of care in other social mammals, especially primates. We can also discern an expectable range of care from humans living in ways consistent with our evolutionary past, to the degree that we can infer this from diverse lines of evidence. Such evidence includes paleoecological reconstructions and contemporary ethnographic studies elucidating a range of adaptations, beginning with nomadic foragers (also known as small-band hunter-gatherers; we use the term *hunter-gatherer* to represent this type of society). Mobile communities like these represent a characteristic social structure for much of human history up until about 10,000 to 15,000 years ago, when more sedentary, settled societies emerged (though hunter-gatherers have coexisted since then as well; Lee and Daly, 2005).

A second question is whether some societies have stepped out of the optimal range for childrearing (Edgerton, 1992). It can be said, for example, that children who are maltreated (i.e., neglected, abused, traumatized) exist outside the optimal range as inferred from their adult dysfunctions, mental disorders, or addictions, all of which are clinically evident (Lanius, Vermetten, and Pain, 2010). But what about those whose care does not reach the legal or clinically relevant levels of neglect or abuse? Are there other, less obvious forms of infant or child caregiving that damage them in more subtle but still significant ways? Although in the past, and to a certain extent even in the present, wide ranges in early life caregiving were considered fairly harmless, increasing evidence shows that traumatic early life experience can be toxic, with lasting effects on physiological and psychological wellbeing (Shonkoff and Phillips, 2000; Shonkoff and Garner, 2012).[1]

Many investigators concur on the importance of having an empirically based, diverse but solid knowledge foundation regarding "healthy" development, in humans and other animals, in order to understand psychopathology (e.g., Cicchetti and Roisman, 2011; Panksepp, 2001). One can always ask how we will know what is abnormal without having a good sense of what the range of normal is. While recognizing the obvious pitfalls and difficulties of proposing an "optimal range" for our species, given humans' great biological and cultural plasticity, this book intends to raise important new questions that challenge certain assumptions about the appropriateness of infant and child care practices, especially in the industrialized West. At the very least we need to start a conversation that moves toward understanding how to identify social caregiving innovations that push infants and children beyond their adaptive limits. Specifically, we hope to shed light on what the

---

[1] The sister book, *Evolution, Early Experience and Human Development*, addresses this question more directly.

evolved, expectable contexts for mammalian and human development really are. What are optimal and suboptimal contexts for human development? What are the effects on children's development and adult wellbeing of the wildly divergent physical and social habitats in which children grow up today, which require behavioral adjustments that were never tested in an evolutionary context?

We do not idolize ancestral forms of care, nor naively sing their collective praises without realizing that the usefulness of evolved behaviors can change through time. Nor do we dismiss the possibility that traits that may have been adaptive at earlier points in our prehistory are not necessarily compatible with present circumstances (but determining what is adaptive or not is difficult). Indeed, we are mindful of Stephen Jay Gould's insightful perspective that evolution is all about functional change with structural continuity. We certainly should not ignore Sarah Hrdy's whimsical but perceptive comments that "[a] mother today, whether in New York, Tokyo or Dacca is not just a gatherer caught in a shopping mall without her digging stick," nor the point that "continuous contact and proximity and carrying may be what infants want but it might not be what mothers want or more importantly what they can provide" (Hrdy 1999, p. 105). We take such observations seriously and know that translating the research presented in this book into "lessons learned" to apply where we can will not be an easy endeavor. But we are also confident that having a strong, empirically based beginning point, a baseline perspective, is the first step in understanding why infants respond and develop as they do. It will help us understand what can go wrong when estranged or biologically novel, current conditions push infants beyond their adaptive limits. To establish a baseline perspective, we begin with our heritage, what we call here the *ancestral context*.

The Ancestral Context

Mobile hunter-gatherer (hereafter, hunter-gatherer) societies represent a lifestyle that many of our ancient ancestors are presumed to have followed before the advent of agriculture about 10,000 to 15,000 years ago. Although archeology and paleontology provide important information about human ancestry, including inheritances from a long line of other animals including nonhuman primates, studies of contemporary hunter-gatherers offer live glimpses into probable components of humanity's past.

Hunter-gatherers are people who gain their sustenance from hunting wild animals and gathering wild plant materials. Anthropologists commonly distinguish between two categories of hunter-gatherers (Bird-David, 1994; Fry, 2006; Ingold, 1999; Kelly, 1995). One category, typified by the Kwakiutl of the American northwest coast and the Ainu of Japan, is variously referred to as *collector* societies, *delayed-return* hunter-gatherers, or *non-egalitarian* hunter-gatherers. They live in relatively permanent, relatively dense villages located near highly concentrated sources of food (commonly fish). These societies are generally organized hierarchically, much like agricultural tribal societies. The other category, which is more common and is believed to reflect a more basal pattern of social demography, includes those referred to as *band* societies, *immediate-return* hunter-gatherers, or *egalitarian* hunter-gatherers. When anthropologists refer to *hunter-gatherers* or to *foragers*, unqualified, they are usually referring to this category, and that is the convention used in this chapter and elsewhere in the book. We note, however, that the hunter-gatherer societies described in this book, while subsisting largely through foraging, do engage in some farming and trading and therefore are not pure hunter-gatherer societies.

During the 20th century, researchers visited and studied dozens of different hunter-gatherer societies, in various remote parts of the world, some of which had been very little influenced by Western or industrialized contact. Examples of such societies are the *Jul'hoansi* (also called the *!Kung*, of Africa's Kalahari Desert), *Hazda* (of Tanzanian rain forest), *Mbuti* (of Congo's Ituri Forest), *Aka* (of rain forests in Central African Republic and Congo), *Efé* (of Congo's Ituri Forest), *Batek* (of Peninsular Malaysia), *Agta* (of Luzon, Philippines), *Nayaka* (of South India), *Aché* (of Eastern Paraguay), *Parakana* (of Brazil's Amazon basin), and *Yiwara* (of the Australian Desert). There are good archaeological reasons to believe that these societies have core patterns similar to those of the human societies that predominated for at least 40,000 years before the development of agriculture, and possibly for much longer (Boehm, 2008). Although these and other hunter-gatherer groups still exist, their cultures have changed considerably in the past few decades because of pressures from the outside world.

Although there is much variability among small-band hunter-gatherer societies, they do share some remarkable similarities. We draw these generalizations from several sources (Lee and Daly, 1999; Fry, 2006, 2013; Hewlett and Lamb, 2005; Ingold, 1999).

Characteristics Shared Across Groups

Wherever they are found, hunter-gatherer societies display several common characteristics. They generally live in groups of about 20 to 50 people, counting children as well as adults. Each group shifts terrain as needed to follow the available game and edible plants, but moves can also be associated with alliance formation and social relationships between groups (Fry, 2006; Gowdy, 1998, 1999). At each campsite to which they move, families build, from natural materials, small, temporary huts, the construction of which usually takes just a few hours. Because the band moves frequently, material goods beyond what a person can easily carry are burdens, so there is very little accumulation of property.

Characteristics of hunter-gatherers include a companionship lifestyle that involves nonexclusive (widely shared) intimacy, characterized by sharing of company, food, residence, and movement (Bird-David, 1994; Gibson, 1985; Ingold,

1999). Cooperation, sharing, and egalitarianism are common values. To survive, individuals within the group, whether or not they are kin (and mostly they are not), cooperate intensely in hunting, gathering, caring for children, and other activities (Hill et al., 2011). They share food and material goods (50% to 80% on average; B. Hewlett, personal communication, July 22, 2013), often following a general rule that nobody in the group should have more than anyone else. Although each group is an independent entity in which group members make all of the group's decisions, boundaries are fluid, and there is generally a spirit of cooperation with nearby groups. Hunter-gatherers also display common childrearing practices that are shared with Old World primates and social mammals generally but have unique features (e.g., alloparental care, extensive cooperation, co-sleeping beyond childhood, pronounced social learning; Hewlett and Roulette, this volume).

Ancestral Childrearing Practices: The Evolved Developmental Niche

The evolved developmental niche (EDN; Narvaez, Wang, Gleason, Cheng, Lefever, and Deng, 2013) for *young* social mammals emerged more than 30 million years ago, and many of the characteristics of that niche remained true for humans (Konner, 2010). For young children, the EDN includes natural childbirth, extensive and infant-initiated breastfeeding, continuous contact with or proximity to caregivers, responsiveness to the needs of the child, free play in nature with multiple-aged playmates, extensive support of the mother–child dyad, and multiple adult caregivers (Hewlett and Lamb, 2005; Hrdy, 2009; Konner, 2005, 2010). The outcomes for the presence or absence of each of these parenting practices have only recently been studied scientifically, and results indicate that not only physiological but also psychological wellbeing is affected (McKenna, Ball, and Gettler, 2007; Narvaez, Gleason et al., 2013; Narvaez, Panksepp, Schore, and Gleason, 2013a,b; Narvaez, Wang, et al., 2013). For example, significant effects on brain development can be observed when breastfeeding does not occur in the first months of life (Deoni et al., 2013).

Today there are extensive conflicts between human biology and culture patterns (Eaton, Shostak, and Konner, 1988). For example, the emergence of the sudden infant death syndrome epidemic in Western industrialized societies was driven by the adoption of untested sociocultural infant care inventions and their underlying social values: having infants sleep in rooms by themselves (i.e., solitary infant sleep), not breastfeeding, and laying infants prone for sleep (to promote deep sleep) all proved to be independent risk factors for sudden infant death syndrome, leading to as many as a half a million infant deaths (Fitzgerald, 1995). There is no doubt, then, that much harm can be done when evolved developmental patterns are abandoned altogether for cultural reasons without exploration of the possible functionally damaging impacts these changes could have. Is there a core set of needs and practices whose absence impedes wellbeing? Section I of this book addresses this question by focusing on several key features of mammalian parenting.

Cultures have shifted over millennia in terms of how much and what kind of support for child development is provided. On one end are the contexts that more closely follow the human developmental niche, which are found often among small-band hunter-gatherers. Although they experience many ecological and physical hardships, some hunter-gatherer groups experience greater social wellbeing than most in modern societies (e.g., Everett, 2009). Section II focuses on case studies of these groups.

On the other end of the spectrum are modern parenting practices, most of which have diverged greatly from the EDN for young children. The high social embeddedness and multi-aged, cooperative lifestyle of hunter-gatherer culture has been replaced, for example, in the United States with extensive social and age-related isolation and a productivity-focused lifestyle. Instead of a village of playful companionship support, many children do not experience characteristics of the EDN for very long—or worse, they are neglected or abused. Felitti and Anda (2005) suggest that child maltreatment has been experienced by the majority of adults in the United States. Indeed, on July 11, 2013, three agencies of the U.S. government sent a letter to state child welfare agencies to alert them about the issue of childhood trauma (U.S. Department of Health and Human Services, 2013). Currently, maltreatment is affecting approximately 1 million children each year (U.S. Department of Health and Human Services, 2012). Including a focus on the effects of early maltreatment will give insight into the extreme cases of the childrearing context. Section III will focus on issues of harm and maltreatment.

This Book

Overall, the interdisciplinary set of contributors to this book addresses contexts for development, with the aim of increasing understanding of basic mammalian, and human, emotional and motivational needs in varied contexts. In chapters 2 and 3 of this book, neurobiological research is reviewed, demonstrating what happens to development when young mammals do not receive beneficial and normative parenting.

In the first section, the needs of mammalian young are addressed. In chapter 2, "Epigenetics of Mammalian Parenting," Frances Champagne details research on mammalian mother–infant interactions which suggests that maternal tactile stimulation has a profound effect on infant neuroendocrine and behavioral development. Among Long-Evans rats, for example, natural variation in maternal licking/ grooming (LG) of pups, a primary forms of tactile stimulation during the postnatal period, leads to profound consequences for offspring: those who receive low compared with high levels of LG have elevated glucocorticoid levels in response to stress, increased fear reactivity, and impaired learning. Moreover, low LG experienced among female offspring is associated with reduced levels of maternal behavior and increased sexual behavior in adulthood. Focusing on epigenetic mechanisms, which are factors that can change the expression of genes without altering the DNA sequence, Champagne provides evidence to support the hypothesis that maternal touch induces long-term effects on offspring's brain development and behavior. For example, the experience of low LG leads to increased DNA methylation of the *ESR1* gene during postnatal development, and the persistence of this epigenetic effect into adulthood renders low-LG female offspring less sensitive to the priming effects of hormones that normally enhance maternal sensitivity. As such, reduced maternal sensitivity results in decreased LG toward the offspring reared by low-LG females, perpetuating a cycle of low maternal care. Implications of the epigenetic effects of early maternal care on child development and parenting are discussed, including their relevance for human development and evolution.

John Bowlby's delineation of the significance of maternal–infant and infant–maternal attachment and his generic "perceptuo-motor mechanisms" that "tie" infants and mothers together are brought to life by the rich, integrative, endocrinological and psychobiological framework used by Amanda Dettmer, Stephen Suomi, and Katie Hinde in chapter 3, "Nonhuman Primate Models of Mental Health: Early Life Experiences Affect Developmental Trajectories." Using a variety of observational, genetic, and physiological data, the authors provide multiple examples of new research explaining and interpreting the underlying neurohormonal transactions that are affected by, and respond to, the primate infant's developmental conditions. These conditions include deficiencies that require compensatory responses, such as by cortisol, which can lead to more fearfulness, increased inhibition, and less play; on the other hand, they include more favorable environments that provide an abundance of maternal and peer-based social support, producing "confidence" and maximal resilience in individuals experiencing stress.

In the book's second section, contributors explore how those who live in conditions comparable to patterns common in human evolutionary history care for their children. The level of access to their informants, and the detailed observations emerging out of their own important established personal commitments and connections to these communities, reflect the very best of ethnographic research and methods. The authors have immersed themselves in the practices of a particular mobile hunter-gatherer society. A focus on hunter-gatherer contexts can assist us in discerning the range of what is normal or how questions concerning what is optimal social development might be developed (in contrast to the focus on Western, educated, industrialized societies that predominates in most contemporary analyses of children's social development; Henrich, Heine, and Norenzayan, 2010). Examining the details of several small-band hunter-gatherer societies regarding parenting, sleeping arrangements, personality, social relations, and morality (and their interconnections) can offer insights into how these factors relate to one another and influence children's development in hunter-gatherer societies.

In chapter 4, "Relationships and Resource Uncertainty: Cooperative Development of Efe Hunter-Gatherer Infants and Toddlers," Gilda Morelli, Paula Ivey Henry, and Steffen Foerster describe the social landscape and development of Efe infants and toddlers. The Efe are pygmy hunter-gatherers in the Ituri Forest, in the northeast portion of Africa's Congo River Basin. Their world is one of uncertainty. Reliable access to nutritious foods is unpredictable, and reliable access to the same people day to day is not assured. Diseases can strike at any time, and it is not uncommon for parents to die before their children are grown. For the Efe, survival depends on sharing and cooperation with others beyond the immediate family (a trait that seems unique to humans) that is built on a history of trustworthy experiences. Morelli and her colleagues present narrative and empirical data showing how Efe infant relationships and trust develop in a highly variable ecology. Efe infancy is intensely social. Infants experience an active social network from birth, and prior research shows that they may be breastfed by other women, not just by their mothers. Infants and toddlers are in nearly constant physical or social contact with people for much of their waking time. They move from partner to partner at rates of roughly once every 3 minutes, and this is flexible as people move in and out of the camp. These young children are very successful at obtaining resources from other members of the forager band as well as visitors. At all ages children experience highly positive affect and reward their partners' engagement with smiles, laughter, and bright-eyed attentiveness. With increasing growth and mobility, toddlers play a more active role in determining with whom they spend time, and their networks grow and diversify, most likely, as a result. Children are active, not passive, partners in developing the trusting relationships that are essential to survival in such an uncertain world.

In chapter 5, "Batek Childrearing and Morality," Karen and Kirk Endicott report on their research in the mid-1970s with the Batek people of Malaysia, who largely followed a nomadic hunter-gatherer lifestyle but also traded forest products for cloth, metal goods, and some food commodities. The Endicotts' description of childrearing practices through adolescence provides a window into how these practices influence the personality of the adults and the culture generally. They describe socialization into nonaggression. For example, like all toddlers, Batek children show signs of aggression or possessiveness, but adults generally react minimally, usually gently redirecting them or using humor to relieve tension. The adults seem to have an understanding that the child will grow out of these impulses, and indeed they do without punishment or admonition. Older children are scared into staying close to camp with threats, as in many cultures, that a bogeyman might come if they do not comply with certain rules. In late childhood and early adolescence, children move into spending more time on sex-typed activities (gathering or hunting with the adult of the same sex). Adolescents set up their own households with each other, not under the direction of adult guidance, until they enter real marriages. Adults generally display enthusiasm, a "confident independence," a sense of responsibility to others, and a "cooperative autonomy," with no apparent personality differences between males and females.

Barry Hewlett and Jennifer Roulette's pioneering study of the social sleeping patterns and arrangements of juveniles, adolescents, and teens, described in chapter 6, "Co-sleeping Beyond Infancy: Culture, Ecology, and Evolutionary Biology of Bed Sharing Among Aka Foragers and Ngandu Farmers of Central Africa," among two well-studied farming and foraging peoples living adjacent to each other in Central Africa reminds us of just how far Western cultural ideologies have departed from our species-wide, universal practice of mothers and children co-sleeping (in some form), with infants breastfeeding throughout the night and older children never sleeping alone. Indeed, throughout the world, most parents would never even imagine the possibility of their infants or children sleeping outside of the company, protection, or social reach of their alloparents, defined either by kin, relationships through marriage, personal preferences, or friendships.

In section III, broader questions about evolution, family, children, and human nature are the focus. In chapter 7, "Environment of Evolutionary Adaptedness, Rough-and-Tumble Play, and the Selection of Restraint in Human Aggression," Douglas Fry addresses the evolution of aggression restraint. Evolution has favored nonlethal aggression in intraspecific competitive interactions in many species. Intraspecific aggression that causes significant harm is rare among animals, including humans in nomadic foraging conditions, and when it occurs it is a personal, not collective, action. Instead, displays of aggression between group collectives cause little physical harm and are characterized by drama and preservation of face. Fry discusses how rough-and-tumble play may be critical for learning aggression restraint because it provides a platform for learning vital social skills such as signaling intentions and maintaining a playful, non–injury-inducing interaction. It provides a way to establish dominance without serious injury.

In chapter 8, Peter Gray presents a "Play Theory of Hunter-Gatherer Egalitarianism." His thesis is that our hunter-gatherer ancestors used play, more or less deliberately, to counteract the tendency to struggle for status and dominance, which was inherited from our primate ancestors, and that this permits the high degree of cooperation and sharing that hunter-gatherer life requires. He explains that play, in all mammals, requires a temporary setting aside of aggressiveness and dominance, and he reviews research suggesting a negative correlation, across primate species, between adult playfulness and steepness of dominance hierarchies. Then, for the rest of the chapter, he reviews research on contemporary hunter-gatherers showing how their social life—including their games and dances, religious practices, approach to productive work, means of enforcing social norms, and approach to children's education—is imbued with the spirit of play. The hunter-gatherer culture represents a social landscape in which play and humor are valued and aggression and status seeking are devalued.

In chapter 9, "Incentives in the Family I: The Family Firm, an Evolutionary/ Economic Theory for Parent–Offspring Relations," Joan Roughgarden and Zhiyuan Song challenge the received view of parent–offspring behavioral conflict with its emphasis on psychological manipulation by offspring of parents for the purpose of getting their needs met (and advancing their genetic fitness). Instead, derived from a social selection model, they emphasize honest communication of needs within the relationship, with a shifting balance of incentives in a type of family "team play." Their cooperative theory better fits the parent–child behavioral data, as well as the social harmony that is found in small-band hunter-gatherer societies.

In chapter 10, "Preliminary Steps Toward Addressing the Role of Nonadult Individuals in Human Evolution," Agustin Fuentes proposes a reconsideration of children in evolutionary theory. Children are often absent, or underrepresented, in our reconstructions of human behavioral evolution. However, there are emerging indications that we can envision nonadults as having substantive impacts in the ways in which early humans interfaced with local ecologies and each other. Modern evolutionary theory provides a toolkit for conceptualizing the role of children in human evolution, especially in the context of niche construction. Through broad cooperation that includes behaviors such as alloparenting, materials collection, and transport for tool making, immatures (children) may have played a critical role. Fuentes suggests that we consider the possibility that immatures are actors alongside adults in creating and shaping the social and ecological inheritance systems that enable behavioral flexibility and extended adaptation. Active participation by children may have been one of the key factors in the long-term success of the genus *Homo*.

In section IV, issues of changed childrearing contexts are addressed, including trauma and abuse. Chapters 11 and 12 describe the extremes for human development, when parents themselves are troubled and unresponsive. In chapter 11, "Child Maltreatment and Early Mother–Child Interactions," Kristin Valentino, Michelle Comas, and Amy Nuttall provide a developmental psychopathology perspective on mother–child interactions among maltreating and nonmaltreating families from infancy through toddlerhood, addressing how a maltreating family environment affects developmental outcomes. Because child maltreatment represents an extreme deviation from the average expected early caregiving environment, the comparison of maltreating and nonmaltreating families serves as an experiment of nature and provides critical information regarding the contribution of early caregiving to young children's development. In particular, early maltreatment is associated with attachment disorganization, decreased maternal sensitivity, and decreased maternal verbal interactions. Moreover, infants and toddlers from abusing families demonstrate persistent deficits in social initiation and autonomous behavior compared with children from neglecting and nonmaltreating families, which underscores the disruption in normative social development associated with an abusive family context. The authors conclude by providing specific examples of translational research interventions for young maltreated children informed by basic research on mother–child interactions during early childhood.

In chapter 12, "Importance of the Developmental Perspective in Evolutionary Discussions of Post-traumatic Stress Disorder," Robyn Bluhm and Ruth Lanius critique theoretical and evolutionary accounts of mental disorders, with an emphasis on post-traumatic stress disorder (PTSD). Focusing on chronic exposure to traumatic stress during early life (i.e., persistent childhood abuse), Bluhm and Lanius present data that demonstrate how early childhood trauma disrupts neural development, and they argue that several key deficits observed in patients with PTSD subsequent to early childhood trauma can be understood through these alterations to neural development and functioning. Thus, in contrast to current theoretical accounts of PTSD, which have largely ignored early life trauma, an alternative account that emphasizes the developmental context is presented.

Eugene Halton, in chapter 13, "From the Emergent Drama of Interpretation to Enscreenment," takes a sweeping view of human evolution. Considering the development of self and the pervasive role of symbol and meaning in human evolution, he reviews the contexts of early development and hunter-gatherer practice, contrasting them with the modern world and highlighting how media and technology act as contemporary socializing agents. Social media and technology have taken such a dominating influence in socialization that they can be viewed as inversions of evolutionarily central socializing practices. In this chapter, Halton lays out how contemporary techno-consumption culture mimics aspects of human behavior and perception related to evolutionary processes, yet subverts their action and outcomes.

The final chapters consider childhood environments and their relation to child flourishing. Tracy Gleason and Darcia Narvaez, in "Childhood Environments and Flourishing," incorporate insights from book chapters, and James McKenna provides a postscript on the larger issues. It is still unclear which biological needs are particularly essential for optimal development, although attending to 30 million years of evolved practices might be a place to start as a baseline for examination. The quality of the early caregiving context has significant ramifications for later physiological and psychological functioning. Central to this nurturing environment are the responsivity of the primary caregiver and the provision of adequately sensitive social and emotional care associated with many positive outcomes. However, flourishing, defined as emotional, psychological, and social wellbeing, along with appropriate physiological regulation and a sociomoral orientation toward others, might require an intense level of caregiving on the part of the community that is atypical in the United States. Attention to caregiving practices common among small-band hunter-gatherer behaviors, which are positively associated with sociomoral development, as well as to the broad social context of early development might provide important steps toward creating proactively moral, prosocial communities.

Conclusion

The interdisciplinary set of contributions to this book provides insight into human development, broad and particular cultural customs, and evolutionary features of social structure in light of human evolution. The integration of eclectic methods and theories breaks previously existing traditional disciplinary boundaries separating anthropology, psychology, sociology, and neuroscience. As a result of cooperative research efforts by scientists from different fields, each discipline is in a strengthened position to find answers to questions that a single discipline working alone might not even have known were important to ask.

The shifting baselines for childrearing that have occurred over generations in settled societies may have long-term effects on the psychology, anthropology, and sociology of subsequent generations. Social environments consistent and inconsistent with ancestral conditions may have long-term effects on individual outcomes. The cultures of mobile hunter-gatherer societies examined here may offer a glimpse at the contexts for child flourishing. With the information provided by these scholars, we may be in a better position to understand what optimal childrearing entails and thereby be able to facilitate changes in social structures and support systems that better foster wellbeing in human development. This next step, however challenging, will require understanding that our evolutionary legacies are relevant to helping us adjust our lifestyles to provide a fit between our more conservative biology and cultures, which can be at odds with one another to greater or lesser degrees. Only our imaginations are stopping us.

References

Bird-David, N. (1994). Sociality and immediacy: Or, past and present conversations on bands. *Man, 29*, 583–603.

Boehm, C. (2008). Purposive social selection and the evolution of human altruism. *Cross-Cultural Research, 42*, 319–352.

Bowlby, J. (1969/1982). *Attachment and loss: Vol. 1: Attachment* (2nd ed.). New York: Basic Books (Original work published 1969).

Bowlby, J. (1980). *Attachment and loss: Vol. 3: Loss: Sadness and depression*. New York: Basic Books.

Bowlby, J. (1988). *A secure base: Parent-child attachment and healthy human development*. New York: Basic Books.

Bronfenbrenner, U. (1979). *The ecology of human development*. Cambridge, MA: Harvard University Press.

Bruner, J. (2000). Foreword. In J. Deloache & A. Gottlieb, *A world of babies: Imagined childcare guides for seven societies* (pp. ix–xii). New York: Cambridge University Press.

Cicchetti, D., & Roisman, G. I. (Eds.) (2011). *The origins and organization of adaptation and maladaptation: Minnesota Symposia on Child Psychology* (Vol. 36). New York: Wiley.

Deloache, J., & Gottlieb, A. (2000). *A world of babies: Imagined childcare guides for seven societies*. New York: Cambridge University Press.

Deoni, S. C. L., Dean III, D. C., Piryatinksy, I., O'Muircheartaigh, J., Waskiewicz, N., Lehman, K., Han, M., & Dirks, H. (2013). Breastfeeding and early white matter development: A cross-sectional study. *NeuroImage, 82C,* 77–86.

Doi, T. (1981). *The anatomy of dependence: The key analysis of Japanese behavior* (J. Bester, English translator) (2nd ed.). Tokyo: Kodansha International.

Eaton, S. B., Shostak, M., & Konner, M. (1988). *The Paleolithic prescription.* New York: Harper and Row.

Edgerton, R. B. (1992). *Sick societies: Challenging the myth of primitive harmony.* New York: Free Press.

Everett, D. (2009). *Don't sleep, there are snakes: Life and language in the Amazonian jungle.* New York: Pantheon.

Felitti, V. J., & Anda, R. F. (2005). *The Adverse Childhood Experiences (ACE) Study.* Atlanta: Centers for Disease Control and Kaiser Permanente.

Fitzgerald, K. (1995). The role of risk factors; How SIDS organizations and the community cope. In Torliev Ole Rognum (Ed.), *Sudden Infant death Syndrome: New Trends in the Nineties* (pp. 119–123). Oslo, Norway: Scandinavian University Press.

Fry, D. P. (2006). *The human potential for peace: An anthropological challenge to assumptions about war and violence.* New York: Oxford University Press.

Fry, D. P. (Ed.) (2013). *War, peace and human nature: The convergence of evolutionary and cultural views.* New York: Oxford University Press.

Georgas, J., Berry, J. W., van de Vijver, F. J. R., Kağitçibaşi, Ç., & Poortinga, Y. H. (2006). *Families across cultures: A 30-nation psychological study.* New York: Cambridge University Press.

Gibson, T. (1985). The sharing of substance versus the sharing of activity among the Buid. *Man, 20,* 391–411.

Gowdy, J. (1998). *Limited wants, unlimited means: A reader on hunter-gatherer economics and the environment.* Washington, DC: Island Press.

Gowdy, J. (1999). Gatherer-hunters and the mythology of the market. In R. B. Lee & R. Daly (Eds.), *The Cambridge encyclopedia of hunters and gatherers* (pp. 391–398). New York: Cambridge University Press.

Henrich, J., Heine, S. J., & Norenzayan, A. (2010). The weirdest people in the world? *Brain and Behavioral Sciences, 33,* 61–135.

Hewlett, B.S., & Lamb, M.E. (2005). *Hunter-gatherer childhoods: Evolutionary, developmental and cultural perspectives.* New Brunswick, NJ: Aldine.

Hill, K.R., Walker, R.S., Božičević, M., Eder, J., Headland, T., Hewlett, B., Hurtado, A.M., Marlowe, F., Wiessner, P., & Wood, B. (2011). Co-Residence patterns in hunter-gatherer societies show unique human social structure. *Science, 331*(6022), 1286–1289. [DOI:10.1126/science.1199071]

Hrdy, S. (1999). *Mother Nature: A History of Mothers, Infants and Natural Selection.* New York: Pantheon.

Hrdy, S. (2009). *Mothers and others: The evolutionary origins of mutual understanding.* Cambridge, MA: Belknap Press.

Ingold, T. (1999). On the social relations of the hunter-gatherer band. In R. B. Lee & R. Daly (Eds.), *The Cambridge encyclopedia of hunters and gatherers* (pp. 399–410). New York: Cambridge University Press.

Kelly, R. L. (1995). *The foraging spectrum: Diversity in hunter-gatherer lifeways*. Washington DC: Smithsonian Institution Press.

Konner, M. (2005). Hunter-gatherer infancy and childhood: The !Kung and others. In B. Hewlett & M. Lamb (Eds.), *Hunter-gatherer childhoods: Evolutionary, developmental and cultural perspectives* (pp. 19–64). New Brunswick, NJ: Transaction.

Konner, M. (2010). *The evolution of childhood*. Cambridge, MA: Belknap Press.

Lanius, R. A., Vermetten, E., & Pain, C. (Eds.) (2010). *The impact of early life trauma on health and disease: The hidden epidemic*. New York: Cambridge University Press.

Lee, R. B., & Daly, R. (Eds.), (2005). *The Cambridge encyclopedia of hunters and gatherers*. New York: Cambridge University Press.

Levine, R. A., & Norman, K. (2001). The infant's acquisition of culture: Early attachment reexamined in anthropological perspective. In C. C. Moore & H. F. Matthews (Eds.). *The psychology of cultural experience* (pp. 83–104). New York: Cambridge University Press.

Main, M. (1995). Recent studies in attachment: Overview, with selected implications for clinical work. In S. Goldberg, R. Muir, & J. Kerr (Eds.), *Attachment theory: Social, developmental and clinical perspectives* (pp. 407–474). Hillsdale, NJ: Analytic Press.

McKenna, J. J, Ball, H., & Gettler, L. T. (2007). Mother-infant co-sleeping, breastfeeding and sudden infant death syndrome: What biological anthropology has discovered about normal infant sleep and pediatric sleep medicine. *Yearbook of Physical Anthropology*, *50*, 133–161.

Narvaez, D., Gleason, T., Wang, L., Brooks, J., Lefever, J., Cheng, A., & Centers for the Prevention of Child Neglect (2013). The Evolved Development Niche: Longitudinal effects of caregiving practices on early childhood psychosocial development. *Early Childhood Research Quarterly*, *28*(4), 759–773.

Narvaez, D., Panksepp, J., Schore, A., & Gleason, T. (Eds.) (2013a). *Evolution, early experience and human development: From research to practice and policy*. New York: Oxford University Press.

Narvaez, D., Panksepp, J., Schore, A., & Gleason, T. (2013b). The value of using an evolutionary framework for gauging children's wellbeing. In D. Narvaez, J. Panksepp, A. Schore, & T. Gleason (Eds.), *Evolution, early experience and human development: From research to practice and policy* (pp. 3–30). New York: Oxford University Press.

Narvaez, D., Wang, L., Gleason, T., Cheng, A., Lefever, J., & Deng, L. (2013). The evolved developmental niche and sociomoral outcomes in Chinese three-year-olds. *European Journal of Developmental Psychology*, *10*(2), 106–127.

Panksepp, J. (2001). The long-term psychobiological consequences of infant emotions: Prescriptions for the 21st century. *Infant Mental Health Journal, 22*, 132–173.

Shonkoff, J. P., & Phillips, D. A. (2000). *From neurons to neighborhoods: The science of early childhood development*. National Research Council, Committee on Integrating the Science of Early Childhood Development. Washington, DC: National Academy Press.

Shonkoff, J. P., Garner, A. S, for the Committee on Psychosocial Childhood, Adoption, and Dependent Care, and Section on Developmental and Behavioral Pediatrics, Dobbins, M. I., Earls, M. F., McGuinn, L.,...& Wood, D. L. (2012). The lifelong effects of early childhood adversity and toxic stress. *Pediatrics, 129*, e232.

U.S. Department of Health and Human Services, Administration for Children and Families, Administration on Children, Youth and Families. (2012). *Child maltreatment*

2011. Retrieved September 2, 2013, from http://www.acf.hhs.gov/sites/default/files/cb/cm11.pdf.

U.S. Department of Health and Human Services. (2013). Letter to state child welfare agencies. Retrieved October 17, 2013, from http://www.medicaid.gov/Federal-Policy-Guidance/Downloads/SMD-13-004.pdf

Williams, G. C. (1966). *Adaptation and natural selection: A critique of some current evolutionary thought.* Princeton, NJ: Princeton University Press.

Epigenetics of Mammalian Parenting

Frances A. Champagne

Development is a dynamic process involving a cascade of cellular and molecular events that ultimately generate our unique characteristics. In mammals, this developmental process occurs within the context of both prenatal and postnatal mother–infant interactions, and there is increasing evidence for the lasting impact of this parental context on neurobiological outcomes. In particular, studies of the effects of parenting on infant development suggest that the tactile aspects of parent–infant interactions play a critical role in growth, self-regulation, and neurobiological maturation (Ardiel and Rankin, 2010; Kuhn and Schanberg, 1998). Just as visual and acoustic stimuli promote the development of the visual and auditory cortex, exposure to touch appears to shape brain systems involved in neuroendocrine function, with implications for response to stress, social behavior, and later life reproductive behavior. These effects may have implications for the parenting behavior of individuals who receive high or low levels of tactile stimulation as infants, leading to the transmission of variation in parenting behavior from one generation to the next (Champagne, 2008).

The mechanism through which the experience of touch becomes encoded into our biology likely involves very complex physiological and cellular pathways (Hellstrom, Dhir, Diorio, and Meaney, 2012). Epigenetic changes may be one critical element within these pathways, allowing for both dynamic changes in response to parent–infant interactions and stable maintenance of the effects of these interactions (Meaney and Ferguson-Smith, 2010). *Epigenetics* refers to those factors that can alter the activity of our genes without altering the underlying DNA sequence. It is increasingly evident that a broad range of experiences occurring throughout the life span can induce epigenetic changes—altering gene expression—and can lead to significant and long-lasting effects on multiple biological systems, including metabolism, immunity, and neuroendocrine function (Champagne, 2010; Jirtle and Skinner, 2007). Epigenetics may also help us to understand the "inheritance" of variation in parental behavior and perhaps give us deeper insights into the adaptiveness and evolutionary significance of parenting. This chapter discusses the importance of touch for infant development and highlights emerging evidence implicating epigenetics as a critical process linking parental behavior to neurobiological and behavioral outcomes within and across generations.

Biological Impact of a Mother's Touch

Tactile stimulation has both immediate and long-term effects on physiological, neurobiological, and psychological outcomes. Within the context of human infant development, much of the evidence for the significant impact of maternal touch comes from studies of premature infants. Intervention studies in which premature neonates within a neonatal intensive care unit are provided with stroking and kinesthetic stimulation indicate that this experience can promote weight gain and improve alertness and behavioral maturation (Field et al., 1986) (Figure 2.1). Despite equivalent levels of caloric intake, infants receiving increased tactile stimulation gain more weight, suggesting improved metabolic efficiency. Similar benefits to growth and development are observed after *kangaroo care*, which involves close skin-to-skin contact between mother and infant (Dodd, 2005; Kaffashi, Scher, Ludington-Hoe, and Loparo, 2013; Ludington-Hoe and Swinth, 1996). This form of tactile stimulation is associated with improved temperature regulation and enhanced growth (Cattaneo et al., 1998). Interestingly, the benefits of increased mother–infant contact have also been observed in mothers. Kangaroo care has been found to increase the amount of positive affect and sensitivity to infant cues in mothers (Feldman, Eidelman, Sirota, and Weller, 2002), promote breastfeeding (Moore, Anderson, Bergman, and Dowswell, 2012), and reduce incidents of maternal rejection of the newborn (Lvoff, Lvoff, and Klaus, 2000). In both mothers and

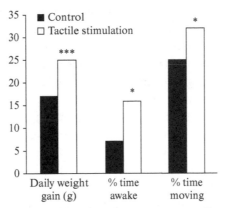

FIGURE 2.1 *Effects of tactile stimulation in premature neonates. Forty infants in the neonatal intensive care unit were provided with stimulation (stroking) for three 15-minute sessions per day for 10 days. Stimulated infants gained more weight, spent more time awake, and engaged in more movement during observations. Values presented are means across the 12-day intervention. ***, p <.001; *, p <.05. (Data from Field et al., 1986).*

fathers, the effects of increased contact with infants can be observed on measures of the peptide hormone oxytocin (Feldman, Gordon, Schneiderman, Weisman, and Zagoory-Sharon, 2010). Oxytocin is involved in lactation, social behavior, and stress responsivity (Gimpl and Fahrenholz, 2001; Ross and Young, 2009) and may contribute to the increased parental bonding associated with increases in parent–infant contact (Keverne and Curley, 2004). Thus, there is a reciprocal benefit to tactile stimulation, which promotes development in the infant and attachment in the parent.

Experimental evidence for the biological impact of mother–infant tactile stimulation is derived primarily from maternal separation/deprivation studies. Across species, prolonged periods of separation between mothers and infants have been found to induce long-term neurodevelopmental deficits in functioning. In humans, studies of institutionalized children indicate that early life social neglect can contribute to growth retardation, impaired attachment, and heightened stress responsivity (Rutter, Kumsta, Schlotz, and Sonuga-Barke, 2012). Recent brain imaging studies suggest significant neurobiological impairments (Chugani, Behen, Muzik, Juhasz, Nagy, and Chugani, 2001; Eluvathingal et al., 2006), including overall reductions in white and gray matter and enlarged amygdala volumes among adolescents who had experienced early life institutionalization (Mehta et al., 2009). Although institutionalization will include a broad range of physical and psychological deprivations that may contribute to these long-term effects, the absence of nurturing touch from a primary caregiver is thought to be one critical element of this early life adversity (Blackwell, 2000). In primates, similar effects are observed among socially isolated or peer-reared infants (Feng et al., 2011; Spinelli, Chefer, Suomi, Higley, Barr, and Stein, 2009; Suomi, 1991). In rodents, pups that experience maternal separation during the postnatal period exhibit heightened response to stress and impaired cognitive functioning in later life (Andersen, Lyss, Dumont, and Teicher, 1999; Lehmann and Feldon, 2000). The short-term effects of this experience include elevated glucocorticoid hormone levels (Stanton, Gutierrez, and Levine, 1988) and reduced levels of ornithine decarboxylase (Pauk, Kuhn, Field, and Schanberg, 1986; Wang, Bartolome, and Schanberg, 1996)—an enzyme that plays a critical role in cell growth and stabilization of DNA (Russell, 1985). When maternally separated pups are provided with tactile stimulation (heavy stroking with a paintbrush), the effects of maternal separation are attenuated such that stroked pups have comparable levels of growth hormone, corticosterone, and ornithine decarboxylase as controls (Pauk et al., 1986). This attenuation is not observed in pups that have received vestibular or kinesthetic stimulation, suggesting a specific role for maternal touch.

Maternal deprivation studies have also been used to demonstrate both the profound deficits in functioning that emerge in response to this experience and the "restorative" effects of tactile stimulation. In rats, maternal deprivation is achieved by rearing pups in the absence of maternal contact but with maintenance of adequate thermal and nutritional levels (artificial rearing, or AR). Much like Harry Harlow's

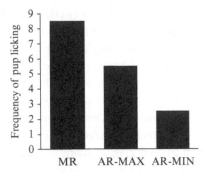

FIGURE 2.2 *Frequency of postnatal pup licking by mother-reared (MR) or artificially reared (AR) female rats. MR females engaged in significantly more pup licking during the early postnatal period compared with AR females. This effect was partially reversed when AR was combined with high levels of tactile stimulation (AR-MAX vs. AR-MIN). (From Gonzalez et al., 2001.)*

maternally deprived rhesus macaques (Harlow, Dodsworth, and Harlow, 1965), pups reared under these conditions exhibit long-term impairments in neurobehavioral outcomes, including impaired social learning (Levy, Melo, Galef, Madden, and Fleming, 2003), reduced attention (Lovic and Fleming, 2004), increased impulsivity (Lovic, Keen, Fletcher, and Fleming, 2011), and increased pain sensitivity (de Medeiros, Fleming, Johnston, and Walker, 2009). AR results in reduced maternal behavior in adulthood (compared with mother-reared offspring), which is partially restored when AR females also receive high levels of tactile stimulation (stroked five times a day, two minutes per pup; Figure 2.2) (Gonzalez, Lovic, Ward, Wainwright, and Fleming, 2001; Melo, Lovic, Gonzalez, Madden, Sinopoli, and Fleming, 2006; Novakov and Fleming, 2005; Palombo, Nowoslawski, and Fleming, 2010). This tactile "intervention" also attenuated maternal deprivation-induced activity/emotionality in an open-field test (Gonzalez et al., 2001), attentional measures (Lovic and Fleming, 2004), impulsivity (Lovic et al., 2011), and amphetamine-induced locomotor behavior (Lovic, Fleming, and Fletcher, 2006). Within the brain, stimulation of maternally deprived pups elevates levels of synaptophysin, neural cell adhesion molecule, brain-derived neurotrophic factor (BDNF), and growth-associated protein 43 (Chatterjee, Chatterjee-Chakraborty, Rees, Cauchi, de Medeiros, and Fleming, 2007), proteins involved in brain development and plasticity. This growing body of evidence highlights both the importance of the social aspects of maternal care and the restorative effects that tactile stimulation can have in the absence of mother–infant interactions.

Although maternal deprivation can be used to demonstrate the impact of maternal care on offspring development, another powerful approach is to assess the effects of natural variations in maternal behavior. Variability in the frequency and quality of care exhibited by mothers during the postpartum period is typical and observed across species (Hane and Fox, 2006; Maestripieri, 1998; Maestripieri and D'Amato,

1991). In humans, indices of maternal sensitivity (Hane and Fox, 2006) and attachment (Raby, Cicchetti, Carlson, Cutuli, Englund, and Egeland, 2012) vary between individuals, and in nonhuman primates, similar variability can be observed on measures of mother–infant contact (Fairbanks, 1989) and rates of maternal rejection (Maestripieri, 1998). In laboratory rodents, despite the controlled conditions of the environment and the limited genetic variability between individuals, there is also considerable variation in maternal care. Observations of Long-Evans rats during the postpartum period indicate that licking/grooming (LG) of pups, one of the primary forms of tactile stimulation during postnatal development, varies significantly between lactating dams (Champagne, Francis, Mar, and Meaney, 2003a). Although a minimal level of LG is necessary to promote pup urination/defecation and moderate body temperature (Gubernick and Alberts, 1983; Hofer, 1975; Ronca, Lamkin, and Alberts, 1993), it is clear that lactating females engage in stable individual differences with regard to the frequency of LG. The long-term consequences of this variation for offspring are profound (Meaney, 2001). In adulthood, offspring that experience low compared with high levels of LG (a two-fold difference in LG) are found to have heightened glucocorticoid levels in response to stress (Liu et al., 1997), decreased exploration of a novel environment (indicating behavioral inhibition) (Caldji, Tannenbaum, Sharma, Francis, Plotsky, and Meaney, 1998), increased fear reactivity (Menard, Champagne, and Meaney, 2004), reduced hippocampal plasticity (Bagot, van Hasselt, Champagne, Meaney, Krugers, and Joels, 2009), and impaired learning/memory (Liu, Diorio, Day, Francis, and Meaney, 2000). LG also induces lasting effects on social and reproductive behavior. Increased dominance and play fighting are observed among offspring that receive low levels of LG (Parent, Del Corpo, Cameron, and Meaney, 2012; Parent and Meaney, 2008). Among female offspring, low levels of LG experienced in infancy predict reduced levels of maternal behavior (Champagne et al., 2003a) and increased sexual behavior in adulthood (Cameron, Fish, and Meaney, 2008b). These physiological and behavioral effects of maternal LG suggest that variation in the tactile aspects of mother–infant interactions can significantly alter development, a finding consistent with evidence from maternal separation and deprivation studies.

The neurobiological effects of maternal LG have also been explored. Offspring reared by mothers that engage in low levels of maternal LG have reduced glucocorticoid receptor (GR) protein and messenger RNA (mRNA) in the hippocampus (Francis, Diorio, Liu, and Meaney, 1999; Liu et al., 1997). Hippocampal GR plays a critical negative-feedback role within the hypothalamic-pituitary-adrenal response to stress (Sapolsky and Meaney, 1986; Sapolsky, Meaney, and McEwen, 1985), and reduced levels of GR may account for the heightened stress responsivity of low-LG offspring. Within the hippocampus, offspring of low-LG compared with high-LG dams also have reduced BDNF and synaptophysin levels (Liu et al., 2000). Low levels of LG are associated with decreased neuronal survival and increased apoptosis within the hippocampus (Bredy, Grant, Champagne, and Meaney, 2003; Weaver, Grant, and Meaney, 2002). Within the amygdala, benzodiazepine receptor density

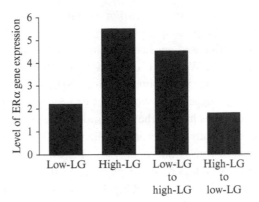

FIGURE 2.3 *Cross-fostering effects on estrogen receptor messenger RNA. Levels of estrogen receptor-alpha (ERα) in the hypothalamus of female rat offspring are elevated in offspring reared by high-LG mothers. Females cross-fostered at birth (from low- to high-LG or high- to low-LG dams) have ERα levels that correspond to their rearing mother's level of LG. (From Champagne et al., 2006.)*

is increased in the offspring of high-LG dams, and within the locus ceruleus, there is increased alpha-2 adrenoreceptor and decreased corticotropin-releasing factor receptor density in high-LG compared with low-LG offspring (Caldji et al., 1998). Within the female offspring of high-LG dams, there is increased oxytocin receptor density in several hypothalamic nuclei and increased estrogen receptor-alpha (ERα) protein and mRNA in the medial preoptic area of the hypothalamus (MPOA), which may account for the increased maternal behavior observed among the female offspring of high-LG dams (Champagne, Diorio, Sharma, and Meaney, 2001; Champagne, Weaver, Diorio, Sharma, and Meaney, 2003b; Francis, Champagne, and Meaney, 2000). Among female offspring of low-LG dams, there is enhanced hypothalamic-pituitary-gonadal function, suggested by increased estrogen sensitivity within luteinizing hormone and gonadotropin-releasing hormone pathways as well as increased ERα in the anteroventral paraventricular nucleus (Cameron, Del Corpo, Diorio, McAllister, Sharma, and Meaney, 2008a). These neuroendocrine effects likely account for the increased sexual receptivity of low-LG offspring. In the case of ERα in the MPOA and hippocampal GR, cross-fostering studies confirm that it is the amount of LG experienced during the postnatal period that accounts for these neurobiological outcomes (Figure 2.3) (Champagne, Weaver, Diorio, Dymov, Szyf, and Meaney, 2006; Francis et al., 1999).

Getting Under the Skin: Epigenetics of Maternal Care

The long-term effects of maternal care on offspring neurobiological and behavioral measures implicate mechanistic pathways that confer both plasticity (changeability in response to maternal separation/deprivation/LG) and stability (maintenance of effects beyond the period of experience). For example, in the case of low versus high LG, the changes in hippocampal GR and hypothalamic ERα mRNA emerge during the postnatal period and are sustained into adulthood (Champagne et al., 2006; Francis et al., 1999; Weaver et al., 2004), even though the mother–infant interactions that characterize the postnatal period are no longer occurring beyond weaning. These findings suggest the involvement of gene regulatory pathways that control the activity of genes in both the short and long term. Epigenetics is a rapidly expanding field of study with broad applications. The term *epigenetics* has historically been used to convey the concept that there are significant interactions between genes and the products of those genes in the development of phenotype (Jablonka and Lamb, 2002). This concept highlights the dynamic interplay between genes and the environment and provides a framework for understanding how our unique characteristics emerge—even in the presence of limited genetic variability. More modern use of this term is applied to the specific molecular mechanisms that can alter the expression or activity of genes without altering the underlying DNA sequence. Despite the genetic "potential" encoded within our DNA, the realization of that potential is an active process that requires physical changes around the DNA that make genes accessible. There are a variety of molecular changes that can either limit this accessibility or enhance the likelihood that genes will become expressed, including DNA methylation, histone modifications, and interference with the process of transcription/translation through noncoding RNAs (Jenuwein and Allis, 2001; Razin, 1998; Sato, Tsuchiya, Meltzer, and Shimizu, 2011).

DNA methylation is a molecular modification directly to DNA. The addition of methyl groups to DNA is a normal process of development and typically limits the accessibility of DNA (Razin, 1998). During the process of DNA methylation, a methyl group is chemically bound to cytosine nucleotides within the gene sequence through the actions of a class of enzymes known as DNA methyltransferases (DNMTs) (Okano, Bell, Haber, and Li, 1999; Turek-Plewa and Jagodzinski, 2005). The importance of this process for normal development is highlighted by studies in which *DNMT1* genes are rendered nonfunctional in mice. Mice lacking DNMTs do not survive beyond embryonic or early postnatal stages of development and have global hypomethylation within the genome (Li, Bestor, and Jaenisch, 1992; Okano et al., 1999). Because of the nature of the chemical bond between methyl groups and cytosine nucleotides, DNA methylation is generally considered a stable epigenetic modification (Turner, 2001), although there is evidence for continued plasticity of DNA methylation patterns across the life span (Miller and Sweatt, 2007; Roth, 2012). A highly dynamic gene regulatory mechanism is post-translational histone modifications. Unlike DNA methylation, these modifications are directed at the histone proteins around the DNA rather than the DNA itself (Turner, 2001). Histones can undergo multiple post-translational modifications in which, for example, acetyl or methyl groups are added to the protein (Jenuwein and Allis, 2001). Because of the interactions between histones and DNA, these modifications can, like DNA methylation, alter the accessibility of DNA to transcription. Noncoding RNAs are also an important epigenetic pathway (Sato et al., 2011). These molecules can interact with DNA, mRNA, and proteins to reduce the activity of genes or the gene products. Collectively, these epigenetic mechanisms allow for a highly dynamic control over genes with implications for the genotype–phenotype relationship.

Evidence for the involvement of epigenetic pathways in the long-term effects of mother–infant interactions is derived primarily from studies of natural variation in maternal care in rats. Hippocampal GR is elevated in the adult offspring of high-LG dams, and this maternal effect has been linked to epigenetic changes within the regulatory region (promoter) of the GR gene (*NR3C1*). Within the *NR3C1* promoter region, offspring that receive low levels of LG have increased DNA methylation and decreased histone acetylation, whereas this region is not highly methylated among the offspring of high-LG dams (Weaver et al., 2004). These adult patterns of DNA methylation/histone acetylation are not observed prenatally or at the time of birth but instead emerge during the period of postnatal mother–infant interactions and persist into adulthood (Weaver et al., 2004). Interestingly, targeting of these epigenetic modifications, with either a histone deacetylase inhibitor (which promotes acetylation) or increased methionine (which increases DNA methylation), reverses the epigenetic effects of postnatal maternal care (Weaver et al., 2004; Weaver et al., 2005).

Further analyses of epigenetic effects within the hippocampus indicate broad epigenetic changes in response to maternal care. Offspring of low-LG dams have elevated levels of DNMT1 mRNA, which may promote widespread increases in DNA methylation within this brain region (Zhang, Hellstrom, Bagot, Wen, Diorio, and Meaney, 2010). In addition to GR, levels of the enzyme glutamic acid decarboxylase (GAD1) are reduced in the offspring of low compared with high-LG dams. Within the *GAD1* promoter region, offspring of low-LG dams have heighted DNA methylation and reduced histone acetylation (Zhang et al., 2010). Within the *GRM1* gene, which encodes the type 1 metabotropic glutamate receptor (mGluR1), the experience of high levels of LG is associated with decreased DNA methylation and increased histone acetylation (Bagot et al., 2012). Analyses of genome-wide gene expression levels in the offspring of high-LG compared with low-LG dams indicate that more than 900 genes are differentially expressed in the hippocampus as a function of maternal LG (Weaver, Meaney, and Szyf, 2006). The overall pattern of decreased gene expression that is observed in the offspring of low-LG dams suggests that, as in the case of *NR3C1, GAD1,* and *GRM1*, there is epigenetic silencing of gene activity as a function of the experience of low maternal care (Figure 2.4).

Within the hypothalamus, the epigenetic effects of maternal care are also apparent and have implications for reproduction. Analysis of levels of DNA methylation within the promoter region of the ERα gene (*ESR1*) in MPOA tissue indicates that offspring of low-LG dams have elevated DNA methylation (Champagne et al., 2006). Interestingly, DNA methylation of *ESR1* can also be manipulated by licking-like tactile stimulation. The MPOA is typically larger in males than females (Gorski, 1978), yet females have higher levels of ERα mRNA and protein

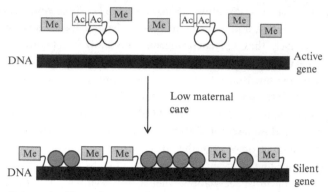

FIGURE 2.4 *Epigenetic effects of maternal care. Low levels of maternal care (LG) can induce gene silencing through increased DNA methylation (binding of methyl groups [Me] to DNA) and removal of acetyl groups (Ac) from histones (circles).*

compared with males in this brain region (Kurian, Olesen, and Auger, 2010). In males, there are elevated levels of DNA methylation within the *ESR1* promoter that may account for the reduced ERα mRNA. However, females can become masculinized (decreased ERα mRNA, increased *ESR1* promoter methylation) by receiving licking-like tactile stimulation (using a paintbrush) during the postnatal period (Kurian et al., 2010). Thus, the tactile experience of mother–infant interactions may shape epigenetic patterns in brain regions that are critical for maternal care and sexual dimorphism.

The epigenetic effects of maternal separation/deprivation have also been demonstrated. In humans, genome-wide levels of DNA methylation have been found to be altered in blood samples taken from institution-raised children. These children have higher overall levels of DNA methylation compared with children raised by their biological parents (Naumova, Lee, Koposov, Szyf, Dozier, and Grigorenko, 2012). These findings are intriguing but are limited by the methodological constraint of using blood rather than brain to assess epigenetic profiles—a limitation that can be overcome in animal studies of early life adversity. In laboratory studies in mice, similar epigenetic dysregulation is observed after maternal separation. Among maternally separated mice, there are increases in hypothalamic vasopressin (AVP) mRNA that persist into adulthood (Murgatroyd et al., 2009). Within the *AVP* gene, DNA methylation is reduced in maternally separated mice at 6 weeks, 3 months, and 1 year of age (Murgatroyd et al., 2009). Increased DNA methylation has also been observed within the *MECP2* (a protein that binds to methylated DNA) and cannabinoid receptor-1 (*CNR1*) genes and decreased DNA methylation within the corticotropin-releasing factor receptor-2 (*CRFR2*) gene consequent to maternal separation (Franklin et al., 2010). Although these studies do not examine the potential reversal of these effects through supplemental tactile stimulation of maternally separated offspring, it seems likely that deprivation of maternal contact is a significant predictor of these epigenetic effects.

The effects of enhanced mother–infant interactions on epigenetic pathways have been observed within laboratory studies in mice. Although prolonged maternal separation from offspring leads to reduced maternal care, brief separations (also called *handling*) may stimulate maternal care, particularly LG, and attenuate offspring response to stress (Lehmann, Pryce, Jongen-Relo, Stohr, Pothuizen, and Feldon, 2002; Meaney et al., 1991). Brief maternal separations have been found to reduce levels of hypothalamic corticotropin-releasing factor mRNA, which may account for the reduced hypothalamic-pituitary-adrenal activity of these offspring. Among handled offspring, protein levels of neuron-restrictive silencer factor are dramatically higher in hypothalamic tissue at postnatal day 9 and throughout adulthood (Korosi et al., 2010). Neuron-restrictive silencer factor was shown to recruit enzymes/proteins involved in epigenetic regulation and may contribute to the epigenetic repression of *CRF* gene expression (Korosi et al., 2010; Seth and Majzoub, 2001; Zheng, Zhao, and Mehler, 2009). Maternal care can also be stimulated through communal rearing, in which multiple lactating females rear offspring in a communal nest (Curley, Davidson, Bateson, and Champagne, 2009). Offspring that have been reared in a communal nest have increased hippocampal histone acetylation at *BDNF* gene promoter regions, and this epigenetic modification may account for the increased BDNF levels observed among communally reared mice (Branchi, Karpova, D'Andrea, Castren, and Alleva, 2011). These findings suggest that there is the potential for mother–infant interventions to recruit epigenetic pathways and enhance physiological and behavioral functioning.

From One Generation to the Next: A Maternal Legacy

Across species, there is evidence for the multigenerational continuity of patterns of maternal care. In humans, parental bonding (an index of the degree of "care" and "overprotectiveness") and attachment style (secure, anxious/resistant, avoidant, disorganized) are consistent across generations, such that individuals with a secure attachment to their own parents have children and grandchildren who tend to be similarly securely attached (Benoit and Parker, 1994; Miller, Kramer, Warner, Wickramaratne, and Weissman, 1997). Cycles of abuse have been reported in humans (Widom, 1989) and monkeys (Maestripieri, Wallen, and Carroll, 1997), and there is evidence suggesting that it is the experience of abuse that perpetuates this cycle. Cross-fostering studies conducted between abusive and nonabusive macaque females indicate that females born to an abusive mother who are cross-fostered to a nonabusive mother are unlikely to be abusive (Maestripieri, 2005). In laboratory rodents, this environmentally driven transmission of abusive behavior is likewise evident and involves epigenetic pathways. Among female rats,

the experience of periods of abusive care (e.g., dragging, burying) during postnatal development is associated with decreased BDNF mRNA within the cortex
and increased DNA methylation within the promoter region of this gene (Roth,
Lubin, Funk, and Sweatt, 2009). Abused females are more likely to engage in abusive behavioral toward their own offspring, and epigenetic effects within the *BDNF*
gene are likewise observed in the offspring of abused females. In humans, the epigenetic "signature" of childhood abuse is also evident within the brain, in the form
of increased *NR3C1* DNA methylation (McGowan et al., 2009) and may be an
important consideration of the transmission of risk for psychological dysfunction
across generations.

There is growing support for the hypothesis that the amount of maternal care
received predicts the amount of maternal care that females engage in toward
their own offspring. Female rats that experience artificial rearing conditions
provide less maternal care toward their own offspring (Gonzalez et al., 2001).
Communal rearing in mice has been demonstrated to increase maternal LG in
the offspring that experienced the communal environment as well as the offspring of communally reared females (Curley et al., 2009). This matrilineal
transmission is also observed when examining the effects of natural variations
in maternal LG (Figure 2.5). In the case of this transmission, it is hypothesized
that the experience of low LG leads to increased DNA methylation of the *ESR1*
gene in MPOA during postnatal development and that the persistence of this
epigenetic effect into adulthood renders low-LG female offspring less sensitive
to the priming effects of hormones that normally enhance maternal responsiveness (Champagne, 2008). This reduced maternal sensitivity results in decreased
LG toward the offspring reared by low-LG females, and thus the cycle continues. These experience-dependent epigenetic effects, combined with the direct

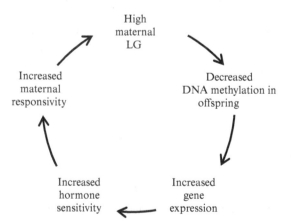

FIGURE 2.5 *Cycle of epigenetic, neuroendocrine, and behavioral changes induced by
maternal LG. This cascade of changes may account for the continuity of variation in
maternal behavior across generations.*

inheritance of epigenetic marks by offspring (Franklin et al., 2010), may under-line the transgenerational continuity of maternal care and risk/resilience to envi-ronmental stressors. These studies have prompted a broader approach to the study of inherited effects and a greater appreciation of the role that mothers have in the inheritance of behavioral variation (Danchin, Charmantier, Champagne, Mesoudi, Pujol, and Blanchet, 2011).

Adapting to the Environmental Context of Parenting

Although it is tempting to draw conclusions regarding the "good" achieved by enhanced maternal care and the "bad" achieved by deprivation of maternal care, it is important to consider the context in which high or low levels of parenting occur. In humans, studies of mother–infant tactile stimulation indicate that depressed moth-ers are less likely to engage in contact with infants (Moszkowski, Stack, Girouard, Field, Hernandez-Reif, and Diego, 2009). In laboratory studies with rodents, mater-nal LG can be enhanced or suppressed by environmental conditions. The experience of physical or social "enrichment"—housing rats in large social groups with toys and opportunities for exploration—during juvenile development leads to increased levels of LG (Champagne and Meaney, 2007). In contrast, social isolation or the experience of stress during pregnancy can reduce levels of LG (Champagne and Meaney, 2006, 2007). Within a communal nest, females engage in higher levels of maternal LG than they would if rearing their offspring in a single nest (Curley et al., 2009). These studies suggest that maternal care exhibits high levels of plasticity, shifting parenting in one direction or the other dependent on the conditions of the environment. To determine whether this plasticity is adaptive, one must consider the gains and costs to offspring of environmentally induced changes in maternal care. In the case of LG, although offspring that receive low levels of maternal LG have heightened stress responsivity and reduced maternal care (Francis et al., 1999), they also possess increased sexual receptivity (Cameron et al., 2008b), which may enhance reproduction. These maternal effects may be conceptualized as inducing different reproductive strategies that are both potentially successful in promoting the growth and survival of subsequent generations (Champagne, 2011). Offspring of low-LG dams also have enhanced cognitive performance and hippocampal plasticity under conditions of stress (Champagne et al., 2008). Taken together, these findings indicate that both low and high maternal care can generate adaptive characteristics in offspring and that the adaptiveness of these characteristics may be dependent on the quality of the environment experienced by offspring (stress vs. no stress). This interpretation is consistent with the theoretical framework of human development proposed by Belsky and colleagues (Belsky, Steinberg and Draper, 1991), wherein the characteristics of the family context give rise to divergent reproductive strategies (early puberty and sexual activity and limited parental investment vs. later sexual activity and greater parental investment) through effects on childrearing.

Future Directions in the Study of Parenting

Although there is growing evidence for the role of epigenetic mechanisms in linking maternal touch to offspring development, there are still many questions remaining regarding the stability and plasticity of these early life effects. In addition to basic research examining the cascade of events that allow the tactile aspects of parenting to shape the brain, translational studies, applying what we know to human infant development, are an important future direction. Intervention studies in neonatal intensive care units and the assessed effects of kangaroo care suggest that significant improvements in infant outcomes can be achieved through enhanced tactile stimulation. The epigenetic basis of this effect has yet to be explored in humans and may be limited by the current inability to study dynamic epigenetic changes within the human brain. Understanding the reciprocal benefits achieved through maternal touch and the psychological and broader environmental influences that increase or decrease a mother's motivation to provide this contact will be particularly important in these future explorations. Although much of the research in this field has been on mothers, fathers can also provide nurturing tactile experiences for infants that may have benefits to later life neurobiological outcomes (Seidel, Poeggel, Holetschka, Helmeke, and Braun, 2011). Study of the complex interplay between mothers, fathers, and offspring may provide critical insights into the epigenetic mechanisms and adaptiveness of mammalian parenting.

References

Andersen, S. L., Lyss, P. J., Dumont, N. L., & Teicher, M. H. (1999). Enduring neurochemical effects of early maternal separation on limbic structures. *Annals of the New York Academy of Sciences, 877*, 756–759.

Ardiel, E. L., & Rankin, C. H. (2010). The importance of touch in development. *Paediatrics & Child Health, 15*(3), 153–156.

Bagot, R. C., van Hasselt, F. N., Champagne, D. L., Meaney, M. J., Krugers, H. J., & Joels, M. (2009). Maternal care determines rapid effects of stress mediators on synaptic plasticity in adult rat hippocampal dentate gyrus. *Neurobiology of Learning and Memory, 92*(3), 292–300.

Bagot, R. C., Zhang, T. Y., Wen, X., Nguyen, T. T., Nguyen, H. B., Diorio, J., et al. (2012). Variations in postnatal maternal care and the epigenetic regulation of metabotropic glutamate receptor 1 expression and hippocampal function in the rat. *Proceedings of the National Academy of Sciences U S A, 109*(Suppl 2), 17200–17207.

Belsky, J., Steinberg, L., & Drape, P. (1991). Childhood experience, interpersonal development, and reproductive strategy: An evolutionary theory of socialization. *Child Development, 62*(4), 647–670.

Benoit, D., & Parker, K. C. (1994). Stability and transmission of attachment across three generations. *Child Development, 65*(5), 1444–1456.

Blackwell, P. (2000). The influence of touch on child development: Implications for intervention. *Infants and Young Children, 13*(1), 25–39.

Branchi, I., Karpova, N. N., D'Andrea, I., Castren, E., & Alleva, E. (2011). Epigenetic modifications induced by early enrichment are associated with changes in timing of induction of BDNF expression. *Neuroscience Letters, 495*(3), 168–172.

Bredy, T. W., Grant, R. J., Champagne, D. L., & Meaney, M. J. (2003). Maternal care influences neuronal survival in the hippocampus of the rat. *European Journal of Neuroscience, 18*(10), 2903–2909.

Caldji, C., Tannenbaum, B., Sharma, S., Francis, D., Plotsky, P. M., & Meaney, M. J. (1998). Maternal care during infancy regulates the development of neural systems mediating the expression of fearfulness in the rat. *Proceedings of the National Academy of Sciences U S A, 95*(9), 5335–5340.

Cameron, N., Del Corpo, A., Diorio, J., McAllister, K., Sharma, S., & Meaney, M. J. (2008a). Maternal programming of sexual behavior and hypothalamic-pituitary-gonadal function in the female rat. *PLoS One, 3*(5), e2210.

Cameron, N. M., Fish, E. W., & Meaney, M. J. (2008b). Maternal influences on the sexual behavior and reproductive success of the female rat. *Hormones and Behavior, 54*(1), 178–184.

Cattaneo, A., Davanzo, R., Worku, B., Surjono, A., Echeverria, M., Bedri, A., et al. (1998). Kangaroo mother care for low birthweight infants: A randomized controlled trial in different settings. *Acta Paediatrica, 87*(9), 976–985.

Champagne, D. L., Bagot, R. C., van Hasselt, F., Ramakers, G., Meaney, M. J., de Kloet, E. R., et al. (2008). Maternal care and hippocampal plasticity: Evidence for experience-dependent structural plasticity, altered synaptic functioning, and differential responsiveness to glucocorticoids and stress. *Journal of Neuroscience, 28*(23), 6037–6045.

Champagne, F., Diorio, J., Sharma, S., & Meaney, M. J. (2001). Naturally occurring variations in maternal behavior in the rat are associated with differences in estrogen-inducible central oxytocin receptors. *Proceedings of the National Academy of Sciences U S A, 98*(22), 12736–12741.

Champagne, F. A. (2008). Epigenetic mechanisms and the transgenerational effects of maternal care. *Frontiers in Neuroendocrinology, 29*(3), 386–397.

Champagne, F. A. (2010). Epigenetic influence of social experiences across the lifespan. *Developmental Psychobiology, 52*(4), 299–311.

Champagne, F. A. (2011). Maternal imprints and the origins of variation. *Hormones and Behavior, 60*(1), 4–11.

Champagne, F. A., Francis, D. D., Mar, A., & Meaney, M. J. (2003a). Variations in maternal care in the rat as a mediating influence for the effects of environment on development. *Physiology and Behavior, 79*(3), 359–371.

Champagne, F. A., & Meaney, M. J. (2006). Stress during gestation alters postpartum maternal care and the development of the offspring in a rodent model. *Biological Psychiatry, 59*(12), 1227–1235.

Champagne, F. A., & Meaney, M. J. (2007). Transgenerational effects of social environment on variations in maternal care and behavioral response to novelty. *Behavioral Neuroscience, 121*(6), 1353–1363.

Champagne, F. A., Weaver, I. C., Diorio, J., Dymov, S., Szyf, M., & Meaney, M. J. (2006). Maternal care associated with methylation of the estrogen receptor-alpha1b promoter and estrogen receptor-alpha expression in the medial preoptic area of female offspring. *Endocrinology, 147*(6), 2909–2915.

Champagne, F. A., Weaver, I. C., Diorio, J., Sharma, S., & Meaney, M. J. (2003b). Natural variations in maternal care are associated with estrogen receptor alpha expression and estrogen sensitivity in the medial preoptic area. *Endocrinology, 144*(11), 4720–4724.

Chatterjee, D., Chatterjee-Chakraborty, M., Rees, S., Cauchi, J., de Medeiros, C. B., & Fleming, A. S. (2007). Maternal isolation alters the expression of neural proteins during development: "Stroking" stimulation reverses these effects. *Brain Research, 1158*, 11–27.

Chugani, H. T., Behen, M. E., Muzik, O., Juhasz, C., Nagy, F., & Chugani, D. C. (2001). Local brain functional activity following early deprivation: A study of postinstitutionalized Romanian orphans. *NeuroImage, 14*(6), 1290–1301.

Curley, J. P., Davidson, S., Bateson, P., & Champagne, F. A. (2009). Social enrichment during postnatal development induces transgenerational effects on emotional and reproductive behavior in mice. *Frontiers in Behavioral Neuroscience, 3*, 25.

Danchin, E., Charmantier, A., Champagne, F. A., Mesoudi, A., Pujol, B., & Blanchet, S. (2011). Beyond DNA: Integrating inclusive inheritance into an extended theory of evolution. *Nature Reviews Genetics, 12*(7), 475–486.

de Medeiros, C. B., Fleming, A. S., Johnston, C. C., & Walker, C. D. (2009). Artificial rearing of rat pups reveals the beneficial effects of mother care on neonatal inflammation and adult sensitivity to pain. *Pediatric Research, 66*(3), 272–277.

Dodd, V. L. (2005). Implications of kangaroo care for growth and development in preterm infants. *Journal of Obstetric, Gynecologic and Neonatal Nursing, 34*(2), 218–232.

Eluvathingal, T. J., Chugani, H. T., Behen, M. E., Juhasz, C., Muzik, O., Maqbool, M., et al. (2006). Abnormal brain connectivity in children after early severe socioemotional deprivation: A diffusion tensor imaging study. *Pediatrics, 117*(6), 2093–2100.

Fairbanks, L. A. (1989). Early experience and cross-generational continuity of mother-infant contact in vervet monkeys. *Developmental Psychobiology, 22*(7), 669–681.

Feldman, R., Eidelman, A. I., Sirota, L., & Weller, A. (2002). Comparison of skin-to-skin (kangaroo) and traditional care: Parenting outcomes and preterm infant development. *Pediatrics, 110*(1 Pt 1), 16–26.

Feldman, R., Gordon, I., Schneiderman, I., Weisman, O., & Zagoory-Sharon, O. (2010). Natural variations in maternal and paternal care are associated with systematic changes in oxytocin following parent-infant contact. *Psychoneuroendocrinology, 35*(8), 1133–1141.

Feng, X., Wang, L., Yang, S., Qin, D., Wang, J., Li, C., et al. (2011). Maternal separation produces lasting changes in cortisol and behavior in rhesus monkeys. *Proceedings of the National Academy of Sciences U S A, 108*(34), 14312–14317.

Field, T. M., Schanberg, S. M., Scafidi, F., Bauer, C. R., Vega-Lahr, N., Garcia, R., et al. (1986). Tactile/kinesthetic stimulation effects on preterm neonates. *Pediatrics, 77*(5), 654–658.

Francis, D., Diorio, J., Liu, D., & Meaney, M. J. (1999). Nongenomic transmission across generations of maternal behavior and stress responses in the rat. *Science, 286*(5442), 1155–1158.

Francis, D. D., Champagne, F. C., & Meaney, M. J. (2000). Variations in maternal behaviour are associated with differences in oxytocin receptor levels in the rat. *Journal of Neuroendocrinology, 12*(12), 1145–1148.

Franklin, T. B., Russig, H., Weiss, I. C., Graff, J., Linder, N., Michalon, A., et al. (2010). Epigenetic transmission of the impact of early stress across generations. *Biological Psychiatry, 68*(5), 408–415.

Gimpl, G., & Fahrenholz, F. (2001). The oxytocin receptor system: Structure, function, and regulation. *Physiological Reviews, 81*(2), 629–683.

Gonzalez, A., Lovic, V., Ward, G. R., Wainwright, P. E., & Fleming, A. S. (2001). Intergenerational effects of complete maternal deprivation and replacement stimulation on maternal behavior and emotionality in female rats. *Developmental Psychobiology, 38*(1), 11–32.

Gorski, R. A. (1978). Sexual differentiation of the brain. *Hospital Practice, 13*(10), 55–62.

Gubernick, D. J., & Alberts, J. R. (1983). Maternal licking of young: Resource exchange and proximate controls. *Physiology and Behavior, 31*(5), 593–601.

Hane, A. A., & Fox, N. A. (2006). Ordinary variations in maternal caregiving influence human infants' stress reactivity. *Psychological Science, 17*(6), 550–556.

Harlow, H. F., Dodsworth, R. O., & Harlow, M. K. (1965). Total social isolation in monkeys. *Proceedings of the National Academy of Science U S A, 54*(1), 90–97.

Hellstrom, I. C., Dhir, S. K., Diorio, J. C., & Meaney, M. J. (2012). Maternal licking regulates hippocampal glucocorticoid receptor transcription through a thyroid hormone-serotonin-NGFI-A signalling cascade. *Philosophical Transactions of the Royal Society of London Series B: Biological Sciences, 367*(1601), 2495–2510.

Hofer, M. A. (1975). Studies on how early maternal separation produces behavioral change in young rats. *Psychosomatic Medicine, 37*(3), 245–264.

Jablonka, E., & Lamb, M. J. (2002). The changing concept of epigenetics. *Annals of the New York Academy of Sciences U S A, 981*, 82–96.

Jenuwein, T., & Allis, C. D. (2001). Translating the histone code. *Science, 293*(5532), 1074–1080.

Jirtle, R. L., & Skinner, M. K. (2007). Environmental epigenomics and disease susceptibility. *Nature Reviews Genetics, 8*(4), 253–262.

Kaffashi, F., Scher, M. S., Ludington-Hoe, S. M., & Loparo, K. A. (2013). An analysis of the kangaroo care intervention using neonatal EEG complexity: A preliminary study. *Clinical Neurophysiology, 124*(2), 238–246.

Keverne, E. B., & Curley, J. P. (2004). Vasopressin, oxytocin and social behaviour. *Current Opinion in Neurobiology, 14*(6), 777–783.

Korosi, A., Shanabrough, M., McClelland, S., Liu, Z. W., Borok, E., Gao, X. B., et al. (2010). Early-life experience reduces excitation to stress-responsive hypothalamic neurons and reprograms the expression of corticotropin-releasing hormone. *Journal of Neuroscience, 30*(2), 703–713.

Kuhn, C. M., & Schanberg, S. M. (1998). Responses to maternal separation: Mechanisms and mediators. *International Journal of Developmental Neuroscience, 16*(3–4), 261–270.

Kurian, J. R., Olesen, K. M., & Auger, A. P. (2010). Sex differences in epigenetic regulation of the estrogen receptor-alpha promoter within the developing preoptic area. *Endocrinology, 151*(5), 2297–2305.

Lehmann, J., & Feldon, J. (2000). Long-term biobehavioral effects of maternal separation in the rat: consistent or confusing? *Reviews in the Neurosciences, 11*(4), 383–408.

Lehmann, J., Pryce, C. R., Jongen-Relo, A. L., Stohr, T., Pothuizen, H. H., & Feldon, J. (2002). Comparison of maternal separation and early handling in terms of their neurobehavioral effects in aged rats. *Neurobiology of Aging, 23*(3), 457–466.

Levy, F., Melo, A. I., Galef, B. G., Jr., Madden, M., & Fleming, A. S. (2003). Complete maternal deprivation affects social, but not spatial, learning in adult rats. *Developmental Psychobiology, 43*(3), 177–191.

Li, E., Bestor, T. H., & Jaenisch, R. (1992). Targeted mutation of the DNA methyltransferase gene results in embryonic lethality. *Cell, 69*(6), 915–926.

Liu, D., Diorio, J., Day, J. C., Francis, D. D., & Meaney, M. J. (2000). Maternal care, hippocampal synaptogenesis and cognitive development in rats. *Nature Neuroscience, 3*(8), 799–806.

Liu, D., Diorio, J., Tannenbaum, B., Caldji, C., Francis, D., Freedman, A., et al. (1997). Maternal care, hippocampal glucocorticoid receptors, and hypothalamic-pituitary-adrenal responses to stress. *Science, 277*(5332), 1659–1662.

Lovic, V., & Fleming, A. S. (2004). Artificially-reared female rats show reduced prepulse inhibition and deficits in the attentional set shifting task—reversal of effects with maternal-like licking stimulation. *Behavioural Brain Research, 148*(1–2), 209–219.

Lovic, V., Fleming, A. S., & Fletcher, P. J. (2006). Early life tactile stimulation changes adult rat responsiveness to amphetamine. *Pharmacology Biochemistry and Behavior, 84*(3), 497–503.

Lovic, V., Keen, D., Fletcher, P. J., & Fleming, A. S. (2011). Early-life maternal separation and social isolation produce an increase in impulsive action but not impulsive choice. *Behavioral Neuroscience, 125*(4), 481–491.

Ludington-Hoe, S. M., & Swinth, J. Y. (1996). Developmental aspects of kangaroo care. *Journal of Obstetric, Gynecologic and Neonatal Nursing, 25*(8), 691–703.

Lvoff, N. M., Lvoff, V., & Klaus, M. H. (2000). Effect of the baby-friendly initiative on infant abandonment in a Russian hospital. *Archives of Pediatric and Adolescent Medicine, 154*(5), 474–477.

Maestripieri, D. (1998). Parenting styles of abusive mothers in group-living rhesus macaques. *Animal Behavior, 55*(1), 1–11.

Maestripieri, D. (2005). Early experience affects the intergenerational transmission of infant abuse in rhesus monkeys. *Proceedings of the National Academy of Sciences U S A, 102*(27), 9726–9729.

Maestripieri, D., & D'Amato, F. R. (1991). Anxiety and maternal aggression in house mice (Mus musculus): A look at interindividual variability. *Journal of Comparative Psychology, 105*(3), 295–301.

Maestripieri, D., Wallen, K., & Carroll, K. A. (1997). Infant abuse runs in families of group-living pigtail macaques. *Child Abuse and Neglect, 21*(5), 465–471.

McGowan, P. O., Sasaki, A., D'Alessio, A. C., Dymov, S., Labonte, B., Szyf, M., et al. (2009). Epigenetic regulation of the glucocorticoid receptor in human brain associates with childhood abuse. *Nature Neuroscience, 12*(3), 342–348.

Meaney, M. J. (2001). Maternal care, gene expression, and the transmission of individual differences in stress reactivity across generations. *Annual Review of Neuroscience, 24*, 1161–1192.

Meaney, M. J., & Ferguson-Smith, A. C. (2010). Epigenetic regulation of the neural transcriptome: The meaning of the marks. *Nature Neuroscience, 13*(11), 1313–1318.

Meaney, M. J., Mitchell, J. B., Aitken, D. H., Bhatnagar, S., Bodnoff, S. R., Iny, L. J., & Sarrieau, A. (1991). The effects of neonatal handling on the development of the adrenocortical response to stress: Implications for neuropathology and cognitive deficits in later life. *Psychoneuroendocrinology, 16*(1–3), 85–103.

Mehta, M. A., Golembo, N. I., Nosarti, C., Colvert, E., Mota, A., Williams, S. C., et al. (2009). Amygdala, hippocampal and corpus callosum size following severe early institutional deprivation: The English and Romanian Adoptees study pilot. *Journal of Child Psychology and Psychiatry, 50*(8), 943–951.

Melo, A. I., Lovic, V., Gonzalez, A., Madden, M., Sinopoli, K., & Fleming, A. S. (2006). Maternal and littermate deprivation disrupts maternal behavior and social-learning of food preference in adulthood: Tactile stimulation, nest odor, and social rearing prevent these effects. *Developmental Psychobiology, 48*(3), 209–219.

Menard, J. L., Champagne, D. L., & Meaney, M. J. (2004). Variations of maternal care differentially influence "fear" reactivity and regional patterns of cFos immunoreactivity in response to the shock-probe burying test. *Neuroscience, 129*(2), 297–308.

Miller, C. A., & Sweatt, J. D. (2007). Covalent modification of DNA regulates memory formation. *Neuron, 53*(6), 857–869.

Miller, L., Kramer, R., Warner, V., Wickramaratne, P., & Weissman, M. (1997). Intergenerational transmission of parental bonding among women. *Journal of the American Academy of Child and Adolescent Psychiatry, 36*(8), 1134–1139.

Moore, E. R., Anderson, G. C., Bergman, N., & Dowswell, T. (2012). Early skin-to-skin contact for mothers and their healthy newborn infants. *Cochrane Database of Systematic Reviews, 5*, CD003519.

Moszkowski, R. J., Stack, D. M., Girouard, N., Field, T. M., Hernandez-Reif, M., & Diego, M. (2009). Touching behaviors of infants of depressed mothers during normal and perturbed interactions. *Infant Behavior and Development, 32*(2), 183–194.

Murgatroyd, C., Patchev, A. V., Wu, Y., Micale, V., Bockmuhl, Y., Fischer, D., et al. (2009). Dynamic DNA methylation programs persistent adverse effects of early-life stress. *Nature Neuroscience, 12*(12), 1559–1566.

Naumova, O. Y., Lee, M., Koposov, R., Szyf, M., Dozier, M., & Grigorenko, E. L. (2012). Differential patterns of whole-genome DNA methylation in institutionalized children and children raised by their biological parents. *Developmental Psychopathology, 24*(1), 143–155.

Novakov, M., & Fleming, A. S. (2005). The effects of early rearing environment on the hormonal induction of maternal behavior in virgin rats. *Hormones and Behavior, 48*(5), 528–536.

Okano, M., Bell, D. W., Haber, D. A., & Li, E. (1999). DNA methyltransferases Dnmt3a and Dnmt3b are essential for de novo methylation and mammalian development. *Cell, 99*(3), 247–257.

Palombo, D. J., Nowoslawski, M., & Fleming, A. S. (2010). Motherless rats show deficits in maternal behavior towards fostered pups. *Developmental Psychobiology, 52*(2), 142–148.

Parent, C. I., Del Corpo, A., Cameron, N. M., & Meaney, M. J. (2012). Maternal care associates with play dominance rank among adult female rats. *Developmental Psychobiology, 55*(7), 745–756.

Parent, C. I., & Meaney, M. J. (2008). The influence of natural variations in maternal care on play fighting in the rat. *Developmental Psychobiology, 50*(8), 767–776.

Pauk, J., Kuhn, C. M., Field, T. M., & Schanberg, S. M. (1986). Positive effects of tactile versus kinesthetic or vestibular stimulation on neuroendocrine and ODC activity in maternally-deprived rat pups. *Life Sciences, 39*(22), 2081–2087.

Raby, K. L., Cicchetti, D., Carlson, E. A., Cutuli, J. J., Englund, M. M., & Egeland, B. (2012). Genetic and caregiving-based contributions to infant attachment: Unique associations with distress reactivity and attachment security. *Psychological Science, 23*(9), 1016–1023.

Razin, A. (1998). CpG methylation, chromatin structure and gene silencing-a three-way connection. *EMBO Journal, 17*(17), 4905–4908.

Ronca, A. E., Lamkin, C. A., & Alberts, J. R. (1993). Maternal contributions to sensory experience in the fetal and newborn rat (Rattus norvegicus). *Journal of Comparative Psychology, 107*(1), 61–74.

Ross, H. E., & Young, L. J. (2009). Oxytocin and the neural mechanisms regulating social cognition and affiliative behavior. *Frontiers in Neuroendocrinology, 30*(4), 534–547.

Roth, T. L. (2012). Epigenetics of neurobiology and behavior during development and adulthood. *Developmental Psychobiology, 54*(6), 590–597.

Roth, T. L., Lubin, F. D., Funk, A. J., & Sweatt, J. D. (2009). Lasting epigenetic influence of early-life adversity on the BDNF gene. *Biological Psychiatry, 65*(9), 760–769.

Russell, D. H. (1985). Ornithine decarboxylase: A key regulatory enzyme in normal and neoplastic growth. *Drug Metabolism Reviews, 16*(1–2), 1–88.

Rutter, M., Kumsta, R., Schlotz, W., & Sonuga-Barke, E. (2012). Longitudinal studies using a "natural experiment" design: the case of adoptees from Romanian institutions. *Journal of the American Academy of Child and Adolescent Psychiatry, 51*(8), 762–770.

Sapolsky, R. M., & Meaney, M. J. (1986). Maturation of the adrenocortical stress response: Neuroendocrine control mechanisms and the stress hyporesponsive period. *Brain Research, 396*(1), 64–76.

Sapolsky, R. M., Meaney, M. J., & McEwen, B. S. (1985). The development of the glucocorticoid receptor system in the rat limbic brain. III. Negative-feedback regulation. *Brain Research, 350*(1–2), 169–173.

Sato, F., Tsuchiya, S., Meltzer, S. J., & Shimizu, K. (2011). MicroRNAs and epigenetics. *FEBS Journal, 278*(10), 1598–1609.

Seidel, K., Poeggel, G., Holetschka, R., Helmeke, C., & Braun, K. (2011). Paternal deprivation affects the development of corticotrophin-releasing factor-expressing neurones in prefrontal cortex, amygdala and hippocampus of the biparental Octodon degus. *Journal of Neuroendocrinology, 23*(11), 1166–1176.

Seth, K. A., & Majzoub, J. A. (2001). Repressor element silencing transcription factor/ neuron-restrictive silencing factor (REST/NRSF) can act as an enhancer as well as a repressor of corticotropin-releasing hormone gene transcription. *Journal of Biological Chemistry, 276*(17), 13917–13923.

Spinelli, S., Chefer, S., Suomi, S. J., Higley, J. D., Barr, C. S., & Stein, E. (2009). Early-life stress induces long-term morphologic changes in primate brain. *Archives of General Psychiatry, 66*(6), 658–665.

Stanton, M. E., Gutierrez, Y. R., & Levine, S. (1988). Maternal deprivation potentiates pituitary-adrenal stress responses in infant rats. *Behavioral Neuroscience, 102*(5), 692–700.

Suomi, S. J. (1991). Early stress and adult emotional reactivity in rhesus monkeys. *Ciba Foundation Symposium, 156*, 171–183; discussion 83–88.

Turek-Plewa, J., & Jagodzinski, P. P. (2005). The role of mammalian DNA methyltransferases in the regulation of gene expression. *Cellular & Molecular Biology Letters, 10*(4), 631–647.

Turner, B. (2001). *Chromatin and gene regulation.* Oxford, UK: Blackwell Science.

Wang, S., Bartolome, J. V., & Schanberg, S. M. (1996). Neonatal deprivation of maternal touch may suppress ornithine decarboxylase via downregulation of the proto-oncogenes c-myc and max. *Journal of Neuroscience, 16*(2), 836–842.

Weaver, I. C., Cervoni, N., Champagne, F. A., D'Alessio, A. C., Sharma, S., Seckl, J. R., et al. (2004). Epigenetic programming by maternal behavior. *Nature Neuroscience, 7*(8), 847–854.

Weaver, I. C., Champagne, F. A., Brown, S. E., Dymov, S., Sharma, S., Meaney, M. J., & Szyf, M. (2005). Reversal of maternal programming of stress responses in adult offspring through methyl supplementation: altering epigenetic marking later in life. *Journal of Neuroscience, 25*(47), 11045–11054.

Weaver, I. C., Grant, R. J., & Meaney, M. J. (2002). Maternal behavior regulates long-term hippocampal expression of BAX and apoptosis in the offspring. *Journal of Neurochemistry, 82*(4), 998–1002.

Weaver, I. C., Meaney, M. J., & Szyf, M. (2006). Maternal care effects on the hippocampal transcriptome and anxiety-mediated behaviors in the offspring that are reversible in adulthood. *Proceedings of National Academy of Science USA, 103*(9), 3480–3485.

Widom, C. S. (1989). Child abuse, neglect, and adult behavior: Research design and findings on criminality, violence, and child abuse. *American Journal of Orthopsychiatry, 59*(3), 355–367.

Zhang, T. Y., Hellstrom, I. C., Bagot, R. C., Wen, X., Diorio, J., & Meaney, M. J. (2010). Maternal care and DNA methylation of a glutamic acid decarboxylase 1 promoter in rat hippocampus. *Journal of Neuroscience, 30*(39), 13130–13137.

Zheng, D., Zhao, K., & Mehler, M. F. (2009). Profiling RE1/REST-mediated histone modifications in the human genome. *Genome Biology, 10*(1), R9.

{ Commentary }

As Time Goes By, a Touch Is More Than Just a Touch

Eric E. Nelson

Development is a complex process involving a multitude of intrinsically released signals mingling with environmental conditions across both space and time (Stiles, 2008). In the midst of this complexity, it is remarkable that real reductionist scientific principles can be revealed, and yet as is evidenced throughout the elegant work summarized in this chapter, they clearly can. Although the breadth and scope of the research characterized by Dr. Champagne is extensive, there are three points in particular that I think deserve further comment.

The first is the important role that sensitive periods play in shaping development. At both phenomenological and mechanistic levels, development and learning have much in common. Both involve adaptation to environmental conditions with mechanisms that act to stabilize coactive circuits (Stiles, 2008), and both are to some extent adaptive. One important difference, however, is that environmental impact is not equipotent across development. The existence of sensitive periods was first demonstrated for the organization of the visual system in development by the Nobel Prize winning work of David Hubel and Torston Wiesel in the 1960s. Since this groundbreaking work, many functional systems have been identified whose development is particularly sensitive to a specific aspect of environmental input for a restricted period of time during development (Kuhl, 2010; Maurer, Lewis, and Mondloch, 2005; Pascalis et al., 2005; Sharma, Nash, and Dorman, 2009). The developmental systems characterized in this overview also appear to fit this model: experience of a specific environmental stimulus in a short maturational window is particularly potent in shaping brain organization.

The breadth of these findings suggests that sensitive periods may be a general principle of development. Although most of the work characterizing sensitive periods has focused on organization of sensory systems in early postnatal life, the findings from the work outlined here and elsewhere (Levine, 2005) demonstrate that emotional systems also undergo sensitive periods of organization. One of the challenges facing the study of development is to identify the timing and input that shape these varied circuits across maturation. The importance of this is highlighted by recent perspectives from psychiatry that most current psychopathologies have developmental roots and can in many ways be construed as developmental in nature (Paus, Keshavan, and Giedd, 2008). The research described here clearly demonstrates that experiences with the mother during the preweaning period influences the organization of stress reactivity and patterns of parental behavior expressed in adulthood. This suggests that particular care be taken in this developmental phase for individuals who live in a high stress environment or who for other reasons may be vulnerable to aberrant development of these systems. Identifying developmental patterns of other systems that have different timing dynamics and are sensitive to different environmental conditions should be an important focus of future developmental work. Moreover, synthesizing and communicating this information to teachers, health care providers, and other key members of society may be an important societal task for developmental psychologists in the coming century.

The second noteworthy point addressed in this chapter is the pervasive impact of somatosensory input in guiding development. To date research has demonstrated that the trajectory of functions as diverse as physical growth, endocrine homeostasis, and parental behavior are modulated by somatosensory input during development. In some ways the pervasiveness of the impact of somatosensory input is not surprising. The somatosensory system is almost certainly the oldest and most evolutionarily conserved sensory system, and the skin is clearly the largest sensory organ; therefore, it makes sense that somatosensory input would have widespread influences on central nervous system function. However, given the varieties of somatosensory experience from thermal pain and gentle scratch to calming pat and erotic stroke, the studies highlighted here likely only represent the tip of the iceberg for organizational influences exerted by varied somatosensory experiences in development. For example, does the experience of pain or hypothermia during development leave a lasting imprint, and what role might the tactile experience of rough-and-tumble play or initial sexual experiences have on shaping subsequent social behavior? In many ways the profound effects induced by the simple tactile experiences associated with licking and stroking that were outlined here beg the question of what developmental effects the large variety of other somatosensory experiences might induce.

In this light the linking of somatosensory experiences to social behavior is particularly noteworthy. There are several indications that the endogenous opioid system which plays a critical role in attenuating somatosensory-associated pain is also a key ingredient in social reward (Nelson and Panksepp, 1998; Panksepp, Nelson, and Bekkedal, 1997), and conversely circuits associated with somatosensory pain may also underlie the affective experience of social rejection (Eisenberger, Lieberman, and Williams, 2003). The tight relationship between social emotion and somatosensory circuits in the brain also suggests the reverse question may be an important one as well—namely how might variations in social experience across maturation affect the development of somatosensation? Some preliminary studies suggest a relationship in this direction might also exist (Blass, Fitzgerald, and Kehoe, 1987; Schneider et al., 2013).

Finally and perhaps most important, the research outlined here highlights the dynamic nature of genes in development. Genes themselves consist of a series of DNA sequences that code for production of specific proteins. Although the specific genetic sequences are inherited and immutable, the activity of specific genes can be affected my many things. The epigenetic effects detailed here are an excellent example of one way in which inherited genetic sequences can be influenced by the environmental context in which they appear. Epigenetic processes like DNA methylation or histone acetylation can result in either transient or lifelong impacts on genetic activity and can profoundly influence the manner in which genes are expressed in the brain. Certainly one of the most important impacts of the research of Frances Champagne and colleagues like Michael Meaney is the demonstration with compelling empirical simplicity of the imperative aspect of the nature–nurture *interaction* (Meaney, 2010). Simply put, there is no "or" in this relationship. I hope that this research will help move the field beyond the untenable idea that one can be understood without the other.

References

Blass, E., Fitzgerald, E., & Kehoe, P. (1987). Interactions between sucrose, pain and isolation distress. *Pharmacology Biochemistry & Behavior, 26*, 483–489.

Eisenberger, N. I., Lieberman, M. D., & Williams, K. D. (2003). Does rejection hurt? An FMRI study of social exclusion. *Science, 302*, 290–292.

Kuhl, P. K. (2010). Brain mechanisms in early language acquisition. *Neuron, 67*, 713–727.

Levine, S. (2005). Developmental determinants of sensitivity and resistance to stress. *Psychoneuroendocrinology, 30*, 939–946.

Maurer, D., Lewis, T. L., & Mondloch, C. J. (2005). Missing sights: Consequences for visual cognitive development. *Trends in Cognitive Science, 9*, 144–151.

Meaney, M. J. (2010). Epigenetics and the biological definition of gene x environment interactions. *Child Development, 81*, 41–79.

Nelson, E. E., & Panksepp, J. (1998). Brain substrates of infant-mother attachment: Contributions of opioids, oxytocin, and norepinephrine. *Neuroscience and Biobehavioral Reviews, 22*, 437–452.

Panksepp, J., Nelson, E., & Bekkedal, M. (1997). Brain systems for the mediation of social separation-distress and social-reward: Evolutionary antecedents and neuropeptide intermediaries. *Annals of the New York Academy of Science, 807*, 78–100.

Pascalis, O., Scott, L. S., Kelly, D. J., Shannon, R. W., Nicholson, E., Coleman, M., et al. (2005). Plasticity of face processing in infancy. *Proceedings of the National Academy of Sciences U S A, 102*, 5297–5300.

Paus, T., Keshavan, M., & Giedd, J. N. (2008). Why do many psychiatric disorders emerge during adolescence? *Nature Reviews Neuroscience, 9*, 947–957.

Schneider, P., Hannusch, C., Schmahl, C., Bohus, M., Spanagel, R., & Schneider, M. (2013). Adolescent peer-rejection persistently alters pain perception and CB1 receptor expression in female rats. *European Neuropsychopharmacology*. doi: 10.1016/j. euroneuro.2013.04.004.

Sharma, A., Nash, A. A., & Dorman, M. (2009). Cortical development, plasticity and re-organization in children with cochlear implants. *Journal of Communication Disorders*, *42*, 272–279.

Stiles, J. (2008). *The Fundamentals of Brain Development Integrating Nature and Nurture*. Cambridge, MA: Harvard University Press.

{ 3 }

Nonhuman Primate Models of Mental Health

EARLY LIFE EXPERIENCES AFFECT DEVELOPMENTAL TRAJECTORIES

Amanda M. Dettmer, Stephen J. Suomi, and Katie Hinde

Introduction

The basic premise that certain early experiences have important consequences for adult functioning has been a central feature of many developmental theories throughout the history of psychiatry, ethology, psychology, and anthropology. More than 100 years ago, Freud argued that events transpiring during an individual's first 3 years have lifelong influences on that individual's personality. One of the most critical contributions to our understanding of child development has been John Bowlby's attachment theory. In the 1960s and 1970s, Bowlby, borrowing concepts from both psychoanalytic and ethological frameworks, formulated a theory of social attachment which had as its most basic premise the notion that all of an individual's social relationships throughout life are influenced in fundamental ways by the initial attachment relationship with one's mother (or other primary caregiver) (Bowlby, 1977). Multiple developmental neuroscience approaches in the 1980s and 1990s expanded our understanding of this important relationship by focusing on long-term neurobiological changes associated with events experienced during early critical or sensitive periods. At the heart of these approaches has been the basic belief that "the child is the father of the man," that is, that early experiences can and do shape adult functioning (Rutter, 1989; Skeels, 1966).

Infant and child development is complex and multifactorial. Significant insights into the effects of early life environment on infants and children can be gained by cross-cultural investigations, especially among small-scale societies that share features with our environments of evolutionary adaptiveness (see chapters 5, 6, and 8). In addition to understanding the breadth and universalities of human development, the study of nonhuman animals provides additional insights. Animal models afford opportunities that are not ethical, logistical, or plausible among human subjects. Experimental manipulation, pedigreed populations, and faster generation times allow for incredible leverage to unlock the genetic, epigenetic, hormonal, neurobiological, and behavioral contexts (and the interactions among them) that influence the biopsychological organization of individuals during early life (also see chapter 2). In the present chapter we review the role the rhesus macaque has played since the mid-19th century in shaping our understanding of maternal contributions, both behavioral and physiological, to infant development. Importantly, although we emphasize maternal and environmental effects in this chapter, infants and juveniles exert agency and are active contributors to their own development by eliciting and affecting the behavior of their caregivers (Fairbanks and Hinde, 2013). Here we summarize studies that showcase, in turn, some of the ways in which early environment influences behavior, cognition, and physiological regulation. We further expand the construct of early environment to include not just the mother's behavioral care of the infant (or consequences of the absence of that caregiving) but also the role of physiological investment—mother's milk. Collectively these studies emphasize the critical organizational effects of early life that shape long-term functioning in offspring.

The Rhesus Monkey

Some of the most compelling evidence in support of this proposition has come from extensive studies of rhesus monkeys (*Macaca mulatta*) carried out over the past half-century, beginning with the pioneering work of Harlow and colleagues (e.g., Harlow and Harlow, 1969). Rhesus monkeys are a highly successful, widely dispersed, and remarkably adaptable species of macaque monkeys. In the wild and in captive environments that provide sufficient space and resources, these monkeys reside in distinctive social groups (troops), each comprising between 2 dozen and 200 individuals. Each troop, large or small, is organized around several female-headed, multigenerational families, plus several immigrant adult males; this species-normative pattern of social organization is derived from the invariant tendency of females to remain in their natal troop for their entire lifetime, and that of males to emigrate from their natal troop around the time of puberty (Altmann, 1962). And yet, there are dramatic individual differences in the temperaments or personalities, as well as in their respective biological correlates, among the members of each rhesus monkey troop. For example, between 15% and 20% of troop members consistently appear to be unusually fearful or anxious in the face of novel or mildly challenging situations or circumstances, accompanied by significant arousal of a number of biological systems, notably the hypothalamic-pituitary-adrenal (HPA) axis (Suomi, 2004). Another 5% to 10% of troop members seem unusually impulsive or aggressive in many of their social interactions with other troop members. Individuals in this latter subgroup tend to have chronically low levels of central serotonin metabolism (Suomi, 2004).

Rhesus monkey infants born in naturalistic social settings spend virtually all of their first postnatal month in intimate physical contact with their mother, during which time a strong and enduring social attachment bond is developed between mother and infant—one that is functionally equivalent to the attachment bonds that human infants in every culture form with their primary caregivers (Bretherton, 1992; Machado, 2013). As they mature, infants spend increasing amounts of time exploring their immediate physical and social environment, typically using their mother as a "secure base," albeit with marked individual differences; for example, excessively fearful infants are reluctant to leave their mother's side and tend to have low rates of exploration during this time, whereas the opposite is usually the case for excessively impulsive individuals (Suomi, 2005).

In their second and third months, rhesus infants begin to develop distinctive social relationships primarily with *peers*—other infants of like age and comparable physical, cognitive, and social capabilities. Following weaning (usually in the fourth and fifth months), play with peers emerges as a predominant social activity for young monkeys and essentially remains so until puberty (Ruppenthal, Harlow, Eisele, and Harlow, 1974). Although play interactions develop in a species-typical pattern, (i.e., progressively more complex, increasingly sex-specific and sex-segregated; Harlow and Lauersdorf, 1974; Suomi, 2009), here too there are marked individual differences in the form and frequency of play behavior. For example, fearful youngsters appear to be shy in these social situations and tend to initiate relatively few playful exchanges with their peers, whereas impulsive individuals seem overly aggressive once they become involved in an initially playful exchange, eventually leading their peers to largely avoid them in the face of potential injury (Suomi, 1991).

Behavioral Consequences of Rearing Experiences and Environment

Individual differences notwithstanding, the general sequence of social development described above—an initial attachment to the mother, a transition involving both exploration increasingly at a distance from the mother and playful social interactions with peers—has consistently been observed in rhesus monkeys growing up either in naturalistic environments or in captive settings that provide unrestricted access to both their biological mothers and same-aged peers (MP rearing). However, when rhesus monkeys are experimentally raised from birth under conditions that prevent or limit access to either mothers or peers, there are significant behavioral and biological consequences. One such rearing condition that has been studied extensively over the past several decades is *peer-only* (PO) rearing. Here, rhesus infants are physically separated from their biological mothers at birth, hand-reared by human caregivers in a neonatal nursery for their first month of life, and then housed with three or four other same-aged peers (cf. Harlow, 1969; Harlow and Harlow, 1969). Typically, after 6 of 7 months of PO rearing, these infants are placed in larger social groups containing both other same-aged PO-reared monkeys and MP-reared age mates, who have just been weaned from their mothers. In many studies both the PO- and MP-reared juveniles are kept together in these large social groups until puberty. Thus, any subsequent behavioral or biological differences between MP- and PO-reared monkeys can ultimately be traced to their experiences in the initial 6 to 7 months of life.

Virtually all PO-reared monkeys rapidly develop "hyperattachments" to one another within days of being placed together, attachments which are basically dysfunctional in that these infants spend significantly more time throughout their initial months clinging to one another than MP-reared monkeys spend clinging to their biological mothers (Suomi, 2009). Perhaps as a result, PO-reared infants tend to appear fearful, explore little, and play significantly less than their MP-reared counterparts during their initial months together. What little mutual play they do exhibit during this period tends to be rudimentary in nature and short-lived in duration, far less complex than routine play bouts among MP-reared monkeys of comparable age.

PO-reared monkeys as a group also exhibit more extreme behavioral and neuroendocrine (HPA) responses to social stressors that occur within the first year of life than do their MP-reared counterparts (Dettmer, Novak, Suomi, and Meyer, 2012; Suomi, 1997). In addition, perhaps because these PO-reared monkeys are essentially experiencing play deprivation even though they are in the continuous presence of potential playmates, as they grow older they become increasingly aggressive, far more so than most of their MP-reared fellow group members (Fahlke, Lorenz, Long, Champoux, Suomi, and Higley, 2000). Importantly, they also consistently exhibit significantly lower cerebrospinal fluid (CSF) 5-HIAA concentrations than MP-reared monkeys from early infancy to early adulthood (Higley, Chaffin, and Suomi, 2011; Shannon et al., 2005), as well as significantly different developmental trajectories of peripheral measures of the neurotrophic factors NGF and BDNF (Cirulli et al., 2011). Furthermore, as adolescents and young adults, they typically consume significantly more alcohol than MP-reared subjects in a "happy hour" situation (Fahlke et al., 2000; Higley, Hasert, Suomi, and Linnoila, 1991). In these respects PO-reared monkeys exhibit not only many of the same behavioral and biological patterns of response to environmental challenge and social stress that have been shown by excessively fearful monkeys but also those of overly impulsive and aggressive monkeys growing up in naturalistic settings (Higley et al., 2011); that is, they are comorbid for both these sets of behavioral and biological features (Suomi, 2009).

Recent neuorimaging studies have demonstrated that PO-reared monkeys also differ significantly from their MR-reared counterparts in many aspects of both brain function and brain structure. For example, PO-reared juveniles exhibit lower serotonin transporter ligand binding potential and cerebral blood flow, as determined by positron emission tomography, in raphe, thalamus, striatum, frontal, and parietal brain regions, than MP-reared monkeys (Ichise et al., 2006; Spinelli et al., 2010). Additionally, magnetic resonance imaging (MRI) studies have revealed larger stress-sensitive brain regions in PO-reared juveniles, particularly the vermis, dorsomedial prefrontal cortex, and dorsal anterior cingulated cortex (but no differences in corpus callosum thickness or hippocampal size; see Spinelli, Chefer, Suomi, Higley, Barr, and Stein, 2009).

Recent data also indicate major differences in susceptibility to adult disease risk in these differentially reared monkeys. Using microarray analyses of messenger RNA expression, Cole and colleagues (Cole, Conti, Arevalo, Ruggiero, Heckman, and Suomi, 2012) found that as early as 4 months of age, PO-reared infants showed enhanced expression of genes involved in inflammation and T-lymphocyte activation, and suppression of genes involved in antimicrobial defenses. Thus, adverse early life experiences appear to not only social behavior and neurobiology but also immunological functioning.

In sum, early life adversity in the from of PO rearing has profound consequences for rhesus monkeys, not only at the levels of behavioral expression and emotional regulation, but also in terms of neuroendocrine output, neurotransmitter metabolism, brain structure and function, and even genome-wide expression. At the phenotypical level, the behavioral and biological features of PO-reared infants resemble those of naturally occurring subgroups of excessively fearful and excessively impulsive or aggressive rhesus monkeys growing up in the wild, and many of those features persist long after the infants' period of exclusive exposure to peers has been completed and they have been living in more diverse social groups.

Early Rearing Experience and Chronic Stress Outcomes

It is well known that early life adversity, especially neglectful or abusive parenting, results in a host of mental and physical health disparities later in life, many of which are associated with exposure to chronic stress. The HPA axis represents the body's primary neuroendocrine stress response system, and as such is responsible for synchronizing the body's responses to perceived or actual stress. The endpoint of the HPA axis is cortisol, the primary stress response hormone in human and nonhuman primates. Cortisol feeds back negatively to the brain to inhibit further activation of the HPA axis, thereby placing a limit on the duration of the stress response. However, chronic activation of the HPA axis is implicated in the development of many diseases and disorders related to maladaptive parenting practices, including post-traumatic stress disorder and anxiety-related disorders, among others. Much research in animals and humans had demonstrated the detrimental yet often preventable role of adverse early experiences on dysregulated HPA activity and the resulting development of anxious behaviors. Most studied among these in nonhuman primates are differential rearing experiments examining the activity and responsivity of the HPA axis. These experiments yield crucial information regarding the physiological and psychosocial consequences of suboptimal or even neglectful childrearing for the offspring, and offer insight into the nature of social relationships. In particular, nonhuman primate studies examining the physiological, cognitive, and behavioral development of infants reared with peers only (PO reared) versus those reared with their mothers in social groups (MP reared) give us an understanding of the evolution of current parenting practices, and what can result from the abandonment of evolved parenting practices, that is, rearing children with their families, surrounded by multiaged relatives and embedded in cultural practices.

A large body of literature exists on studies of acute stress with respect to early life rearing, but these studies are limited in their ability to assess the long-term physiological consequences of early parenting practices. Past studies have relied on measures of cortisol in blood plasma, saliva, CSF, urine, and feces. Each of these "point" measures provides a window into HPA activity, with blood plasma, saliva, and CSF reflecting activity within the past 15 minutes and urine and feces reflecting activity up to the past 24 hours. Owing in large part to the inherent qualities of these media for assessing cortisol—namely, their circadian variability, low long-term stability, and vulnerability to environmental disturbances (Meyer and Novak, 2012)—nonhuman primate studies examining the effects of early life stress on these measures of cortisol have been difficult to interpret. Early studies indicated that infant peer-reared (PR) monkeys aged 1 to 6 months exhibited similar basal plasma cortisol levels to mother-reared (MR) monkeys, but lower stress reactivity (Clarke, 1993). However, subsequent studies found the reverse, namely that PO-reared monkeys had *lower* basal plasma cortisol levels than MP-reared monkeys at 2 months of age (Capitanio, Mendoza, Mason, and Maninger, 2005; Shannon, Champoux, and Suomi, 1998), and *larger* cortisol increases after repeated stress (Higley, Suomi, and Linnoila, 1992). Finally, one study found that CSF basal or stress-related cortisol did not differ between PO- and MP-reared monkeys. Thus, although these studies have demonstrated differential effects of early parenting practices on later acute stress physiology, the overall impact has been difficult to ascertain. The inconsistency in HPA axis activity in PO-reared monkeys may be due in part to differing PR protocols across laboratories (Capitanio et al., 2005; Shannon et al., 1998; Winslow, Noble, Lyons, Sterk, and Insel, 2003), but they may also be due to the variability of cortisol samples. Additionally, repeated sampling, often invasive in nature, is required to provide a rough composite index of cortisol levels over time (Meyer and Novak, 2012). To address these limitations, in the Laboratory of Comparative Ethology, we have been studying the effects of differential rearing on chronic HPA axis activity and associated psychosocial development in rhesus monkeys.

Recently a new instrument has been developed for assessing HPA activity over long-term time scales. In 2006, an assay for measuring cortisol in the hair of rhesus monkeys was developed and validated (Davenport, Tiefenbacher, Lutz, Novak, and Meyer, 2006). This work demonstrated that cortisol was readily quanitifiable in hair and that hair cortisol levels were positively correlated with salivary cortisol values. Importantly, hair cortisol was significantly elevated compared with baseline after these monkeys were subjected to the major life stressor of relocation (Davenport, Lutz, Tiefenbacher, Novak, and Meyer, 2008). Since the development of this assay, hair cortisol has been assessed in many animal species, including humans, and has been related to levels of perceived stress (Kalra, Einarson, Karaskov, Van Uum, and Koren, 2007). Moreover, several studies in nonhuman primates (rhesus macaques, bonnet macaques, vervets) have demonstrated that hair cortisol is elevated in subjects undergoing significant stress (Davenport et al., 2006; Davenport et al., 2008; Fairbanks, Jorgensen, Bailey, Breidenthal, Grzywa, and Laudenslager, 2011; Laudenslager, Jorgensen, Grzywa, and Fairbanks, 2011; see Meyer and Novak, 2012, for a review). Human studies, too, have shown that hair cortisol is a reliable biomarker of chronic stress in neonates (Yamada et al., 2007), children (Vanaelst et al., 2013), and adults (Dettenborn, Tietze, Bruckner, and Kirschbaum, 2010; Karlén, Ludvigsson, Frostell, Theodorsson, and Faresjö, 2011; Russell, Koren, Rieder, and Van Uum, 2012). Thus, we can use the hair cortisol assay to determine the long-term physiological and psychosocial implications of adverse early rearing so as to better understand the effects of nonancestral forms of parenting on child outcomes.

Exposure to chronic circulating glucocorticoids, whether by repeated exogenous administration or by exposure to repeated stressors, is detrimental to cognitive functioning in humans and animals alike (Lupien, McEwen, Gunnar, and Heim, 2009). In particular, the hippocampus, which functions in the formation of declarative and spatial memories, is particularly vulnerable to chronic stress (Conrad and Bimonte-Nelson, 2010). To determine whether hair cortisol serves as a reliable biomarker for cognitive development in developing rhesus monkeys, we assessed 32 infant monkeys beginning at 14 days of age on Piagetian object permanence tasks (which are reliable measures of emerging cognition: Sackett, Ruppenthal, Hewitson, Simerly, and Schatten, 2006; Wise, Wise, and Zimmerman, 1974). Testing continued through 3 to 4 months of life. Hair samples were collected at 14 days and again at 6 months of age; cortisol for the 6-month hair sample was assayed to provide a retrospective analysis of cumulative glucocorticoid exposure over the previous 5.5 months (which included object permanence testing). We found that hair cortisol concentrations significantly predicted object permanence performance in infant monkeys, such that infants with higher hair cortisol throughout the testing period required more test sessions to complete the tasks and were significantly older upon reaching criterion (Dettmer, Novak, Novak, Meyer, and Suomi, 2009). Since this study, others have also demonstrated a similar relationship between hair cortisol and cognitive functioning in adults (Saleem et al., 2013), indicating that hair cortisol is a reliable biomarker for stress-related cognitive performance. Importantly, the subjects in our study were all nursery-reared (NR) infants, suggesting that suboptimal early life experiences may have long-term consequences for cognitive development; however, we need to determine the relationship between chronic cortisol levels and cognitive development in MP-reared monkeys to ascertain whether this relationship holds only for NR infants. Studies are underway in our laboratory to conduct cognitive testing on infant MP-reared monkeys in their social housing pens, as well as on NR infants, and we aim to elucidate the relationship between hair cortisol and emerging cognition in this more normative population.

Hair cortisol has also recently proved to be a reliable biomarker of some mental health disorders in adults (Staufenbiel, Penninx, Spijker, Elzinga, and van Rossum, 2012; Steudte et al., 2013). In particular, higher hair cortisol has been associated with major depression and bipolar disorder (although this relationship only held for individuals with late age of onset), whereas generalized anxiety disorder, panic disorder, and post-traumatic stress disorder have been associated with lower hair cortisol (Staufenbiel et al., 2012; Steudte et al., 2013). However, all of these studies have been conducted in adults, and thus far no studies have aimed to elucidate the relationship between hair cortisol and the *emergence* of mental health disorders. We studied 61 infant rhesus monkeys prospectively for the first 2 years of life to determine the influences of early life experience on (1) the development of anxious behaviors in adolescence after the imposition of the major life stress of housing relocation at 8 months of age, (2) chronic stress levels across development as assessed by hair cortisol, and (3) the ability of hair cortisol to predict anxious behavior. We studied three groups of monkeys exposed to different rearing conditions: MP reared, PO reared, and surrogate-peer (SP) reared. PO-reared monkeys were reared in a nursery together 24 hours per day, whereas SP-reared monkeys were reared in a nursery in single cages with cloth-covered surrogates and given 2-hour play sessions with three other peers per day. Hair samples were assessed at 6, 12, 18, and 24 months, and composite anxiety scores were calculated at the same time points to reflect total anxious behavior over the preceding 6 months. The effects of early life experience were striking. Across the first 2 years of life, PO-reared monkeys exhibited the most anxious behaviors, followed by SP-reared then MP-reared infants (Dettmer et al., 2012). Notably, PO-reared monkeys exhibited elevated anxiety for up to 1 year after the relocation stress (i.e., up to 18 months of age), whereas MP- and SP-reared monkeys did not differ at this age (Figure 3.1a). Different patterns of hair cortisol levels emerged for each rearing group. PO-reared monkeys exhibited the highest hair cortisol at 6 months (just before relocation), maintained elevated levels at 12 months (just after relocation), and saw cortisol levels gradually decrease over the next year. SP-reared infants' hair cortisol was similar to that of MP-reared infants at 6 months (just before relocation) but sharply rose at 12 months (just after relocation), remained elevated at 18 months, and declined by 24 months to values indistinguishable from MP- and PO-reared infants. MP-reared infants seemed the most unaffected by the major life stress of relocation because their hair cortisol values showed no change from months 6 to 12. Further, their hair cortisol values decreased sharply from months 12 to 18 and remained low at 24 months, indicating that these animals experienced the lowest amounts of chronic stress across development and particularly after a major life stress (Figure 3.1b). These findings

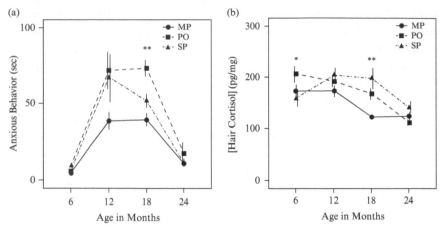

FIGURE 3.1 *Rearing differences in anxious behavior and hair cortisol concentrations across the first two years of life. (a) **PO > MP = SP (p < 0.001). (b) *PO > MP = SP (p < 0.05); **PO = SP > MP (p < 0.01). Data shown as mean + SEM.*

further support the notion of maternal buffering and indicate that being reared in a family-like environment provides later physiological and behavioral coping benefits.

The second main finding from this study was that hair cortisol predicted the emergence of anxious behavior, but *only for at-risk infants.* PO-reared infants only, but not SP- or MP-reared infants, showed a strong positive correlation between hair cortisol taken at 6 months (just before relocation) and anxious behavior at 12 months (just after relocation; r_s = .75, p < .001). Furthermore, 6-month hair cortisol predicted anxious behavior through 18 months as well, but again only for PO-reared infants (r_s = .47, p < .05). Thus, it appears that hair cortisol is a useful biomarker for the development of anxious behavior for populations already at risk for developing such problems. Taken together, our studies using hair cortisol indicate that it is a reliable measure of chronic stress, particularly in individuals exposed to adverse early rearing conditions, and that it serves as a reliable predictor of cognitive and emotional development in young nonhuman primates. Hair cortisol is thus likely to become increasingly valuable in the search for valid biomarkers of stress-related and psychiatric disorders.

Mother's Milk and Infant Behavioral Outcomes

Mothers provide not just the early postnatal social environment but also the postnatal physiological environment. This is most notably through the production of milk, which serves to provide nourishment, immunofactors, and hormonal signals (Hinde and German, 2012). There is a rich literature on how maternal behavioral care of the infant influences offspring behavior (Fairbanks and Hinde, 2013;

Machado, 2013; Vandeleest and Capitanio, 2012; see also chapter 2 of this volume), much less is understood about how mother's milk contributes to offspring behavioral development (Hinde, 2013; Hinde and Capitanio, 2010). Mother's milk contains building blocks for neurodevelopment, such as the fatty acids that are integral to neurodevelopment (Milligan, 2013). Mother's milk also provides the calories infants use for their behavioral activity, which affords them the experiential learning that contributes to neuronal connectivity (Dauncey, 2013). Several studies have also demonstrated that "maternal-origin" hormones in milk, specifically glucocorticoids, bind to receptors in the neonate and exert influences on their neurobiology (Miller et al., 2013; reviewed in Hinde, 2013). These influences may persist into adulthood, although at this time long-term effects are only known from rodent models. Recent data from humans and rhesus monkeys show correlations between mother's milk glucocorticoids and infant temperament, but substantially more research is needed to understand how mother's milk programs infant behavior.

Since the 1980s, Angelucci, Catalani, and Casolini's research group in the Department of Human Physiology and Pharmacology, University of Rome, has conducted a series of experiments on mother's milk glucocorticoids and consequences for offspring. Their studies indicate that ingestion of glucocorticoids through mother's milk contributes to the organization—and therefore regulation—of the HPA axis in offspring into juvenility and adulthood, with important implications for their behavior and cognition. In their study design, rat dams consumed glucocorticoids in their water, increasing glucocorticoids in their blood and their milk. As juveniles, individuals who ingested elevated glucocorticoids through their mother's milk had better spatial memory as assessed by performance in a Morris water maze (Casolini, 1997; Catalani et al., 1993). Moreover, juvenile pups that ingested glucocorticoids engaged in more social play than did controls (Cinque, Zuena, Catalani, Giuli, Tramutola, and Scaccianoce, 2012). In adulthood, these individuals demonstrated less anxiety during stress challenges (Catalani, Casolini, Scaccianoce, Patacchioli, Spinozzi, and Angelucci, 2000; Catalani et al., 2002; Meerlo, Horvath, Luiten, Angelucci, Catalani, and Koolhaas, 2001). Individuals exposed to elevated glucocorticoids in mother's milk showed better regulation of the HPA axis during these challenges, and in males this was apparently mediated by glucocorticoid receptor density in the hippocampus (Catalani et al., 2000). Although females showed similar behavioral and physiological effects as males, the neurobiological mechanism remains unknown—females exposed to glucocorticoids did not have higher density of glucocorticoid receptors in their hippocampus (Catalani et al., 2002). Taken together though, these rodent studies demonstrate empirically that hormones in mother's milk shape behavioral outcomes in offspring, but that the neurobiological pathways may differ for sons and daughters. Notably, these studies did not investigate maternal behaviors that are implicated in offspring outcome, most specifically arched-back nursing and licking and grooming (see chapter 2).

Two studies from rhesus monkeys show some parallels with the rodent model (reviewed in detail in Hinde, 2013). In a sample of 44 rhesus monkey mothers, Sullivan and colleagues (Sullivan, Hinde, Mendoza, and Capitanio, 2011) found substantial individual variation in cortisol concentrations in mother's milk in the outdoor breeding colony at the California National Primate Research Center. Infants whose mothers produced higher concentrations of cortisol in milk were characterized as more "Confident," a factor score derived from systematic ratings of confident, bold, active, curious, and playful trait adjectives (described in detail in Hinde and Capitanio, 2010). However, this main effect was due to a strong effect for sons—milk cortisol concentrations did not predict "Confident" factor scores for daughters (Sullivan et al., 2011). Assessment of milk cortisol concentrations and infant temperament ratings were conducted simultaneously. In another study in the same population, infant "Confident" temperament at 3 to 4 months of age was correlated with earlier available milk energy—the number of calories in the milk that mothers synthesized (Hinde and Capitanio, 2010). Mothers who produced higher available milk energy at 1 month postpartum, when rhesus infants show marked increases in behavioral activity and exploration, had sons and daughters who were characterized as more "Confident" months later. This result suggests that in rhesus monkeys, mother's milk exerts an organizational effect on infant temperament reminiscent of the effects found in rodents.

At the time of this chapter's submission, to the best of our knowledge, only a single study of breast milk cortisol concentrations in humans and infant temperament has been published. Among 52 breastfeeding mothers, Grey and colleagues (Grey, Davis, Sandman, and Glynn, 2012) discovered that higher concentrations of cortisol in breast milk were associated with greater "Negative Affectivity" in the infant. This is a composite score of the infant's tendency toward fear, sadness, discomfort, anger/frustration, and reduced soothability, as reported by the infant's mother. These cross-sectional results were not explained by other factors such as maternal depression or perceived stress. And most interestingly, the effect was a result of an effect in daughters—the relationship between milk cortisol concentrations and negative affectivity was not present in sons. This result is particularly intriguing because the human results differ so markedly from the animal studies, both in that there are stronger effects in daughters than sons and that the effect is toward what could be considered a *less confident* temperament.

Taken together, the above studies on mother's milk reveal that the physiological pathway from mother to infant is not restricted to the role of the placental interface during prenatal life (Rutherford, 2013), but rather continues postnatally in the form of mother's milk. Moreover, given that this postnatal period is when the infant develops behaviorally and participates in contingent social interactions, mother's milk may play a pivotal role in the organization of infant temperament. However, we must be exceedingly cautious in the interpretation of these studies to date. Importantly, the concentration of glucocorticoids in milk is correlated with nutritional aspects of milk—most notably concentrations of fat and protein

(Sullivan et al., 2011)—and possibly also milk volume. However, most studies have investigated milk glucocorticoids in a vacuum from the other bioactives in milk, problematic for apportioning a programming role to glucocorticoids alone (Hinde, 2013). Future research should simultaneously investigate milk hormones and milk energy in concert as well as across time, identifying critical developmental windows. Lastly, a more holistic understanding of the mother–infant dyad is needed that integrates behavioral care and physiological investment to understand whether these have additive or multiplicative effects on infant outcomes.

Conclusion

Rhesus macaques provide an important bridge between the elegant experimental rodent work and the predominantly "epidemiological" research among humans. Results derived from research conducted in rhesus macaques are particularly translational because of our many shared features—an extended developmental time period characterized by the formation of close and long-lasting social bonds, within a complex community, in which the social dynamic requires nuanced social behavior and cognitive abilities. All together, recent research studies on the effects of early rearing experience on physiological, cognitive, and behavioral development inform the long-term consequences of child maltreatment and of parenting practices in general. Specifically, the results presented here demonstrate the superiority of practices in which infants are reared within family units embedded in a broader social context, in which they interact with both peers and nonparental adults and have exposure to family and societal cultural practices. Such a context is without doubt the "IEEA"—infant environment of evolutionary adaptedness.

References

Altmann, S. A. (1962). A field study of the sociobiology of rhesus monkeys, *Macaca mulatta*. *Annals of the New York Academy of Sciences, 102*, 338–435.

Angelucci, L., Patacchioli, F. R., Chierichetti, C., & Laureti, S. (1983). Perinatal mother-offspring pituitary-adrenal interrelationship in rats: Corticosterone in milk may affect adult life. *Endocrinology Experiments, 17*(3–4), 191–205.

Bowlby, J. (1977). The making and breaking of affectional bonds. I. Aetiology and psychopathology in the light of attachment theory. *British Journal of Psychiatry, 130*, 201–210.

Bretherton, I. (1992). The origins of attachment theory: John Bowlby and Mary Ainsworth. *Developmental Psychology, 28*(5), 759–775.

Capitanio, J. P., Mendoza, S. P., Mason, W. A., & Maninger, N. (2005). Rearing environment and hypothalamic-pituitary-adrenal regulation in young rhesus monkeys (*Macaca mulatta*). *Developmental Psychobiology, 46*, 318–330.

Casolini, P., Cigliana, G., Alemà, G. S., Ruggieri, V., Angelucci, L., & Catalani, A. (1997). Effect of increased maternal corticosterone during lactation on hippocampal corticosteroid receptors, stress response and learning in offspring in the early stages of life. *Neuroscience, 79*(4), 1005–1012.

Catalani, A., Casolini, P., Cigliana, G., Scaccianoce, S., Consoli, C., Cinque, C., et al. (2002). Maternal corticosterone influences behavior, stress response and corticosteroid receptors in the female rat. *Pharmacology, Biochemistry and Behavior, 73*(1), 105–114.

Catalani, A., Casolini, P., Scaccianoce, S., Patacchioli, F. R., Spinozzi, P., & Angelucci, L. (2000). Maternal corticosterone during lactation permanently affects brain corticosteroid receptors, stress response and behaviour in rat progeny. *Neuroscience, 100*(2), 319–325.

Catalani, A., Marinelli, M., Scaccianoce, S., Nicolai, R., Muscolo, L. A., Porcu, A., et al. (1993). Progeny of mothers drinking corticosterone during lactation has lower stress-induced corticosterone secretion and better cognitive performance. *Brain Research, 624*, 209–215.

Cinque, C., Zuena, A. R., Catalani, A., Giuli, C., Tramutola, A., & Scaccianoce, S. (2012). Maternal exposure to low levels of corticosterone during lactation increases social play behavior in rat adolescent offspring. *Reviews in the Neurosciences, 23*(5–6), 723–730.

Cirulli, F., Reif, A., Herterich, S., Lesch, K. P., Berry, A., Francia, N, et al. (2011). A novel BDNF polymorphism affects plasma protein levels in interaction with early adversity in rhesus macaques. *Psychoneuroendocrinology, 36*(3), 372–379.

Clarke, A. S. (1993). Social rearing effects on HPA axis activity over early development and in response to stress in rhesus monkeys. *Developmental Psychobiology, 26*, 433–446.

Cole, S. W., Conti, G., Arevalo, J. M., Ruggiero, A. M., Heckman, J. J., & Suomi, S. J. (2012). Transcriptional modulation of the developing immune system by early life social adversity. *Proceedings of the National Academy of Sciences USA, 109*(50), 20578–20583.

Conrad, C. D., & Bimonte-Nelson, H. A. (2010). Impact of the hypothalamic-pituitary-adrenal/gonadal axes on trajectory of age-related cognitive declines. *Progress in Brain Research, 182*, 31–76.

Dauncey, M. J. (2013). Genomic and epigenomic insights into nutrition and brain disorders. *Nutrients, 5*, 887–914.

Davenport, M. D., Tiefenbacher, S., Lutz, C. K., Novak, M. A., & Meyer, J. S. (2006). Analysis of endogenous cortisol concentrations in the hair of rhesus macaques. *General and Comparative Endocrinology, 147*, 255–261.

Davenport, M. D., Lutz, C. K., Tiefenbacher, S., Novak, M. A., & Meyer, J. S. (2008). A rhesus monkey model of self-injury: Effects of relocation stress on behavior and neuroendocrine function. *Biological Psychiatry, 63*, 990–996.

Dettmer, A. M., Novak, M. F., Novak, M. A., Meyer, J. S., & Suomi, S. J. (2009). Hair cortisol predicts object permanence performance in infant rhesus macaques (*Macaca mulatta*). *Developmental Psychobiology, 51*, 706–713.

Dettmer, A. M., Novak, M. A., Suomi, S. J., & Meyer, J. S. (2012). Physiological and behavioral adaptation to relocation stress in differentially reared rhesus monkeys: Hair cortisol as a biomarker for anxiety-related responses. *Psychoneuroendocrinology, 37*, 191–199.

Dettenborn, L., Tietze, A., Bruckner, F., & Kirschbaum, C. (2010). Higher cortisol content in hair among long-term unemployed individuals compared to controls. *Psychoneuroendocrinology, 35*, 1404–1409.

Fahlke, C., Lorenz, J. G., Long, J., Champoux, M., Suomi, S. J., & Higley, J. D. (2000). Rearing experiences and stress-induced plasma cortisol as early risk factors for excessive alcohol consumption in nonhuman primates. *Alcoholism, Clinical and Experimental Research, 24*(5), 644–650.

Fairbanks, L. A., Jorgensen, M. J., Bailey, J. N., Breidenthal, S. E., Grzywa, R., & Laudenslager, M. L. (2011). Heritability and genetic correlation of hair cortisol in vervet monkeys in low and higher stress environments. *Psychoneuroendocrinology, 36*, 1201–1208.

Fairbanks, L. A., & Hinde, K. (2013). Behavioral response of mothers and infants to variation in maternal condition: Adaptation, compensation and resilience. In K. B. H. Clancy, K. Hinde, & J. N. Rutherford (Eds.), *Building babies: Primate developmental trajectories in proximate and ultimate perspectives* (pp. 281–302). New York: Springer.

Grey, K. R., Davis, E. P., Sandman, C. A., & Glynn, L. M. (2012). Human milk cortisol is associated with infant temperament. *Psychoneuroendocrinology, 38(7)*, 1178–1185.

Harlow, H. F. (1969). Age-mate or peer affectional system. In D. S. Lehrman & R. A. Hinde (Eds.), *Advances in the study of behavior* (p. 333). New York: Academic Press.

Harlow, H. F., & Harlow, M. K. (1969). Effects of various mother-infant relationships on rhesus monkey behaviors. *Determinants of Infant Behavior, 4*, 15–36.

Harlow, H. F., & Lauersdorf, H. E. (1974). Sex differences in passion and play. *Perspectives in Biology and Medicine, 17*(3), 348–360.

Higley, J. D., Chaffin, A. C., & Suomi, S. J. (2011). Reactivity and behavioral inhibition as personality traits in nonhuman primates. In A. Weiss, J. E. King, & L. Murray (Eds.), *Personality and temperament in nonhuman primates* (pp. 285–311). New York: Springer.

Higley, J. D., Hasert, M. F., Suomi, S. J., & Linnoila, M. (1991). Nonhuman primate model of alcohol abuse: Effects of early experience, personality, and stress on alcohol consumption. *Proceedings of the National Academy of Sciences U S A, 88*(16), 7261–7265.

Higley, J. D., Suomi, S. J., & Linnoila, M. (1992). A longitudinal assessment of CSF monoamine metabolite and plasma cortisol concentrations in young rhesus monkeys. *Biological Psychiatry, 32*, 127–145.

Hinde, K. (2013). Lactational programming of infant behavioral phenotype. In K. B. H. Clancy, K. Hinde, & J. N. Rutherford (Eds.), *Building babies: Primate developmental trajectories in proximate and ultimate perspectives* (pp. 187–207). New York: Springer.

Hinde, K., & Capitanio, J. P. (2010). Lactational programming? Mother's milk predicts infant temperament and behavior. *American Journal of Primatology, 72*, 522–529.

Hinde, K., & German, B. (2012). Food in an evolutionary context: Insights from mother's milk. *Journal of the Science of Food and Agriculture, 92*, 2219–2223.

Ichise, M., Vines, D. C., Gura, T., Anderson, G. M., Suomi, S. J., Higley, J. D., & Innis, R. B. (2006). Effects of early life stress on [11C] DASB positron emission tomography imaging of serotonin transporters in adolescent peer-and mother-reared rhesus monkeys. *Journal of Neuroscience, 26*(17), 4638–4643.

Kalra, S., Einarson, A., Karaskov, T., Van Uum, S., & Koren, G. (2007). The relationship between stress and hair cortisol in healthy pregnant women. *Clinical and Investigative Medicine, 30*, E103–E107.

Karlén, J., Ludvigsson, J., Frostell, A., Theodorsson, E., & Faresjö, T. (2011). Cortisol in hair measured in young adults—A biomarker of major life stressors? *BMC Clinical Pathology, 11*, 12.

Laudenslager, M. L., Jorgensen, M. J., Grzywa, R., & Fairbanks, L. A. (2011). A novelty seeking phenotype is related to chronic hypothalamic-pituitary-adrenal activity reflected by hair cortisol. *Physiology and Behavior, 104*, 291–195.

Lupien, S. J., McEwen, B. S., Gunnar, M. R., & Heim, C. (2009). Effects of stress throughout the lifespan on the brain, behavior, and cognition. *Nature Reviews, 10*, 434–445.

Meerlo, P., Horvath, K. M., Luiten, P. G., Angelucci, L., Catalani, A., & Koolhaas, J. M. (2001). Increased maternal corticosterone levels in rats: Effects on brain 5-HT1A receptors and behavioral coping with stress in adult offspring. *Behavioral Neuroscience, 115*(5), 1111–1117.

Machado, C. J. (2013). Maternal influences on social and neural development in macaque monkeys. In Clancy, K. B. H., Hinde, K., & Rutherford, J. N., (Eds.), *Building babies: Primate developmental trajectories in proximate and ultimate perspectives* (pp. 259–279). New York: Springer.

Meyer, J. S., & Novak, M. A. (2012). Minireview. Hair cortisol: A novel biomarker of hypothalamic-pituitary-adrenocortical activity. *Endocrinology, 153*, 4120–4127.

Miller, D. J., Wiley, A. A., Chen, J. C., Bagnell, C. A., & Bartol, F. F. (2013). Nursing for 48 hours from birth supports porcine uterine gland development and endometrial cell compartment-specific gene expression. *Biology of Reproduction, 88*(1), 4.

Milligan, L. A. (2013). Do bigger brains mean better milk? In K. B. H. Clancy, K. Hinde, & J. N. Rutherford (Eds.), *Building babies: Primate developmental trajectories in proximate and ultimate perspectives* (pp. 209–231). New York: Springer.

Ruppenthal, G. C., Harlow, M. K., Eisele, C. D., & Harlow, H. F. (1974). Development of peer interactions of monkeys reared in a nuclear-family environment. *Child Development, 45*(30), 670–682.

Russell, E., Koren, G., Rieder, M., & Van Uum, S. (2012). Hair cortisol as a biological marker of chronic stress: Current status, future directions and unanswered questions. *Psychoneuroendocrinology, 37*, 589–601.

Rutherford, J. N. (2013). The primate placenta as an agent of developmental and health trajectories across the life course. In K. B. H. Clancy, K. Hinde, & J. N. Rutherford (Eds.), *Building babies: Primate developmental trajectories in proximate and ultimate perspectives* (pp. 27–53). New York: Springer.

Rutter, M. (1989). Pathways from Childhood to Adult Life. *Journal of Child Psychology and Psychiatry, 30*(1), 23–51.

Sackett, G. P., Ruppenthal, G., Hewitson, L., Simerly, C., & Schatten, G. (2006). Neonatal behavior and infant cognitive development in rhesus macaques produced by assisted reproductive technologies. *Developmental Psychobiology, 48*, 243–265.

Saleem, M., Herrmann, N., Swardfager, W., Oh, P. I., Shammi, P., Koren, G., et al. (2013). Higher cortisol predicts less improvement in verbal memory performance after cardiac rehabilitation in patients with coronary artery disease. *Cardiovascular Psychiatry and Neurology*, doi: 10.1155/2013/340342.

Shannon, C., Champoux, M., & Suomi, S. J. (1998). Rearing condition and plasma cortisol in rhesus monkey infants. *American Journal of Primatology, 46*, 311–321.

Shannon, C., Schwandt, M. L., Champoux, M., Shoaf, S. E., Suomi, S. J., Linnoila, M., & Higley, J. D. (2005). Maternal absence and stability of individual differences in CSF 5-HIAA concentrations in rhesus monkey infants. *American Journal of Psychiatry, 162*(9), 1658–1664.

Skeels, H. M. (1966). Adult status of children with contrasting early life experiences: A follow-up study. *Monographs of the Society for Research in Child Development, 31*(3), 1–65.

Spinelli, S., Chefer, S., Carson, R. E., Jagoda, E., Lang, L., Heilig, M., et al. (2010). Effects of early-life stress on serotonin$_{1A}$ receptors in juvenile rhesus monkeys measured by positron emission tomography. *Biological Psychiatry, 67*(12), 1146–1153.

Spinelli, S., Chefer, S., Suomi, S. J., Higley, J. D., Barr, C. S., & Stein, E. (2009). Early-life stress induces long-term morphologic changes in primate brain. *Archives of General Psychiatry, 66*(6), 658.

Staufenbiel, S. M., Penninx, B. W., Spijker, A. T., Elzinga, B. M., & van Rossum, E. F. (2012). Hair cortisol, stress exposure, and mental health in humans: A systematic review. *38*(8), 1220–1235.

Steudte, S., Kirschbaum, C., Gao, W., Alexander, N., Schönfeld, S., Hoyer, J., & Stalder, T. (2013). Hair cortisol as a biomarker of traumatization in healthy individuals and post-traumatic stress disorder patients. *Biological Psychiatry, 74*(9), 639–646.

Suomi, S. J. (1991). Up-tight and laid-back monkeys: Individual differences in the response to social challenges. In Brauth, S., Hall, W., Dooling, R., (Eds.), *Plasticity of development* (27–56). Cambridge, MA: MIT Press.

Suomi, S. J. (1997). Early determinants of behaviour: Evidence from primate studies. *British Medical Bulletin, 53*(1), 170–184.

Suomi, S. J. (2004). How gene-environment interactions shape biobehavioral development: Lessons from studies with rhesus monkeys. *Research in Human Development, 1*(3), 205–222.

Suomi, S. J. (2005). Mother-infant attachment, peer relationships, and the development of social networks in rhesus monkeys. *Human Development, 48*(1–2), 67–79.

Suomi, S. J. (2009). How gene-environment interactions shape biobehavioural development: Lessons from studies with rhesus monkeys. *Research in Human Development, 1*(3), 205–222.

Sullivan, E. C., Hinde, K., Mendoza, S. P., & Capitanio, J. P. (2011). Cortisol concentrations in the milk of rhesus monkey mothers are associated with confident temperament in sons, but not daughters. *Developmental Psychobiology, 53*, 96–104.

Vanaelst, B., Michels, N., De Vriendt, T., Huybrechts, I., Vyncke, K., Sioen, I., et al. (2013). Cortisone in hair of elementary school girls and its relationship with childhood stress. *European Journal of Pediatrics, 172*(6), 843–846.

Vandeleest, J. J. & Capitanio, J. P. (2012). Birth timing and behavioral responsiveness predict individual differences in the mother–infant relationship and infant behavior during weaning and maternal breeding. *American Journal of Primatology, 74*, 734–746.

Winslow, J. T., Noble, P. L., Lyons, C. K., Sterk, S. M., & Insel, T. R. (2003). Rearing effects on cerebrospinal fluid oxytocin concentration and social buffering in rhesus monkeys. *Neuropsychopharmacology, 28*, 910–918.

Wise, K. L., Wise, L. A., & Zimmerman, R. R. (1974). Piagetian object permanence in the infant rhesus monkey. *Developmental Psychology, 10*, 429–437.

Yamada, J., Stevens, B., de Silva, N., Gibbins, S., Beyene, J., Taddio, A., et al. (2007). Hair cortisol as a potential biologic marker of chronic stress in hospitalized neonates. *Neonatology, 92*, 42–49.

{ Commentary }

Look How Far We Have Come

A BIT OF CONSILIENCE IN ELUCIDATING THE ROLE OF CAREGIVERS IN RELATIONSHIP TO THEIR DEVELOPING PRIMATE INFANTS AND CHILDREN

James J. McKenna

Okay, so I admit it. I still recall coincidentally watching, as an 11-year-old boy, on black-and-white television a nationwide 1960 special hosted by CBS reporter Charles Collingwood called "Mother Love" (Charles Collingwood and Harry F. Harlow, for CBS Television Network, Carousel Films).

Featured on the screen was a very "stage-struck" Professor Harry Harlow who discussed and showed clips of his social experiments on orphaned rhesus macaque infants. His work disproved or at least made suspect one version of Freudian "drive theories" which was predicated on the idea that infants learn to "love" (read, "attach") by collapsing their positive feelings toward being fed and feeling full with the individual responsible for providing that feeling—their mother. Harlow offered a significant corrective to this idea when he demonstrated that even baby monkeys will choose (or prefer) "contact comfort" (soft, terrycloth, surrogate mother bellies) to cold and uncomfortable, wire-rim "mothers" who offer food but not any kind of emotional security derived apparently through their cuddliness. It would seem, then, for nonhuman primates, who are born more mature at birth than are human infants, but not by much, that the "take-home message" was clear and unequivocal: never leave nonhuman primate infants alone! Perhaps more than other mammals, they need, desire, and seek out contact, preferring even a fake, inert, substitute caregiver above food. Ironically, it is only among the least neurologically mature primates of all—human infants, and those specifically living in Western industrialized societies—that the critical importance and advantages of sustained contact, day and night, comes to be considered problematic, if not dangerous, at least in regard to nighttime sleep and feeding arrangements (Konner, 2010; McKenna and McDade, 2005).

What a Difference a Few Decades Can Make

As chapter 3, for which I was given the privilege to comment on, makes clear, during the past especially 30 years or so, a sea change has occurred in the extent to which especially psychological and anthropological methods and theories have been joined at the proverbial intellectual hip, specifically looking for and exposing critical linkages between what looks on the surface to be disparate, functionally disconnected adaptive systems, but instead proves to be anything but that.

It surely was not always this way; that is, this appreciation of the complementarity of psychological and anthropological research leading to joint research efforts by scientists whose degrees span both disciplines, as is the case with Dettmer, Suomi, and Hinde. And perhaps it takes someone that has lived professionally through part of this time period to recognize how significant and productive this change really is. Consider that at the end of the 1950s, field studies of monkeys and apes were still rather sparse. But during the 1960s and 1970s, after heeding the call from the likes of such luminaries as anthropologist Sherwood Washburn at Berkeley and ethologist Robert Hinde at Cambridge, what seemed like a virtual army of young biological anthropologists were packing up their knapsacks, notebooks, and binoculars and heading to the forests of Central and South America, Africa, and Asia to document naturalistic primate behavior.

Whether in anthropology or psychology, those of us who stayed closer to home and worked with animals under semi-natural conditions (housed in outside pens) or within laboratories on developmental issues requiring experimental procedures or manipulations were rather looked down on by our field-bound colleagues. There was general agreement that the increased "stress" that captivity imposed on the animals limited what kind of data could be collected. But more than that, it was presumed, and rightly so, at least to a degree, that formulation especially of evolutionary models or research questions examining how and why particular primate behaviors emerged and functioned were problematic because captive animals were not being subjected to the full range of selective pressures that shaped their present or past behavior. At the time, I think it fair to say, a not-so-invisible elephant separating psychological and anthropological primatology was always in the room: in a word, and with some element of false pride, admittedly, anthropologists gloated something like, "We all know it is the 'field' and nothing less, from which all good primate behavior science will grow."

Right! Surely, the emerging understandings of proximate behavioral and physiological mechanisms and subsystems involving the hypothalamic-pituitary-adrenal axis, the HPA, presented by Dettmer et al., framed and contextualized by evolutionary questions, principles, and explanations, serve presently as an effective historical yardstick to measure just how far both psychology and anthropology have come. It is clear that a form of "consilience" about which Wilson (1998) speaks—that is, the gradual dissolution of strict discipline or theoretical boundaries that comes with the integration of diverse methodologies wrapped around evolutionary-based questions—is at play. This convergence of fields, he predicted, should, as is in evident in chapter 3, truly bridging the social and the biological with the neurological sciences. And...

Don't Forget That Underlying Every Social Relationship There Is...

The idea that underneath every social relationship, perhaps every interaction, bidirectional "neurohormonal traffic" flows, accompanying and accommodating it, may at first seem like an insight demanding the facetious "duh" reaction. But the linkages between social relationships, the underlying neurobiology, and mammalian physiology did not appear quite so obvious or so relevant two or three decades ago. In fact, in my mind, this reality was not really appreciated until the completion of hundreds of deprivation studies examining specifically what happens when that "neural traffic" underlying the relationship of two "attached" individuals suddenly isn't there. This research caused a dramatic, historically important shift in research away from looking at long-term psychosocial behavioral effects of attachment loss without also examining the more immediate changes in brain architecture and, more relevant here, the physiological consequences and the role that the endocrine system plays in regulating and compensating for that loss.

Aspects of the diverse, often deleterious physiological effects of separation, then, at this time came to be identified and appreciated in new ways, especially in the laboratories of John Capitanio, Tiffany Field, John Kauffman, Leonard Rosenblum, Stephan Suomi, and Martin Reite, all of whom made major contributions. Across a wide spectrum of Old World and New World primates, a range of sometimes unexpected deleterious changes in sleep patterns, heart rate, weight gain, and immune efficiency, as well as alterations in thermoregulation, cardiopulmonary physiology, and respiration, all induced by unexpected (or unusual) social changes in the environment of an infant or child were being documented. Studies of the role of a species social structure (e.g., bonnet vs. pig-tailed macaques) showed dramatically how the availability of alloparents and other aspects of social life determined whether anaclitic depression would set in or infants could survive sudden mother loss and, finally, how, even following a mere 3-day separation, the cortisol levels of mother–infant dyads never could or ever did return to baseline, or preseparation, levels (Kaufmann and Rosenblum, 1967).

And What Kind of Brain Should Be Grown?

With so much brain yet to grow at birth, it is not at all surprising that among primates there is great sensitivity to early social experiences and relationships, whether natural or induced experimentally. These experiences, as Dettmer et al. make clear, are proving to be remarkably consistent and determinative as to what kind of brain to grow, whether confident or fearful, or explorative or inhibited, or sad and sullen or zestful and eager. This latter "type," zestful and eager, not surprisingly among monkeys, seems to be associated with infants raised under more "normal" social circumstances in which consistent maternal buffering and support, along with access to others, especially peers, is possible, from whom so much seems to be gained. Dettmer et al. describe significant behavioral differences between infants raised more normally and "peer-only raised" or nursery-raised infants, with differential amounts of cortisol seemingly produced, especially when faced with new circumstances. Peer-only raised animals, who fared the least well developmentally on cognitive and other tests revealing more fearfulness, exhibit the highest cortisol levels at least in novel "stressful" situations, having in the early years also exhibited "hyperattachments" to one another but also, and because of it, failed to play, or at least to learn how to play and, basically, how and when to engage socially with others.

Consequent to these unnatural experiences, these peer-only raised monkeys became more aggressive as young adults—as if to compensate? If anything can be inferred from Dettmer and colleagues' brief synthesis of this current research, it is that through bodily sensory modalities, neonatal and juvenile brains are very good at quickly detecting that something is missing and what needs to be compensated for; and while not always ideal or optimal in the long run, these behavioral responses substitute for minimal needs not being met, making the best out of a bad situation, perhaps in anticipation of a future that holds those same "bad conditions" as constants.

In How Many Roles, and in How Many Ways, Do Hormones Function, Beyond the Simple "Up or Down," "Good or Bad" Regulatory Concept?

One of many fascinating insights to be inferred here is just how difficult it is to functionally pigeon-hole what any particular hormone, especially cortisol, does and when it does it, and to whom. As was pointed out by Dettmer et al. cortisol is generally positively related to stress, as a way to perhaps "rise to the occasion" to overcome whatever appears challenging and requires emotional remediation. But just as cortisol "rises to the occasion," it also feeds back negatively to the brain to inhibit further activation of the HPA axis, thereby placing a limit on the duration of the stress response. After reading reviews of much cortisol-based research, it seems difficult, if not naive, to attribute any singular, simple functional role to cortisol, and to remember how important it is not to think of cortisol in terms of being necessarily the good or bad hormone, the cause or cure, especially in regard to understanding the origins of human mental disorders, but much, much more

I suspect. This is because the data show that while higher cortisol levels are being detected across time in hair samples of those experiencing major depression and late-onset bipolar disease, for example, at least among adults, in other diseases such as anxiety disorders, panic disorders, and post-traumatic stress disorders, cortisol is found in much lower concentrations, so Dettmer et al. point out.

Hence, the variety and significance of "up or down" regulation is not at all simple to predict or interpret across different behavioral and disease domains. Indeed, even *what* specific concentrations mean functionally can vary depending on the sex and age of an individual, whether an infant, child or adult. In other words, not confusing the "effects" of cortisol with disease origins, and not jumping too quickly to interpret its role as being helpful or harmful, is necessary. A review of research reminds us also that cortisol plays a critical role in allostasis, that is, restoring physiological systems to some kind of homeostasis, the interpretation of which can be especially tricky given the plurality of conditions and processes that altogether confound regulation, such as quality of sleep, immune and reproductive status, and its synergisms with other hormones, all of which are factors central to defining proper research questions needed eventually to sort out the varied, multifaceted roles of cortisol.

Breast Milk Composition, Energetic Yield, and Delivery: The Underappreciated Fundamental Beginning Point for "Hidden" Regulatory Mechanisms Relevant to Primate Behavioral Development

During my own career I have spent many years studying and writing about the immediate and long-term behavioral and physiological consequences of human infants in Western societies being deprived of their mother's breast milk, the sensory and cognitive richness of breast milk delivery, and the effects of sleeping alone without the presence of a caregiver, mother, or other (McKenna, Ball, and Gettler, 2007). Not surprisingly, I was therefore most excited to learn of Hinde's (2013) and Hinde and Milligans' (2011) path-breaking research on breast milk and the possibility of postweaning developmental behavioral organizing effects caused (at least in part) by its specific composition and energetic yield (see also Clancy et al., 2013).

Indeed, Hinde's studies show the value of combining long-term, *observational* data collection (traditional primate behavior) with the use of reliable biomarker methodologies tracking offspring hormonal exposures and maternal milk volumes, to name but two, in relationship to the development of brain architecture and behavioral characteristics or proclivities. Altogether, Hinde and colleagues are documenting potentially new ways to conceptualize Bowlby's often-used term, "the infant's tie to its mother," and vice versa, that must include an appreciation of how breast milk facilitates neuronal connectivity, while providing just the right kinds and quality of fatty acids integral to the *pace* and *quality* of neurodevelopment, and while also producing the specific types and quantities of calories needed for maximal energy yield compatible with (perhaps) species-specific behavioral activities that facilitate particular kinds of learning.

Also of interest are Hinde's explorations of how (or if) and for whom breast milk glucocorticoids, in combination with other bioactives, bind with particular receptors in the brain, potentially influencing infant temperament, and therein "programing" or at least *inclining* infants toward particular "styles" and emotional responses (less fearfulness?) coincident with different kinds of social engagements.

Hinde's work among the rhesus monkeys builds on research by her colleagues and even earlier work on rodents, as Dettmer et al. describe in full. For example, and as reported, an earlier study by colleagues at the University of California, Davis Primate Research Center of 44 rhesus monkey infants showed that especially male infants, whose mothers produced higher concentration of cortisol in milk, became more "confident" using a systematically applied, multivariable ranking system (and adjectives like confident, bold, active, curious, and playful). In her own study of that same group, though switching altogether to a new variable, available milk energy, Hinde and her coauthor found that both sons and daughters of rhesus mothers who produced higher available milk energy yields showed behavioral activities and exploration levels that ranked them, similarly, as "confident."

Both of these studies on the rhesus monkeys, although in different ways, are reminiscent of the effects of breast milk composition on rodent infant temperament (anxiety to stress) and cognitive skills first elucidated by researchers in the early 1990s. It was discovered that, as juveniles, rodent pups who ingested elevated levels of glucocorticoids in their mothers' milk had better spatial memory, as reflected by superior performances on maze tests that were interpreted by the authors as reflecting better cognitive skills. More recently, researchers have found that juvenile pups that ingested glucocorticoids engaged in more social play than did controls. As summarized by Dettmer et al., in adulthood these same individuals displayed less anxiety during relocation (another kind of stress test) and overall exhibited better regulation of the HPA axis during this challenge. Interestingly, at least in males, but not females, further research revealed that this response was mediated by enhanced glucocorticoid receptor density in the hippocampus (Sullivan et al., 2011).

In light of these studies on the types of social relationships and individual personalities or temperaments that mothers' milk potentially helps to organize, I, too, especially endorse Rutherford's (see Clancy et al., 2013) inference. She suggests that we must appreciate that the physiological pathway from mother to infant is not restricted to the role of the placental interface experienced only during prenatal life but rather continues postnatally in the form of mothers' milk. Bowlby would most certainly endorse this statement, too, as would those of us who have explored the physiological regulatory effects of mother–infant co-sleeping and breastfeeding among humans (Bretherton, 1992; McKenna et al., 2007). I would only add: we must appreciate that, for humans, along with the content of breast milk itself, the sensory, emotionally and cognitively rich context by which that milk is delivered are quite potentially significant developmentally and throughout the breastfeeding years. Recall that during this period, breastfeeding sessions increase the time mothers and infants spend together and what and how much is communicated between them, along with what is, perhaps, practiced by the infant in regard to a range of social signals, cues, turn-taking, and communicative acts, providing an inestimable opportunity for learning how and what to feel and why, while also learning how to adjudicate, essentially, the desires and wants of others.

References

Bowlby, J. (1951). *Maternal care and mental health*. World Health Organization Monograph Serial Number 2.

Bretherton, I. (1992). The origins of attachment theory: John Bowlby and Mary Ainsworth. *Developmental Psychology, 28*, 759–775.

Clancy, K. B. H., Hinde, K., & Rutherford, J. N. (Eds.) (2013). *Building babies: Primate developmental trajectories in proximate and ultimate perspectives*. New York: Springer.

Hinde, K. (2013). Lactational programming of infant behavioral phenotype. In: K. B. H. Clancy, K. Hinde, & J. N. Rutherford (Eds.), *Building babies: Primate developmental trajectories in proximate and ultimate perspectives* (pp. 187–207). New York: Springer.

Hinde, K., & Milligan, L. M. (2011). Primate milk synthesis: Proximate mechanisms and ultimate perspectives. *Evolutionary Anthropology, 20*, 9–23.

Konner, M. (2010). *The evolution of childhood*. Cambridge, MA: Belknap Press of Harvard University Press: Boston

McKenna, J. J, Ball, H., & Gettler, L. T. (2007). Mother-infant co-sleeping, breastfeeding and sudden infant death syndrome: What biological anthropology has discovered about normal infant sleep and pediatric sleep medicine. *Yearbook of Physical Anthropology, 50*, 133–161.

McKenna, J, J., & McDade, T. (2005). Why babies should never sleep alone: A review of the co-sleeping controversy in relationship to SIDS, breast feeding and bedsharing. *Paediatric Respiratory Reviews, 6*, 134–152.

Rutherford, J. (2013). The primate placenta as an agent of developmental and health trajectories across the life course. In: K. B. H. Clancy, K. Hinde, & J. N. Rutherford (Eds.), *Building babies: Primate developmental trajectories in proximate and ultimate perspectives*. New York (pp. 27–33): Springer

Sullivan, E. C., Hinde, K., Mendoza, S. P., & Capitanio, J. P. (2011). Cortisol concentrations in the milk of rhesus monkey mothers are associated with confident temperament in sons, but not daughters. *Developmental Psychobiology, 53*, 96–104.

Wilson, E. O. (1998). *Consilience: The unity of knowledge*. New York: Knopf.

Evolution's Baseline: Hunter-Gatherer Contexts

4

Relationships and Resource Uncertainty

COOPERATIVE DEVELOPMENT OF EFE
HUNTER-GATHERER INFANTS AND TODDLERS

Gilda Morelli, Paula Ivey Henry, and Steffen Foerster

4.15.06: Eleven-month-old Uese sits wide-eyed in her aunt's lap as men, women, boys, and girls stream from the forest into the bright light of the freshly cleared camp. Cheerful greetings and song meet the newcomers as they are helped to ease baskets and infants to the ground. Babies are cuddled by people they do not know or do not remember; with a bit of humored coaxing, toddlers are directed to shake hands, and older children bring water to the travelers. In time, they sit and share news, and voices blend with the sound of bees circling above.

First one and then several men untie bundles of honey, and pieces of dripping comb make their way across camp. It is difficult to keep track of the flow—honey received from one person is then shared with another, and in minutes all are eating, seemingly content with their share.

Uese is amazed by the rich sweetness in her mouth. As her mother opens a roasted yam, she steps unsteadily to her side. Her mother breaks off a small warm piece and says a few quiet words to Uese, placing it into her waiting hand. Uese toddles to a young girl, newly arrived, and breaks off a piece, offering an equal morsel in out-stretched hand. Smiling, the girl accepts, and together they watch the animated sto-rytelling of men nearby. A boy grins at Uese and breaks from the group, scooping her onto his hip. Her brow knits, uncertain how to respond to her cousin, not remembering their last camp together. Sensing her concern, he distracts her with a flowering vine and carries her about camp. Uese's mother disappears into the forest to retrieve fresh antelope from her husband's unmarried nephew, in recognition of meals the family has shared with him in the past. Uese's cousin sets her down beside her sister, who is weav-ing a basket for tomorrow's foray.

The day fades as women shingle last leaves on new huts; others return from the forest with bedding and firewood. A neighbor beckons Uese to come see the baby she nurses—a newborn whose mother has not yet returned from gathering. Uese perches on her thigh and fingers the baby's tiny hands. When her own mother returns to the hearth, Uese feels very hungry and fusses, reaching for her breast. Saying nothing, her mother kneels next to the fire and blows on the fading embers. As they burst into flames, her mother sits, and Uese climbs into her lap and begins to nurse hungrily. Water begins to boil for the rest of the family's meal.

Abruptly, an angry voice complains from across the camp, and all are reminded of the dispute that once split the group. Voices soften, and the gentle rhythm from a finger piano eases the tension. When Uese's sucking slows with sleepiness, she is laid into the arms of an old relative, whose own children have long since died. Draped there also is a small orphaned boy, now in the woman's care. Uese's mother and sister join a group of women on the other side of camp.

Darkness sets in, and a drum beats to the laughter of girls, a decade's span in age, sitting arms entwined. Men rub aching feet and store their bows and arrows in the rafters of huts; women confer about the search for food. Many will go to "kilima ya njala"—hill of hunger—a forest patch dense with yams where innumerable generations have foraged when other foods are scarce. Tomorrow, though, they will go because it is close; and happily, as the abundant honey affirms that many weeks of poor returns are, for now, finally behind them.

This vignette describes experiences typical of the Efe of the Ituri Forest, who over generations have hunted and foraged a broad stretch of tropical forest on the northeastern edge of the vast Congo River Basin. It exemplifies the pace of the continuously shifting social and physical landscape of hunter-gatherer child experience, as well as the influence of multiple cooperative relationships on Efe children's ability to secure resources. Honey season is a celebratory time, and even more so when game is plentiful. Sharing abounds, moods are raised as families and friends reconnect after months apart, and vestiges of past conflicts are forgotten. Other times are challenging for the Efe. When rains are heavy, foraging becomes difficult and food scarce. Smaller camps lie fragmented across the high ground between swollen rivers, and poor returns are guarded from exchange obligations by the rain that forces hearths inside.

The unpredictability of resources is a part of Efe life across the life span, influencing wellness and behavior. But its effects can be especially profound for babies as they leave a niche buffered by breast milk and continuous contact. These children are increasingly heavy and energetically costly to carry, but they are not able to independently follow their mothers when they gather food. And they are not as good as their older and more skilled social players at competing for resources.

The Efe adapt to shifts in resource availability by changing residency and camp location, and by sharing unpredictable returns in flexible social networks calibrated to individual and cooperative needs. These interpersonal networks develop over a lifetime of association with family, clan, and other Efe. Efe babies are centered within social networks from birth, and they access food and other interests by active social participation. Through these early experiences, and from observation, imitation, and instruction in valued patterns of behavior, Efe babies develop crucial cooperative competencies to strategically garner resources from others. Over time, they develop the more complex skills required to be economically and reproductively successful partners in social networks that they will depend on throughout their lives.

Chapter Background and Overview

More than 25 years have passed since Tronick et al. first reported the significant breadth and intensity of cooperation in Efe infant care now known to characterize their social landscape from birth into early childhood (Ivey, 2000; Morelli and Tronick, 1987; Tronick, Morelli, and Ivey Henry, 1992; Tronick, Morelli, and Winn, 1987). At the time, the highly social nature of Efe infancy was viewed as an extreme, even odd, outlier to the canonical expectation that human infants develop primarily under the sole care of mothers, graduating into the broader community later in childhood. This premise privileged the patterns of care and social interaction characteristic of middle-class communities in the United States and Western Europe (Arnett, 2008) and continues to retain special influence as *the* human evolutionary legacy (Morelli and Ivey Henry, in press). Now, however, a sea change has occurred in hunter-gatherer research demonstrating both the prevalence of shared developmental assistance and the universal energetic need of human mothers for it (Hewlett and Lamb, 2005; Hrdy, 2005; Kramer and Ellison, 2010). This progress has been critical to the vibrant synthesis of work to understand the ecological conditions that favor human cooperative solutions to inherent genetic evolutionary conflicts. The emergence of human cooperation from behavioral flexibility, shared risks, and shared genes established the reliable patterns of resource and information exchange from which human life history, and culture, developed (Alvard, 2009; Gurven, 2004; Hill et al., 2011; Kaplan, Hill, Lancaster, and Hurtado, 2012).

We return to research on Efe babies with these theoretical advancements as backdrop to examine Efe life history and ecological circumstances, past and present, that favor the cooperative patterns of babies' relationships and their developing capacity to participate in them to secure resources. We describe the nutritional, physical, and social ecology of Ituri Forest life to frame more clearly the uncertainties and tradeoffs of Efe child growth and development and the behavioral adaptations that characterize Efe relationships. Then we examine babies' social networks and resource acquisition from infancy through the toddler period.

Efe Adaptive Landscape

The Efe are one of the oldest and most genetically diverse extant lineage of modern humans (Hammer, Woerner, Mendez, Watkins, and Wall, 2011; Patin et al., 2009), and one of the few remaining traditional African pygmy groups inhabiting the Congo Basin of sub-Saharan Africa (Bailey and DeVore, 1989). African

pygmies were long considered fragments of a homogeneous population, but ancestral pygmies diverged into two distinct clusters during climactic retraction of the
Congo forest about 27 thousand years ago. Since then, there has been little gene
flow between the western (Aka, Baka, Bakola, Biaka) and eastern (Efe, Mbuti,
Asua, Batwa, Babinga) clusters, and variable cultural and genetic assimilation with
neighboring populations (Bahuchet, 2012; Hewlett, 1996). The Efe remain distinct
in their lack of genetic admixture (perhaps accounting for the lowest average stature of any human population), their primary subsistence use of bow and arrow, and
only sporadic engagement in market economies. Efe subsistence and social ecology closely mirror that in which human biology—and social dependence—evolved,
providing a rare window into the ontogeny of cooperative dexterity demanded by
foraging life. The ancestry of Efe pygmies, together with evidence of wetter and
highly variable ecosystems during the period of human evolutionary emergence
(Magill, Ashley, and Freeman, 2013a, 2013b), reframes their place in the central
story of human social and biological evolution.

The Ituri Forest, ancestral home of the Efe, lies along the northeastern rim of
the Congo Basin and was once part of a large forest archipelago providing rare
ecological continuity during the period of hominid evolution (Mercader, 2002). The
Efe maintain a predominantly foraging lifestyle. Men hunt and gather in groups
and solitarily; women gather, mostly in groups and often with children. In some
years, the Efe journey to the forest-savanna margins in search of food. The diverse
and verdant nature of African tropical forests, however, belies significant temporal and spatial unpredictability of preferred foods (Foerster, Cords, and Montfort,
2012; Wilkie, 1987), risks for micronutrient deficiency and food toxicity (Davies,
2013), marked leanness of most protein sources (Siren and Machoa, 2008), and a
scarcity of carbohydrates (Hladik, 1993).

Like hunter-gatherers elsewhere, Efe gained access to new resource patches
through contact with horticulturalists (Kelly, 1995) believed to have migrated into
the Ituri Forest about 2 thousand years ago with the introduction of bananas
(Vansina, 1990). Their descendants, including the Lese, live in villages that dot the
road transecting the forest. The clan-based, interpersonal exchange system of Efe
forager and Lese farmer men has been described as symbiotic, but may be better characterized as a mixture of cooperation, conflict, interdependence, and mis-
trust (Wilkie and Curran, 1993). The formalized but flexible pattern of reciprocity
offers advantages to Lese in the form of Efe labor, especially during short-duration
high-need periods of clearing, planting, and harvesting of crops. In return, Efe
are given limited access to garden yields, but are expected to share highly valued
resources of meat and honey. In recent decades, the alliance has grown fragile as
Lese gardens and villages retracted with the disrepair of roads and dwindling markets across the Ituri. Even with fewer Lese partners and more meager harvests, the
Efe, unlike a number of other foragers (Dounias and Froment, 2011), have not
adopted farming.

In addition to the unpredictability of food, the Congo is rife with pathogens and trauma hazards (Dounias and Froment, 2011). Strong positive selection on immune-related genes in pygmy populations, for example, bears evidence of a long history of exposure to disease-producing agents (Lachance et al., 2012). High exposure to pathogens through activities strongly associated with zoonotic infections and infectious disease is a significant cause of death among foragers (Gurven and Kaplan, 2007), including the Efe (Bailey, 1991a). Young children are at special risk for harm, given their small size, immature immune systems, and precarious skills.

Adaptation to Ecological Uncertainty

NUTRITIONAL UNCERTAINTY

The Efe, like all pygmies, share a suite of biological and social adaptations in response to nutritional uncertainty common in rainforest environments. Nutritional pressure is a central hypothesis of pygmy stature (Perry et al., 2007) because small body size reduces caloric demands of cell growth and maintenance (Kuzawa, 2007; Stearns, 1992). Along with slower growth rates from early childhood (Bailey, 1991a) through puberty, a long history of adaptation to limited nutritional resources (Becker, Verdu, Hewlett, and Pavard, 2010) is evidenced in selection pressure on growth hormone sensitivity, bone cell turnover, breast milk lipid composition, and starch metabolism (Lachance et al., 2012; Perry et al., 2007). Micronutrient deficiencies and food toxicities also pose unique challenges for reproduction and growth during infancy, a time of significant sensitivity to variation in nutritional access and quality (Kuzawa and Bragg, 2012; Spencer and Palmer, 2012). Iodine, for example, is scarce in tropical forests but crucial to both successful pregnancy and child growth and survival (Branca and Ferrari, 2002; Davies, 2013). Improved iodine uptake is evident among Efe and other pygmies (Dormitzer and Ellison, 1989; Herraez et al., 2009), and although it is contained in breast milk, it cannot be banked for future use (Zimmermann, 2011).

Efe babies are very small at birth, averaging only 2.4 kg, but are exceptionally fat for their size (Tronick and Winn, 1992), suggesting critical resource pressures very early in Efe infancy. Although human young are protected from nutritional variation in maternal milk supply by the adaptive insurance of fat deposits in the first half-year of life (Dettwyler 1992), this safeguard weakens as growth outpaces milk production at about 6 to 9 months of age and babies require additional foods to maintain growth and health (Kuzawa, 1998). By their first birthday, babies come into increasing competition with siblings over food resources that parents and other cooperative producers bring to the hearth (Gurven, Stieglitz, Hooper, Gomes, and Kaplan, 2012). The synergies of small size and immature systems heighten disease risks in the first year, and the Efe infant mortality rate of 22% in our study is similar to that reported for the Aka of the Central African Republic and Twa in Uganda (Ohenjo et al., 2006) and the 23% average for hunter-gatherers (Marlowe, 2005).

The transition from infancy into childhood is one of the most critical windows of selection pressure in human development (Bogin, 1999; Kuzawa, 2007). Human young are weaned into a buffered, energetic environment where they continue to be provisioned. They also grow for an extended period before reaching puberty, a derived pattern of human childhood This longer period of slow physical growth affords greater cognitive capacities, including the development of complex foraging skills to extract resources in ecologically unpredictable environments (Kaplan, Lancaster, and Robson, 2003) and the honing of social skills for coalitional relationships on which they will depend (Flinn, Quinlan, Coe, and Ward, 2008). As for a number of forager populations (Blurton Jones, 1993; Bock, 2005; Draper, 1976; Kaplan and Dove, 1987), Efe children are highly constrained in their ability to secure adequate food for themselves until young adulthood, placing strong demands on skills to secure resources from their social environment. The extent and duration of constraint across Efe childhood and vulnerability of early growth to perturbation are evident in the differential growth achieved in early childhood as a majority of the adult variance in Efe size is attained in the first 5 years (Bailey, 1991a).

Across the life span, forager social adaptations characterized by sharing and cooperative efforts reduce individual variance in access to energetic resources (Gurven, 2004). The high daily variability of Efe subsistence returns (Bailey and Peacock, 1988) strengthens the value of relationships through which children and adults can secure more predicable flows of resources. For example, Efe men more often hunt cooperatively, achieving lower individual return rates, but increasing the chance of returning from a hunt with some food to share (Bailey, 1991b). And, the specialized economic efforts of Efe wives and husbands smooth otherwise highly variable returns consumed at the hearth, consistent with evolutionarily arguments for the human pairbond (Bailey and Aunger, 1989).

The Efe increase the probability of successful returns in other ways by reducing search costs of patchily distributed resources (Hein and McKinley, 2012) and by averting the risk for conflict with others (Wolf and McNamara, 2013). They scan the forest constantly as they travel, stopping to peer into the canopy, kick over logs, and probe cavities for resources and information predicting when fruit will ripen, a nesting animal will return, or new bee colony will be formed. They scan social resources in this way as well, testing for reciprocity of prior exchanges and offering new ones. The Efe travel between camps to learn about the movements of others, and check in at villages to catch the wind of possible exchange opportunities, all while avoiding long intrusions that wear out welcomes and test conflicting interests. The information that Efe obtain as they interact in their physical and social world is critical to resource providers, and information foraging across a broad niche increases the flow of opportunities for interaction within social networks.

SOCIAL UNCERTAINTY

Although Efe life is densely social, children may not have reliable access to those who may be most likely to invest in their welfare by the tether of close kinship. The high prevalence of parasites, infectious diseases, and injury increases the likelihood that, at times, caregivers will not be well enough to care for children or may die. Estimates of mortality for most African pygmy populations are relatively high, and we expect the same for the Efe. The death of an adult was often a close personal loss, and nearly 20% of all children up to 17 years of age had lost a mother or a father. Although children who lose a parent are quickly absorbed into another family of close kin, the social and psychological salience of loss and resulting shift in the demands of children's dependency radiate through the community. A unique and sensitive study of mortality experience of Aka pygmy adolescents found that they remembered an average of 24 deaths and could recount very intimate and frightening details of most. They experienced the strongest sense of grief with the loss of biological kin who were a source of comfort, safety, and security (Hewlett and Lamb, 2005).

Ecologically-specific energetic, morbidity and mortality risks are likely a continuous factor shaping Efe biology and behavior. Chisholm (1996) argues that environments of high mortality risk present children with important cues regarding the precariousness of social resources on which they depend, and poor resource access may accentuate the ill effects of this uncertainty even further (Ellis, Boyce, Belsky, Bakermans-Kranenburg, and van Ijzendoorn, 2011; Griskevicius, Delton, Robertson, and Tybur, 2011). Living with chronic social uncertainty has immediate and long-term impacts on development (Flinn, Nepomnaschy, Muehlenbein, and Ponzi, 2011) and can produce response strategies that are risk aversive and geared to minimizing variance across opportunities rather than avoiding social contact altogether (Nettle, 2009). For example, Efe children's uncertain access to important sources of care may promote broad solicitation of relationships during childhood. After the death of a parent and a period of mourning, Efe children often go away to live with a relative for some time in an effort to help them to move on from the experience. As in cases of fostering and migraton, children must manage new caregivers, camps, and circumstances often without others with whom they have established relationships. Migration, morbidity, and mortality are salient and recurring social landscapes of Efe interdependency across the lifespan that both increase and ameliorate social variation.

Uncertainty and Cooperative Relationships

The mobility and flexibility of cooperative hunter-gatherer residence and economic pursuits also hedge against unpredictable access to resources (Hill, Walker, et al. 2011; Kaplan, Schniter, Smith, and Wilson, 2012), and present new cooperative opportunities for sharing the demands of child care between diverse members of the group (Sear and Mace, 2008). Efe mothers, like other foraging mothers, greatly rely on others for help, but caregiver characteristics do not predict the overall amount of time infants spend with caregivers (Ivey Henry, Morelli, and Tronick, 2005). Kin are usually among the first to help with infant care (Briga, Pen, and Wright, 2012; Hamilton, 1975), and cultures provide a rich environment to learn kinship delineations and expectations for interpersonal, familial, and group level investment and exchange (Alvard, 2003).

Cooperation goes well beyond kinship. Residence is a key element of forager social organization (Hill et al., 2011; Kramer and Greaves, 2011), and familiarity is an important cue in cooperative relationships signaling potential for future sharing and trust (Harrison, Sciberras, and James, 2011). Hunter-gatherer resident patterns, however, are transient, marked by frequent changes in camp size, location, and composition. Efe camps may be as small as a few families located close to Lese gardens or as large of 30 to 35 people grouped in patrilineally affiliated clans located deep in the forest. And camps may be as close as 10 minutes from each other, or many hours' walk apart. These shifts expand and contract Efe children's access to other, with new social encounters with the shifting demographics that may accompany residential flexibility.

The variable nature of resource access for human adults and children alike places high demands on the development of social skills. Children must develop flexible capacities to learn about, manage, and negotiate cooperative and competitive relationships; to navigate shifting social networks; to predict intentions and future behaviors; and to adapt accordingly (Flinn et al., 2011; Fonagy, Gergely, and Target, 2007). The ability to discern the trustworthiness of others is central to recognizing and developing favorable patterns of exchange while minimizing and eliminating unfavorable ones, and is necessary for the evolution of stable social networks (Fowler and Christakis, 2010). Trust develops from trustworthy experiences and underlies cooperative relationships built on social and resource exchange. For Efe children, over time, some of these relationships will develop into closer and more intimate ones.

Ecological uncertainty should pressure for early development of capacities for social capture of resources and cooperative exchange due to energetic constraints on mothers as well as on children. The biological and social dependency of human reproduction on cooperative investment by others (Lancaster and Kaplan, 2010) implies that the same is true for children's development. Children's active pursuit of investment through the relationships they develop should be considered cooperative development, and, similar to adults, strategic and sensitive to ecological variation.

Research Objective

We explore the ontogeny of Efe social relationships across the first 2 years of life by examining infants' and toddlers' involvement in social networks and the cooperative opportunities they provide that extend beyond the mother's care. Our interest is to describe transitions over time in Efe child sociality, with their increasing physical (e.g., locomotor) independence from caregivers and growing need for nutritional resources beyond breast milk. These features strongly determine child resource-seeking capacity as well as vulnerability to variation in food and protective resources. We follow two lines of inquiry in our analysis. The first asks about children's social networks. We examine children's physical and social contact with people and changes in their social landscape by considering partners in terms of number, kinship, time engaged, and consistency. The second asks about trustworthy experience. We examine solicitations for and offers of resources. For both lines of inquiry, we examine children's affective state.

Data Collection and Query

The Efe in our study area number about 500 people and form 18 hunter-gatherer bands scattered across an area of approximately 900 square kilometers. The information we report in this chapter comes from a 2-year study of the development and behavioral ecology of Efe children in 51 camps. In the observational piece of this study, we (Ivey Henry) observed 20, 4- to 21-month-olds using focal subject sampling technique. Observations took place in two blocks of time over 2 consecutive days, from the time the child left the hut until about noon, and from afternoon until sunset. In each block of time, each child was observed for four 15-minute sessions separated by 45 minutes. In total, 2 hours of data were collected on each child at each age group (eight sessions total). All observations were recorded in real time using a tablet computer. This allowed the recording of duration of each event accurate to the second and the duration and sequencing of co-occurring events. Among the events recorded were all child behaviors, maternal location and activity, activity of others engaged with the child, and proximity of others to the child. Behavioral codes were developed over many years of experience living and working with the Efe and talking with the people we studied (Morelli and Ivey Henry, 2004).

INFANT AND TODDLER AGE GROUPINGS

Increasing physical independence from caregivers and growing nutritional need bring children into contact with resources—and resource holders—in new ways. At the same time, the child's size, ability to move through the landscape, and demand for food and transport have energetic and time allocation implications for caregivers and other social partners (Konner, 2005). Because these qualities are important to Efe child social experiences, they form the basis of our age groupings. Physical and nutritional changes occur along with changes in social, emotional, and cognitive competences, however, we do not rely on conventional age-dependent developmental markers because they are increasingly questioned as cross-culturally appropriate characterizations of human variation (Broesch, Callaghan, Heinrich, Murphy, and Rochat, 2010; Super, Harkness, Barry, and Zeitlin, 2011).

We examine the development of children's social experiences across four age periods: younger infants (4- to 6-month-olds; $N = 10$; mean age, 5 months), older infants (7- to 11-month- olds; $N = 14$; mean age, 9 months), younger toddlers (12- to 15-month-olds; $N = 16$; mean age, 14 months), and older toddlers (18- to 21-month-olds; $N = 7$; mean age, 20 months). *Younger infants* are physically very dependent on their caregivers. Although they may have experience of other foods, they receive almost all of their nutrition from breast milk. They are capable of sitting on their own, but are almost always in the laps of others and cannot stand or move about without help. *Older infants* still rely mostly on breast milk for nutrition, but require more nutrition than milk alone can provide (Kuzawa, 2007). They may eat with siblings, but mothers often preferentially feed them independent of family meals. They stand but generally depend on the support of others to bring people and resources in close range. *Younger toddlers* walk quite easily around camp, but are unsteady on the uneven ground of a forest trail. At this age they move with significant independence from caregivers in camp, but are not agile enough to quickly follow older children. *Older toddlers* continue to nurse, but share fully in meals served around the hearth. They more readily follow and join the activities of other children in camp, and mothers increasingly leave them in camp when foraging.

All efforts were made to observe children over the first 24 months of life. But longitudinal studies of hunter-gatherer children are challenged by all the rigors of data collection among traditional cultures with the added unpredictability of forager mobility. Given this, and the distribution of child age at the start of the study, four children were observed once, seven twice, and nine three times in the course of the study period.

INFANT AND TODDLER SOCIAL NETWORKS

We considered as partners all people engaged physically (e.g., holding, leaning directly against, carrying) and/or socially (e.g., talking, directing, playing) with a child. We grouped social partners into one of four partner category types based on kinship affiliation given the role of genetic relatedness in determining others' investment in dependent young and in cooperative exchanges across the lifespan. In descending order of estimated relatedness with the child are (1) *family*, including the child's nuclear family (except mothers) and extended family members at. 125 shared genetic relatedness or greater (i.e., fathers, siblings, first cousins, aunts, uncles, grandparents, and great grandparents); (2) *clan*, including individuals sharing any known paternal or maternal genetic relatedness less than. 125; (3) *unrelated Efe*, including individuals with no identified genetic kinship other than being Efe; and (4) *Lese* farmers. Demographic data were gathered as part of a larger longitudinal study of the population and reconfirmed during each camp visit before data collection. Paternity is unknown but accepted as informed by camp members. Although Efe children are gregarious and may have multiple partners simultaneously, we consider concurrent engagements with a maximum of two partners because children at the ages studied rarely engaged with three or more partners.

EXPECTED INFANT AND TODDLER PATTERN OF ASSOCIATION

Efe family members are expected to be among the most trusted of caregivers, and mothers are likely to solicit child care assistance from those dependent on her for provisioning such as siblings and foster children. As an extension of greater experience with family members, infants and toddlers may approach them more often for resources. And given close kinship, family members are expected to respond more favorably in return, especially if caregiving demands are not high. More distal kin such as *clan members* are likely to reside in camp. A number of economic and social cooperative relationships are established through clan membership. And mothers are likely to regard clan members as an opportunity for future benefits for themselves or their offspring, especially as infants grow and demonstrate increasing vigor and independence.

Unrelated Efe are expected to be less engaged in direct contact with infants and toddlers than family or clan because more closely related young are likely to be the recipients of their attention and investment. However, cooperation among Efe includes many individuals other than kin, and genetic relatedness does not fully predict the care that infants receive (Ivey, 2000). Most unrelated Efe living in the camps studied were women (77%) who had married into the band (i.e., affines), comprising two and sometimes three generations of endogamy. An older woman may have known the baby's father as a child, and a younger woman may know the mother as a peer. Although adult Efe females in a camp are much less likely to be kin than are males, they spend much of their lives together or in nearby camps foraging, living as neighbors, and sharing deep friendships, often intergenerationally. Other unrelated members of camp include children who may or may not have parents in camp and visitors such as unmarried young men in search of a mate. Some of these, especially children, may rely on the good will of residents for food and protection, and kindness towards children (and usefulness to their mothers) may help secure them. A small number of unrelated camp members are transient passers-by.

Lese farmers' appearance in the social sphere of Efe infants and toddlers is highly transient and seasonal, and is associated with adult relationships. Such brief encounters occurred in villages or gardens, or when Efe joined in village celebrations. Yet, insofar as they are a part of the social scene, they contribute to the social demands children must learn to negotiate. As a result, Lese are included in analyses that examine social landscape complexity.

ANALYTIC APPROACH

We rely largely on descriptive statistics because our goal is to describe patterns of social experiences. Data for each child were averaged across the eight 15-minute observation sessions, and these averages were used to create age-group mean scores for the measures reported. For each measure involving partner types, only children involved with the partner type under consideration were included in the calculation. We report separately on mothers and exclude their data elsewhere, except where noted, because of our interest in care that extends beyond mothers. To increase the reliability of measures, for each child we include a partner category if it is made up of five or more individuals, and we include solicitations and requests when three or more were made.

Results and Discussion

OPENING SCENES OF SOCIAL LIFE

In previous research, we observed that the first to hold a newly born baby are the women and children in the mother's hut, who assist with the birth and provide emotional support to her. The newborn is passed tenderly from one person to the next, until all have seen and held him, then taken outside and placed into the hands of the people waiting to meet this new camp member (men, by custom, do not attend births but remain in camp). The mother is among the last to hold her baby, an hour or two after birth, and during the next few days, even though she nurses the baby, another lactating woman or two nurse the baby as well (Morelli and Tronick, 1987).

In the months that follow, Efe mothers largely determine the character of their babies' social connections by allowing the people they trust to take care of them (Hrdy, 2009). They influence their baby's exposure to and perspective of others by their own relationships, visiting with and working side by side others—baby in tow—and situating homes and hearths next to particular family and friends in cooperative and supportive relationships. But mothers alone do not determine the full extent of the early connections babies develop. Babies seek out others with smiles, sounds, and gestures; and others seek out babies to play, hold, and carry. Their social world also expands as they travel on the hips and backs of others in camp, on trails, to other camps or villages, and with mothers while they are working. Once toddling (about 9 to 10 months of age), babies are better able to contact others on their own, and over the following year they are increasingly physically independent of their mothers and other caregivers. The research on which we report strengthens the view that the social life of Efe infants and toddlers is dynamic and complex, and expands on it by examining other features of their social networks and their involvement in them.

INFANTS' AND TODDLERS' SOCIAL NETWORK

Social Network Structure

Prior research on Efe infancy demonstrated that the number of different people in physical or social contact with babies was high and increased with age (Tronick et al., 1992). Consistent with this work, we found that in a 2-hour period, younger infants (4- to 6-month-olds) were in contact, on average, with 9 different people, whereas older toddlers (18- to 21-month-olds) had 14 different partners, including mothers (Figure 4.1; Table 4.1).

Variation among babies was high; some were in contact with as many as 20 different social partners, and others with as few as 3. The 2 babies with the fewest social partners were observed in camps that were very small (5 and 7 members) and located near or in gardens during brief periods when camp members helped their Lese exchange partners with agricultural work. This is in line with previous research showing that group size and composition is an important determinant of the availability and diversity of Efe camp members, predicting the number of care-givers, but not the amount of time that babies received care (Ivey, 2000).

Family members were comparably represented in the social networks of infants and younger toddlers, and as expected made up a greater proportion of partners than clan or unrelated Efe (Figure 4.2; see Table 4.1). As toddlers grew, their social

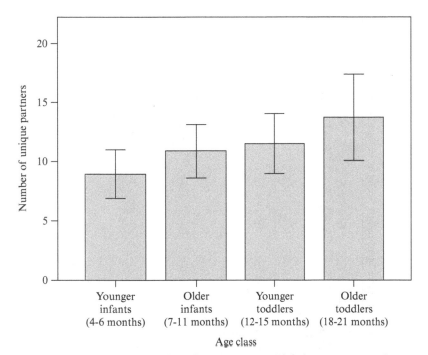

FIGURE 4.1 *Mean (±95% CI) number of unique partners Efe babies were in social or physical contact with per 2-hour observation period.*

TABLE 4.1 Descriptive Measures of Social or Physical Contact

Measure	Partner Type*	Statistic	Younger Infants (4–6 mos)	Older Infants (7–11 mos)	Younger Toddlers (12–15 mos)	Older Toddlers (18–21 mos)
Number of unique partners per 2-hour period*	All partners	Mean ± SE	8.9 ± 0.9	10.9 ± 1	11.5 ± 1.2	13.7 ± 1.5
		Median	8.5	11	11	13
		95% CI	6.9–10.9	8.6–13.1	9–14.1	10.1–17.4
		N	10	14	16	7
Percentage of nonmaternal partners in category based on count of all partners†	Family	Mean ± SE	48.5 ± 8.9	46.3 ± 6.6	47.1 ± 5.4	34.3 ± 7.1
		Median	42.725	46.43	50	30
		95% CI	28.3–68.7	32.1–60.5	35.4–58.8	17–51.7
		N	10	14	15	7
	Clan	Mean ± SE	33 ± 5.8	35 ± 3.5	42.5 ± 6.3	40 ± 9
		Median	31.665	36.36	46.15	27.27
		95% CI	19.2–46.8	27.3–42.8	28.7–56.2	18.1–62
		N	8	11	13	7
	Unrelated Efe	Mean ± SE	27.3 ± 4.8	24 ± 3.1	14.9 ± 1.6	19.6 ± 6.6
		Median	18.18	25	15.48	14.29
		95% CI	15.4–39.2	17.1–30.8	11.4–18.4	1.3–37.8
		N	7	11	12	5

Percentage of observation time spent with different partner types	Family	Mean ± SE	33.3 ± 6.9	24.7 ± 4.6	32 ± 5	39.9 ± 7.6
		Median	22.29	23.47	29.44	34
		95% CI	17.8–48.8	14.7–34.6	21.3–42.6	21.2–58.6
		N	10	14	15	7
	Clan	Mean ± SE	10.6 ± 4.7	9.7 ± 2.9	13.1 ± 5.3	12.3 ± 4
		Median	4.66	5.07	4.07	5.54
		95% CI	−0.4–21.6	3.3–16.2	1.5–24.6	2.5–22
		N	8	11	13	7
	Unrelated Efe	Mean ± SE	12.7 ± 3.8	9.7 ± 2.4	9.4 ± 3.3	2.6 ± 0.7
		Median	7.63	12.07	4.82	2.49
		95% CI	3.3–22.1	4.4–15	2.2–16.6	0.7–4.5
		N	7	11	12	5

* Family: partners other than the mother with a relatedness coefficient of 0.125 or more; clan: partners more distantly related, including patrilineal and matrilineal clan; unrelated Efe: partners not identified as kin of subject or of unknown relatedness.

† For each measure involving partner types, only babies involved with the partner type under consideration were included in the calculation. Because each infant could have a different selection of partner types in a given age group (e.g., some interacted with cousins, some did not), averages calculated across infants do not add up to 100% across partner types.

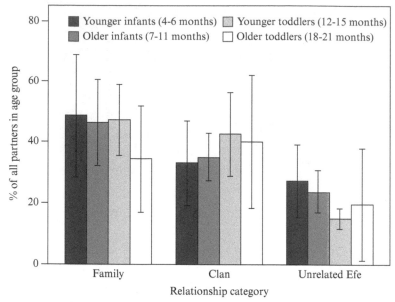

FIGURE 4.2 *Distribution of partners in social or physical contact across different partner types. Plotted is the mean (±95% CI) percentage of all social partners accounted for by each partner category. Family: partners other than the mother with a relatedness coefficient of 0.125 or more; Clan: partners more distantly related, including patrilineal and matrilineal clan; Unrelated Efe: partners not identified as kin of subject or of unknown relatedness. Babies without a given partner type available were not considered in calculations.*

networks expanded to include clan; and for older toddlers, the proportion of social partners that were family or clan was similar across infants.

Unrelated Efe representation in social networks of babies was highly variable, with no distinct age trend, but on average they accounted for a smaller proportion of social partners compared to clan members.

As anticipated, family members spent two to three times more time with infants and toddlers than did clan members or unrelated Efe, and the time family spent with them did not change dramatically with age (Figure 4.3; see Table 4.1). Clan members and unrelated Efe spent a similar proportion of time with infants and younger toddlers. For clan, the time they invested changed little for older toddlers; for unrelated Efe, time with older toddlers dropped considerably.

The social world of Efe infants and toddlers is strongly influenced by the spatial patterning of associations determined by mother and trusted caregivers, and by their ability to navigate camp. Family members are likely to share a hearth or have one close to the baby's family, and mothers can easily put their babies in the laps of close-by family members while setting a fire or attending to another child. Dependents who are able to keep up with their mothers on foraging trips typically accompany them to help care for infants. But kinship alone does not determine

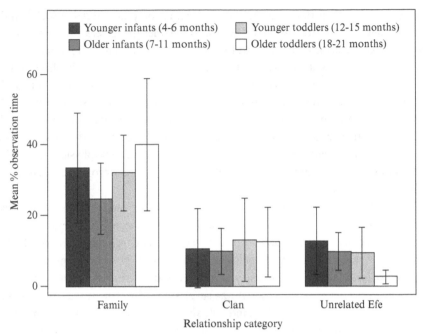

FIGURE 4.3 *Mean (±95% CI) percentage of observed time Efe babies were in social or physical contact with different partner types. For definitions of relationship categories, see Figure 4.2.*

where adults locate hearth. Friendships are important, especially among women (Fisher, 1987), which may help explain baby contact beyond association by kinship. Women are the most frequent people not related to mothers in contact with babies, and they provide help when most needed for the smallest of babies, whose care is more physically demanding and requires strength and experience (Ivey, 2000). As babies become more independent and seek out company on their own, it appears that they choose a different set of social partners. They may visit with camp members, who take pleasure welcoming them, and they may be found at the edges of older children's play, or on the lap of a great uncle while he checks his hunting gear. The graduation of hunter-gatherer children from the toddler period into peer groups is well described (Draper, 1976), but indications of this transition are evident among the Efe much earlier than previously expected.

Social Network Consistency

We learned from prior research that very young Efe infants changed social partners often, with the rate of change increasing over the first 18 weeks of life. Three-week-olds, for example, were transferred to a person, on average, 3.7 times an hour; 18-week-olds 8.3 times an hour (Tronick et al., 1987). As partners change, babies are pressed to adjust to different interactional styles, and this likely facilitates

the social capabilities that allow babies to navigate complex and dense social landscapes (Stern, 1977; Tronick, 1980). We asked whether there were similar opportunities for babies as they grew up, and found that social movement from one partner
to another continues at a rapid pace throughout the first 2 years of life. Infants and
toddlers, on average, experienced a change in social partners every 3 minutes regardless of age, and differences among them at each age group were small (Table 4.2).
The average time from one partner to the next for younger infants (4- to 6-month
olds) ranged from 2 to 4 minutes; for older toddlers (18- to 21-month-olds), it was 1
to 3 minutes. The regularity of this pattern under highly variable physical and social
conditions of Efe life underscores the robustness of social turnover as a feature of
Efe baby experience.

Efe mobility, camp fissions and fusions, and mortality and migration all serve as
disruptors of social stability and are expected to present significant shifts in opportunities and constraints on babies' social networks and development of social relationships. When we considered babies who were observed in two consecutive age
groups, we found that the consistency of infants' and toddlers' social networks (i.e.,
the same person in both age groups) was surprisingly low. On average, in a 2-hour
period, only one out of every three individuals was observed in contact with babies
across two consecutive age groups. There were differences, however, among social
partner categories in partner consistency. Efe babies experienced more predictable
access to the same family members over time. Mean consistency ranged from 62%
to 69%, and exceeded 50% for the majority of babies (see Table 4.2). Most consistent partners were fathers and siblings; less so, cousins and grandparents; and least,
aunts and uncles. By comparison, only 20% of clan members or unrelated Efe were
the same in two consecutive age groups for infants and toddlers. For Efe babies, the
significant departures and reunions in their emotional experience may not occur on
a familial level as much as on a level of group residency. Social relationships with
many others may be explored and enjoyed intensely, and then after some absence,
renewed again.

Three probable factors that relate to the low consistency of partners are changes
in camp mobility, composition, and labor allocation associated with high seasonal-
ity of resource availability. For example, of the consecutive age group comparisons
made, 76% involved a change in camp size of 30% or more. In addition, there were
significant changes in seasonal pursuits and camp distance from road across age
group comparisons. These shifts dramatically influence the potential players in the
social landscape for babies (and their mothers).

The quickness with which Efe babies' social partners changed moment to
moment and the likelihood that people in contact with them would not be the same
from one age group to the next provide opportunities for learning how to manage
a fluid social scene of partners with diverse characteristics, permanency, and interests. The social knowledge gained from involvements with the many and varied
people in contact with babies allow them to learn what they must do, and provide to
others, to secure resources reliably. All of this suggests that sophisticated capacities

TABLE 4.2 Descriptive Measures of Social Consistency

Measure	Partner Type	Statistic	Younger Infants (4–6 mos)	Older Infants (7–11 mos)	Younger Toddlers (12–15 mos)	Older Toddlers (18–21 mos)
Interval (min) between partner change	All partners[*]	Mean ± SE	2.4 ± 0.2	1.7 ± 0.2	3.3 ± 0.4	2.3 ± 0.2
		Median	2.2	1.6	3.05	2.1
		95% CI	2.5–4.1	1.9–2.8	2–2.9	1.3–2.2
		N	16	7	10	14
Percentage of all unique partners across two consecutive age groups who appear in both groups	All nonmaternal partners	Mean ± SE		28.7 ± 3.9	32.1 ± 3.7	26.8 ± 3.7
		Median		33	29	28
		95% CI		19.7–37.6	23.5–40.7	16.5–37.1
		N		9	9	7
	Family	Mean ± SE		61.6 ± 7	65.1 ± 12.6	68.9 ± 9
		Median		60	67	60
		95% CI		45.5–77.6	36.1–94.1	46.9–90.8
		N		9	9	7
	Clan	Mean ± SE		0 ± 0	6.3 ± 3.3	12.1 ± 6.1
		Median		0	0	0
		95% CI			-1.2–13.9	-2.9–27.1
		N		9	9	7
	Unrelated Efe	Mean ± SE		10.3 ± 7.2	19.1 ± 12.4	4.7 ± 4.7
		Median		0	0	0
		95% CI		-6.3–26.9	-10.1–48.4	-6.8–16.3
		N		9	8	7
	Lese	Mean ± SE			7.4 ± 4.6	
		Median			0	
		95% CI			-5.3–20.1	
		N		4	5	4

[*] Mothers and Lese included in calculation

to develop social networks and negotiate conflict may be a much earlier feature of social development than appreciated, and the socially interdependent and uncertain life they live are likely similar to those in the human past.

Social Networks and the Child's Positive Affective Experience

Although it might be expected that a lack of continuity in individual social partners—and caregivers—would place high demands on infant capacity to regulate physiological and affective state, Efe babies appeared sanguine about their fast-paced and fluid social experiences, and they seemed to enjoy the exposure and learning that multiple partners provide. They were in good moods—smiling, laughing, bright eyed, and attentive—for most of the time observed, regardless of age (85% to 94% mean observation time). Moreover, their positive affective state varied little by partner type, even though stability of individual partners over time was low for all but family; and similarly aged babies varied little on this measure (Table 4.3). Their amiable and fun moods may make their engagement a pleasing experience, which likely encourages continued contact and sustained involvement with others (Sroufe, 2005), and as such, may be the means by which babies and partners learn about each other, commitments strengthen, and trust develops.

As Efe babies hone capabilities that allow them to move fluidly in and out of partnerships with others, they are likely to find negotiating their variable social landscapes difficult at times. The potential psychological cost of socially and emotionally demanding engagements may be lessened in at least two ways. One is by regularities in important aspects of care others provide. The public nature of Efe life makes examples of good care visible to all. Older children are counseled (by anyone) about appropriate caregiving, which improves their caregiving well before they are more fully responsible for care. Even less experienced adults are offered gentle advice. With constant watchfulness by many, partners are accountable in ways that they are not in other cultures, including Western cultures. All of this makes for more reliable social partners for babies, and more consistency in the care they receive even when the caregivers themselves are inconsistently available. With this may come feelings of familiarity and of safety and certainty that lie at the root of close relationships (Sroufe, 1979).

Moreover, the energetic and opportunity costs and psychological demands of infant caregiving are in part ameliorated by the distribution of work across caregivers and the elevated attention given to those who are engaged with Efe young. Caregivers are expected to be attentive or else not interact with babies, and dependents that compete for parental food and attention are expected to be tolerant and gentle. If a baby becomes overly challenging or the caregiver has a competing interest or demand at the time, there is no constraint on, or penalty for, passing the baby to someone more experienced at comforting or who is free of other tasks. The interdependency of Efe life nurtures intergenerational and intragenerational cooperation, enhancing infant experience of relationships by enhancing that of caregivers as well. Rather than a stand-alone child care system confined to the period of

TABLE 4.3 Descriptive Measures of Positive Affect

Measure	Partner Type	Statistic	Younger Infants (4–6 mos)	Older Infants (7–11 mos)	Younger Toddlers (12–15 mos)	Older Toddlers (18–21 mos)
Percentage of observation time in positive affect	All nonmaternal partners	Mean ± SE	87.5 ± 1.5	85.9 ± 2.2	84.9 ± 4.1	94.1 ± 1.3
		Median	87.4	88.6	90.5	93.5
		95% CI	84.2–90.8	81.1–90.8	76.1–93.7	91–97.2
		N	10	14	16	7
Percentage of observation time with partner type that infants were in positive affect	Family	Mean ± SE	83.8 ± 2.9	82.3 ± 5.3	87.4 ± 2.2	94.3 ± 1.5
		Median	82.3	88.8	87.4	95.1
		95% CI	77.3–90.4	70.8–93.8	82.6–92.2	90.6–98.1
		N	10	14	14	7
	Clan	Mean ± SE	94.5 ± 2.2	79.1 ± 4.4	92.9 ± 4.4	95.9 ± 1.6
		Median	95.1	81.6	100.0	95.0
		95% CI	88.9–100.2	69.4–88.9	83.1–102.6	91.9–99.9
		N	6	11	12	7
	Unrelated Efe	Mean ± SE	82.1 ± 5.6	87 ± 3	95.6 ± 1.8	100 ± 0
		Median	88.5	86.5	100	100
		95% CI	68.4–95.7	80.3–93.7	91.6–99.7	91.6–99.7
		N	7	11	12	5

infant dependency, over the course of development, Efe infants' iterative experiences with the people who care for them—paused by departures and renewed in later seasons—become *relationships*.

TRUSTWORTHINESS OF SOCIAL PARTNERS

The vulnerability of hunter-gatherer babies, intensified by ecological unpredictability, should favor early abilities to judge the safety and reliability of nutritional and social resources, especially given the competing interests of human parents with multiple young (Chisholm, 1996; Simpson and Belsky, 2008). From an early age, babies are able to assess the care they receive, judge others based on this and what they see, and act on these evaluations (Einav and Robinson, 2011; Hamlin and Wynn, 2011, 2012). Young babies may intuit as trustworthy care that meets their security/protective and biological needs (e.g., Fonagy et al., 2007; Simpson and Belsky, 2008); but later their understanding of trustworthiness becomes more cultural in nature. Social partners, in turn, signal their interests in cooperative exchange by investments of time, energy, and kindness in infant care, providing to children information about their trustworthiness as social partners. This benevolence signals to the child shared social interests in their welfare and the availability and distribution of resources in the social environment (Szczesniak, Colaco, and Rondon, 2012).

Learning whom to trust is fundamental to developing and sustaining long-term cooperative relationships and to managing conflictual ones. Trust of others rests on trustworthy experiences of them (Yamagishi, 2011). There are many ways Efe babies directly experience the trustworthiness of others; being picked up caringly or played with gently are examples. What is more, the perceptions babies have of people through their direct involvement with them may be amplified by watching how they are with others. Here, we examine the people with whom infants and toddlers experience low levels of distress and from whom they receive resources as signs of their trustworthiness.

The Social Experience of Distress

Distress compromises babies' attentional and physiological processes (Morasch and Bell, 2011) and is energetically demanding (Wells and Davies, 1996). Because of this, the experience of prolonged periods of distress when with others may provide a strong signal to babies that their social partners are not adequate or reliable. And, as a result, babies' views of them as trustworthy may be undermined. The Efe respond rapidly to infant cries with calm attempts to quiet the child by meeting their immediate needs. They become very concerned when babies are distressed for no apparent reason and interpret it as a sign of poor health. Eighteen-week-olds who are difficult to console are returned more quickly to their mothers than are other babies, a wise choice given that mother's milk is most likely to comfort them and help them recover from illness (Tronick et al., 1987; Winn, Morelli, and Tronick, 1990). At times, infant distress is tolerated for a little while in the course of care or brief competing tasks, knowing that the baby's unhappiness is temporary and not associated with harm.

This responsive and patient caregiving may be why Efe babies rarely showed signs of distress, as measured by fussing, crying, and fretting. Infants and younger toddlers overall spent an average of 7% to 9% of time distressed, older toddlers about half of this time (Table 4.4). When with family, clan, and unrelated Efe, the percentage of time in distress was similar and low for each age group and declined noticeably for older toddlers (from 9% to 12%, to 4% to 6%). Although abilities and demands change dramatically over the first 2 years of life, average distress bouts were consistently brief—averages ranged from only 11 to 20 seconds.

Reliability of Resources

Infants' and toddlers' perceptions of social partners as dependable rests in part on receipt of resources asked for and offered. Successful requests may strengthen perceptions, deepen social connections, and affect future asking. They may also provide opportunities to enter into new exchange partnerships. Offers made in the absence of requests may be one way others demonstrate good will towards babies and shape the contours of their social matrices. Willing partners in the exchange are likely to act preferentially towards one another over time, which is what 3-year-olds did by directing altruistic acts to those likely to reciprocate (Olson and Spelke, 2008). This ask-and-offer, give-and-take process is core to early reciprocity and later cooperation.

Requests to Others for Resources

Efe infants require others to meet almost every need. They ask for food and protection, help with walking or dressing, transport, shared communications, and attention to someone or something. And most times, they get what they ask for (Table 4.5). About three out of every four requests made by Efe infants and toddlers were responded to favorably (on average, 70% to 75% success). The exception was younger infants, who experienced a low success rate of 47%. Many refusals were for objects that were not appropriate for infants to have, such as a sharp tool, or uncooked food.

Remarkably, whom Efe babies asked did not appear to determine the success they enjoyed. The percentage of successful requests, on average, did not differ by kinship of the sharing partner; this was true at each age group and across age groups (see Table 4.5). Efe babies may enjoy such consistency of success across partners independent of shared kinship interests because favors requested are not usually costly—a steady hand to help negotiate steps around the fire, a call for another to watch other children at play, or a piece of food. Physically demanding activities such as carrying a baby require more effort but are often of short duration and only brief energetic costs to others. Widely shared displays of cooperation may produce

TABLE 4.4 Descriptive Measures of Distress

Measure	Partner Type	Statistic	Younger Infants (4–6 mos)	Older Infants (7–11 mos)	Younger Toddlers (12–15 mos)	Older Toddlers (18–21 mos)
Percentage of observation time in distress	All nonmaternal partners	Mean ± SE	8.4 ± 1	9.1 ± 0.7	7.4 ± 0.9	3.6 ± 0.8
		Median	9.3	9.6	6.7	3.9
		95% CI	6.1–10.7	7.5–10.7	5.5–9.3	1.7–5.6
		N	10	14	16	7
Percentage of observation time with partner type that infant was in distress	Family	Mean ± SE	13.7 ± 2.3	15 ± 4.9	10 ± 1.6	4 ± 1
		Median	15.7	10.0	9.6	4.1
		95% CI	8.5–18.8	4.3–25.6	6.5–13.5	1.6–6.3
		N	10	14	14	7
	Clan	Mean ± SE	6.3 ± 2.2	19.2 ± 3.3	12.1 ± 4.5	
		Median	5.3	17.7	10.8	
		95% CI	0.3–12.3	11.8–26.6	−0.5–24.7	
		N	5	10	5	4
	Unrelated Efe	Mean ± SE	15.2 ± 5.8	16.3 ± 2.6	9.2 ± 2.1	
		Median	8.5	13.5	9.3	
		95% CI	1–29.3	10–22.5	3.5–15	
		N	7	8	5	0
Mean distress bout duration (seconds) with partner type	Family	Mean ± SE	15.6 ± 2	13.1 ± 1.3	16.1 ± 1.9	13 ± 1.5
		Median	16.6	12.0	14.5	14.3
		95% CI	11.1–20.1	10.3–15.8	11.9–20.2	9.3–16.6
		N	10	14	14	7
	Clan	Mean ± SE		18 ± 2.3	19 ± 4.8	
		Median		16.4	14.1	
		95% CI		12.9–23.1	5.7–32.3	
		N	4	10	5	4
	Unrelated Efe	Mean ± SE	20.3 ± 6.1	15.7 ± 1.4	12.3 ± 1.9	
		Median	11.5	14.7	12.5	
		95% CI	5.4–35.3	12.4–19.1	7–17.5	
		N	7	8	5	0

TABLE 4.5 Descriptive Measures of Requests for and Offers of Goods and Services with Different Partner Types

Measure	Partner Type	Statistic	YoungerInfants (4–6 mos)	OlderInfants (7–11 mos)	YoungerToddlers (12–15 mos)	OlderToddlers (18–21 mos)
Percentage success of all requests made to different partner types	All nonmaternal partners	Mean ± SE	47.3 ± 4.7	69.5 ± 3	74.7 ± 3.2	73.1 ± 2.8
		Median	42.9	69.0	76.3	71.4
		95% CI	36.8–57.9	63.1–76	68–81.4	66.2–80
		N	10	14	16	7
	Family	Mean ± SE	45.7 ± 5.9	62.9 ± 4.7	69.1 ± 6.2	64.5 ± 7.7
		Median	45.0	58.3	71.4	69.7
		95% CI	31.8–59.7	52.6–73.3	55.6–82.7	45.6–83.4
		N	8	12	12	7
	Clan	Mean ± SE	49.3 ± 12.5	72.2 ± 11.7	73.2 ± 9.9	
		Median	37.5	77.8	73.1	
		95% CI	14.6–84	42.1–102.2	47.7–98.6	
		N	5	6	6	3
	Unrelated Efe	Mean ± SE		65.9 ± 8.9		
		Median		65.3		
		95% CI		43.1–88.7		
		N	4	6	3	1
Percentage of all offers received that were made by different partner types	Family	Mean ± SE	34.9 ± 6.6	28.1 ± 3.1	34 ± 7.4	30.5 ± 5
		Median	33.7	26.3	25.0	26.6
		95% CI	20–49.8	21.3–34.9	18.1–49.8	18.2–42.8
		N	10	14	15	7
	Clan	Mean ± SE	25 ± 7.4	16.6 ± 4.3	15.5 ± 3.6	18.4 ± 5.6
		Median	20.2	10.3	10.0	13.9
		95% CI	5.9–44	7–26.1	7.4–23.7	4.8–32.1
		N	6	11	11	7
	Unrelated Efe	Mean ± SE	23.3 ± 5.7	14.8 ± 4	17.9 ± 4	
		Median	19.1	9.6	15.4	
		95% CI	8.8–37.8	5.8–23.7	8.7–27.1	
		N	6	10	9	3

benefits for all Efe social partners, given significant interdependencies across the life span, a shared ecology of uncertainty, and the public nature of most social interactions. For infants and toddlers, these trustworthy experiences may inspire a sense of safety and certainty that extend to family, clan, and unrelated Efe and lay ground for judgments about whom to trust, and whom parents trust with the child.

Offers of Resources From Others

What babies asked for were mirrored in what others offered, suggesting that Efe babies learn about the availability of resources in the social environment through requests. Although the percentage of offers made by family, clan, and unrelated Efe changed little with the age of the child, family members accounted for more of the offers made to older infants and toddlers, on average, compared with clan and unrelated Efe, who did not differ from one another (see Table 4.5). The proximity of family members, and therefore their ability to anticipate needs in advance of requests, may in part explain differences between kin in offers. Many offers included resources and activities near the hearth, such as eating, dressing, washing, and comforting a baby. Moreover, the social cost of not initiating engagement in the first place may be very different from not responding to a baby's request. The differences among partner types in their response to requests and offers suggests that the complex and perhaps conflicting signals of care and cooperative intent make for especially complex social environments in which infants must strategically navigate.

Predicting Infant Success Securing Resources

The rate at which babies encounter new partners is a less well-studied feature of social networks, and it is remarkably high in Efe infants and toddlers. Given this, we looked more closely at the role of encounter rate and success in securing resources from requests. We found that more rapid turnover of social partners was associated with greater success (Figure 4.4), underscoring the active role that Efe babies play in acquiring resources from highly variable social networks. Infants may trigger shifts in social partners behaviorally (reaching out) or affectively (smiling or fussing); toddlers may do so by moving on their own, from one partner to the next, and by verbalizing their interests.

Under conditions of high resource variance, the benefits of developing positive experiences and avoiding being burdensome in partner encounters may lay the ground for strategies to move more continuously through the social network, initiating broader and more rapid partner shifts. Changing partners at a fast pace, and the baby's ability to do so in a positive and socially productive way, distributes the cost of resource sharing with babies across many people and allows caregivers to return to activities that compete with child care with ease. There may be tradeoffs, however, such that gains of broad exposure to many partners must be balanced with the investment of time with particular partners to develop more intimate relationships.

Encounter rate is likely to be sensitive to camp size and composition, which change with ecological conditions. Camp size may relate negatively to encounter

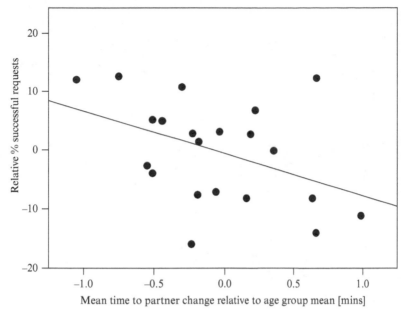

FIGURE 4.4 *Relationship between mean interval between partner changes in minutes and mean percentage of Efe babies' requests that were successful. Both measures were first expressed relative to the mean across subjects in each age group by subtracting the mean across babies in a given age group from each individual score, and these centered values were then averaged across age groups for each baby to give an overall relative measure independent of age. Infants who encountered different partners more frequently per unit observation time (i.e., had shorter than average intervals between partner changes) had greater than average success in getting their needs met (r = −0.43, P = 0.05, N = 21 infant means).*

rate, but camp composition may affect this relation. And resource-seeking strategies may be sensitive to both. Infants and toddlers may engage others in small camps that they may not engage in larger camps, where preferred partners are more likely available. We continue to explore predictors of success, including Efe infant strategy, and factors that may play a role in the relation.

EFE MOTHERS

Compared with other family members, Efe mothers spent more time observed with infants and younger toddlers. But this difference disappeared for older toddlers, with mothers and family spending about 35% (Table 4.6) and 39% (see Table 4.1; see Figure 4.3) of time with older toddlers, respectively.

Mothers continue to spend similarly low percentages of time with 24-month-olds and 36-month-olds (Tronick et al., 1992). This decline might have to do with toddlers' abilities to engage others on their own and with the reduced availability of mothers because mothers were less likely to be within sight of toddlers than infants.

TABLE 4.6 Descriptive Measures of Efe Mother Social or Physical Contact

Measure	Statistic	Younger Infants (4–6 mos)	Older Infants (7–11 mos)	Younger Toddlers (12–15 mos)	Older Toddlers (18–21 mos)
Percentage of all partner time in contact with mother	Mean ± SE	55.9 ± 6.8	60.3 ± 5.4	49.4 ± 4.2	35 ± 7.3
	Median	46.1	56.5	45.6	33.0
	95% CI	40.4–71.4	48.6–72	40.5–58.4	17–52.9
	N	10	14	16	7
Percentage of observation time with mother that infant was in positive affect	Mean ± SE	89.5 ± 2.2	86.5 ± 2	82.6 ± 4.4	91.1 ± 3.4
	Median	90.6	86.9	87.0	93.0
	95% CI	86.7–96.2	82.6–91.4	73.9–92.5	85–99.5
	N	10	14	16	7
Percentage of observation time with mother that infant was in negative affect	Mean ± SE	4.5 ± 0.9	7.1 ± 1.1	8.6 ± 1.4	5 ± 2
	Median	3.3	5.9	9.0	4.1
	95% CI	2.4–6.6	4.9–9.4	5.6–11.6	0.1–9.8
	N	10	14	16	7
Mean duration (seconds) of distress bouts while with mother	Mean ± SE	16.4 ± 1.7	13.6 ± 1.1	15.2 ± 1	13.9 ± 2.4
	Median	16.2	13.6	15.3	16.3
	95% CI	12.5–20.4	11.2–16	13–17.4	8.1–19.7
	N	10	14	16	7
Percentage of successful requests to mother	Mean ± SE	49.9 ± 5.7	71.8 ± 3.8	77.9 ± 2.9	71.8 ± 8.7
	Median	57.1	73.8	79.9	85.7
	95% CI	37.1–62.7	63.6–80	71.6–84.2	50.6–93
	N	10	13	16	7
Percentage of offers made to infants accounted for by mother	Mean ± SE	25.6 + −5	26.5 ± 4.4	22.8 ± 3.3	14.8 + −4.9
	Median	21.6	26.4	19.4	11.2
	95% CI	14.4–36.8	17–36	15.8–29.8	2.8–26.7
	N	10	14	16	7

All mothers were observed in contact with babies from one age to the next, yielding consistency scores of 1, compared with the lower consistency scores of close family (about 65%). Other than these, few differences were noted in the measures we reported between mothers, close family, clan, and unrelated Efe.

Reflections on Cooperative Care and Infant Development

Efe babies are born into an intensely social world made up of networks of cooperative relationships that are critical to the survival of all. They benefit from these relationships by the care they receive and other resources they gain, and by the opportunities social engagements present to learn about others and to develop social ties that increase the security of accessing resources in the future. To do this, infants and toddlers must be able to adapt to the many changes in social partners and to discern people worthy of trust. And they must act in ways that sustain others' involvement with and interest in them. Their health and survival hinge quite immediately on doing so.

We cast light on the genesis of cooperative relationships by examining babies' social networks in the first 2 years of life. With age, networks grew in size and diversified. Family member presence in infant networks was strong across age groups, and clan member presence strengthened as babies grew older. Family contact time was consistent across age groups, and infants and toddlers could count on being with the same family members, but not with the same clan member or unrelated Efe, as they moved from one age group to the next. Shifts in social landscape brought babies into contact with many people and allowed them to learn and practice complex behaviors for developing, sustaining, and renewing relationships. The facility with which they did this and the willingness of others to engage them even while they grew heavier and more dependent on others for food and protection (given their increased mobility) were aided by their overall good disposition, which made it pleasurable for others to be with them.

That Efe infants and toddlers experience such rapid change in partners is noteworthy because it is as yet an undescribed feature of care among foraging groups. Quick turnover in partners affords advantages to them, and it did not appear energetically costly when distress was considered. A fast paced, broad network may lead to skills that allow babies to adapt to a fluid social scene and to enter into relationships with people, kin, and others, familiar and not. All of this may open up different social options that let babies hedge their bets in the face of uncertainty. It does the same for social partners. With information garnered from engagements with babies, they are able to invest judiciously in those whom as dependents are in need of scarce and often fleeting resources and whom as adults may be future cooperative partners.

Efe infants and toddlers experience people beyond the family as trustworthy, and this may be bolstered by what they observe. With many people worthy of trust,

Efe babies are expected to feel safe and secure in the knowledge of certain resources in their presence and perhaps in their absence as well. Given the safety that their social world engenders, the freedom for them to try new associations, and the favorable experiences they commonly enjoy with people they have just met or do not remember, Efe babies may well perceive unfamiliar people as trustworthy. Because of this, they should be more likely to risk new engagements in the hope for new resources and new information.

We are not certain if the social engagements in which Efe babies were involved beyond the mother developed into attachment relationships. We expect many did. It is a challenge to narrow conceptions of attachment to mother alone when there are no hunter-gatherer mothers we know of solely responsible for infant care (see, e.g., Quinn and Mageo, in press). Aka babies, for example, direct attachment behaviors to a good portion of the people who care for them other than their mothers (Meehan and Hawks, in press). And these babies experience little distress on their mothers' return when these preferred caregivers are available to them. This led Meehan and Hawks to conclude that babies developed multiple attachment relationships, up to six for some infants.

The highly variable social and environmental conditions that selected for human cooperative reproduction and the tradeoffs experienced by forager parents in the coordination of economic productivity and care of multiple young imply that the same uncertainties selected for *cooperative attachment* of infants to others as well. Given the life-span dependence of humans on sharing and reciprocity, evolutionary pressures on development should favor much greater social potential than Western science and culture have expected from children (or adults). The remarkable specialization of human biology and behavior on cooperative resource captures requires a shift in our view from *social* development to *cooperative* development.

References

Alvard, M. S. (2003). The adaptive nature of culture. *Evolutionary Anthropology Issues News and Reviews, 12,* 136–149.

Alvard, M. S. (2009). Kinship and cooperation. *Human Nature: An Interdisciplinary Biosocial Perspective, 20,* 394–416.

Arnett, J. J. (2008). The neglected 95%: Why American psychology needs to become less American. *American Psychologist, 63,* 602–614.

Bahuchet, S. (2012). Changing language, remaining pygmy. *Human Biology, 84,* 11–43.

Bailey, R. C. (1991a). The comparative growth of Efe Pygmies and African farmers from birth to age 5 years. *Annals of Human Biology, 18,* 113–120.

Bailey, R. C. (1991b). *Efe: The behavioral ecology of Efe Pygmy men in the Ituri Forest, Zaire.* Ann Arbor, MI: University of Michigan Press.

Bailey, R. C., & Aunger, J. R. (1989). Significance of the social relationships of Efe pygmy men in the Ituri Forest, Zaire. *American Journal of Physical Anthropology, 78,* 495–507.

Bailey, R. C., & DeVore, I. (1989). Research on the Efe and Lese populations of the Ituri Forest, Zaire. *American Journal of Physical Anthropology, 78,* 459–471.

Bailey, R. C., & Peacock, N. R. (1988). Efe pygmies of northeast Zaire: Subsistence strategies in the Ituri Forest. In I. de Garine & G. A. Harrison (Eds.), *Coping with uncertainty in food supply* (pp. 88–117). Oxford, UK: Oxford University Press.

Becker, N. S. A., Verdu, P., Hewlett, B., & Pavard, S. (2010). Can life history trade-offs explain the evolution of short stature in human pygmies? A response to Migliano et al. (2007). *Human Biology, 82,* 17–27.

Blurton Jones, N. (1993). The lives of hunter-gatherer children: Effects of parental behavior and parental reproductive strategy. In M. E. Pereira & L. A. Fairbanks (Eds.), *Juvenile primates: Life history, development and behavior* (pp. 367–415). New York: Oxford University Press.

Bock, J. (2005). What makes a competent adult forager? In B. Hewlett & M. Lamb (Eds.), *Hunter-gatherer childhoods: Evolutionary, developmental, and cultural perspectives* (pp. 109–128). New York: Aldine de Gruyter.

Bogin, B. B. (1999). Evolutionary perspective on human growth. *Annual Review of Anthropology, 28,* 109–153.

Branca, F., & Ferrari, M. (2002). Impact of micronutrient deficiencies on growth: The stunting syndrome. *Annals of Nutrition and Metabolism, 46*(Suppl. 1), 8–17.

Briga, M., Pen, I., Wright, J. (2012). Care for kin: Within-group relatedness and allomaternal care are positively correlated and conserved throughout the mammalian phylogeny. *Biology Letters, 8,* 533–536.

Broesch, T. L., Callaghan, T., Heinrich, J., Murphy, C., & Rochat, P. (2010). Cultural variations in children's mirror self-recognition. *Journal of Cross-Cultural Psychology, 42,* 1018–1029.

Chisholm, J. S. (1996). The evolutionary ecology of attachment organization. *Human Nature, 7,* 1–38.

Davies, B. E. (2013). Deficiencies and toxicities of trace elements and micronutrients in tropical soils: Limitations of knowledge and future research needs. *Environmental Toxicology and Chemistry, 16,* 75–83.

Dettwyler, K. A. (1992). Infant feeding practices and growth. *Anthropology, 21,* 171–204.

Dormitzer, P. R., & Ellison, P. T. (1989). Anomalously low endemic goiter prevalence among Efe pygmies. *American Journal of Physical Anthropology, 78,* 527–531.

Dounias, E., & Froment, A. (2011). From foraging to farming among present-day forest hunter-gatherers: Consequences on diet and health. *International Forestry Review, 13,* 294–304.

Draper, P. (1976). Social and economic constraints on child life among the !Kung. *Anthropology Faculty Publications, Paper 13,* 200-217.

Einav, S., & Robinson, E. J. (2011). When being right is not enough: Four-year-olds distinguish knowledgeable informants from merely accurate informants. *Psychological Science, 22,* 1250–1253.

Ellis, B. J., Boyce, W. T., Belsky, J., Bakermans-Kranenburg, M. J., & van Ijzendoorn, M. H. (2011). Differential susceptibility to the environment: An evolutionary- neurodevelopmental theory. *Development and Psychopathology, 23,* 7–28.

Fisher, J. (1987). *Shadows in the forest: Ethnoarchaeology among the Efe Pygmies.* Ph.D. Dissertation. Berkeley, CA: University of California at Berkeley.

Flinn, M. V., Nepomnaschy, P. A., Muehlenbein, M. P., & Ponzi, D. (2011). Evolutionary functions of early social modulation of hypothalamic-pituitary-adrenal axis development in humans. *Neuroscience and Biobehavioral Reviews, 35,* 1611–1629.

Flinn, M. V., Quinlan, R. J., Coe, K., & Ward, C. V. (2008). Evolution of the human family: Cooperative males, long social childhoods, smart mothers, and extended kin networks. In C. A. Salmon & T. K. Shackelford (Eds.), *Family relationships: An evolutionary perspective* (pp. 16–31). New York: Oxford University Press.

Foerster, S., Cords, M., & Monfort, S. L. (2012). Seasonal energetic stress in a tropical forest primate: Proximate causes and evolutionary implications. *PLoS ONE, 7,* 501–508.

Fonagy, P., Gergely, G., & Target, M. (2007). The parent-infant dyad and the construction of the subjective self. *Journal of Child Psychology and Psychiatry, 48,* 288–328.

Fowler, J. M., & Christakis, N. A. (2010). Cooperative behavior cascades in human social networks. *Proceedings of the National Academy of Sciences U S A, 107,* 5334–5338.

Griskevicius, V., Delton, A. W., Robertson, T. E., & Tybur, J. M. (2011). Environmental contingency in life history strategies: The influence of mortality and socioeconomic status on reproductive timing. *Journal of Personality and Social Psychology, 100,* 241–254.

Gurven, M. (2004). To give and to give not: The behavioral ecology of human food transfers. *Behavioral and Brain Sciences, 27,* 543–583.

Gurven, M., & Kaplan, H. (2007). Longevity among hunter-gatherers: A cross-cultural examination. *Population and Development Review, 33,* 321–365.

Gurven, M., Stieglitz, J., Hooper, P. L., Gomes, G., & Kaplan, H. (2012). From the womb to the tomb: The role of transfers in shaping the evolved human life history. *Experiments in Gerontology, 47,* 807–813.

Hamilton, W. (1975). Innate social aptitudes of man: An approach from evolutionary genetics. In R. Fox (Ed.), *Biosocial anthropology* (pp. 113–153). London: Malaby Press.

Hamlin, J. K., & Wynn, K. (2011). Young infants prefer prosocial to antisocial others. *Cognitive Development, 26,* 30–39.

Hamlin, J. K., & Wynn, K. (2012). Who knows what's good to eat? Infants fail to match the food preferences of antisocial others. *Cognitive Development, 27,* 227–239.

Hammer, M. F., Woerner, A. E., Mendez, F. L., Watkins, J. C., & Wall, J. D (2011). Genetic evidence for archaic admixture in Africa. *Proceedings of the National Academy of Sciences U S A, 108,* 15123–15128.

Harrison, F., Sciberras, J., & James, R. (2011). Strength of social tie predicts cooperative investment in a human social network. *PLoS ONE, 6,* e18338.

Hein, A. M., & McKinley, S. (2012). Sensing and decision-making in random. *Proceedings of the National Academy of Sciences U S A, 109,* 12070–12074.

Herraez, D., Bauchet, M., Tang, K., Theunert, C., Pugach I., Li, J., et al. (2009). Genetic variation and recent positive selection in worldwide human populations: Evidence from nearly 1 million SNPs. *PLoS ONE, 4,* e7888.

Hewlett, B. L. (2005). Vulnerable lives: The experience of death and loss among the Aka and Ngandu adolescents of the Central African Republic. In B. S. Hewlett & M. E. Lamb (Eds.), *Hunter-gatherer childhoods: Evolutionary, developmental and cultural perspectives* (pp. 322–342). New Brunswick, NJ: Aldine Transaction.

Hewlett, B. S. (1996). Cultural diversity among African pygmies. In S. Kent (Ed.), *Cultural diversity among twentieth-century foragers: An African perspective* (pp. 1–16). Cambridge, UK: Cambridge University Press.

Hewlett, B. S., & Lamb, M. E. (Eds.) (2005). *Hunter-gatherer childhoods: Evolutionary, developmental, and cultural perspectives.* New Brunswick, NJ: Aldine Transaction.

Hill, K. R., Walker, R. S., Bozicevic, M., Eder, J., Headland, T., Hewlett, B., et al. (2011). Co-residence patterns in hunter-gatherer societies show unique human social structure. *Science, 331,* 1286–1289.

Hladik, C. M. (1993). *Tropical forests, people and food: Biocultural interactions and applications to development.* Paris; Carnforth, UK; Pearl River, NY: UNESCO, Parthenon Publishing Group.

Hrdy, S. (2005). *Comes the child before man: How cooperative breeding and prolonged postweaning dependence shaped human potentials.* In B. S. Hewlett & M. E. Lamb (Eds.), *Hunter-gatherer childhoods: Evolutionary, developmental and cultural perspectives* (pp. 65–91). New Brunswick, NJ: Aldine Transaction.

Hrdy, S. (2009). *Mothers and others: The evolutionary origins of mutual understanding.* Cambridge, MA, Harvard University Press.

Ivey Henry, P., Morelli, G., & Tronick, E. (2005). Child caretakers among Efe foragers of the Ituri Forest. In B. S. Hewlett & M. E. Lamb (Eds.), *Hunter-gatherer childhoods: Evolutionary, developmental and cultural perspectives* (pp. 191–213). New Brunswick, NJ: Aldine Transaction.

Ivey, P. (2000). Cooperative reproduction in Ituri Forest hunter-gatherers: Who cares for Efe infants? *Current Anthropology, 41,* 856–866.

Kaplan, H., & Dove, H. (1987). Infant development among the Ache of eastern Paraguay. *Developmental Psychology, 23,* 190–198.

Kaplan, H., Hill, K., Lancaster, J., & Hurtado, A. M. (2012). A theory of human life history evolution: Diet, intelligence, and longevity. *Evolutionary Anthropology, 9,* 156–185.

Kaplan, H., Lancaster, J. B., & Robson, J. B. (2003). Embodied capital and the evolutionary economics of the human lifespan. *Population and Development Review, 29,* 152–182.

Kaplan, H., Schniter, E. E., Smith, V., & Wilson, B. J. (2012). Risk and the evolution of human exchange. *Proceedings of the Royal Society B: Biological Sciences, 279,* :2930–2935.

Kelly, R. L. (1995). *The foraging spectrum: Diversity in hunter-gatherer lifeways.* Washington, DC: Smithsonian Institution Press.

Konner, M. (2005). Hunter-gatherer infancy and childhood: The !Kung and others. In B. S. Hewlett & M. E. Lamb (Eds.), *Hunter-gatherer childhoods: Evolutionary, developmental and cultural perspectives* (pp. 19–64). New Brunswick, NJ: Aldine Transaction.

Kramer, K., & Ellison, P. T. (2010). Pooled energy budgets: Resituating human energy allocation trade-offs. *Evolutionary Anthropology, 19,* 136–147.

Kramer, K., & Greaves, R. (2011). Postmarital residence and bilateral kin associations among hunter-gatherers: Pumé foragers living in the best of both worlds. *Human Nature, 22,* 41–63.

Kuzawa, C. (1998). Adipose tissue in human infancy and childhood: An evolutionary perspective. *Yearbook of Physical Anthropology, 41,* 177–209.

Kuzawa, C. (2007). Developmental origins of life history: Growth, productivity, and reproduction. *American Journal of Human Biology, 19,* 654–661.

Kuzawa, C., & Bragg, J. M. (2012). Plasticity in human life history strategy. *Current Anthropology, 53,* 369–382.

Lachance, J., Vernot, B., Elbers, C. C., Ferweda, B., Froment, A., Bodo, J.-M., et al. (2012). Evolutionary history and adaptation from high-coverage whole-genome sequences of diverse African hunter-gatherers. *Cell, 150,* 457–469.

Lancaster, J. B., & Kaplan, H. S. (2010). Embodied capital and extra-somatic wealth in human evolution and human history. In M. P. Muehlenbein (Ed.), *Human evolutionary biology* (pp. 439–455). Cambridge, UK: Cambridge University Press.

Magill, C. R., Ashley, G. M., & Freeman, K. H. (2013a). Ecosystem variability and early human habitats in eastern Africa. *Proceedings of the National Academy of Sciences U S A, 110,* 1167–1174.

Magill, C. R., Ashley, G. M., & Freeman, K. H. (2013b). Water, plants, and early human habitats in eastern Africa. *Proceedings of the National Academy of Sciences U S A, 110,* 1175–1180.

Marlowe, F. W. (2005). Hunter-gatherers and human evolution. *Evolutionary Anthropology, 14,* 54–67.

Meehan, C., & Hawks, S. (in press). Cooperative breeding and attachment among the Aka foragers. In N. Quinn and J. Mageo (Eds.), *Cross-cultural challenges to attachment theory.* Hampshire, UK: SPA Palgrave.

Mercader, J. (2002). Forest people: The role of African rainforests in human evolution and dispersal. *Evolutionary Anthropology Issues News and Reviews, 11,* 117–124.

Morasch, K. C., & Bell, M. A. (2011). Self-regulation of negative affect at 5 and 10 months. *Developmental Psychobiology, 54,* 215–221.

Morelli, G., & Ivey Henry, P. (2004). Field work: More than a trip to the field. *Cross-cultural Psychology Bulletin, 38,* 10–17.

Morelli, G., & Ivey Henry, P. (in press). Afterword. In N. Quinn and J. Mageo (Eds.), *Cross-cultural challenges to attachment theory.* Hampshire, UK: SPA Palgrove.

Morelli, G., & Tronick, E. (1987). Perinatal practices: A biosocial perspective. In M. Reite & T. Field (Eds.), *Psychobiology and early development* (pp. 293–322). New York: Academic Press.

Nettle, D. (2009). An evolutionary model of low mood states. *Journal of Theoretical Biology, 257,* 100–103.

Ohenjo, N., Willis, R., Jackson, D., Nettleton, C., Good, K., & Mugarura, B. (2006). Health of indigenous people in Africa. *Lancet, 367,* 1937–1946.

Olson, E. R., & Spelke, E. S. (2008). Foundations of cooperation in young children. *Cognition, 108,* 222–231.

Patin, E., Laval, G., Barreiro, L. B., Salas, A., Semino, O., Santachiara-Benerecetti, S., et al. (2009). Inferring the demographic history of African farmers and pygmy hunter-gatherers using a multilocus resequencing data set. *Proceedings of the National Academy of Sciences USA, 5,* 1000448.

Perry, G. H., Dominy, N. J., Claw, K. G., Lee, A. S., Fiegler, H., Redon, R., et al. (2007). Diet and the evolution of human amylase gene copy number variation. *Nature Genetics, 39,* 1061–4036.

Quinn, N., & Mageo, J. (Eds.) (in press). *Cross-cultural challenges to attachment theory.* Hampshire, UK: SPA Palgrove.

Sear, R., & Mace, R. (2008). Who keeps children alive? A review of the effects of kin on child survival. *Evolution and Human Behavior, 29,* 1–18.

Simpson, J. A., & Belsky, J. (2008). Attachment theory within a modern evolutionary framework. In J. Cassidy and P. R. Shaver (Eds.), *Handbook of attachment: Theory, research, and clinical applications* (pp. 131–157). New York: Guilford Press.

Siren, A., & Machoa, J. (2008). Fish, wildlife, and human nutrition in tropical forests: A fat gap? *Interciencia, 33,* 186–193.

Spencer, P. S., & Palmer, V. S. (2012). Interrelationships of undernutrition and neurotoxicity: Food for thought and research attention. *NeuroToxicology, 33,* 605–616.

Sroufe, L. A. (1979). The coherence of individual development: Early care, attachment, and subsequent developmental issues. *American Psychologist, 34,* 834–841.

Sroufe, L. A. (2005). Attachment and development: A prospective, longitudinal study from birth to adulthood. *Attachment and Human Development, 7,* 349–367.

Stearns, S. C. (1992). *The evolution of life histories.* New York: Oxford University Press.

Stern, D. (1977). *The first relationship.* Cambridge, MA: Harvard University Press.

Super, C. M., Harkness, S., Barry, O., & Zeitlin, M. (2011). Think locally, act globally: Contributions of African research to child development. *Child Development Perspectives, 5,* 119–125.

Szczesniak, M., Colaco, M., & Rondon, G. (2012). Development of interpersonal trust among children and adolescents. *Polish Psychological Bulletin, 43,* 50–58.

Tronick, E. (1980). On the primacy of social skills. In D. B. Sawin, L. O. Walker, & J. H. Penicuff (Eds.), *The exceptional infant: Psychosocial risks in infant environment transactions* (pp. 144–158). New York: Brunner/Mazek.

Tronick, E., Morelli, G., & Ivey Henry, P (1992). The Efe forager infant and toddler's pattern of social relationships: Multiple and simultaneous. *Developmental Psychology, 28,* 568–577.

Tronick, E., Morelli, G. A., & Winn, S. (1987). Multiple caretaking of Efe (pygmy) infants. *American Anthropologist, 89,* 96–106.

Tronick, E., & Winn, S. (1992). The neurobehavioral organization of Efe (Pygmy) infants. *Journal of Developmental and Behavioral Pediatrics, 13,* 421–424.

Vansina, J. (1990). *Paths in the rainforests: Toward a history of political tradition in equatorial Africa.* Madison, WI: University of Wisconsin Press.

Wells, J. C. K., & Davies, P. S. W. (1996). Relationship between behavior and energy expenditure in 12-week-old infants. *American Journal of Human Biology, 8,* 465–472.

Wilkie, D. (1987). *Impact of swidden agriculture and subsistence hunting on diversity and abundance of exploited fauna in the Ituri Forest of northeastern Zaire.* Unpublished Ph.D. Dissertation. Amherst, MA: University of Massachusetts.

Wilkie, D. S., & Curran, B. K. (1993). Historical trends in forager and farmer exchange in the Ituri rain forest of northeastern Zaire. *Human Ecology, 21,* 389–417.

Winn, S., Morelli, G., & Tronick, E. (1990). The infant and the group: A look at Efe caretaking practices. In J. K. Nugent, B. M. Lester, & T. E. Brazelton (Eds.), *The cultural context of infancy* (pp. 87–109). Norwood, NJ: Ablex.

Wolf, M., & McNamara, J. M. (2013). Adaptive between-individual differences in social competence. *Trends in Ecology & Evolution, 28*(5), 253–254.

Yamagishi, T. (2011). *Trust: The evolutionary game of mind and society.* New York: Springer.

Zimmermann, M. B. (2011). The role of iodine in human growth and development. *Seminars in Cell and Developmental Biology, 22,* 645–652.

{ Commentary }

Social Connectedness Versus Mothers on Their Own

RESEARCH ON HUNTER-GATHERER TRIBES HIGHLIGHTS THE LACK OF SUPPORT MOTHERS AND BABIES RECEIVE IN THE UNITED STATES

Kathleen Kendall-Tackett

In Morelli, Henry, and Foerster's compelling chapter on life among the Efe, we read the story of infants born into a world where life is uncertain and premature death is common. In order to survive, infants must form attachments with multiple adults: some kin, others not. Right from birth, mothers have other women present who will help care for their new babies. Mothers know that they are not on their own, and that others in the tribe will help them tend their babies. Babies' cries are viewed as communication, and will be answered promptly. If a baby does not settle, tribe members presume that the baby is possibly sick, and he is often brought to mother to nurse.

This chapter wonderfully describes the importance of having a wide range of people available to support a mother and baby. Responsive parenting is modeled by others in the community, and even non-kin take responsibility for caring for the children in the tribe. Mothers in this culture are not left alone to fend for themselves, as there are plenty of role models and people to provide practical help. The result is responsive and loving infant care.

In Contrast, What New Mothers in the U.S. Face

The picture of the life in this tribe could not be more different than the postpartum experience of many American mothers. And the lack of support women receive often starts with the birth itself. In one large nationally representative U.S. sample, 9% of women have met full criteria for posttraumatic stress disorder, with an additional 18% showing symptoms (Beck, Gable, Sakala, & Declercq, 2011). In another U.S. study, 46% of women described their birth experiences as "traumatic" (Alcorn, O'Donovan, Patrick, Creedy, & Devilly, 2010). They use words like "horrific," "degrading," and "barbaric" to describe the actions of their health care providers (Elmir, Schmied, Wilkes, & Jackson, 2010). These experiences often have lasting effects, and women may experience depression, anxiety, or PTSD as a result (Beck, 2004, 2011).

After a woman has her baby in the USA, the mother-focused support received, which may have been high while pregnant, rapidly declines. Typically, a woman is discharged from the hospital 24 to 48 hours after a vaginal birth, or 2 to 4 days after a cesarean section. She may or may not have anyone to help her at home—chances are no one at the hospital has even asked. Her mate will probably return to work within the week, and she is left alone to make sure she has enough to eat, to teach herself to breastfeed, and to recuperate from birth. The people who provided attention during her pregnancy are no longer there, and the people who do come around are often more interested in the baby. There is the tacit—and sometimes explicit—understanding that she is not to "bother" her medical caregivers unless there is a medical reason, and she must wait to talk to her physician until her six-week postpartum checkup. There probably are resources in her community, but she has no idea where they are and often feels too overwhelmed to seek them out for herself. So she must fend for herself as best she can.

Once home, many American mothers experience profound social isolation, living in a culture where babies and children are barred from many activities, and where women might be harassed, or publicly scorned, for breastfeeding in public. So they stay home, thereby increasing their isolation. If they do venture out, they often feel compelled to use formula so they can feed their babies discreetly, thereby placing them on the slippery slope to full-time formula use, compromising their infants' health along the way (Kendall-Tackett, 2010a, 2010b).

Not surprisingly, many women find the postpartum period to be extremely stressful. One popular book written for new mothers describes this transition as "the reverse Cinderella—the pregnant princess has become the postpartum peasant" with a "wave of the obstetrician's wand" (Eisenberg, Murkoff, & Hathaway, 1989, p. 546). (Here are some comments mothers have shared with me about community support:

> *I felt like I didn't matter. I felt like they weren't interested in me after I had my baby. My husband said, "Of course they are not interested. You've had your baby."*
>
> *After the birth, I had several people tell me that the most important thing was that I had a healthy baby. Yes, that is important. But what about me? No one pays attention to the fact that you've had major surgery. They would have paid more attention if you had had your appendix out.*

It is unlikely that Americans would ever seek to be like hunter-gatherers, with their extensive web of connections. But we *can* learn from them. They are doing a much better job in caring for mothers and babies, and the result is babies, children, and adults who can weather extreme life events, such as the high rate of parental death, and still maintain their mental health.

The good news is that change may be on the way. A grass-roots movement has begun that seeks to meet the needs of postpartum women. The word *doula*—from the Greek word for servant—is becoming part of our vocabulary. A *postpartum doula* is someone who takes care of postpartum women by providing practical and emotional assistance. The postpartum doula movement is in response to the lack of postpartum care available from traditional care providers (Webber, 2012).

The type of care new mothers need is so foreign to most of us, that we need some details about what this entails. How might this look when carried out in an American family? In the following account, Postpartum Doula Salle Webber, author of *The Gentle Art of Newborn Family Care,* describes the types of support and assistance that new mothers need (Webber, 1992).

> *In my work as a Doula, my focus is on the mother. I want to provide whatever it is that she needs to feel comfortable, nourished, relaxed, and appreciated: to facilitate a harmonious transition for both mother and child in those profound first days and weeks after birth. A mother needs someone who cares about how many times the baby woke to nurse in the night, how many diapers were changed, how her breasts are feeling. She may need her back massaged or her sheets changed, or she may need someone to provide an abundant supply of water or tea, salads ready-made in the refrigerator, a bowl of cut-up fruit. She needs to be able to complain about how little her mate understands what she's going through, and perhaps, some gentle reminders of all the contributions he has made. She needs someone to hold the baby so she can take a shower or even go to the bathroom; someone to answer the phone when she's napping; someone to water her plants or garden, to clean the kitchen and bathroom, to keep up on the family's laundry. She may have many questions and concerns that only an experienced mother can understand. She needs patience and kind words and a clean and calm environment. (p. 17)*

While most mothers in the USA do not get the care and support they need (though other Western and traditional societies do better), postpartum care can make a significant difference. Many are surprised that this decidedly "low-tech" intervention can work. But as Morelli and colleagues have shown, when this care is routine and what mothers experience, it can indeed be effective.

In conclusion, the style of ongoing and postpartum support modeled by the hunter-gatherer tribes is something Western cultures can learn from. Women can make a comfortable and peaceful transition into motherhood, even when faced with severe hardship and deprivation. It is time that we recognize and meet the needs of postpartum women. The health of our mothers and babies depend on it.

References

Alcorn, K. L., O'Donovan, A., Patrick, J. C., Creedy, D., & Devilly, G. J. (2010). A prospective longitudinal study of the prevalence of post-traumatic stress disorder resulting from childbirth events. *Psychological Medicine, 40*, 1849–1859.

Beck, C. T. (2004). Birth trauma: In the eye of the beholder. *Nursing Research, 53*(1), 28–35.

Beck, C. T. (2011). A metaethnography of traumatic childbirth and its aftermath: Amplifying causal looping. *Qualitative Health Research, 21*. doi: 10.1177/1049732310390698

Beck, C. T., Gable, R. K., Sakala, C., & Declercq, E. R. (2011). Posttraumatic stress disorder in new mothers: Results from a two-stage U.S. national survey. *Birth, 38*(3), 216–227.

Eisenberg, A., Murkoff, H.E., & Hathaway, S.E.(1989). *What to expect the first year.* New York: Workman.

Elmir, R., Schmied, V., Wilkes, L., & Jackson, D. (2010). Women's perceptions and experiences of a traumatic birth: A meta-ethnography. *Journal of Advanced Nursing, 66*(10), 2142–2153.

Kendall-Tackett, K. A. (2010a). Breastfeeding beats the blues. *Mothering, Sept/Oct,* 60–69.

Kendall-Tackett, K. A. (2010b). *Depression in new mothers: Causes, consequences and treatment options, 2nd Edition.* London: Routledge.

Webber, S. (1992). Supporting the postpartum family. *The Doula, 23,* 16–17.

Webber, S. (2012). *The Gentle Art of Newborn Family Care.* Amarillo, TX: Praeclarus Press.

5

Batek Childrearing and Morality
Karen L. Endicott and Kirk M. Endicott

Although contemporary and recent nomadic hunting and gathering societies are not living fossils from the Stone Age, as they are sometimes depicted in popular media, they do provide the closest analogy we have to the way of life our ancient ancestors followed before the advent of agriculture about 10,000 years ago. Understanding that way of life is crucial to our understanding of human nature, for it is the context in which the biology and behavior of our species evolved. Archaeologists, human pale-ontologists, and geneticists have made great strides in extracting information from the physical remains of early hominins and ancient cultures, but many gaps remain in what we can know from such evidence alone. We believe that the ethnographic anal-ogy, if used carefully, can generate testable hypotheses and plausible reconstructions that can help to fill some of those gaps (but see Wylie, 1985, on the limitations of the ethnographic analogy in archaeology). In this chapter, we describe the childrearing practices and their consequences of the Batek people of Peninsular Malaysia, many of whom continue to follow a nomadic hunting and gathering way of life, in hope of casting some light on the probable practices of our remote ancestors.

The Batek

The Batek are 1 of 19 cultural-linguistic groups of Orang Asli (Malay for "original people") in Peninsular Malaysia. They live in the lowland tropical rainforest in a contiguous area where the states of Pahang, Kelantan, and Terengganu meet, an area that encompasses the 4343–square kilometer national park, Taman Negara. Since the 1970s, the forests in the Batek homeland outside Taman Negara have been clear-cut or selectively logged and replaced by oil palm plantations or degraded secondary forest. Now roughly one-third of the approximately 1500 Batek De' (the largest language group called Batek) live in temporary camps in the primary rain-forest of Taman Negara at any one time, and the other two-thirds live in settle-ments on the periphery of the park, although many individuals move back and forth between the two environments from time to time (Tacey, 2013, p. 240; T. P. Lye, personal communication, March 16, 2013).

This chapter is based mainly on 5 months of research we carried out over a 9-month period in 1975 to 1976 in the upper Lebir River watershed of Kelantan, which was then mostly covered by primary rainforest. In those days, the 84 Batek living there were fully nomadic. They occupied two to four camps that changed size and composition continually as people moved in and out of existing camps and as camp groups split and merged and moved to new locations every week to 10 days. The average population of the camps we lived in was 34, including 11 adult men, 9 adult women, and 14 children younger than age 14. At that time the Batek were relatively isolated from the outside world. The only regular contact they had with outsiders was with small parties of Malay traders, who came up the river in outboard motorboats about once a month to obtain forest products, and with employees of the Department of Aboriginal Affairs, who came less frequently at irregular intervals. Few of the Batek had spent any substantial amount of time outside the forest, and only one boy had spent a few months at school at a government settlement on the lower Lebir River. Certainly most Batek knew little or nothing about the childrearing practices of the Malays or other non–Orang Asli Malaysian ethnic groups.

The Batek economy was based on a mixture of hunting and gathering and collecting forest products—mostly large- and small-diameter rattan, the vine-like stems of climbing palms—which they traded for such goods as rice, flour, sugar, tea, tobacco, cloth, and metal pots and knives (see K. M. Endicott, 1984, 1995, 2005; Endicott and Bellwood, 1991; Endicott and Endicott, 2008, for details of the Batek economy). Batek have long traded forest products to outsiders, although the particular products in demand have varied over the years. In March and April of 1976, they participated briefly in a Department of Aboriginal Affairs–sponsored horticulture project, clearing a patch of forest and planting a few fast-growing crops such as maize, but they abandoned the project as soon as the rations provided ran out. Their main source of protein was arboreal game, such as leaf monkeys, gibbons, squirrels, and birds, which men—alone or in small groups—killed by means of bamboo blowpipes and poisoned darts. Although women were not prohibited from blowpipe hunting, few of them pursued it after childhood. However, women did bring in appreciable amounts of meat in the form of small burrowing animals, such as bamboo rats, and fish, which they caught with hooks and lines obtained through trade. The carbohydrate staples of the foraging diet were wild tubers (*Dioscorea* spp.) and vegetables, such as mushrooms and palm hearts, and seasonal fruits and honey. Women in small parties of three or four, together with their small children, gathered wild tubers almost daily. Men also dug up tubers if they came across a promising source while hunting or collecting rattan. Men, who slightly outnumbered women in the adult population, brought in 34% of the tubers by weight, whereas women accounted for the remaining 66% (Endicott and Endicott, 2008, p. 87). Most adult men and adolescent boys also took part in collecting rattan, and some women who did not have young, dependent children did so as well. Small-diameter rattans could simply be pulled down from the forest

canopy and cut into standardized lengths, but large-diameter rattan required someone (usually a man) to climb a tree and cut the vine loose from its crown of leaves.
They alternated collecting rattan with hunting and gathering wild foods, and both
activities were integrated smoothly within the nomadic foraging round. During the
study period, the upper Lebir Batek obtained about 58% of their calories from
wild sources and 42% from traded foods, mainly rice (Endicott and Endicott, 2008,
p. 97). The Batek economy in 1975 and 1976 differed most significantly from the
economies of our ancient ancestors in including cultivated foods, metal tools, and
cloth obtained through trade with outsiders.

The basic unit of Batek society was the conjugal family, consisting of a married
couple and their dependent children. (For details of Batek marriage and divorce,
see below.) Couples were potentially independent economically, at least for limited
periods of time, and husbands and wives together decided where to live and what
kind of work to do. However, the unit of long-term survival was the camp, which
usually consisted of five to eight conjugal families living in separate palm-thatched
lean-to shelters. Although camp composition changed almost continually, camps
had a moral unity that was expressed most vividly in the obligation to share any
food—animal or vegetable, foraged or traded—that people obtained in excess of
their daily needs. We often saw children carrying portions of food from one shelter to another, even when the occupants already had their own supply. The direct
participation of each individual in the camp sharing network enabled unmarried,
divorced, or widowed persons to augment their own food-getting efforts and gain
direct access to foods they may not have been able to procure themselves, and it
provided people with food when their own food-getting labors failed, a frequent
enough occurrence in foraging societies.

Although Batek highly valued their individual autonomy, they also cooper-
ated voluntarily in many work and social activities, including performing rituals
(K. M. Endicott, 1979). No one had any authority over anyone else, but there were
some informal leaders—who might be men or women—who exercised some influence in group decisions. However, no one had the right to coerce anyone else in any
way, and violence of any kind was absolutely forbidden. Thus the social environment in which Batek children grew up was one in which everyone had great personal autonomy, but also an obligation to respect, help, and cooperate with others
regardless of age or gender (K. M. Endicott, 2011; Endicott and Endicott, 2008).

Batek Childrearing Practices

During pregnancy, there were no prohibitions on a woman's eating habits or on her
activities. She continued her normal activities, including sexual relations, for as long
into her pregnancy as she felt able.

Although we did not have the opportunity to observe a birth during our fieldwork, people explained their practices to us. Unless labor began unexpectedly,

Batek babies were born in special lean-to shelters set in the forest away from the camp. The shelter had a floor of split bamboo, sticks, or bark and some sticks stuck diagonally through the floor for the expectant mother to lean against. She sat with her knees drawn up and a cloth covering her abdomen and thighs. A midwife, usually an experienced older woman, and a few other women assisted in bringing the baby into the world. The midwife massaged the mother's abdomen and received the baby in her hands when the mother pushed it out. The midwife placed the baby between the mother's feet and then bathed the mother and baby with cool water to prevent fever. She cut the umbilical cord with a splinter of bamboo, wrapped the baby in a cloth, and placed it at the mother's breast. When the mother felt strong enough to walk, she returned to her family shelter in camp. For the next 3 or 4 days, she returned regularly to the birth hut to keep a fire burning beside the placenta, which was left covered by a pandanus leaf mat, to prevent the mother or baby from incurring a fever.

Infancy (birth to 18 months) was a time of indulgence and constant physical contact for children of both sexes. An infant's cries were always heeded by a parent or any adult or child nearby. The infant spent most of its time with its mother, being carried in a cloth sling on the mother's back or at her breast so that the baby could nurse on demand. At night, the infant slept next to the mother. Breastfeeding might continue for 3 or 4 years unless a subsequent pregnancy caused the mother's milk supply to dry up. Otherwise, children were allowed to take the breast as long as they wanted to, although soft foods and later solid foods were added to their diets as soon as their teeth began to come in.

Fathers also played an important part in the social life of infants (K. L. Endicott, 1992). Fathers held, cuddled, and chattered to their sons and daughters with as much obvious enjoyment as mothers showed. Fathers as well as mothers bathed their children, cleaned up their excrement, and took them outside camp to relieve themselves. They often made toys—such as blowpipes, swings, and climbing ladders—for their children's amusement. While in camp, fathers often carried their babies in a sling on their back and let the babies sit on their laps while sitting in their shelters. Other camp members also took an active interest in the babies, admiring and cuddling them, reciting rhymes for their amusement, and lavishing affection on them. The Batek said they desire male and female babies equally, and their affectionate behavior toward infants of each sex supports this claim.

From about 2 to 6 years old, boys and girls spent much time together doing the same activities. Two- and three-year-olds of both sexes tended to stay close to their mothers. Mothers at this time, however, began to foster independence in their children by not heeding every cry, letting children deal with their own minor frustrations and difficulties, and intervening primarily when their cries indicated pain, fear, or intense frustration. Children were not cuddled quite as frequently as during infancy, especially if the mother had a new baby. By about 3½ to 4 years of age, most children ranged farther from their mothers, playing in mixed-sex groups, often with 5- and 6-year-olds, without direct supervision from adults or older children.

As long as the children remained within earshot, they were allowed to do almost anything they pleased. Activities included chopping trees with bush knives, building fires, pretending to cook or actually cooking small amounts of rice or other food, digging as if digging for tubers, climbing trees, gathering sticks as if they were rattan, "moving camp," building miniature shelters, and other activities imitative of the skills they saw performed by adults inside and outside camp. Adults did not normally participate in children's play activities. Both boys and girls learned various skills by imitation and practice, without direct instruction or suggestion from adults. During these early years, children also began to participate directly in the sharing network of the camp by helping to distribute plates of food to other families in camp. This was one of the few jobs young children were actively given.

All young boys and girls frequently accompanied their mothers on tuber-collecting trips, babies being carried and older children walking behind. Although the presence of children did not usually hinder the women's foraging success, mothers sometimes tried to leave some of their children behind in camp. Adults who were resting or working in camp were usually happy to look after other families' children. Batek sometimes spoke of the children in camp as if they belonged to the camp group as a whole, referring to all of them as "our children." However, older children were not called on to look after younger ones, mainly because parents considered the older children unreliable and likely to leave their young charges unattended.

Play and play groups were flexible. Whenever children decided to do a particular activity, other interested children spontaneously joined in. No child was excluded from play by other children. Youngsters who could not keep up because of their age and more limited abilities simply dropped out of the play and found something else to do. Sometimes one child consistently initiated an activity, but often play flowed from one activity to the next, according to the whim of the ever-changing group. A typical sequence of play began with the children swimming in a shallow stream, changed to jumping off logs into the stream, shifted to running after each other in a "tiger chasing Batek" game (children switched roles at will), reverted back to swimming, and ended up with pretending to be motorboats traveling up and downstream until the children gradually drifted off to their own or each other's shelters to rest. Each activity in this sequence lasted about 10 minutes. (See the DVD packaged with Endicott and Endicott, 2008, for scenes of children at play.) Leisure activities in camp included grooming each other and singing. There was little parental interference in play, except to correct children if they were breaking prohibitions against particular acts (termed *lawac*), such as laughing at butterflies, which were thought to provoke the thundergod, Gobar, and the earth deity, Ya', into causing a devastating thunderstorm and flood (K. M. Endicott, 1979). This was a major way children learned about the Batek world view.

Children's play was strikingly noncompetitive. Games did not have actual rules; children simply created and then repeated activity patterns as they went along. Play was not structured to produce teams of winners and losers. Even in constructive play, when children made darts or other items, there was little if any concern with producing "the best" objects, each child simply working at his or her own level of proficiency. The noncompetitive nature of play paralleled the noncompetitive nature of adult work activities, on which most play was based.

From about 6 to 8 years old, children practiced more intensively the skills they would later use as adults, learning more about their environment and culture through direct observation and questioning of adults and some informal instruction from them. In camp they observed hunters making blowpipes and darts, and they saw them shooting birds and squirrels nearby. The children, including girls, tried to make darts and might borrow someone's blowpipe to try them out close to camp. They also practiced fishing, digging tubers, catching frogs, and other food-getting activities, often with considerable success. Although parents did not expect children to produce food, the youngsters enjoyed doing so when they could, and they also enjoyed cooking and sharing it with their friends. Swimming, pretending to move camp, singing, dancing, and other activities done in early childhood continued to form part of the activities of the older children. Imitating animal sounds, learned from hunters, was a favorite activity. As in their early years, the older children spent much of their time in mixed-sex groups because they had similar interests.

Between ages 8 and 10, children usually moved out of the family shelter. This was often a practical necessity because the floor space of the typical lean-to shelter measured only about 5 by 7 feet, and younger siblings would take precedence in the family bed. At first the older children would construct a small shelter near or even attached to the family shelter and would continue to eat at the family hearth. Adolescents often banded together in separate shelters, where they sometimes cooked their own food, while at other times eating with their natal families. The occupants of these adolescent group-shelters might be all boys, all girls, or a mixture of both. During adolescence, youngsters began experimental sexual relations, which sometimes led to "trial marriages" of varying durations. Parents expected this to happen and were not greatly concerned. Parents expected their children to become more independent as they physically matured.

By 8 to 9 years of age, a change in the interests and activity-group composition could be seen. Boys spent more and more of their time hunting birds and squirrels increasingly far from camp and spent more of their in-camp hours making darts and drying their blowpipes. After about age 10, boys also began to accompany older boys or men on the hunt. Girls gradually spent less time making darts as the boys increased their out-of-camp hunting activities. Instead, girls accompanied women more frequently on gathering trips, not as children tagging along, but rather as workers in their own right. Often girls went with women other than their own mothers. In camp, girls began to be taught (not necessarily by their mothers) how to weave baskets and mats of pandanus leaves, a skill that required considerable practice.

By about 12 years of age, the frequency of boys accompanying hunters and girls going with women on their activities was so great that they were essentially already following adult behavior patterns. Some girls continued to hunt casually near camp, but as far as we know, they rarely if ever actually accompanied skilled hunters on hunts. Batek believed that females had naturally weaker breath than males and were therefore less suited than males to becoming serious blowpipe hunters. Boys still accompanied their mothers on gathering trips whenever they wished, but they usually took along their blowpipes and spent their time shooting at birds and squirrels, rather than digging for tubers. Boys and girls also began to participate in rattan work during this time.

A striking characteristic of the gradual change from the mixed-sex play groups and identical activities of childhood to the frequently single-sex work groups and complementary activities of adulthood was that it happened without overt pressure, coercion, or direct influence from adults. Children seemed to adopt appropriate gender-role behaviors of their own accord. They were undoubtedly influenced by seeing very positive role models in women as well as men. Batek were gender egalitarian in the sense that neither males nor females as groups had control over the other sex and neither sex was accorded greater value than the other by society as a whole (K. L. Endicott, 1979; Endicott and Endicott, 2008). Both men and women appeared to be self-confident, enthusiastic about their activities, high spirited, and generally satisfied with their work and lives. Batek did not downgrade or differentially evaluate the activities of either sex, nor did they impose gender-specific behaviors on individuals. Batek children, then, had no obvious reason not to readily adopt the behavior patterns of their own sex group, even though the activities usually associated with the other sex were not actually prohibited to them.

For Batek, the transition from childhood to adulthood was unmarked by puberty ceremonies, challenges, or deals, religious inductions, or secret ceremonies, which serve to differentiate stages of life and separate the sexes in many other societies. Growing up entailed the acquisition of adult skills and eventually a change to the role of spouse. The life stages were noted linguistically rather than ceremonially. There were separate terms for infant, child, female youth, male youth, parent of young children, and old person. The only gender-specific terms were those used when a person underwent obvious physical maturation.

By about 14 to 16 years of age, the Batek were no longer just children and novices in their activities, but rather were essentially adults. By then, they lived in separate shelters from their parents, and they had begun to engage in trial marriages. Their food-getting activities took a serious turn from the practice and play of the early years to the productivity expected of adults.

By their late teens or early 20s, most Batek entered into socially recognized marriages (Endicott and Endicott 2008, pp. 55–61). These often followed a series of trial marriages and sexual liaisons. Although parents sometimes tried to influence their children's marriage choices, people made their own decisions about whom to marry. They said that marriages were based on mutual attraction, love (*sayegn*), and physical desire (*hawa'*). Marriage was defined by a couple moving in together in a separate lean-to shelter and accepting the responsibilities of married life, not necessarily by means of a ritual. They began to cooperate in food getting and to share their meals, and they started to use respectful terms of reference and address for their affines and to follow proper avoidance behaviors toward them. At the beginning of a marriage, the couple might provide a small feast for camp members, exchange small gifts, and give gifts to their new parents-in-law, whom they were obligated to help for the first few years of marriage, but this too was up to the wishes of the individuals involved. Often the newly married couple lived near the wife's parents for the first year, but later they might move to the husband's parents' camp (if different) or to another camp entirely.

Divorce, which was marked mainly by the couple ceasing to live together, was almost as frequent as marriage in the early years of adulthood. Although couples were less likely to divorce after having children, that was not unusual either. When a couple with children divorced, breastfeeding infants and very young children remained with the mother, whereas older children would choose which parent to live with or might alternate between them. Because the parents often lived in the same camp, the children's access to both parents was easy. When the parents remarried, as they almost always did, the new spouse took on a parental role toward the children that continued even if they in turn divorced. Children normally called their parents' new spouses *bah* ("uncle, male relative of parents' generation") or *be'* ("aunt, female relative of parents' generation"), but referred to them as their *pa' tiri'* ("stepfather") or *na' tiri'* ("stepmother"). Thus, the more divorces and remarriages their biological parents went through, the more quasi parents the children acquired, which no doubt enhanced the security of children in a society in which either or both parents might die at any time.

SOCIALIZATION INTO NONAGGRESSION

A striking feature of adult Batek society, and one to which children had to be socialized, was the absence of aggression and violence (K. L. Endicott, 1979; K. M. Endicott, 2013). Writers on nonaggressive and nonviolent societies generally accept that all people, even those living in nonviolent societies, experience aggressive feelings at some point during their lives (see, e.g., Dentan, 1978; Draper, 1978; Marshall, 1976, p. 288; Montagu 1978). The earliest training in nonaggression that Batek children received took place between the ages of 1 and 2 years. Children of this age who hit out at each other in annoyance or even in the wild animation of play were simply retrieved by their mothers or other adults and separated. This was done without comment from the mothers, who then tried to interest each child in some new activity. With toddlers and older children, parents might explicitly tell them not to annoy each other and might intervene to separate them if necessary.

Batek toddlers seemed to have "classic" toddler tendencies. They might act possessively about an object, be it a stick or a portion of food, and might hit others who came too close while they had the object. Children gradually learned to over-come this aggressive possessiveness, however. Parents did not generally admonish children about being possessive, which would have drawn attention to it, but simply ignored it. They said that young children did not know any better, that they were *budo' lagi'*, "still ignorant." Parents seemed to think that children would simply grow out of possessiveness and aggressive behavior. Sometimes they laughed at aggressive behavior, making what seemed important to the child appear to be trivial and amusing. This also served to ease the tension of the situation. Aggression could also be calmed by others distracting the child. If a child was seen to be about to hit someone, others might cry out "*ala'!*" which roughly means "Hey!" Whatever method was used, no direct comments about the aggressive act or lessons about the right or wrong of the act were made. Parents normally did not punish children for aggressive acts, although very occasionally, one might strike a child to teach her not to hit others. The Batek appeared to think that a better way of handling children's aggression was to minimize reaction to it and let children learn at their own pace that acting aggressively was just not something people do. As children became more cognizant of adult behavior, they realized that adults did not hit each other or act possessively about food or objects. They also saw that adults vented their anger or frustration verbally rather than physically. The absence of an adult aggression model for Batek children to follow was probably the greatest factor in socializing children to be nonaggressive.

THE BASAL HUMAN CHILDREARING PATTERN

Recently, scholars have tried to determine which childrearing practices are most common in nomadic hunting and gathering societies, with the implication that they probably also existed in early hominin and archaic *Homo sapiens* groups. Narvaez and Gleason, drawing on studies by such scholars as Melvin Konner (2010), sum-marize those features thus:

> "...early life experience for hominids involved (1) touch, being held or kept near others constantly; (2) caregiver prompt and appropriate responses to fusses, cries, and needs; (3) breastfeeding on demand frequently (2 to 3 times/ hour initially) and on average 2 to 5 years; (4) cosleeping close to caregivers; (5) multiple alloparents, that is, frequent care by individuals other than moth-ers (fathers and grandmothers in particular); (6) multiage free-play groups in nature; (7) high social embeddedness; and (8) natural childbirth...." (2013, p. 314; see also Hewlett and Lamb 2005, p. 15)

Batek childrearing practices fit that pattern closely. The question is: Why?

The Batek we knew did not express a coherent, all-inclusive theory or philoso-phy of how children should be raised. The closest term in Batek to our term "chil-drearing" is *perigos*, which means merely "to give life." Our impression is that they viewed most, if not all, of their childrearing practices as common-sense solutions to practical problems of life. They had no alternatives to such practices as natural childbirth and breastfeeding, and they would have seen no reason to limit breast-feeding to a fixed schedule. Similarly, the alternatives to carrying babies and sleep-ing with them in the family shelter would have unnecessarily exposed the babies to hazards, given the absence of clean, safe places to put them. Alloparenting helped solve the practical problem of how to care for children when a parent had to be away, although it also expressed the Batek feeling that the health and survival of babies was partially the responsibility of the entire camp group and the baby's kin group. Batek sometimes expressed anxiety about the possible decline in their popu-lation, referring especially to such continuing threats as malaria and occasional epidemics of communicable diseases. Multiage play groups seemed inevitable given the small child population of a forest camp, and people would have seen no reason to separate children by age. The only listed feature on which the Batek presented a partial exception was that of caregivers promptly responding to babies' fusses, cries, and needs. Certainly Batek did so during the first year or so of a baby's life, but after that, they gradually began to let the child cope with minor problems on its own. This may have reflected a deliberate policy of letting children learn by doing and helping them to achieve greater independence from adults. We were surprised that parents allowed babies not yet able to walk to play with bush knives and fire, a practice that has been noted for some other nomadic hunter-gatherers (Hewlett and Lamb, 2005, p. 15). No doubt this sometimes led to cuts and burns, but it also resulted in children becoming incredibly good at practical skills at an early age.

Child, Adolescent, and Adult Relationships

The basic relationship between Batek children and adults was one of mutual affec-tion and respect. Parents and other adults were very caring and protective toward young children, but they also gave them the freedom to do what they wanted to do. Parents were indulgent toward their children, never denying them anything that they wanted or that the parents themselves enjoyed. For example, we were aston-ished at first to see toddlers smoking miniature cigarettes. If a child ruined some family possession in the course of play, the parents simply shrugged it off.

Children were openly affectionate toward both parents. Attachments to fathers appeared to be equal in intensity to those with mothers. It was not uncommon for a man's young son or daughter to wail despairingly for him when he left camp to hunt. Such cries went up for mothers, too, if they tried to go off to work without taking their children along.

Although parents molded their children's behavior through example, verbal cor-rection, or spontaneous reactions, parents had no real authority over their children. Parents expected that children would not obey them if they did not want to. This was accepted in much the same way that Western parents accept that "boys will be boys." Batek parents normally did not strike their children, unless they felt it was a last resort for teaching children not to hit others. When children's behavior annoyed parents, they might yell at them to stop, but this often had no effect. Children were more likely to heed if a parent said he or she was upset or angry about the behavior. Fathers were no more successful at controlling their children's behavior than mothers.

The main way parents in this largely nonviolent society tried to control the behavior of their children was by invoking the authority Batek culture projected onto nonhuman or non-Batek third parties: the thundergod Gobar, tigers, and outsiders. Gobar was the authority figure for both adults and children because he punishes transgressions of the proper social and cultural order with thunderstorms. Parents reminded children, often while they were playing, that certain acts were prohibited (*lawac*), and gradually children learned to avoid those acts. Parents also used the tiger as an authority figure and bogeyman to prompt or scare children into proper behavior. Although the fear of tigers had some basis in the real physical threat tigers posed to the Batek, it was also intensified by the use of the tiger as a bogey figure. If a child wandered too far from camp, for example, a parent might call out "Tiger, tiger!" so that the child would run back to camp. This taught children to be aware of potentially dangerous situations and also served as a means of controlling children. The other bogeyman parents used to influence children's behavior was the outsider (*gob*), a role in which we were sometimes cast. Parents might tell a child that the *gob* would come, or if present, was watching, if a child did certain things or continued to misbehave.

Adults generally respected the autonomy of adolescents. Some parents tried to influence their children's choices of spouses, but it was up to the youngster to decide whether to obey. Some did, and others did not. Occasionally, we heard an adult lecturing a group of adolescents about something he or she thought they should do. The youngsters would listen and then do whatever they wished.

Social Personality

We did not conduct any standardized personality tests on the Batek, so our observations on this topic are impressionistic. Although most Batek shared personality traits promoted by their socialization practices—such as adventurousness, independence, friendliness, cheerfulness, and generosity—there was also a tolerance for personal quirks and eccentricities. Nevertheless, the range of personality types was probably narrower than that found in modern complex societies, in which people come from diverse backgrounds and life experiences. Unlike in societies in which the two sexes are treated and valued differently, in Batek society there were no obvious male or female personality types. The intolerance of aggression prevented males from developing aggressive or dominating personalities, as is common in many societies. Conversely, women were not submissive or meek. Their socialization led individuals toward a confident independence coupled with a sense of responsibility toward others, rather than creating vastly different masculine and feminine personality types.

People seemed to tolerate some cases of antisocial behavior, probably for the sake of group solidarity. For example, one man who had once worked for the Department of Aboriginal Affairs was considered somewhat "wicked" (Malay *jahat*) because he and his wife kept a small supply of rice for emergencies rather than sharing it with the camp group. One man was said to sometimes lie to get his way and to be irresponsible. He ran up a large debt with a rattan trader and then expected other relatives to help him pay it off. We heard of one case of a mother beating one of her young children unconscious with a piece of bamboo when she was angry with her husband for supposedly making advances toward another woman. We were told that she had actually killed two of her children in the past in similar fashion. People said that she was somewhat "insane," and that she was prone to losing all self-control when angry. Most of the time, however, she seemed very sweet and caring, and before hearing of that incident, we had considered her a model mother.

Moral Culture

All human societies develop rules of proper behavior—some explicit, and others implicit. Proper behavior is encouraged and rewarded by social approval, whereas improper behavior is condemned and punished by human agents, superhuman beings, or invisible forces. Moral rules, according to some Western scholars, prohibit actions that are wrong in some absolute sense. Philosopher Bernard Gert (2005, p. 10) distinguishes moral rules from legal, religious, and prudential rules and from codes of conduct of specific groups, which may actually be immoral (e.g., Nazi "morality"). However, in actual practice such moral rules are often entwined with other kinds of rules, as when they are justified by religious beliefs and enforced by laws. For our purposes, we regard morality as "concerned with the behavior of people insofar as that behavior affects others; it prohibits the kind of conduct that harms others and encourages the kind of conduct that helps them" (Gert, 2005, p. 9; see also De Waal, 1996, pp. 207–208).

The behavior of well-socialized Batek could be seen as governed—or at least strongly influenced—by a set of explicit and implicit moral rules, some in the form of prosocial obligations, and others in the form of prohibitions against antisocial behavior. Both obligations and prohibitions were enforced by diffuse social pressure and divine punishments meted out by superhuman beings. Some teasing was used, but only in good humor, because seriously hurting another person's feelings was thought to cause them physical harm (see below).

Batek did not express their obligations to others in the form of an explicit list, but they can be deduced from childrearing practices, approval and disapproval of certain actions, sanctions against certain actions, and observable behaviors. Batek "ethical principles" or "moral obligations" appear to be the following: respect others, help others (including share food), be self-reliant, be nonviolent, and be noncompetitive (K. M. Endicott, 2011, pp. 66–75; see also Endicott and Endicott, 2008, pp. 42–51). Our discussion above of Batek childrearing practices gives some idea of how children internalized these obligations as they grew up. Because no Batek person had formal authority over anyone else, no one was in a position to punish anyone else for failing to fulfill any of these moral obligations. However, Batek were sensitive to the opinions of others and were susceptible to pressure from negative talk and direct criticism. We were told that for a serious offense, such as killing someone, the group would abandon the offender, running away if necessary. In addition, Batek believed that if a person mistreated someone else, the victim might incur a disease called *ke'oy*, in which the heart becomes hot and the person falls into deep depression (K. M. Endicott, 1979, pp. 107, 109–110; 2011, p. 68; Endicott and Endicott, 2008, pp. 45–46). People believed that *ke'oy* could lead to physical breakdown and death if untreated. The most effective treatment for *ke'oy* was for someone, preferably the offender, to lightly cut his own leg, wipe some blood on some leaves, rub the leaves on the chest of the ailing person to cool the heart, and then throw away the leaves, taking the poison of the disease with them. People's fear of being accused of causing someone to suffer an attack of *ke'oy* served as a powerful incentive to avoid mistreating others.

Batek also observed a large number of prohibitions against acts that were thought to offend the superhuman beings. *Lawac* acts were thought to anger the thundergod, who would cause a violent thunderstorm to strike the offender's camp, and the earth deity, who would cause a flood to well up from the underground sea and dissolve the earth beneath the camp. The prohibited acts included laughing at certain animals (e.g., leeches), cooking certain combinations of foods over a single fire, pouring certain kinds of blood into streams, flashing a mirror in the sun, and making a booming sound by banging a section of bamboo on the surface of a stream. It was also *lawac* for anyone to have sexual relations with a relative closer than first cousin. (Unlike some other Orang Asli groups, Batek allowed marriage between first cousins.) The thundergod was thought to punish sexual breaches by sending a thunderstorm or a crippling disease to afflict the offender. To stop punitive thunderstorms, people—usually the offender—performed a "blood sacrifice," scratching their shin with a knife, mixing some blood with water, and throwing the mixture upward to the thundergod and downward to the earth deity (K. M. Endicott, 1979, pp. 68–79).

Another category of prohibited acts, called *tolah* (Malay *tulah*), included a large number of socially disruptive and disrespectful acts, such as spitting on someone, urinating in a stream above a bathing place, and calling an older relative by her personal name rather than a kin term or teknonym. Violence was considered a *tolah* act and, if serious, *lawac* as well. *Tolah* acts were punished by the creator god, Tohan (cf. Malay *tuhan*), causing the offender to have an accident or sending a disease that would cause the offender to become paralyzed and eventually die. If the offense were serious, the superhuman beings would refuse to take the person's shadow-soul after death, thus dooming the offender to roam the earth as a ghost.

Moral Behavior

The Batek system of moral obligations encouraged a behavior pattern that we term "cooperative autonomy," as distinct from the "competitive autonomy" of such peoples as the New Guinea highlanders and what Americans call "rugged individualism"—self-reliance unhampered by obligations to others. Although Batek were free in principle to do whatever they might have wanted without interference from others, their long-term survival depended on the support of a group that would help them in times of need. Anyone who chose to violate one of their moral obligations risked angering their camp group. The habit of helping others (e.g., sharing surplus food) was engrained in people by the time they reached maturity. People had empathy for others and concern for the welfare of others, especially fellow camp members and close relatives who might have been living elsewhere. This does not mean that there was no room for disputes and differences of opinion. The moral principles were not entirely consistent with each other. For example, the right to move at will to another camp would sometimes conflict with a person's obligation to help close relatives in the original camp. There were also some ambiguities in how the principles should be applied. For example, we heard an argument between two adolescent girls and two boys who had been living in the same shelter over whether the girls should have saved some fruit for the boys, who were out hunting when the fruit came into camp. Individuals and couples usually took account of what other camp members wanted to do before making their own decisions, if only to ensure that they did not end up camping alone, which would have been dangerous. Discussions took place every day in camp about what people wanted to do and where they wanted to go, and the composition of work groups varied from day to day.

Because the Batek did not have leaders with the authority to settle disputes, people usually thrashed out their complaints verbally, in public arguments to which anyone could contribute. If a consensus developed that one disputant was in the wrong, camp members would try to convince that person to alter their behavior or to make amends to the other disputant, but applying too much pressure always risked causing the person who was blamed to incur *ke'oy*. If bad feelings persisted, the disputants always had the option of moving to another camp, the classic escape valve in nomadic foraging societies. Violence between adults was almost nonexistent. We heard that two men had once gotten into a physical fight over the wife of one of the men, but respected elders managed to calm the conflict and convince the men to let the woman decide.

Wellbeing

Batek childrearing methods and social practices seem to have produced well-adjusted individuals who were generally happy, emotionally secure, and self-confident. Of course, individuals were subject to emotional ups and downs depending on events in their lives, such as the death of a child. (We estimated that about 25% of Batek children were stillborn or died within the first 2 years after birth, usually from malaria or gastrointestinal problems.) But whenever someone suffered such a misfortune, they could count on the emotional support of the other members of the camp group.

The tone of everyday life in Batek camps and work parties was usually upbeat (see the DVD packaged with Endicott and Endicott, 2008, for scenes from daily life). An element of adventure pervaded daily activities, and people did not make a firm distinction between work and play (cf. Gray, 2009). People seemed to enjoy the challenges of hunting, fishing, and searching for and harvesting wild foods. On average, men worked at food-getting only about 29 hours a week and women about 20 hours, thus leaving plenty of time for leisure activities in camp. Adults could be as playful as children. For example, once a couple of men drew mustaches and beards on their faces with charcoal and pretended to be Tamil shopkeepers. In the evenings, after eating, people usually sat by their fires repairing their blowpipes, making darts, weaving mats, or grooming each other's hair to remove lice. They also visited back and forth at each other's shelters. Sometimes small groups would sing into the night. The fear of punitive thunderstorms did not fill people with constant dread. Few thunderstorms passed directly over a camp, and in any case, people seemed confident that performing the blood sacrifice would cause any that did to abate. They normally ignored thunder in the distance.

One important activity that reinforced their group solidarity and confidence was the singing and trancing sessions that they usually performed before the fruit season, to ask the superhuman beings for abundant fruit, and at the end of the fruit season, to thank them for the fruit that had been sent (K. M. Endicott, 1979, pp. 150–155). Such rituals were also performed occasionally to solicit the help of the superhuman beings in treating a seriously ill person. These rituals engaged almost everyone in camp, and preparations took as long as a week. Men and women together constructed a huge thatch lean-to shelter over a large dancing platform made of logs and sheets of tree bark. Men also constructed a log drum, a green log about 5 inches in diameter suspended from rattan straps, which was beaten with sticks. Women made body decorations of rattan, pandanus, fragrant leaves, and flowers. By the night of the ritual, the camp had swollen in size as people from other camps on the upper Lebir assembled at the ritual site. During the ritual, two or three people would beat a rhythm on the log drum, and a large number of other people would dance around the platform in a circle while singing songs to the superhuman beings. The songs and the fragrant odors of the body decorations were thought to attract the superhuman beings to the ceremony. Shamans and others would sit in the center and eventually go into trance, sending their shadow-souls on journeys to the land of the superhuman beings above the firmament and beneath the earth, where they would ask the superhuman beings for fruit or help in curing. These singing sessions might last for the entire night. They left the participants with a renewed feeling of security and confidence in the support of the superhuman beings.

Conclusion

We have shown how the Batek prepared their children for the cooperative autonomy that helped them thrive as nomadic forest-dwelling hunter-gatherers and traders. The Batek seemed very satisfied with their way of life, and they rejected attempts by the Department of Aboriginal Affairs to induce them to settle down and become swidden farmers. Many people told us that when we came back in the future, we would always find them deep in the forest, not in government-sponsored settlements.

The Batek childrearing method corresponds closely to the model that has been hypothesized to have been followed by our ancient hominin ancestors. The Batek case study also should alert us to the probable importance of religious beliefs in the moral systems of archaic *Homo sapiens,* even though hard evidence of early religions is hard to find. The elaborate religions of the Aboriginal Australians give ample evidence that hunter-gatherers with simple technologies can have complex systems of beliefs and rituals (see, e.g., Tonkinson, 1991). In the absence of political hierarchy, supernatural sanctions punishing antisocial behavior may well have been crucial for maintaining the social cohesion necessary for survival in the world of ancient humans. The universal existence of religion in human cultures attests to the tendency of humans to project meaning onto places, objects, and events in the world around them. It is but a small further step to imagine that the cosmos is populated by superhuman beings who take note of human actions and can punish misbehavior by means of accidents, illness, death, and even thunderstorms.

Acknowledgments

Our research in 1975 and 1976 was generously funded by the Department of Anthropology in the Research School of Pacific Studies at The Australian National University. In Malaysia, the research was made possible by the kind permission of the Jabatan Hal Ehwal Orang Asli and the Economic Planning Unit. We sincerely thank our Batek friends who made that research and our earlier and later research trips possible.

References

Dentan, R. (1978). Notes on childhood in a nonviolent context: The Semai case (Malaysia). In A. Montagu (Ed.), *Learning non-aggression: The experience in non-literate societies* (pp. 94–143). New York: Oxford University Press.

De Waal, F. (1996). *Good natured: The origins of right and wrong in humans and other animals.* Cambridge, MA: Harvard University Press.

Draper, P. (1978). The learning environment for aggression and anti-social behavior among the !Kung (Kalahari Desert, Botswana, Africa). In A. Montagu (Ed.), *Learning non-aggression: The experience in non-literate societies* (pp. 31–53). New York: Oxford University Press.

Endicott, K. L. (1979). *Batek Negrito sex roles.* M.A. thesis. Canberra: Australian National University, Department of Prehistory and Anthropology.

Endicott, K. L. (1992). Fathering in an egalitarian society. In B. Hewlett (Ed.), *Father-child relations: Cultural and biosocial contexts* (pp. 281–295). Hawthorne, NY: Aldine de Gruyter.

Endicott, K. M. (1979). *Batek Negrito religion: The world-view and rituals of a hunting and gathering people of peninsular Malaysia.* Oxford, UK: Clarendon Press.

Endicott, K. M. (1984). The economy of the Batek of Malaysia: Annual and historical perspectives. *Research in Economic Anthropology, 6,* 29–52.

Endicott, K. M. (1995). Seasonal variations in the foraging economy and camp size of the Batek of Malaysia. In R. Talib and C. B. Tan (Eds.), *Dimensions of tradition and development in Malaysia* (pp. 239–258). Kuala Lumpur: Pelanduk Publications.

Endicott, K. M. (2005). The significance of trade in an immediate-return society. In T. Widlock & T. Wolde (Eds.), *Property and equality.* Vol. 2: *Encapsulation, commercialization, discrimination* (pp. 79–89). Oxford, UK: Berghahn Books.

Endicott, K. M. (2011). Cooperative autonomy: Social solidarity among the Batek of Malaysia. In T. Gibson & K. Sillander (Eds.), *Anarchic solidarity: Autonomy, equality, and fellowship in Southeast Asia* (pp. 62–87). New Haven, CT: Yale University Council on Southeast Asia Studies.

Endicott, K. M. (2013). Peaceful foragers: The significance of the Batek and Moriori for the question of innate human violence. In D. Fry (Ed.), *War, peace, and human nature: The convergence of evolutionary and cultural views* (pp. 243–261). New York: Oxford University Press.

Endicott, K. M., & Bellwood, P. (1991). The possibility of independent foraging in the rain forest of Peninsular Malaysia. *Human Ecology, 19,* 151–185.

Endicott, K. M., & Endicott, K. L. (2008). *The headman was a woman: The gender egalitarian Batek of Malaysia.* Long Grove, IL: Waveland Press.

Gert, B. (2005). *Morality: Its nature and justification* (revised ed.). New York: Oxford University Press.

Gray, P. (2009). Play as a foundation for hunter-gatherer social existence. *American Journal of Play, 1,* 476–522.

Hewlett, B., & Lamb, M. (2005). Emerging issues in the study of hunter-gatherer children. In B. Hewlett, & M. Lamb (Eds.), *Hunter-gatherer childhoods: Evolutionary, developmental and cultural perspectives* (pp. 3–18). New Brunswick, NJ: Transaction Publishers.

Konner, M. (2010). *The evolution of childhood.* Cambridge, MA: Belknap Press.

Marshall, L. (1976). *The !Kung of Nyae Nyae*. Cambridge, MA: Harvard University Press.

Montagu, A. (1978). Introduction. In A. Montagu (Ed.), *Learning non-aggression: The experience of non-literate societies* (pp. 3–11). New York: Oxford University Press.

Narvaez, D., & Gleason, T. (2013). Developmental optimization. In D. Narvaez, J. Panksepp, A. Schore, & T. Gleason (Eds.), *Evolution, early experience and human development: From research to practice and policy* (pp. 307–325). New York: Oxford University Press.

Tacey, I. (2013). Tropes of Fear: The Impact of Globalization on Batek Religious Landscapes. *Religions, 4,* 240-266. Retrieved from www.mdpi.com/journal/religions.

Tonkinson, R. (1991). *The Mardu Aborigines: Living the dream in Australia's desert* (2nd ed.) Fort Worth, TX: Holt, Rinehart and Winston, Inc.

Wylie, A. (1985). The reaction against analogy. *Advances in Archaeological Method and Theory, 8,* 63–111.

{ Commentary }

Parenting in the Modern Jungle
Michael Jindra

Few things get Americans going like parenting practices. Witness the huge debate over Amy Chua's *Battle Hymn of the Tiger Mother*, or debates and recriminations over Lenore Skenazy's *Free-Range Kids*, amid all the other countless missives on parenting. The insight provided by these controversies is often limited by the lack of historical and cross-cultural perspectives. This is indeed what the Endicotts offer us, with their fine descriptions of Batek life. To flesh out some of the implications for contemporary debates over parenting practices, let me first give a brief "lay of the land" of these popular debates, with a focus on the wide diversity of parenting practices, and then we can see how the Batek fit into this, and what it may mean.

Diana Baumrind's conception of three (authoritative, authoritarian, permissive) parenting styles (1991) is a major touchstone, which was followed by a slew of other works that attempt to delineate different parenting styles such as nurturant. "Authoritative" seems to be one of the most recommended practices/terms, as in the recommendation for "authoritative communities" in the 2003 report of the *Commission on Children at Risk*.

The more popular writing on parenting practices, however, portrays a more contentious reality, and more divergence in actual recommended practices. At the extremes, we have a hyperparenting "Tiger Mother" style exemplified by Amy Chua, which is blasted by Margaret K. Nelson (2010) as "parenting out of control," but whose more moderate version is charitably called "concerted cultivation" by Annette Lareau (2011, p. 2ff). This "cult of childhood success" (Kottak and Kozaitis, 2002) includes numerous planned enrichment activities for children and an ongoing use of experts and advice to manage the "business" of raising children and to ensure their future success. Some families put intense pressure on youth to perform well in school, with substantial lifelong effects on educational attainment and income and wealth levels. Another feature of this, however, is overprotectiveness and the refusal to let kids venture out and explore on their own because of fears over security. New Yorker Skenazy (2009) reports many episodes of being pilloried for her perceived neglect, and as a father of three boys, I can attest to a few similar incidents, such as being chewed out by a mom in a wealthy suburban Chicago mall (surely the modern equivalent of the jungle) for letting my 5-year-old confront his fear of an escalator alone while I observed from below.

At the other end, we have "natural growth," Lareau's (2011, p. 3ff) generous euphemism for a laissez-faire style found in lower income groups that can verge on the negligent. It does have some parallels with the Batek style, but it does not train kids very well to become self-sufficient adults in a technocratic society. It can produce more independent, less whiny kids, but also makes it very hard for those kids to have the option to "succeed" in contemporary terms because media (and especially) television are heavily used, and books and language learning are neglected. In fact, this style of parenting contributes to the "education gap" that exists before kids even get to school, and for which early education programs like Head Start are designed. In other words, the childrearing patterns have increasingly diverged into a hyperachieving one of nervous parents trying to get their kids into elite schools and on the road to economic success (but with the potential drawbacks mentioned above), and one that is passive and entertainment oriented, with kids left alone with TVs and video games, unengaged. According to survey research, higher income parents tend to regulate the use of electronic gadgets more than lower income families (Rideout, Foehr, and Roberts, 2010). This process is surely a significant contributor to the inequality of our time.

In between, however, we have more moderate and mixed practices—and those families that mix discipline and limitations on entertainments (not so much an issue with the Batek) with freedom and exposure to activities that prepare kids to play positive roles in communities. Indeed, an ethnography of contemporary parenting would have to take in a wide range of possibilities, including, as my students tell me, distinguishing between console (e.g., *Xbox*) households and nonconsole ones, or more specifically those with the popular and violent videogame *Call of Duty* and those without. One could also add policies related to television, meals, play time, friends, chores, bed times, and a host of other activities, where by family policies like this seem to cohere with the more "authoritative" approaches.

Given the wide range of parenting practices, where do the Batek fit and are there lessons for us here? Amid the blizzard of contemporary parenting advice, Lenore Skenazy's (2009) missives on "free-range kids" are probably the closest to what we see among the Batek. Skenazy is highly critical of overprotective American parents and the whole culture of safety that is partly created by media scares. She uses a healthy dose of cross-cultural examples and anecdotes, including David Lancy's (2008). *The Anthropology of Childhood,* to argue that American children are not given enough independence, to the point that parents like her are called "bad moms" for letting 10-year-old kids take public transportation by themselves, or walk to parks independently. Our kids learn to maneuver in their environments, just like the Batek. But the problem is that too many parents let fear limit the environments of their children. Eventually you get timid kids turning into adults who are afraid to venture off campus in college.

Unlike the Batek, who are small scale and relatively egalitarian and undifferentiated, we live in a world of tremendous diversity and complexity that requires coordination, so our styles cohere more with "tight" cultures rather than the "loose" cultures like the Batek (Gelfand et al., 2011). In some ways, it makes sense that we have turned upper- and middle-class kids into little lawyers by allowing them to negotiate with their parents, manipulate them, and look for loopholes in household rules and work, a skill my oldest has learned. This kind of assertiveness prepares kids well for corporate life, but it can also create entitled, aggressive kids. It doesn't inculcate the classic virtues, unless specific efforts are made to counter the assertiveness and sense of entitlement.

At the same time, we need to keep in mind our heritage in environments like the Batek, and the basic structures our evolutionary biology has attuned us to: rich, relational, prosocial environments, as Narvaez, Panksepp, Schore, and Gleason (2013) point out. The more isolated environments of wealthier communities can be more risky for youth development unless parents allow time for unstructured relations and play to develop. Too high a concern for security can isolate kids, compared with a more "free-range" approach that gives kids independence and bonding and physical play with multiple others. The latter fits better with our evolved heritage, as demonstrated among the Batek.

References

Baumrind, D. (1991). Parenting styles and adolescent development. *The encyclopedia of adolescence*, *2*, 746–758.

Gelfand, M. J., Raver, J. L., Nishii, L., Leslie, L. M., Lun, J., Lim, B. C., et al. (2011). Differences between tight and loose cultures: A 33-nation study. *Science*, *332*(6033), 1100–1104.

Kottak, C. P., & Kozaitis, K. A. (2002). *On being different: Diversity and multiculturalism in the North American mainstream*. Boston: McGraw-Hill College.

Lancy, D. F. (2008). *The anthropology of childhood: Cherubs, chattel, changelings*. Cambridge, UK: Cambridge University Press.

Lareau, A. (2011). *Unequal childhoods: Class, race, and family life, with an update a decade later*. Berkeley, CA: University of California Press.

Narvaez, D., Panksepp, J., Schore, A. N., & Gleason, T. R. (2013). The value of using an evolutionary framework for gauging children's wellbeing. In D. Narvaez, J. Panksepp, A. Schore & T. Gleason (Eds.), *Evolution, early experience and human development: From research to practice and policy* (pp. 3–30). New York: Oxford University Press.

Nelson, M. (2010). *Parenting out of control: Anxious parents in uncertain times*. New York: NYU Press.

Rideout, V. J., Foehr, U. G., & Roberts, D. F. (2010). Generation M2. *Media in the lives of 8 to 18 year olds*. Retrieved October 23, 2013 from http://kaiserfamilyfoundation.files.wordpress.com/2013/04/8010.pdf.

Skenazy, L. (2009). *Free-range kids, giving our children the freedom we had without going nuts with worry*. Hoboken NJ: John Wiley & Sons.

6

Cosleeping Beyond Infancy

CULTURE, ECOLOGY, AND EVOLUTIONARY BIOLOGY OF BED SHARING AMONG AKA FORAGERS AND NGANDU FARMERS OF CENTRAL AFRICA

Barry S. Hewlett and Jennifer W. Roulette

Introduction

The term *cosleeping* is generally used both by academics, including medical researchers, and the public in general to refer to infants sleeping with or near their mothers or parents, on the same or different surfaces, but at least close enough for participants to detect and respond to each others' sensory signals and cues (McKenna, 1993). It is difficult to explain why infant cosleeping has in recent years become of great interest, but it could be a result of a cultural shift to breastfeed among Western industrialized mothers because breastfeeding is functionally interdependent with cosleeping (Gettler and McKenna, 2010). That is, because cosleeping makes breastfeeding so much easier for mothers, including allowing mothers to get more sleep (Volpe and McKenna, 2012), breastfeeding often is soon followed various forms of cosleeping. In Western societies, conversations largely revolve around whether cosleeping is safe, or at the very least what causes particularly one form of cosleeping, bed sharing, to be dangerous and how risks can be avoided (Ball and Volpe, 2012).

Although infant cosleeping is also considered in this chapter, as are issues of safety, though of a different kind, here we focus mainly on what is less well known: cosleeping throughout the juvenile period, from birth through adolescence. We specifically examine (in detail) the contexts of similarities and differences between two small-scale cultures, the Aka foragers and the Ngandu farmers.

Anthropologists and others have pointed out that infant cosleeping is nearly cross-culturally universal (Barry and Paxson, 1971; Konner and Super, 1987; McKenna, 1986; Morelli, Rogoff, Oppenheimer, and Goldsmith, 1992) and that it has a deep phylogenetic history—that is, infant cosleeping is practiced by all Old World monkeys and apes (Konner, 2010; McKenna, Ball, and Gettler, 2007). In so far as infant cosleeping facilitates breastfeeding and decreases the risk for sudden infant death (Gettler and McKenna, 2010), clearly it has adaptive value, especially when one considers that the human infant is born neurologically the least mature primate of all and consequently is unable to thermoregulate (keep warm) efficiently enough to sleep alone. But what about sleep patterns after weaning? Mother–infant cosleeping is common in our closest biological relatives, the great apes, but little attention has been given to cosleeping beyond weaning among either humans or nonhumans. What we do know is that field studies with higher primates suggest that sharing a nest or space with the mother beyond weaning occurs but is not common (e.g., Anderson, 1984).

Primatologists define ape juveniles as prepubertal animals (Pereira, 1993) with the capability to forage and sleep separately from their mothers (Parker, 1999). The birth of a new sibling increases the likelihood that ape juveniles move out of their mother's nest, build their own nest, and sleep separately but nearby (e.g., Horvat and Kraemer, 1982). Chimpanzee infants are weaned at about 5 years old and usually sleep in a separate nest by 6 years old, whereas gorilla infants are weaned at 3 to 4 years old and sleep in a separate nest shortly thereafter (Watts and Pusey, 1993). Before weaning, great ape infants engage in nest-constructing play (Fruth and Hohmann, 1993; Goodall, 1962, 1968; MacKinnon, 1974; Schaller, 1963) and are able to build their own nest shortly after weaning. As great ape juveniles become increasingly self-sufficient, they seldom return to sleep near their mother's nest (Anderson, 1984, 1998). Among a species of lesser apes, the gibbons, "group members usually slept in separate trees, and except for females with infants, they never shared a sleeping space" (Reichard, 1998, p. 35).

Is human cosleeping beyond weaning consistent or inconsistent with our higher primate cousins? Are humans similar to apes, slowly moving into separate nests after weaning, or are they relatively unique, having juveniles continue to cosleep beyond weaning? Existing cross-cultural studies suggest humans are similar to the apes. A recent summary of the cross-cultural literature on cosleeping beyond the age of weaning (age 3 to 4 years) found that 10% to 23% of 5- to 11-year-old children co-slept, and only 2% to 4% of adolescents shared a space with others (Yang and Hahn, 2002). A minority of children past weaning co-slept, and this number declined substantially with age. However, most of the studies in the review were from urban industrialized cultures.

Anthropologists and developmental psychologists have conducted excellent overviews (Worthman and Melby, 2002) and quantitative studies of cosleeping beyond infancy, but existing field data are limited in that most of the studies have taken place in relatively modern, high-density, highly stratified cultures such as India (Shweder, Jensen, and Goldstein, 1995), Japan (Caudill and Plath, 1966; Latz, Wolf, and Lozoff, 1999), Korea (Yang and Hahn, 2002), China (Liu, Liu, and Wang, 2003), and Egypt (Worthman and Brown, 2007). Most of the families in these studies had access to electricity or other sources of energy to heat their homes, and they did not have to worry about animal predators invading their homes. Police and other state-level services were also available to help support parents in their role as protector of the safety and survival of their children.

Systematic and quantitative studies of cosleeping in relatively egalitarian hunter-gatherer or other small-scale cultures, which characterized most of human history, do not exist. Even if cosleeping beyond infancy exists in small-scale cultures, we do not know how frequently it occurs, the contexts in which it occurs, whom children sleep with, or what impact age and sex may have.

Theoretically, researchers use culture (i.e., preferences, values, and ideologies) to explain intercultural variability in cosleeping (Lozoff, Wolf, and Davis, 1985; McKenna, 2000). Shweder et al. (1995, p. 21) begin their comparative article on Indian and U.S. cosleeping by stating, "Our central claim is that the universal practice of determining 'who sleeps by whom' in a family household is a symbolic action, or nonverbal vehicle of meaning, that both expresses and realizes some of the deepest moral ideals of a cultural community." Several cosleeping studies compare a non-Western culture (e.g., Mayan, Indian, Japanese, Korean) with middle-class U.S. culture and often conclude that cultural preferences, values, or beliefs explain the cross-cultural variability—that is, non-Western cultures believe it is essential to promote the development of family bonds and interdependent relationships in their children and therefore co-sleep with their children, whereas Western parents value the development of independence and self-reliance and therefore place children in their own beds to help promote these parental cultural ideals. Most of the cosleeping researchers recognize that ecological constraints (e.g., size of house, number of rooms in a house, and climate) play some role in cosleeping, but most view house ecology as secondary. Many cite Caudill and Plath's (1966) classic study which clearly demonstrated that cosleeping among the Japanese was more about the moral imperative to co-sleep, specifically to foster familial interdependence, rather than the spatial ecology of a house, that is, the number of available rooms.

Our study of cosleeping differs from previous research in three ways. First, it compares cosleeping among two non-Western and non–socioeconomically stratified cultures—Aka foragers and Ngandu farmers. Anthropologists and developmental psychologists would characterize both groups as "interdependent" cultures, in part, because family bonds and social networks are highly valued in both groups, so it is not possible to apply the standard cultural explanation given above to cosleeping differences between the groups. Second, the study looks at cosleeping beyond infancy and across the juvenile period. As already mentioned, existing studies focus on infants and young children. Finally, the study is relatively distinct in that interactions between culture, evolutionary biology, and ecology are considered in explaining intercultural and intracultural diversity in cosleeping. Culture and ecology, to some degree, are considered in previous studies, but relatively minimal attention has been given to the evolutionary or biological component. This study was initiated to answer the following basic questions: How often does cosleeping occur in childhood (0 to 18 years)? Who co-sleeps with children? How do ecology (size of bed, heat sources), cultural ideologies (that distinguish the Aka and Ngandu), and evolutionary biology (genetic relatedness, incest considerations) influence cosleeping? Although limited by sample size and study duration, this may well be the first study of its kind to provide preliminary observations and insights regarding the nature and contexts of cosleeping beyond infancy in humans.

Ethnographic Locale and Contexts

The data for the paper come from Aka hunter-gatherers and Ngandu farmers in the southern forests of the Central African Republic. About 40,000 Aka live in the tropical rainforests in northern Republic of Congo and southern Central African Republic, but about 2,000 live in and around the village study area. About 15,000 Ngandu live mostly in the Central African Republic, and about 4,000 live in the study area. The Aka in this study have complex economic, ritual, and kinship relationships with the Ngandu (Hewlett, 1991).

To understand cosleeping among the Aka and Ngandu, it is essential to have an understanding of their foundational schema—cultural values and ways of thinking and feeling that pervade most domains of daily life. The Aka live in camps of 25 to 35 people and move camps several times a year. They rely on a wide variety of hunting and gathering techniques (see Hewlett, 1991, for greater detail). Three foundational schema pervade the lives of the Aka and many other hunter-gatherers: egalitarianism, autonomy, and sharing. An *egalitarian* way of thinking means others are respected for what they are, and it is not appropriate to draw attention to oneself or judge others as better or worse. Men and women, young and old, are viewed as relatively equal and have similar access to resources. Respect for an individual's *autonomy* is also a core cultural value and foundational schema. One does not coerce or tell others what to do, including children. Men and women, young and old, do pretty much what they want. If they do not want to hunt that day, they do not do it; if an infant wants to play with a machete, she is allowed to do so. A giving or *sharing* way of thinking also pervades hunter-gatherer life; Aka share 50% to 80% of what is acquired hunting and gathering, they share it with everyone in camp, and they share every day. Sharing of child care is also extensive; for instance, 90% of Aka mothers reported that other women nursed their young babies (Hewlett and Winn, 2014).

The Ngandu live in villages of 50 to 200 individuals and domesticate manioc, corn, plantains, and peanuts. They exchange some of their crops for meat and other forest products of the Aka. Women plant, maintain, and harvest the fields and provide the majority of the calories to the diet, whereas men fish, hunt, and trade. Foundational schema among the Ngandu include gender and age hierarchy, communalism, and material-economic dimensions to social relations. Women should defer to the requests of men, and the young should be respectful and listen to those older than them, whether older brothers and sisters or parents. The Ngandu are patrilocal and patrilineal and have strong clan organization. *Communalism* refers to the cultural value placed on putting the needs of the group, generally clan members or the extended family, over the needs of an individual. The third foundational schema refers to the thoughts and feelings that interpersonal relations should have economic or material components. Material and economic dimensions of relationships are on par with or greater than social and emotional aspects of relationships. Just liking the person or just being a kind person is not enough to sustain a relationship. This contrasts with Aka relationships, in which greater emphasis is placed on social-emotional bonds.

Sanctions exist for foundational schema. Among the Aka, others will tease and joke about individuals' sexual, dancing, or singing abilities if they starts to act better than others or draw attention to themselves. If a child does not share, others make sounds, gestures, or comments. One Aka adolescent girl's earliest memory was of her mother giving her a bowl of food to share with others; she was hungry and ate all of it. Her mother said she was stingy, others teased her, and she started to cry (B. L. Hewlett, 2013). Children often hear stories about how people who do not share properly face sanctions (e.g., illness, death, death of a child, person who did not share was a sorcerer). Among the Ngandu, sanctions for not listening to or respecting parents or older individuals can also be harsh and may include corporal punishment. One adolescent girl said that one day she was asked by her mother to help in the fields, but she decided instead to go fishing with her friends. When she returned, her mother said, "if you do not want to help, you do not want to live here." She was kicked out of the house and went to live with her grandmother.

Habitus and Daily Life

Habitus (Bourdieu, 1977) refers to the daily, lived experiences of people. The habitus is shaped by the foundational schema described above and helps to contextualize the cosleeping study.

INTIMACY

Physical and emotional proximity are particularly important to the Aka (Hewlett, 1991; Hewlett, Fouts, Boyette, and Hewlett, 2011). When the Aka sit down in the camp, they are usually touching somebody. In terms of holding during infancy and early childhood, forager infants are held 91% of the day, whereas farmer infants are held 54% of the day (Hewlett, Lamb, Leyendecker, and Schölmerich, 2000). Forager 2-, 3-, and 4-year-olds were held 44%, 27%, and 8% of daylight hours, respectively, whereas farmer children of the same age were held 18%, 2%, and 0% of the day (Fouts and Brookshire, 2009).

The importance of emotional proximity to others is illustrated in two studies. In a study of conflicts between toddlers and older juveniles among Central African hunter-gatherers and farmers, Fouts and Lamb (2009) found that hunter-gatherer toddlers were substantially more likely to have conflicts over staying close to older juveniles, whereas farmer toddlers were more likely to have conflicts with older juveniles over competition for objects or over the older juvenile hitting the toddler, which never occurred among the hunter-gatherer toddlers. This study illustrates early acquisition and manifestations of cultural values—emotional proximity to others among the Aka and the economic-material dimensions of social relations among the Ngandu.

In another study, Aka and Ngandu adolescents were asked about their experiences and feelings about the death and loss of friends and relatives (B. L. Hewlett, 2005). Forager expressions of grief emphasized their the love and emotional connections to the person, whereas farmer expressions of grief focused on what the lost relative gave or provided them, and the grief was often diminished once objects of the deceased were given to the adolescent.

AUTONOMY

Aka children do pretty much what they want during the day, whereas farmer children are affected by the control of parents and older children. For instance, one study showed that Aka 3- to 4-month-old infants took the breast on their own to nurse during 58% of feeding bouts, in comparison to only 2% of feeding bouts among the Ngandu. Ngandu mothers decided when to nurse, not the infant. At weaning, hunter-gatherer mothers said the child decided when he or she wanted to wean, whereas farmer mothers said they decided when to wean and often used dramatic techniques, such as putting red fingernail polish on their nipples and telling their child it was blood in order to get the child to stop nursing. Hunter-gatherer mothers said that if they initiated the weaning, it would cause the child to get sick, whereas the farmers said that nursing too long causes the child to become lazy (Fouts, Hewlett, and Lamb, 2001). These are just a few examples of how foundational schema affect daily life—Aka parents respect the autonomy of the child, whereas Ngandu parents direct some parts of the child's daily life.

TRUST OF OTHERS

The development of trust in others is important to some degree in all cultures, but the socialization for trust in several others is particularly pronounced among the Aka, which makes sense given their extensive sharing and giving. Aka infants and young children are breastfed on demand, averaging about four bouts per hour, whereas farmers average about two bouts per hour. Young Aka infants are often breastfed by women other than their mother, generally aunts and grandmothers (but sometimes even fathers offered their breast). Grandmothers who hold infants for long periods may breastfeed a young infant, whereas fathers with a fussy infant may offer their breast to an infant. Among the Ngandu, breastfeeding by other women is thought to cause infant sickness and was not practiced except under unusual circumstances (see Hewlett and Winn, 2014, for details of allomaternal nursing). Studies show that Aka caregivers are significantly more likely than

Ngandu caregivers to respond to infant crying and that Ngandu infants cry significantly longer and more frequently than do Aka infants (Hewlett et al., 1998, 2000). As mentioned above, Aka infants and young children were held twice as often as Ngandu, and this additional holding came from many different people—fathers, grandmothers, siblings, and others. In early infancy, mothers provide the most care, but all others together provide more holding than do mothers (Hewlett, 1991).

MIXED ADULT–CHILD GROUPS

Konner (2010) indicates that after weaning, hunter-gatherer children move from a relationship with their mother to relationships with children in mixed-age playgroups. Our data question this representation and indicate that parents and other adults are frequently around children and even adolescents. Time with parents and other adults, generally grandparents, gradually declines with age, but in comparison with the Ngandu, the Aka spend considerably less time in child-only groups. Behavioral observations indicate that Aka children were much more likely to be proximal (defined as within an arm's distance) to more categories of people and parents and other adults than were Ngandu (Hewlett et al., 2011). By age 4 to 5 years, hunter-gatherers are still proximal to parents and adults 33% of the time, whereas farmer children are proximal to them only 6% of the day. Farmer children at this age spent most of their day, 59% of their time, in child-only groups, whereas hunter-gatherer children spent only 18% of their day in proximity to child-only groups (Fouts and Lamb, 2009). In another study, children in late childhood spent more time in mixed-age groups, but they were still within visual range of an adult 81% of the day, and parents and other adults were the nearest neighbor (defined as those equally close to the child) 33.1% of the day (Boyette, 2013).

Aka and Ngandu Homes and Beds

Aka homes are usually constructed by women in 2 to 3 hours; they are generally dome shaped, made of bent saplings and large phrynium leaves, and about 6 feet in diameter and 3 feet tall (Figure 6.1). Aka also make rectangular homes of saplings and leaves, but these are often temporary structures made by males. A distance of 1 or 2 feet separates Aka homes, and the entire camp of five to seven homes is relatively compact, often occupying an area about 1,000 ft^2. The homes do not have doors, and children easily move between homes. By contrast, Ngandu homes are rectangular, about 20 × 30 feet on average, with mud walls and a thatch or a tin roof (Figure 6.2). Men construct the homes over several weeks or months, and the homes are anywhere from 10 to 100 feet apart from each other. They have doors that can be locked or secured, so fewer people, including children, move between homes. Interior rooms of Ngandu homes may have a wooden or cloth door for privacy.

FIGURE 6.1 *Entrance to an Aka home with hunting net hanging inside.*

Table 6.1 summarizes the demography of the Aka and Ngandu homes in the study. Ngandu homes were larger, having about three bedrooms on average, and not surprisingly had more individuals per home, more beds per home, and fewer individuals per delimited space (room for Ngandu, home for Aka) than did Aka. Ngandu homes can be large, but only 15% (three homes) of the Ngandu homes had more than three bedrooms. Ngandu homes were also more likely to include extended (30% of Ngandu homes) or polygynous (15% of Ngandu homes) families. None of the Aka homes had these arrangements within a home; a second wife or extended family members had their own homes.

FIGURE 6.2 *Typical Ngandu home.*

TABLE 6.1 Demography of Aka and Ngandu Homes

	Aka	Ngandu
Number of homes observed	38	20
Number of adults in all homes	66	63
Number of children <18 years old in all homes	84	74
Total number of individuals	150	137
Mean age of fathers	40.4	38.3
Mean age of mothers	37.8	32.3
Mean number individuals per home	3.9 (range, 1–7)	7.2 (range, 3–20)
Mean number of rooms per home	1 (all one-room)	2.7 (range, 1–6)
Mean number of people per room (Ngandu) or home (Aka)	3.9 (range, 1–7)	2.8 (range, 1–9)
Mean number of beds per home	1.7 (range, 1–3)	3.5 (range, 1–8)

Aka beds are constructed from logs, leaves, or skins. Log beds can be on the ground or up off the ground by a few inches. It takes a few minutes to make a bed of leaves or skins and an hour or so to make a log bed off the ground. The Ngandu bed frame is made of logs, and the sleeping surface is usually made of woven strips of a forest liana or bamboo. Ngandu beds are generally a foot or more above the ground. Several people in the village make beds, they take several days to construct, and they cost about $3 to $5 U.S. Neither group uses pillows.

It should be noted that it does not take long to build an Aka home or bed. If an Aka wants to sleep alone, it is easy to make a new bed, and it only takes a few hours to build a new home. Although women usually build camp homes, both boys and girls by age 10 years know how to build their own home (men make rectangular or lean-to homes, and women build the sturdier dome-shaped homes).

Methods

The first phase of this study began in 2005 and concentrated initially on the Aka foragers. The first author (BH) replicated Shweder et al.'s (1995) methodology and variable classification (at least part of it) with the Aka because no such study had ever been conducted with a hunter-gatherer population. Shweder et al. relied on adults' and children's reports of who slept next to whom. But in this study, BH walked down a trail shortly after sunrise to visit homes and asked people in each home to explain precisely where they slept and why they slept in that particular place. Sketch maps of sleeping arrangements were drawn, beds were measured, and Shweder's coding technique was used to record age and gender of who slept next to who (e.g., M45 D7 S10 F48 means a 45-year-old mother slept next to her 7-year-old daughter, who slept next to her 10-year-old brother, who slept next to the 48-year-old father) in each bed. BH walked down a particular trail into the forest and recorded data on every home in 7 successive camps along the trail. To evaluate changes over time, 6 homes were visited 4 consecutive days, 10 homes were visited 3 consecutive days, and 14 homes were visited twice. The summary data (e.g., frequency of bed sharing, who sleeps next to children) presented in the study are based on the first observation day. When the Aka research was completed, we decided to conduct a comparative study with the neighboring Ngandu farmers. We thought the contrast would be useful because both groups occupy the same natural environment—the tropical forest—speak similar or the same languages, and observe each other on a regular basis. If one particular way of cosleeping was more "adaptive" in this environment, members of each group had plenty of opportunities to observe members of the other group and modify their behaviors. Twenty of 32 Ngandu homes in one section of the village were visited one time.

Terminology

Considerable variability exists in how researchers define cosleeping. In general, it is defined as a practice whereby individuals sleep close to each other—either in the same bed, touching each other, or within an arm's reach of each other (e.g., when an infant sleeps in a separate crib or mat, but is within an arm's reach of the parents). Bed sharing is therefore one type of cosleeping whereby individuals share the same bed, mat, leaves, or hammock. Because most studies have been conducted with infants and young children in low-fertility populations, the assumption is often that the child is touching the mother or parents. Bed sharing is the focus of this study, and unless noted otherwise, the term *cosleeping* means bed sharing. We also use the term *co-rooming* to refer to situations in which individuals share a room but are in separate beds.

The term *small-scale culture* refers to groups that make a living by hunting and gathering, simple farming (slash-and-burn farming; no irrigation or intensive agriculture), or agropastoralism (raising domesticate animals along with some simple farming) and lack stratified political-economic classes or castes. The terms *hunter-gatherers* and *foragers* are synonymous.

Results

FREQUENCY OF BED SHARING

As Table 6.2 shows, cosleeping (in the form of bed sharing) was clearly normative for both ethnic groups and universal up to age 7 years. Bed sharing declined slightly with age, especially among the Ngandu and particularly with adolescents, but 67% of adolescents in both groups were still bed sharing. None of the Aka children slept in a bed in their own home, whereas 5% of Ngandu children, mostly adolescents, slept in a bed in their own room. This study is a snapshot in time, and anyone who

TABLE 6.2 Percentage of Aka and Ngandu children (0–18 Years), Infants (0–1 Years), Young Children (2–6 Years), Middle-Aged Children (7–11 Years), and Adolescents (12–18 Years) Who Bed-Shared, Co-roomed, or Had Their Own Bed in Their Own Room

	Aka (*n* = 84)	Ngandu (*n* = 74)
Bed-shared—overall	89%	82%
Infants	100%	100%
Young children	100%	96%
Middle-aged children	93%	78%
Adolescents	67%	67%
Co-roomed: separate bed, but share room or home—overall	11%	12%
Infants	0%	0%
Young children	0%	4%
Middle-aged children	7%	17%
Adolescents	33%	17%
Alone: own bed in separate room or home—overall	0%	5%
Infants	0%	0%
Young children	0%	0%
Middle-aged children	0%	6%
Adolescents	0%	17%

has worked with the Aka knows that, on occasion, children, adolescents in particular, may sleep in a different home they build on their own.

For comparative purposes, Table 6.3 summarizes cosleeping prevalence data from as many cross-cultural quantitative studies as we could find. It is obvious that infant and early childhood cosleeping is relatively common in East Asia and among some socioeconomic groups within the United States, but with the exception of rural Mayan infants, none of the prevalence rates comes close to that found with the Aka and Ngandu. Yovsi and Keller (2007) conducted a study of cosleeping among the Nso of Cameroon and state that they are a cosleeping culture, giving the impression of normative cosleeping in infancy, but they do not provide prevalence rates. Table 6.4 demonstrates the relative lack of data on older children and adolescent cosleeping and suggests that Egyptian adolescent cosleeping rates are not that different from those of Aka and Ngandu. Egyptian adolescents are similar to the Ngandu (and unlike Aka) in that they seldom co-sleep with their parents or other adults. Overall, Aka and Ngandu prevalence rates for most ages appear to be higher than those found in other cultures.

DENSITY OF BED SHARING

Table 6.5 reports bed size in relationship to the number of people sharing them. Only 34 of 49 Aka beds were examined because it was not possible to accurately measure beds made of leaves or skins, that at times resembled a loose and undefined space on the ground. We were able to measure 69 of 70 Ngandu beds. Aka beds were particularly small and dense; the average Aka person had 4.4 square feet to sleep

TABLE 6.3 Cosleeping Studies From Birth to Age 6 Years

Samples	Age	Definitions[a, b]	Bed Sharing	Co-rooming	Reference
White middle-class mothers living in a U.S. city with infants 2 to 28 months ($n = 18$)	0–3 mo After 6 mo	Include others (not exclusively parents)	0.0 11.0	83.3 11.0	Morelli, Rogoff, Oppenheim, & Goldsmith (1992)
Guatemalan Mayan mothers living in a rural community with infants 12 to 22 months ($n = 14$)	0–3 mo After 6 mo		100.0 100.0	0.0 0.0	
1993–2000 Nighttime caregivers of infants born in the U.S. within 7 months before annual interviews ($n = 8,453$)		Said "adult" bed (not parental bed)—usually at night, 2 weeks preceding the interview	9.2	·	Willinger, Ko, Hoffman, Kessler, & Corwin (2003)
1993–1994 ($n = 2,123$)			5.8	·	
1995–1996 ($n = 2,100$)			7.5	·	
1997–1998 ($n = 2,126$)	0–7 mo		10.7	·	
1999–2000 ($n = 2,228$)			12.5	·	
Black ($n = 524$)			27.9	·	
Asian/other ($n = 282$)			20.9	·	
Hispanic ($n = 467$)			12.4	·	
White ($n = 7,278$)			7.2	·	
Predominantly Asian countries/regions (P-A)			64.7	86.5	
China (CN) ($n = 7,505$)			67.6	88.7	
Hong Kong (HK) ($n = 1,049$)			27.6	67.1	
India (IN) ($n = 3,982$)			72.6	88.3	
Indonesia (ID) ($n = 967$)			70.7	81.9	
South Korea (KR) ($n = 1,036$)			61.4	83.4	
Japan (JP) ($n = 872$)			69.7	88.1	
Malaysia (MY) ($n = 997$)		Behaviors in the last 2 weeks	44.0	84.1	Mindell, Sadeh, Wiegand, Hwei How, & Goh (2010)
Philippines (PH) ($n = 1,034$)	0–36 mo		65.1	86.6	
Singapore (SG) ($n = 1,001$)			35.9	73.7	
Taiwan (TW) ($n = 896$)			60.2	88.4	
Thailand (TH) ($n = 988$)			77.2	94.5	
Vietnam (VN) ($n = 1,000$)			83.2	94.3	
Predominantly Caucasian countries (P-C)					
Australia (AU) ($n = 1,073$)			8.6	27.0	
Canada (CA) ($n = 501$)			12.4	15.1	
New Zealand (NZ) ($n = 1,081$)			5.8	17.8	

(continued)

TABLE 6.3 (Continued)

Samples	Age	Definitions[a, b]	Bed Sharing	Co-rooming	Reference
United Kingdom (UK) (*n* = 800)			5.0	26.0	
United States (US) (*n* = 4,505)			15.1	21.8	
Predominantly-Caucasian (P-C) countries: Australia, Canada, New Zealand, U.K., U.S.			11.8	22.0	
	0–2		.	58.0[c]	
	3–5		.	47.0[c]	
	6–8		.	21.0[c]	
	9–11		.	17.0[c]	
	12–17		.	11.0[c]	
	18–23		.	8.0[c]	
	24–36			6.0[c]	
1984–1989 Norwegian children control group (*n* = 375)			4.0	.	Arnestad, Andersen, Vege, & Rognum (2001)
1990–1992 control group	0–36 mo		7.0		
1993–1998 control group			15.0		
White U.S. children (*n* = 90)			19.2	16.0	
African-American U.S. children (*n* = 94)		Three times a week for the month preceding the interview	57.8	47.2	Wolf, Lozoff, Latz, & Paludetto (1996)
White U.S. children breastfed 6 months or more (*n* = 51)	6–48 mo		16.0	3.9	
Italian children (*n* = 66)			42.4	75.8	
Japanese children (*n* = 62)			58.1	67.7	
Japanese children (*n* = 56)		All or part of night, three or more times a week for the month preceding the interview	59.0	.	Latz, Wolf, & Lozoff (1999)
White U.S. children (*n* = 61)	6–48 mo		15.0	.	
Cleveland U.S. urban (*n* = 150) children between 1 and 4 yr (white and African American)	6–48 mo	More than once during the previous month before the interview	53.0	.	Lozoff, Wolf, & Davis (1984)
White children			35.0		
African American children			70.0		
U.S. white Americans bed-sharing (*n* = 83) and co-rooming (*n* = 96)		All night and more than once during the previous month	6.0	10.0	Lozoff and Klaus (p.c.) cited in Schachter et al. (1989)
	6–48 mo	Part night	18.0	.	
U.S. African-Americans co-rooming and bed sharing (*n* = 30)		All night	46.0	50.0	
		Part night	13.0	.	

(continued)

TABLE 6.3 (Continued)

Samples	Age	Definitions[a, b]	Bed Sharing	Co-rooming	Reference
Urban Hispanic-American, East Harlem, New York City, U.S. ($n = 210$)	6–48 mo	The parent had to be sleeping— more than 1 night per month and for more than 1 hour per day	21.0	80.0	Schachter, Fuchs, Bujur, & Stone (1989)
Basque women reflecting on their childhood ($n = 201$)	0–2 yr 3–5 yr	Presence of co-room. No measurement parameters (how many times in a week/month)	. .	22.7 22.5	Crawford (1994)
Taiwan—subset who reported environmental factors that influence children's sleep ($n = 29$)	0–6 yr	Sleeping with parents (no specifics)	37.9		Chou (2007)
Total Californian sample Euro-American families ($n = 205$)	5 mo 3 yr 4 yr 5 & 6 yr 5 mo 3 & 4 yr 5 yr 6 yr	No measurement parameters (how many times in a week/month)	35.0 7.0 10.0 4.0 9.0 6.0 6.0 3.0	. . . .	Okami, Weisner, & Olmstead (2002)
U.S. California countercultural family lifestyle ($n = 154$)	Before 6 yr		13.2	.	
U.S. California conventional family lifestyles ($n = 51$)	Before 6 yr		2.0	.	
Worcester, Massachusetts, U.S. children ($n = 303$)		At least once during the previous 2 months	55.0	.	
	2–3 yr	At least once per month	16.0	.	Madansky & Edelbrock (1990)
		Once per week	15.0	.	
		Several times per week	14.0	.	
		All the time	11.0	.	
U.S.—17 EHS programs across the country ($n = 944$)	1 yr 2–3 yr	Presence of bed sharing at annual follow-up	21.9 26.1	.	Barajas et al. (2011)

(continued)

TABLE 6.3 (Continued)

Samples	Age	Definitions[a, b]	Bed Sharing	Co-rooming	Reference
White, middle- and upper-income private patients in Greater Cleveland area, U.S. infants 2–5 yr old (*n* = 119)	0–1 yr		0.0	3.0	
	After 1 yr		0.0	1.0	
Black, lower middle, and lower income clinic patients in Cleveland, U.S. with infants 2–5 yr old (*n* = 166)	0–1 yr	Presence of bed sharing	13.0	42.0	Litt (1981)
	After 1 yr		16.0	9.0	
Swiss children longitudinally followed between 1974 and 2001 (*n* = 493)	3 mo	Definition does not include body contact. Behavior 3 months before each follow-up interview. At least once per week	5.9	.	Jenni, Singgeler Fuhrer, Iglowstein, Molinari, & Largo (2005)
	9 mo		6.6	.	
	3 yr	Every night	12.8	.	
	4 yr	At least once per week	38.1	.	
	2–7 yr[d]	At least once per week for 1 or more years	44.1	.	
Korean families, city of Busan (*n* = 427): co-sleepers (*n* = 377) and non–co-sleepers (*n* = 50)	1–7 yr[d]	Bed sharing and room sharing have about the same meaning in Korea. More than three times a week for all of the night	50.9	49.1	Yang & Hahn (2002)
	12–36 mo		85.0[c]		
	37–60 mo		80.0[c]		
	61–84 mo[d]		70.0[c]		
Eastern Kentucky Appalachian children (*n* = 107)	2 mo–18.5 yr[d]	No measurement parameters (how many times in a week/month)	35.6		Abbott (1992)
	2 yr and younger		71.0		
	2 yr, 1 mo to 4 yr		47.0		
	4 yr, 1 mo to 5 yr		13.3		

(*continued*)

TABLE 6.3 (Continued)

Samples	Age	Definitions[a,b]	Bed Sharing	Co-rooming	Reference
Egyptian family members—urban Cairo and a village, Marhum, Tanta District, Lower Egypt (*n* = 614)	2–10 yr[d]	Sleep events in a 7-day period. Definitions include other family members not solely parent and child	77.4	84.0	Worthman & Brown (2007)
Subset: age-stratified patterns of cosleeping in Egyptian families (*n* = 428)		Sleep events (parent–child cosleeping)	34.0	.	
		Parent–child cosleeping at night (males)	21.0	.	
		Parent–child cosleeping at night (females)	51.0	.	

[a]*Bed sharing* is defined as parents and children sleeping in body contact with each other in the same bed for the majority of the night. Studies grouped children who co-slept with their parents occasionally or in extraordinary circumstances with non–co-sleepers. In the table, we present additional information regarding a study's bed-sharing definition.
[b]Refers to children *co-rooming*—sleeping in their parent's room in a separate bed or space. In the table, we present additional information about a study's co-rooming definition.
[c]We estimated the findings highlighted in a figure.
[d]The age range reported includes children older than 6 years.

TABLE 6.4 Cosleeping Studies of Children 6 Years and Older

Samples	Age	Definitions[a,b]	Bed Sharing	Co-rooming	Reference
Basque women reflecting on their childhood (*n* = 201)	6 yr and older	Presence of co-rooming. No measurement parameters (how many times in a week/month)	.	20.8	Crawford (1994)
Chinese elementary-school children (*n* = 517)	7–13 yr	A child's usual behavior within the recent weeks	18.2	18.4	Liu, Liu, & Wang (2003)
	7–13 yr, boys		15.1	.	
	7–13 yr, girls		21.0	.	
	7 yr		55.8	.	
	8 yr		39.6	.	
	9 yr		18.4	.	
	10 yr		19.0	.	
	11–13 yr		7.2	.	

TABLE 6.4 (Continued)

Samples	Age	Definitions [a, b]	Bed Sharing	Co-rooming	Reference
Chinese elementary-school children ($n = 517$)	Grades 1–5	A child's usual behavior within recent weeks	26.4	21.6	Liu, Liu, Owens, & Kaplan (2005)
Swiss children longitudinally followed between 1974 and 2001 ($n = 493$)	8 yr	Definition does not include body contact. Behavior 3 months before each follow-up interview. Bed sharing every night.	5.1	.	Jenni, Singgeler, Iglowstein, Molinari, & Largo (2005)
		At least once a week	21.2	.	
Eastern Kentucky Appalachian children ($n = 107$)	5 yr, 1[c] mo to 9 yr	No measurement parameters (how many times in a week/month)	18.5		Abbott (1992)
	12 yr		One boy slept with his siblings in a separate bed in the parental bedroom.		
Egyptian family members ($n = 614$)—from urban Cairo and a village, Marhum, Tanta District, Lower Egypt	10–20 yr[d]	Sleep events in a 7-day period. Definitions include other family members, not solely parent–child cosleeping	60.1	77.6	Worthman & Brown (2007)
Subsample: age-stratified patterns of cosleeping in Egyptian families ($n = 428$)		Sleep events (parent–child cosleeping)	7.0	.	
		Parent–child cosleeping at night (males)	0.0	.	
		Parent–child cosleeping at night (females)	16.0	.	

[a]Regular bed sharing is defined as parents and children sleeping in body contact with each other in the same bed for the majority of the night. Studies grouped children who co-slept occasionally or in extraordinary circumstances with non–co-sleepers. In the table, we present additional information about a study's bed-sharing definition.

[b]*Co-rooming* refers to children sleeping in their parent's room in a separate bed or space. In the table, we present additional information about a study's co-rooming definition.

[c]The age range reported includes children younger than 6 years.

[d]The age range reported includes adults older than 18 years.

TABLE 6.5 Bed Sizes and Density of Bed Sharing

	Number of Beds Measured	Proportion of Single Beds in Sample	Mean Size of Beds	Mean Space per Person	Relationship Between Size of Bed and Number of Individuals in Bed
Aka	34	0.15	10.71 ft² (0.99 m²)	4.37 ft² (0.41 m²)	$R^2 = 0.56$**
Ngandu	69	0.35	22.33 ft² (2.07 m²)	12.84 ft² (1.19 m²)	$R^2 = 0.09$**
U.S. (queen bed)			33.33 ft² (3.10 m²)	16.65 ft² (1.55 m²) (2 people)	
t-Test between Aka and Ngandu			$t = -9.9^a$(101 df)	$t = -9.6^a$(84 df)	

(about a 1- × 4-foot space). By comparison, the average middle-class American individual sharing a queen-sized bed has almost four times as much space—16.7 square feet. Aka bed size was highly correlated to the number of people in a bed, and the number of people in the bed explained 56% of the variability in Aka bed size. A statistically significant relationship also existed among the Ngandu, but it only explained 9% of the variability. This is primarily a result of Ngandu individuals, usually older adult males, sleeping alone in large beds. Ngandu beds are significantly larger than Aka beds, and Table 6.6 shows that more people on average slept in Aka than in Ngandu beds.

WHO SHARES A BED WITH A CHILD?

Figure 6.3 considers with whom infants, young children, middle-aged children, and adolescents shared a bed. First, although seldom emphasized in previous studies, children in both groups generally co-slept with genetically related kin—parents, grandparents, or siblings. None of the Ngandu children and only 4% of Aka children slept with someone who was not genetic kin. The importance of biological kin cosleeping was clearly evident with Ngandu in polygynous homes or where the mother or father had children from a previous marriage—children from the same mother and father slept separately (own beds and rooms, if available) from other children. This study is only a slice in time; our long-term informal observations are generally consistent with this result, but field researchers know that on occasion

TABLE 6.6 Number and Age of People in Measured Beds

	Mean Number of Adults	Mean Number of 0- to 11-Year-Olds	Mean Number of 12- to 18-Year-Olds	Mean Total Number of People in Bed
Aka	1.23	1.03	0.41	2.70
Ngandu	0.94	0.84	0.24	2.01
t-Test between groups	$t = 1.96^a$ (70 df)	$t = 1.07$ NS (67 df)	$t = 1.28$ NS (55 df)	$t = 2.87^b$ (54 df)

[a] $p<.05$
[b] $p<.01$

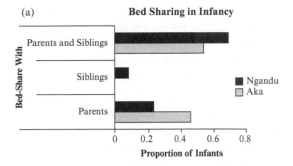

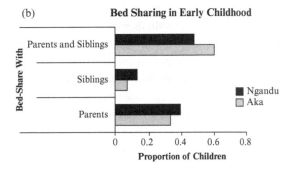

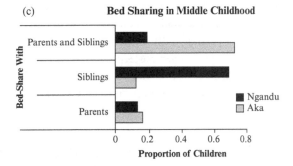

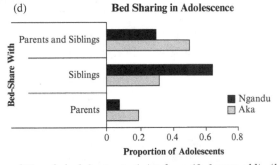

FIGURE 6.3 *Aka and Ngandu bed sharing in (a) infancy (0–1 years old), (b) early childhood (2–6 years old), (c) middle childhood (7–11 years old), and (d) adolescence (12–18 years old).*

children, especially adolescents when they travel, co-sleep with nongenetically related individuals. Second, although grandparents can be important caregivers in small-scale cultures, only 8.0% of Aka children and 9.8% of Ngandu children shared a bed with a grandparent, usually, but not always, the grandmother. The "parent" category in Figure 6.3 includes the limited number of grandparents who co-slept with children.

Figure 6.3 reflects the facts that (1) infants and young children in both groups frequently co-slept with parents and siblings and (2) Aka middle-aged children and adolescents were more likely than Ngandu children of the same age to co-sleep with parents or both parents and siblings, whereas Ngandu children in these age categories were more likely to co-sleep with siblings.

Table 6.7 examines the sex of individuals with whom children share a bed with and whom they are touching. Children who bed-share may not actually be touching others in a bed because they may be placed on the edge of the bed, touching only one person, or may sleep with several people, touching only the two people immediately next to them. Touching is therefore a subcategory of bed sharing in Table 6.7.

The table shows that children in both groups and of all ages regularly bed-shared and slept next to both males and females. Infants bed-shared less with males than females, but by early childhood, sex differences were minimal in both groups. Ngandu males (mostly fathers) bed-shared and touched infants and young children less than Aka males did, but the differences disappeared in middle childhood and adolescence because Ngandu children bed-shared with male siblings and Aka bed-shared with male siblings and adults (fathers).

It should be noted that Aka father cosleeping with infants is underestimated because several fathers did not sleep in the same bed with their wife and infant because they wanted to decrease the temptation to have sex with their wives, which

TABLE 6.7 Proportion of Individuals Who Bed-Share/Sleep Next to (i.e., Touch) Children

	Males (All Ages)	Females (All Ages)	Both Males and Females
Infants			
Aka	.50/.50	1.00/1.00	.50/.42
Ngandu	.42/.25	1.00/1.00	.42/.25
Young Children			
Aka	.78/.56	.83/.72	.61/.33
Ngandu	.62/.30	.91/.87	.43/.26
Middle-Aged Children			
Aka	.69/.65	.88/.65	.62/.31
Ngandu	.71/.64	.79/.64	.50/.29
Adolescents			
Aka	.64/.43	.79/.64	.43/.07
Ngandu	.83/.67	.58/.33	.33/.17

TABLE 6.8 Percentage of Children by Gender and Age Who Slept Next to Their Parents

	Aka	Ngandu
Early Childhood		
Mother slept next to daughter	80%	75%
Mother slept next to son	46%	27%
Father slept next to son	38%	7%
Father slept next to daughter	40%	25%
Middle Childhood		
Mother slept next to daughter	40%	25%
Mother slept next to son	45%	0%
Father slept next to son	27%	0%
Father slept next to daughter	20%	0%
Adolescence		
Mother slept next to daughter	33%	50%
Mother slept next to son	0%	0%
Father slept next to son	20%	0%
Father slept next to daughter	0%	0%

is taboo until the infant is able to walk well. If parents have sex before this time, the infant can get sick and die. Consequently, fathers made beds next to their wives and infants, but the bed was often within an arm's reach of the family. He was in a separate bed, so it was not bed sharing and not considered in this table, but it does fall within the usual definition of cosleeping, in which case the Aka rate of father cosleeping in infancy would be above 80%.

Table 6.8 examines the frequency with which mothers and fathers slept next to their children of the same and opposite sex in the three age groups. Aka mothers and fathers slept next to their children more frequently than Ngandu parents at all ages except adolescence, when Ngandu mothers were somewhat more likely to sleep next to their daughters than were Aka mothers. Mothers in both ethnic groups were more likely to sleep next to their children than were fathers. Ngandu fathers never slept next to their older children, whereas 20% to 30% of Aka fathers slept next to their older sons or daughters. The table also provides empirical support for Aka and Ngandu cultural beliefs in the incest taboo (parents should not sleep next to their sexually mature adolescent of the opposite sex): Aka and Ngandu fathers never slept next to their adolescent daughters, and Aka and Ngandu mothers never slept next to their adolescent sons.

SLEEPING IN YOUR OWN BED

Children in both groups sometimes slept in their own beds. Ten Aka children (12% of all Aka children), and 13 Ngandu children (18% of all Ngandu children) slept in their own beds during the observation period. Eighty percent of these Aka children were male, and 80% were adolescents; whereas among the Ngandu, 62% were male, and 38% were adolescents. Aka adolescents often slept on some leaves in their parents' home next to the fire. Solitary sleeping among the Ngandu is influenced, in part, by the number of rooms in a house; only 15% of Ngandu homes had four or more bedrooms, but 54% of the children in their own beds lived in these larger homes. It is important to remember that among the Aka, sleeping in your own bed seldom means you are very far from someone because Aka homes are small.

WHERE DO MOTHER AND FATHER SLEEP?

Taken together, the data indicate that children often sleep with at least one parent, especially among the Aka. But it is not clear where husband and wife sleep on the bed in relation to their children—do they sleep next to each other with children to the side or do they place the children between them? The Shweder et al. study (1995) gives the impression that husband and wife sleeping next to each other may not be important in non-Western cultures. He finds that Americans view the husband–wife couple as "sacred" in that they almost always sleep next to each other regardless of the number of beds in a house, but that by comparison the Indian husband and wife regularly slept apart. Another cross-cultural study by the Whitings (1975) also suggests that hunter-gatherer couples should sleep together more than horticultural couples, such as the Ngandu, because (1) foragers are mobile, and it takes more time and energy to build separate places for husband and wife to sleep each time they move than it does for sedentary farmers; and (2) foragers are less likely than farmers to have strong clan organization and warfare to defend stored food items and are therefore less likely to have separate sleeping locations for males. The Whitings also found that couples were more likely to sleep apart in warmer climates and together in colder climates (i.e., where winter temperatures drop below 50° F).

Our data do not support the Whitings' predictions. Aka forager couples slept "apart" (separate beds) 44% of the time, whereas only 7% of Ngandu farming couples slept apart. Thirty-two percent of the Aka cases involved couples with young infants and, as described above, fathers made beds within an arm's reach next to or perpendicular to the bed with mothers and infants. In the other 12% of cases, husband and wife had their own beds next to each other, and each parent slept with some of their children. In our view, Aka couples are, by classic definition, cosleeping in most cases, as are most Ngandu couples. The Ngandu do have strong patriclans and value aggressive males, but these conditions do not lead to separate sleeping locations. Also, as mentioned, Aka homes are quick and easy to build, so if husband and wife want to sleep apart, it does not take much time to make it happen.

We did not take ambient temperatures during the night, so it is difficult to evaluate the role of temperature in husband–wife cosleeping. According to Whitings' climate hypothesis, husbands and wives in both groups should sleep apart, but this is not the case.

Mixed evidence existed for Shweder et al.'s suggestion that husband–wife proximity is not as important in non-Western contexts. Contrary to his predictions and unlike the Indian setting, husband and wife in both ethnic groups co-slept, either in the same bed or within an arm's reach of each other. But at the same time and consistent with Shweder et al.'s representation in India, Aka and Ngandu husband and wife often did not sleep next to each other even though they may have been sharing a bed or within an arm's reach of each other—48% of Aka couples and 33% of Ngandu couples who shared a bed did not sleep next to each other because their children slept between them.

Other Aka and Ngandu differences existed in husband–wife sleeping arrangements. Middle-aged Ngandu couples with middle-aged children or older often slept in a bed separate from their children (27% of Ngandu husband–wife sleeping arrangements), whereas Aka couples never did this. This is why older Ngandu children were more likely than Aka children to sleep with siblings. Ngandu couples with young children were more likely than Aka couples (33% Ngandu couples, 8% Aka couples) to sleep next to each other, with the child or children sleeping next to the mother; Aka parents were more likely to put the children between them.

FIRES AND THERMOREGULATION

Heat and protection from predators or biting insects (e.g., ants, flies, mosquitoes) are important functions of fire at night. Keeping warm at night is important for evening sleeping, even in the tropical forest. The Aka stay warm by keeping a fire going all night or using a cotton cloth, which is often worn today by Aka women. The person next to the fire is responsible for keeping it going during the night. Table 6.9 examines who slept next to the fire, and it is usually the father or mother.

TABLE 6.9 Who Sleeps Next to the Fire? Cultural Models or Patterns About When Father, Mother, and Children Sleep Next to the Fire (*N* = 64)

Cultural Model	Number of Cases Consistent With Prediction	Number of Cases Inconsistent With Prediction
The father sleeps next to the fire when his wife and children share the bed with him, or he sleeps in his own bed because he has an infant or has several children (3 or more).	23	0
The mother/grandmother sleeps next to the fire when (a) the father is in his own bed, (b) the father is not present, or (c) she is divorced or single.	21	4
If children sleep next to the fire, it is usually a male child older than 7 years; he simply decides to sleep next to the fire alone or with other male children.	11	5

The table evaluates three cultural models, or predictions, about who should sleep next to the fire. If a husband shares a bed with his wife and children, he should usually sleep next to the fire. His wife sleeps on the other side of the bed with children in between them, and she has a cloth to keep her warm. He keeps the fire going, which is near the front of the home so that if predators or other threats arrive, he is the first to deal with them. This prediction and the other father prediction in the table were consistent with all cases of fathers next to the fire. The prediction for mothers being next to the fire was correct 84% of the time. Three of the four exceptions were when the father shared the bed but the mother slept next to the fire rather than the father, often because she wanted to because she was cold. The prediction for when children sleep next to the fire was correct 69% of the time. The exceptions included four cases in which female children older than 7 years decided to sleep in their own bed or with others next to the fire. In the other case, an 8-year-old boy slept next to the fire with his father next to him.

Most Aka adolescents co-slept, but 33% of them slept in their own bed, but not in their own home by themselves. During the day, Aka girls may build small homes and stay in them much of the day, and boys may build shelters with a bed, but when it comes time to sleep, they move into their parents' home because of the warmth provided by the fire or sleeping next to others. It takes considerable time and energy to collect enough firewood and keep a fire going all night. Several teenagers said they ended up sleeping in their parents' house because they got cold.

Today the Ngandu seldom use fires in their homes to provide heat or protection. When the first author started to conduct research in the early 1970s, it was normative among the Ngandu, but today most families have kerosene lanterns that provide light, but not much heat, and several cotton cloths. Families try to keep the lanterns burning during of the night, not so much for heat but rather for protection from others (both spiritual and physical) who may try to enter their house. Flashlights are available and used to check disturbances in or outside the home. All members of the family have cotton sheets to help keep them warm.

CHANGING SLEEPING ARRANGEMENTS

Thirty Aka homes were observed for up to 4 consecutive days for a total of 82 home observations. Sixteen of the homes had some change (e.g., change of bed or who slept next to whom) in sleeping arrangements. Forty-one days with at least one change in the home's sleeping arrangements were possible (i.e., from observation day 1 to observation day 2) and the survey found 25 homes with at least one change in sleeping arrangement from the previous day (61% of possible days). This limited survey indicated that changes in Aka sleeping arrangements occur regularly— about every other day.

LOCAL EXPLANATIONS FOR SLEEPING ARRANGEMENTS

Worthman (2007, p.133) states that, "who sleeps with whom reflects the social order and informs the emotional-regulatory content of relationships." What happens at night reflects and is consistent with cultural values and ways of thinking and feeling. The foundational schema and habitus described in the first section of the chapter represent the social and social-emotional nature of relationships in these two ethnic groups, and they dramatically affected cosleeping arrangements and how people explained why individuals slept where they did.

The Aka

When asking Aka parents why children slept where they did, the standard answer was, "this is where the child wants to sleep." For instance, a 12-year-old boy started the evening in a *bokala* home (constructed by and occupied by adolescent males), but got cold and decided on his own to move back into his parents' home. An 8-year-old girl who was sleeping next to her mother moved across camp to sleep with her father's first wife because she said she loved her. In another case, an elderly grandmother was sleeping alone in her own home and when asked why she was alone said, "I prefer the grandchildren to sleep with me but they no longer come." This contrasts with a 10-year-old boy who said, "I prefer to sleep with my grandmother because I love her; she gives me a lot and takes good care of me." Another 6-year-old boy who shared a bed with his 9-year-old sister and parents said, "I love her [mother] so much I want to be next to her." His father slept in the same bed, but two people away. Many of the changes in sleeping arrangements have to do with individuals moving to be closer to someone else or to get closer to the fire.

The flexibility and variability in Aka bed-sharing arrangements are similar to the daily changes that take place in camp composition—individuals or families move in and out of camp every day. This is, in part, why it is easy to move into an Aka camp—changes occur daily, so it not unusual for someone, including an anthropologist, to move in. According to the Aka, most of the variability of who sleeps by whom is based on individual choice and reflects foundational schema. It is important to respect the autonomy of each individual; status differences are minimal, so no individual can command another what to do (i.e., age egalitarianism), and individuals are expected to give, which may mean sharing proximity.

Infants, of course, do not decide where to sleep, and parents often put them between them to keep them warm, so they will not roll into the fire, and as one Aka father said, "I put our baby between us so he can get the smell of his mother and can turn and get my smell."

Aka parents said that they co-slept with their children because children should always sleep next to them. As mentioned in the habitus section of the paper, staying physically close to each other is a core feature of Aka daily life. They also said they kept their children between them to keep them warm and protect them from any dangers. Parents said they wrap their legs over their children to keep them warm.

In terms of why Aka fathers were most likely to be next to the fire, they said fathers should be closest to the opening of the home for protection from leopards, strangers, or other dangers in addition to keeping the fire going throughout the night. Although this was generally the case, mothers said, and observational data confirmed, that they would not hesitate to change positions with their husband so that they could be next to the fire. Again, the respect for autonomy and minimal status hierarchy (i.e., gender egalitarianism) contributed to the flexibility.

The Ngandu

Ngandu explanations for sleeping arrangements also reflected foundational schema. When parents were asked why children slept in particular beds, they consistently said this is where they told children to sleep or this is where they put them. When a grandmother was asked why her grandson was sleeping with her, she said she had brought him to her home; he did not decide on his own. Ngandu parents regularly command their children to do particular tasks, and this includes where to sleep.

Like the Aka, several Ngandu said they placed infants between them so as "not to invite sex" and maintain the postpartum sex taboo. If they have sex before the infant walks well, the infant can get sick and die. In terms of having an infant and younger children between them, they said it was to keep them warm and so that the "children can rest comfortably." A few other parents said infants and young children were placed between them so that they would not fall out of the bed (Ngandu beds can be a foot or more off the ground).

In terms of why some children were in separate beds, some parents said their children kept fighting, so they put them in separate beds, whereas others said their children were big and needed their own bed.

It is also important to note that when Ngandu parents were asked why their children sleep between them, they said there was no reason, this is simply the way they did it. Anthropologists are often looking for cultural rationale, but for many people it is a matter of habit and social learning without an explicit rationale.

Finally, like the Aka, several Ngandu said that the father should sleep closest to the door to protect the family.

Discussion

The study identified both similarities and differences in bed sharing among the Aka foragers and Ngandu farmers.

SIMILARITIES BETWEEN GROUPS

1. Bed sharing after weaning was normative for children in both groups, even into adolescence. Humans in small-scale cultures were relatively distinct

from other higher primates in their cosleeping patterns after weaning, whereas humans in most modern, high-density, highly stratified, urban industrialized cultures were somewhat closer to the great ape patterns in that juveniles often slept separately after the age of weaning.

2. Children in small-scale cultures bed-shared with genetically related kin, primarily parents and siblings. Grandparents seldom bed-shared with children.
3. Children of all ages regularly bed-shared and slept next to both males and females.
4. Parents never co-slept next to their sexually mature adolescent of the opposite sex.
5. Husband and wife in both ethnic groups co-slept, either in the same bed or within an arm's reach of each other. Even though husband and wife with young children often co-slept, they did not always sleep next to each other because their children were placed between them.
6. Mothers in both ethnic groups were more likely to sleep next to their children than were fathers.

DIFFERENCES BETWEEN GROUPS

1. Aka hunter-gatherer homes, living spaces, and beds were substantially more proximal, smaller, and denser (i.e., more people per unit space) than were Ngandu farmers'.
2. Middle-aged and adolescent Aka children were more likely than Ngandu children to sleep with parents and siblings, whereas Ngandu children of the same age seldom slept with parents and were more likely to sleep with only siblings. Ngandu parents often stopped sleeping with children in middle childhood.
3. Aka fathers were more likely to sleep next to their older children than were Ngandu fathers.
4. Aka children often made the decisions about where to sleep at night, whereas Ngandu parents usually told their children where to sleep.

EXPLAINING COMMONALITIES

Why is cosleeping beyond infancy and young childhood common and normative in these small-scale cultures? The prevalence of cosleeping at all ages appears to be greater in these two small-scale cultures than that found in other cultures. The differences are especially pronounced after infancy. The variability may result from differential risks for child morbidity and mortality. Parents in previous cosleeping studies in the United States, Japan, China, Korea, and India had access to relatively modern medical care for their children (e.g., vaccination programs, antibiotics), and children were not raised in environments where predators or poisonous snakes were potential threats. Juvenile (younger than 15 years) mortality rates among the Aka and Ngandu are 30% to 45%, so many parents lose one-third to one-half of their children on average before they reach age 15 years. By comparison, mortality rates for children younger than 15 years in the above-mentioned countries are less than 8%. Substantial differences also exist in total fertility rates; Aka and Ngandu women have four to six children in their lifetimes, whereas women in the urban industrialized countries of previous studies have one to three live births. Many families in the urban industrialized cultures also have access to electricity or other sources of heat, in addition to an array blankets and other material items to keep warm.

For most of human history and in small-scale societies today, children who co-sleep after weaning are probably more likely to survive than children who do not co-sleep. Children who do not co-sleep are at a greater risk for morbidity and mortality caused by predators, poisonous snakes, and strangers entering camp, and do not have others to help with thermoregulation. Cosleeping beyond infancy is adaptive in this context.

As Shweder et al. (1995) found in India, cosleeping beyond infancy protects and monitors vulnerable juveniles as well as keeping them warm. Parents often place children between them for these purposes. Cosleeping in these contexts is part of parental investment; parents invest time and energy throughout the night to help ensure their children's safety and warmth. Parental investment through cosleeping in urban industrialized settings is substantially reduced because of lower risks for morbidity and mortality and the availability of alternative sources of heat.

An evolutionary perspective (i.e., enhancing inclusive fitness) also helps to explain why cosleeping generally occurs with genetically related individuals and why incest avoidance with cosleeping is a human universal. The finding that mothers are somewhat more likely to co-sleep than fathers is also consistent with evolutionary explanations in which parental investment theory indicates men and women have different reproductive strategies (Trivers, 1972). Women invest somewhat more time in energy cosleeping next to children, whereas some fathers sometimes sleep in a nearby bed closer to the front of the home to protect the family.

Like the Aka and Ngandu, incest avoidance was an important criterion in predicting Indian cosleeping patterns (Shweder et al., 1995), but Aka and Ngandu were different from the Indian study in that "female chastity," that is, not allowing adolescent females to sleep alone, was not an issue in either group.

We were somewhat surprised to find that children infrequently co-slept with grandparents, given the attention paid to the "grandmother hypothesis" (Hawkes et al., 1998). This may be because adult mortality is also high in both groups, and relatively few grandmothers are available given the relatively large number of children per woman.

EXPLAINING INTRACULTURAL AND INTERCULTURAL VARIATION

Foundational schema among the Aka, egalitarianism and respect for autonomy, and the Ngandu, sex and age hierarchy, contributed to intercultural variability in various dimensions of cosleeping. Aka values of autonomy and age egalitarianism were reflected in Aka children's decisions about where they wanted to sleep, whereas the Ngandu value of showing respect and deference to parents was reflected in parents making decisions about where their children should sleep.

Ngandu age hierarchy was also demonstrated in the fact that older parents often stopped sleeping with middle-aged children, whereas Aka parents continued to co-sleep with their older children and some adolescents. Higher status accorded men compared with women among the Ngandu was also evident in that fathers were especially unlikely to co-sleep with middle-aged and adolescent children, whereas this was not pronounced among Aka fathers. These cultural differences in gender and age roles contributed to the fact that middle-aged and adolescent children were much more likely than their Aka counterparts to co-sleep with siblings rather than mixed-age and mixed-sex groups. These differences are also reflected during daylight hours because Ngandu children are much more likely than Aka children to spend the day with other children, whereas Aka children are more likely to spend time with both adults and children.

Aka also highly value physical proximity to others, and this was reflected in the size of their beds and the average space each person had in a bed. The average Ngandu bed was twice the size of any Aka bed, and an average Ngandu person had about three times more space in a bed on average than did an Aka individual. Aka were also more likely than Ngandu to have more people in a bed, even though their beds were smaller on average.

Greater economic wealth influenced intracultural variation among the Ngandu. Three of the 20 Ngandu homes were occupied by relatively wealthy individuals— the former mayor, a retired schoolteacher with a pension, and a merchant. These homes were larger, had more rooms and beds, and consequently had more individuals sleeping alone in their own bed in their own room, or in their own bed with others in the room.

The expansion of family also influences intracultural diversity, as reflected by the fact that as more children are born, modifications take place in sleeping arrangements. For example, in both groups, young couples with an infant often put the infant between them. As more children arrive, Aka beds get bigger (strong relationship between number of people in a bed and bed size) to accommodate the increase in family size, whereas among the Ngandu, older children are placed with their siblings. When children become adolescents, some Aka boys and girls build their own homes, but they often return to their parents' home because it takes time and energy to keep a fire going. They get cold and return to their parents' home. In both groups, a minority of adolescents slept in their own bed.

It is worth pointing out that the size of houses and beds illustrates some of the dynamic ways that new or novel social or physical environments are created by participants who alter, or reconstruct, the niche to which all members must then become adjusted, either in an acute or long-term way, an example of *cultural niche construction.* Existing literature often discusses house size (e.g., number of beds or rooms in the house) as an "ecological constraint" in regard to intracultural cosleeping decisions, but in reality, these features were subjected to the same cultural processes (i.e., they were adopted or chosen) and were contiguous with specific socially transmitted and learned behaviors—becoming part of the niche to which members of the group continue to adjust or adapt. We mention this only because culture and ecology are often separate discussions of cosleeping, but they clearly influence each other.

SPECULATION ON SOCIAL-EMOTIONAL DIMENSIONS OF COSLEEPING

The evolutionary scenario for cosleeping beyond infancy in small-scale cultures may make some sense, but one has to ask, Why do the great apes not co-sleep with their juveniles after weaning? Would it not increase juvenile survival? It is beyond the scope of this chapter to adequately address this question, but we propose an additional evolutionary and adaptive explanation. Critical differences exist between ape and human juveniles after weaning. Ape juveniles start to forage on their own, provisioning from their mother is minimal, and sharing food with others is rare. By contrast, human juveniles after weaning continue to be provisioned and cared for by parents and other adults. Humans are cooperative breeders, but apes are not; and extensive food and child care sharing are integral to forager life, whereas this is not the case among our higher primate cousins. Apes do not need to learn to cooperate and share, but it is essential among humans. How do children learn to cooperate and share so extensively? We suggest that the close physical proximity and regular cosleeping throughout the juvenile stage contributed substantially to the coevolution of theory of mind and empathy and the consequent trust necessary for extensive cooperation and sharing beyond the nuclear family.

Today cosleeping, in general, and beyond infancy, in particular, is in decline possibly because sharing, cooperation, and trust are simply not as important as they once were in hunter-gatherer societies. If regular cosleeping is associated with the development of trust, sharing, and cooperation, the subsequent predictions follow (*arrows* refer to which group should practice cosleeping more than the next group):

1. Hunter-gatherers → farmers → urban industrialists
2. Interdependent cultures → independent cultures
3. Poor → wealthy

Although speculative, our goal is to stimulate additional research on cosleeping beyond infancy, especially in small-scale cultures.

IMPLICATIONS FOR WESTERN PARENTS

1. Cosleeping or bed sharing after infancy appears to be normative in the small-scale cultures that likely characterized most of human history, so it should not be considered unnatural, deviant, or unusual. At a minimum, we suggest that human bodies and minds are adapted to cosleeping beyond the age of weaning. Based on our reading of the limited number of ethnographic descriptions of cosleeping beyond infancy in hunter-gatherers, the way of life that characterized most of human history, cosleeping beyond infancy appears to be common, as it was in this study. However, little is known about the costs or benefits of cosleeping beyond infancy in the modern context.
2. We do not know the adaptive value or design of cosleeping after weaning in contemporary urban industrialized cultures. Research in urban industrialized cultures has shown that cosleeping in infancy promotes successful breastfeeding and may lead to a lower prevalence of sudden infant death syndrome (Gettler and McKenna, 2010).
3. We do not know about the social-emotional dimensions of cosleeping beyond infancy. Bed sharing likely enhances trust of self and self with others (i.e., secure and safe while sleeping) as well as intimate knowledge and understanding of others with whom one co-sleeps. For parents in today's world, cosleeping beyond infancy may provide an additional opportunity to spend time with their children.

Conclusion

Although the sample size and length of study are admittedly limited, this is the first systematic study of cosleeping beyond infancy in a hunter-gatherer and a small-scale farming culture. Our study suggests that cosleeping beyond infancy may be common in the high fertility mortality small-scale cultures that characterized most of human history. Future studies with more attention given to the ethnography of sleeping arrangements, typically ignored in most cross-cultural research, will be needed to affirm or correct the speculations we have put forth here. We hope that this work will stimulate just such needed additional research.

Acknowledgments

We want to acknowledge and sincerely thank the Aka and Ngandu families for allowing us into their daily lives, research assistants Auban Mongosso and Edward Mboula, and Bonnie Hewlett and Scott Calvert for their insightful comments on early drafts of the paper.

References

Abbott, S. (1992). Holding on and pushing away: Comparative perspectives on an Eastern Kentucky child-rearing practice. *Ethos, 20,* 33–65.

Anderson, J. R. (1984). Ethology and ecology of sleep in monkeys and apes. *Advances in the Study of Behavior, 14,* 156–229.

Anderson, J. R. (1998). Sleep, sleeping sites, and sleep-related activities: Awakening to their significance. *American Journal of Primatology, 46,* 63–75.

Ball, H. L., & Volpe, L. E. (2012). Sudden infant death syndrome (SIDS) risk reduction and infant sleep location—moving the discussion forward. *Social Science and Medicine, 79,* 84–91.

Barajas, G. R., Martin, A., Brooks-Gunn, J., & Hale, L. (2011). Mother-child bed-sharing in toddlerhood and cognitive and behavioral outcomes. *Pediatrics, 128,* 339–347.

Barry, H., & Paxson, L. M. (1971). Infancy and early childhood: Cross-cultural codes. *Ethnology, 10,* 466–508.

Bourdieu, P. (1977). *Outline of a theory of practice.* Cambridge, UK: Cambridge University Press.

Boyette, A. H. (2013). *Social learning in middle childhood among Aka foragers and Ngandu farmers.* Doctoral dissertation. Washington State University, Pulman, WA.

Caudill, W., & Plath, D. W. (1966). Who sleeps with whom? Parent-child involvement in urban Japan families. *Psychiatry, 29,* 344–366.

Chou, Y. (2007). Survey of sleep in infants and young children in northern Taiwan. *Sleep and Biological Rhythms, 5,* 40–49.

Crawford, C. J. (1994). Parenting practices in the Basque country: Implications of infant and childhood sleeping location for personality development. *Ethos, 22,* 42–82.

Fouts, H. N., Hewlett, B. S., & Lamb, M. E. (2001). Weaning and the nature of early childhood interactions among Bofi foragers in Central Africa. *Human Nature, 12,* 27–46.

Fouts, H. N., & Brookshire, R. (2009). Who feeds children? A child's-eye-view of caregiver feeding patterns among the Aka foragers in Congo. *Social Science and Medicine, 69,* 285–292.

Fouts, H. N., & Lamb, M. E. (2009). Cultural and developmental in toddlers' interactions with other children in two small-scale societies in central Africa. *Journal of European Developmental Science, 3,* 259–277.

Fruth, B., & Hohmann, G. (1993). Ecological and behavioral aspects of nest building in wild bonobo (*Pan paniscus*). *Ethology, 94,* 113–126.

Gettler, L. T., & McKenna J. J. (2010). Never sleep with baby? Or keep me close keep me safe: Eliminating inappropriate "safe infant sleep" rhetoric in the United States. *Current Pediatric Reviews, 6,* 71–77.

Goodall, J. (1962). Nest building behavior in the free ranging chimpanzee. *Annals of the New York Academy of Sciences, 102,* 455–467.

Goodall, J. (1968). Behavior of free-ranging chimpanzees in Gombe Stream Reserve. *Animal Behavior Monographs, 124,* 272–308.

Hawkes, K., O'Connell, J. F., Jones, N. G., Alvarez, H., & Charnov, E. L. (1998). Grandmothering, menopause, and the evolution of human life histories. *Proceedings of the National Academy of Sciences USA, 95,* 1336–1339.

Hewlett, B. L. (2005). Vulnerable lives: Death, loss and grief among Aka and Ngandu adolescents of the Central African Republic. In B. S. Hewlett & M. E. Lamb (Eds.), *Hunter-gatherer childhoods: Evolutionary, developmental and cultural perspectives* (pp. 322–342). New Brunswick, NJ: Aldine Transaction.

Hewlett, B. L. (2013). *Listen, here is a story: Ethnographic life history narratives from Aka and Ngandu women of the Congo basin.* Cary, NC: Oxford University Press

Hewlett, B. S. (1991). *Intimate fathers.* Ann Arbor, MI: University of Michigan Press.

Hewlett, B. S., Lamb, M. E., Leyendecker, B., & Schölmerich, A. (2000). Internal working models, trust, and sharing among foragers. *Current Anthropology, 41,* 287–297.

Hewlett, B.S., Lamb, M.E., Shannon, D., Leyendecker, B, & Schölmerich, A. (1998). Culture and early infancy among central African foragers and farmers. *Developmental Psychology, 34,* 653–651.

Hewlett, B. S., Fouts, H. N., Boyette, A. H., & Hewlett, B. L. (2011) Social learning among Congo Basin hunter-gatherers. *Philosophical Transactions of the Royal Society B* (U.K.), *366,* 1168–1178.

Hewlett, B. S., & Winn, S. L. (in press). Allomaternal nursing in humans. *Current Anthropology.*

Horvat, J. R., & Kraemer, H. (1982). Behavioral changes during weaning in captive chimpanzees. *Primates, 23,* 488–499.

Jenni, O. G., Fuhrer, H. Z., Iglowstein, I., Molinari, L. & Largo, R. H. (2005). A longitudinal study of bed sharing and sleep problems among Swiss children in the first 10 years of life. *Pediatrics, 115,* 233–240.

Konner, M. J. (2010). *The evolution of childhood: Relationships, emotion, mind.* Cambridge, MA: Harvard University Press.

Konner, M. J., & Super, M. (1987). Sudden infant death syndrome: An anthropological hypothesis. In C. M. Super (Ed.), *The role of culture in developmental disorder* (pp. 95–108). San Diego, CA: Academic Press.

Latz, S., Wolf, A. W., & Lozoff, B. (1999). Cosleeping in context: Sleep practices and problems in young children in Japan and the United States. *Archives of Pediatrics and Adolescent Medicine, 153,* 339–46.

Litt, C. J. (1981). Children's attachment to transitional objects: A study of two pediatric populations. *American Journal of Othopsychiatry, 51,* 131–139.

Liu, X., Liu, L., & Wang, R. (2003). Bed sharing, sleep habits, and sleep problems among Chinese school-aged children. *Sleep, 26,* 839–844.

Liu, X., Liu, L., Owens, J. A., & Kaplan, D. L. (2005). Sleep patterns and sleep problems among schoolchildren in the United States and China. *Pediatrics, 115,* 241–249.

Lozoff, B., Wolf, A. W., & Davis, M. S. (1984). Cosleeping in urban families with young children in the United States. *Pediatrics, 74,* 171–182.

Lozoff, B., Wolf, A., & Davis, N. S. (1985). Sleep problems seen in pediatric practice. *Pediatrics, 75,* 477–483.

MacKinnon, J. (1974). The behavior and ecology of wild orangutans (*Pongo pygmaeus*). *Animal Behaviour, 22,* 3–74.

McKenna, J. J. (1986). An anthropological perspective on Sudden Infant Death Syndrome (SIDS): The role of parental breathing cues and speech breathing adaptation. *Medical Anthropology, 10,* 9–92.

McKenna, J. J. (1993). Cosleeping. In M. A. Carskadon (Ed.), *Encyclopedia of Sleep and Dreaming* (pp. 143–148). New York: MacMillan Publishing Co.

McKenna, J. J. (2000). Cultural influences on infant and childhood sleep biology and the science that studies it: Toward a more inclusive paradigm. In J. Laughlin, C. Marcos, & J. Carroll (Eds.), *Sleep and breathing in children: A developmental approach* (pp. 99–130). New York: Marcel-Dekker.

McKenna, J. J., Ball. H., & Gettler, L. H. (2007). Mother-infant cosleeping, breastfeeding and SIDS: What biological anthropology has discovered about normal infant sleep and pediatric sleep medicine. *Yearbook of Physical Anthropology, 50*, 133–161.

Mindell, J. A., Sadeh, A., Wiegand, B., How, T. H., & Goh, D. Y. T., (2010). Cross-cultural differences in infant and toddler sleep. *Sleep Medicine, 11*, 274–280.

Morelli, G. A., Rogoff, B., Oppenheimer, D., & Goldsmith, D. (1992). Cultural variations in infants' sleeping arrangements: The question of independence. *Developmental Psychology, 28*, 604–613.

Okami, P., Weisner, T. S., & Olmstead, R. (2002). Outcome correlates of parent-child bed-sharing: An eighteen-year longitudinal study. *Developmental and Behavioral Pediatrics, 23*, 244–253.

Parker, S. T. (1999). The life history and development of great apes in comparative perspective. In S. T. Taylor & R. W. Mitchell (Eds.), *The mentalities of gorillas and orangutans: Comparative perspectives*. Cambridge, UK: Cambridge University Press.

Pereira, M. E. (1993). Juvenility in animals. In M. E. Pereira & L. A. Fairbanks (Eds.), *Juvenile Primates: Life history, development, and behavior* (pp. 17–27). Oxford, UK: Oxford University Press.

Reichard, U. (1998). Sleeping sites, sleeping places, and presleep behavior of gibbons (*Hylobates lar*). *American Journal of Primatology, 46*, 35–62.

Schachter, F. F., Fuchs, M. L., Bujur, P. E., & Stone, R. K. (1989). Cosleeping and sleep problems in Hispanic-American urban young children. *Pediatrics, 84*, 522–530.

Schaller, G. (1963). *The mountain gorilla: Ecology and behavior.* Chicago: University Press.

Shweder, R. A., Jensen, L. A., & Goldstein, W. M. (1995). Who sleeps with whom revisited. In J. J. Goodnow, P. J. Miller, & F. Kessel (Eds.), *Cultural practices as contexts for development* (pp. 21–39). San Francisco: Jossey-Bass.

Trivers, R. (1972). Parental investment and sexual selection. In B. Campbell (Ed.), *Sexual selection and the descent of man, 1871-1971* (pp. 136–179). Chicago: Aldine.

Volpe, L. E., Ball, H. L., & McKenna, J. J. (2013). Nighttime parenting strategies and sleep-related risks to infants. *Social Science and Medicine, 79*, 92–100.

Watts, D. P., & Pusey, A. E. (1993). Behavior of juvenile and adolescent great apes. In M. E. Pereira & L. A. Fairbanks (Eds.), *Juvenile primates: Life history, development, and behavior* (pp. 148–171). New York: Oxford University Press.

Willinger, M., Ko, C. W., Hoffman, H. J., Kessler, R. C., & Corwin, M. J. (2003). Trends in infant bed sharing in the United States, 1993-2000: The National Infant Sleep Position Study. *Archives of Pediatric and Adolescent Medicine, 157*, 43–49.

Wolf, A., Lozoff, B., Latz, B., & Paludetto, R. (1996). Parental theories in the management of young children's sleep in Japan, Italy, and the United States. In S. Harkness, C. M. Super (Eds.), *Parents' cultural belief systems* (pp. 364–384). New York: Guilford Press.

Worthman, C. M., & Brown, R. A. (2007). Companionable sleep: Social regulation of sleep and cosleeping in Egyptian families. *Journal of Family Psychology, 21*, 124–135.

Worthman, C. M., & Melby, M. K. (2002). Toward a comparative developmental ecology of human sleep. In M. A. Carskadon (Ed.), *Adolescent sleep patterns: Biological, social and psychological influences* (pp. 69–117). New York: Cambridge University Press.

Yang, C. K., & Hahn, H. M. (2002). Cosleeping in young Korean children. *Journal of Developmental and Behavioral Pediatrics, 23*, 151–157.

Yovsi, R. D., & Keller, H. (2007). The architecture of cosleeping among wage-earning and subsistence farming Cameroonian Nso families. *Ethos, 35*, 65–84.

Intertwining the Influences of Culture and Ecology Broadens a Definition of the Importance of Closeness in Care
Wendy Middlemiss

In their work, Hewlett and Roulette help us to consider co sleeping as a context of care, a foundation for socialization, and an aspect of our developmental niche. This is a helpful focus for a topic that is often considered in regard to none of these concerns. As Hewlett and Roulette note, "culture and ecology are often separate discussions of cosleeping, but they clearly influence each other." In this research, the authors provide a window into the influences of culture and ecology in their description of cosleeping in the Aka and Ngandu communities.

Of particular note in regard to current Western views of cosleeping are the sleeping contexts in the Ngandu community. Parallel to many urban industrialized communities, increases in wealth and access to larger space were associated with decreases in frequency of bed sharing or cosleeping—with children at the age of middle childhood and older often sleeping away from parents. This bears resemblance to changes evidenced in many Western societies with industrialization. More wealth, more space, less contact between mothers, fathers, and their children.

Interestingly, however, the Ngandu community described differs in a very fundamental way from Western societies, with distinct dissimilarities evidenced in the interactions of culture and ecology. In the Ngandu community, ecological changes were associated with adaptations in some aspects of the sleeping context. However, with these adaptations, the cultural base of shared sleeping spaces was retained—thus retaining continued support for the development of cooperative and shared experiences through continued shared sleep space with siblings. Thus, in comparison to many Western societies, the need for interaction, that is, the provision of closeness; the building of a cooperative understanding; and the meeting of children's and parents' needs for warmth and safety did not dissipate with the added wealth and space. With this continued cosleeping, the Ngandu families retained an important element of their cultural milieu—allowing, as the authors propose, a sleeping context that supports the "coevolution of theory of mind and empathy and the consequent trust necessary for extensive cooperation and sharing beyond the nuclear family."

When we turn to Western urban industrialized communities' beliefs regarding cosleeping, we quickly move from a question of whether cosleeping beyond infancy is normative to a question of whether cosleeping at any age is acceptable. This shift in focus moves away from the consideration of cosleeping as a context of care to a view of cosleeping as a practice that may undermine healthy development of needed skills. Ironically, and sadly, in this refocusing of the role of cosleeping, we shift away from acknowledging the importance of the shared, cooperative, trusting interactions, the developmental niche of infants that identifies these interactions as essential to biological and emotional growth and wellbeing. This aspect of care and consideration of related implications is lost to the goal of independent functioning.

A review of the current literature around cosleeping clearly bears out these differences in views between Western and Ngandu communities. In Western communities, cosleeping and bed sharing are defined as maladaptive (Simard et al., 2008), intrusive, resulting from parents' inability to set limits (Weinraub et al., 2012), and dangerous (see American Academy of Pediatricians policies for summary). The basis for these distinctions does not consider issues of socioemotional development or the necessary interaction between caregiver and child to assure health and development. Thus in Western cultures, consideration of sleep arrangements is divorced from considerations of the benefits and the normative nature of these close, responsive interactions. This framework for building of infants' capacity for independent regulation is attempted on a stark foundation of independent care from early ages. As Hewlett and Routlette note, and science will readily confirm, this early nonresponsiveness to need is associated with less positive social and emotional health at later years.

The divorcing of the normative practices of responsiveness and protection of young from sleeping practices results in parents' reports of confusion, discomfort, and distress (Huey and Middlemiss, 2012), with chosen sleep arrangements devoid of shared sleep and responsiveness at nighttime. The confusion stems from the conflict between a normative drive to be responsive as a way to build a sense of trust and cooperativeness and mandates to encourage self-settling sleep at extraordinarily young ages. This disconnect between caring and the cultural message to remain distant generates stress related to engaging in a behavior that does not resonate with the contextual, necessary role of parent as protector and provider (Middlemiss, Granger, Goldberg, and Nathans, 2012).

Little time is spent considering how this cultural focus has developed—even less time is spent considering the cost. However, when we look at the research, there are strong indicators that taking away parents' flexibility in providing care that may be determined appropriate or inappropriate based on considerations other than independence, causes stress for mothers (Middlemiss et al., 2012; Morgenthaler et al.,

2006) and may constrain interactions that build that necessary attachment, which will underlie children's developing strengths—emotionally and socially.

The beauty of Hewlett and Roulette's work is that it provides us the opportunity to step back from the view of cosleeping common in Western cultures. When we step back and look, we can see so much about how the Western view may have come to the fore and what may be the costs for our children's and societies' wellbeing. With a broader frame, we ask different questions because we take ourselves out of a standard cultural explanation. Lessons may be learned if we look carefully at the care choices in the Ngandu communities. Despite a focus on compliance, hierarchy based on age and gender, and living spaces contributing to greater likelihood of sleeping alone, there is still an extended cosleeping period and an assurance of a setting in which infants and young children are kept close for safety and care.

Thus, as the Ngandu gained in prosperity, they retained a balance between the larger space and the developmental niche of early care and socialization. In this way, the choices regarding sleep weren't focused away from infants' development and fragility, and they weren't focused away from parents' and communities' natural propensity for early care to support later strengths.

References

Huey, E., & Middlemiss, W. (2012, November). *The role of civility in parent-practitioner communications related to infant care.* Paper presented at the Association of Moral Educators, San Antonio, TX.

Middlemiss, W., Granger, D. A., Goldberg, W. A., & Nathans, L. (2012). Asynchrony of mother–infant hypothalamic-pituitary-adrenal axis activity following extinction of infant crying responses induced during the transition to sleep. *Early Human Development, 88,* 227–232.

Morgenthaler, T. I., Owens, J., Alessi, C., Boehlecke, B., Brown, T. M., Coleman, J. Jr., et al. (2006). Practice parameters for behavioral treatment of bedtime problems and night wakings in infants and young children. *Sleep, 29,* 1277–1281.

Simard, V., Nielsen, T. A., Tremblay, R. E., Boivin, M., & Montplaisir, J. Y. (2008). Longitudinal study of bad dreams in preschool-aged children: Prevalence, demographic correlates, risk and protective factors. *Sleep, 31*(1), 62–70.

Weinraub, M., Bender, R. H., Friedman, S. L., Sussman, E. J., Knoke, B., Bradley, R., et al. (2012). Patterns of developmental change in infants' nighttime sleep awakenings from 6 through 36 months of age. *Developmental Psychology, 48,* 1511–1548.

Contexts for the Evolution of Families and Children

7

Environment of Evolutionary Adaptedness, Rough-and-Tumble Play, and the Selection of Restraint in Human Aggression

Douglas P. Fry

The observation that aggressive behavior is widespread in the animal kingdom suggests that it has evolved to fulfill survival and reproductive functions. Intraspecific aggression, in comparison with predation, tends to be much less bloody. There are exceptions to this generalization, such as when a langur male, taking over a harem, practices infanticide against his predecessor's offspring, or when a female praying mantis begins to devour her mate during copulation—but for the most part, conspecifics do not attempt to kill each other (Hrdy, 1977; Huntingford and Turner, 1987).

The thesis of this chapter is that natural selection has favored the restrained use of aggression in humans. Intraspecific killing has been selected against. Although obviously homicides occur, they can be viewed as the exception, not the rule. In support of this thesis, the first observation is that aggression within numerous other species reflects restraint and nonlethal patterns, thus showing that curtailed or limited aggression has been favored by natural selection in many different contexts (Maynard Smith, 1974; Maynard Smith and Price, 1973). Consequently, there is a precedent for the evolutionary argument that restrained aggression has been positively selected in humans. Second, a careful examination of aggression within nomadic forager societies—the social context that most closely approximates the conditions under which humans evolved—supports the thesis about the restrained nature of most human aggression.

Using extant nomadic forager data to glean insights about the evolutionary past and human nature, we will see that homicides are very rare in some nomadic band societies and occur from time to time in others. Importantly, when killings do occur, the motives are very personal, not collective. Nomadic forager societies are not warlike (Fry, 2006, 2007; Fry and Söderberg, 2013; Kelly, 1995; Lee and Daly, 1999; Reyna, 1994). In fact, there are numerous features of nomadic forager social organization that militate strongly against warfare. The types of aggression that tend to occur at the band level of social organization probably have been typical in the human evolutionary past. A central focus of this chapter is to consider the reasons that the killing of other humans may well have been selected against as humankind evolved. The chapter also considers the possible role of rough-and-tumble play (R&T) in learning restrained patterns of aggression during the course of development. Research on animals and human children suggests that R&T may be important in the learning of social skills, such as how to assess an opponent's strength, how to signal submission, and how to keep from sustaining serious injuries during a fight (Einon and Potegal, 1991; Pellegrini, 1993, 1995; Pellis and Pellis, 2007, 2009).

Reconstructing the Environment of Evolutionary Adaptedness

One way to gain inferences about the environment of evolutionary adaptedness (EEA) is to use a process called nomadic hunter-gatherer analogy. For most of their evolutionary past, humans lived as nomadic foragers. Therefore, the best societies to examine with the goal of gaining insights about the EEA are extant nomadic foragers (Bicchieri, 1972; Marlowe, 2005, 2010). The goal is to look for recurring patterns across such societies, with the explicit assumption that features which characterize mobile hunter-gatherers in current times across a variety of habitats are likely to have been regular features in the EEA as well (Fry, 2006).

Nomadic hunter-gatherers live in bands whose composition varies as people transfer regularly among groups. Nomadic foragers have few material possessions, are politically egalitarian, and tend to be widely dispersed. Lacking authoritative leadership, nomadic band societies nonetheless manage to deal with much conflict through avoidance, discussion, group meetings, contests, ostracism, and other non-violent or aggression-limiting ways (Boehm, 1999; Fry, 2000, 2006, 2007, 2011; Fry and Söderberg, 2013).

Disputes tend to be personal, such as between two men over a woman (Fry, 2006, 2007; Fry and Söderberg, 2013; Reyna, 1994; Service, 1966). The most common reasons for homicide are avenging the death of a close family member and competition over a woman (Fry, 2011; Fry and Söderberg, 2013). Another reason for homicide in some nomadic band societies is that band members do not tolerate overly aggressive persons; recidivist killers and otherwise dangerous persons may be executed for the public good (Balikci, 1970; Boehm, 1999; Fry, 2011; Lee, 1979, 1993). Most disputes in nomadic forager societies, however, are nonlethal, and many conflicts involve no physical aggression at all. A typical response to conflict within a band is for one party to simply leave the group and join another band. Nomadic foragers are famous for voting with their feet (Fry and Söderberg, 2013).

Nomadic hunter-gatherer bands tend not to engage in war or have militaristic value orientations (Fry, 2006, 2007, 2011; Steward, 1968; Kelly, 1995, Table 8.1). After spending much of his career studying nomadic foragers, Steward (1968, p. 334) explains that warfare is almost nonexistent among nomadic hunter-gatherers for a variety of reasons:

> "First, the primary groups [small bands] that comprise the larger maximum bands intermarry, amalgamate if they are too small or split off it too large. Second,...there is no more than a tendency for primary groups to utilize special areas. Third, most so-called 'warfare' among such societies is no more than revenge for alleged witchcraft or continued interfamily feuds. Fourth, collecting is the main resource in most areas. Primary bands did not fight one another, and it is difficult to see how a maximum band could assemble its manpower to defend its territory against another band or why it should do so."

Wolf (2001, p. 196) notes that the Ju/'hoansi [or San], Shoshone, and Walbiri live in some of the least abundant environments on earth, but in times of environmental stress these groups do not go to war. Instead, they share:

> "Among some human groups organized conflict between groups is absent or rare, and we can perhaps specify the conditions that account for the absence of war among them. All three populations—San, Shoshoneans, Walbiri— live in environments where strategic resources are widely scattered and sea- sonably variable. To survive, a person periodically needs to gain access to resources in other locations, and he gains such access through ties of kinship, marriage, friendship, and exchange."

The amount of interpersonal physical aggression in forager band societies var- ies from one group to the next. Ethnographers describe killings in some nomadic band societies. On the other hand, other mobile foragers, such as the Paliyan of India (Gardner, 2004, 2013) and the Batek Semang of Malaysia (Endicott, 1979, 2013), have nonviolent value systems, and physical aggression, including homicide, is extremely rare. For one sample of 21 nomadic band societies, ethnographers assessed homicides to be uncommon in one-third of the sample (seven societies), describing killings as rare, very rare, never mentioned to occur, none known, and unknown (Fry, 2011; Fry and Söderberg, 2013).

Next three types of natural selection pressures that may have favored restraint against intraspecific killing will be considered. Two of these also apply within ani- mal species more generally, but the third hypothesized selection pressure against killing may be uniquely human (Fry and Szala, 2013).

Natural Selection Favors Restrained Intraspecific Aggression

Aggression has both evolutionary costs and benefits. Costs include physical inju- ries; mortality; harming one's own kin if they are opponents; losing friends and supporters through damaged relationships; draining time and energy away from other necessary pursuits such as obtaining food, finding mates, or being vigilant for predators; and being ostracized from the social group as a troublemaker (Archer and Huntingford, 1994, p. 10; Bernstein, 2007, 2008; Boehm, 1999; Hamilton, 1971; Riechert, 1998, p. 82; Service, 1966). On the other hand, evolutionary benefits of aggression include obtaining resources such as food, territory, and mates; safeguarding one's offspring and oneself from attack; and achieving or maintaining dominance in a social hierarchy, which in turn correlates with access to resources or mates (Alcock, 2005; Archer, 1988; Wilson, 1975, pp. 242–243). In short, aggression serves a variety of evolutionary functions that vary from species to species (Alcock, 2005; de Waal, 1989; Wilson, 1975). The overall conclusion is that aggression can be risky, but it also can be beneficial to individual fitness in certain circumstances (Fry, Schober, and Björkqvist, 2010). Natural selection can be seen as shaping the aggressive behavior of a species over many generations to maximize fitness benefits and minimize costs. This principle applies not only to other species but also to humans.

Most intraspecific aggression in the animal world is nonlethal (Alcock, 2005; Hinde, 1974, p. 268; Kokko, 2008; Maynard Smith and Price, 1973). Nonetheless, on occasion injuries sustained during a fight can result in death, as reported, for example, among chimpanzees, hyenas, and lions (Alcock, 2005; Schaller, 1972; Wilson, 1975, p. 246; Wilson and Wrangham, 2003). Blanchard and Blanchard (1989, p. 104) explain that "In evolutionary terms...successful individuals will be those with techniques which enable them to avoid agonistic situations involving serious possibilities of defeat or injury." And Bernstein agrees (2008, p. 60): "The potential costs of fighting are such that natural selection has favored individuals that avoid taking risks when the cost to themselves is likely to exceed the benefits of anything obtained by engaging in that interaction." Consideration of intraspecific competitive and aggressive behavior across species reveals a variety of ways that individuals minimize risks (Fry et al., 2010). First, noncontact displays are used in place of actual fighting. For example, among elephant seals, threats outnumber fights by about 60:1 (Le Boeuf, 1971). Second, when fighting does occur, it often consists of ritualized aggression, wherein serious injuries and death are unlikely, such as in the head-butting contests for which ungulates are renowned. Third, animals practice avoidance and hence eliminate the possibility of confrontations. For instance, lions simply avoid members of other prides (Schaller, 1972).

As Darwin (1998) observed, most of the intraspecific aggression in the animal kingdom occurs between males. Intraspecific male–male aggression usually does not entail all-out fighting, but rather reflects various types of restraint (Archer and Huntingford, 1994; Bernstein, 2007; Eibl-Eibesfeldt, 1961; Kokko, 2008; Le Boeuf, 1971; Riechert, 1998, p. 65). That is, animal aggression rarely involves "total war," as Maynard Smith and Price call it (1973, p. 15), "but instead intraspecific conflicts are usually of a 'limited war' type, involving inefficient weapons or ritualized tactics that seldom cause serious injury to either contestant." Natural selection seems to have favored individuals who "follow the rules" of ritualized fighting so as not to expend unnecessary energy or to increase unnecessarily the risk for injury. This point is illustrated by the data showing that out of 1,314 agonistic interactions between pairs of male caribou, 1,308 were ritualized sparring matches between animals who followed the rules of restrained engagement, compared with a mere six bouts of escalated fighting (Alcock, 2005). This is a ratio of 1 escalated fight to every 218 ritualized contests.

Triumph of Restraint: Display and Tournament Contests in Nonhuman Animals

In a classic article, Maynard Smith (1974) distinguishes between two kinds of ritualized contests, which he calls displays and tournaments. Displays reduce the risk for injury to nil because they involve no physical contact between adversaries. Side-blotched lizards, for example, perform push-up displays toward their opponents; male tarantula hawk wasps engage in aerial displays, flying upward side-by-side for many meters before diving back to earth, repeating the process many times over (Alcock, 2005). Red dear stags engage in reciprocal roaring displays as they compete for mating privileges (Archer, 1988; Archer and Huntingford, 1994). The roaring displays may escalate to parallel walking displays wherein the deer visually assess each other's size and strength, still without making any physical contact.

Red deer also illustrate tournament contests; if neither animal yields after roaring and parallel walking displays, the final element of competition entails an antler-wrestling tournament (Archer and Huntingford, 1994). Tournaments are energetically expensive compared with roaring and walking displays, and the possibility of injury, although unlikely, does exist (Riechert, 1998).

As Kokko (2008, p. 55) points out, "There is an optimal level of aggression, rather than more being always better." With rare exceptions, animals follow the rules of restraint rather than escalating to more risky types of fighting. Competing giraffes batter each other with their necks and heads until one gives up (Alcock, 2005). Maynard Smith and Price (1973, p. 15) describe how mule deer "fight furiously but harmlessly by crashing or pushing antlers against antlers, while they refrain from attacking when an opponent turns away, exposing the unprotected side of its body." Generally speaking, once an opponent submits or tries to flee, prolonging a struggle serves no useful purpose; to the contrary, failing to respect a loser's submission signals may lead to escalation, a greater chance of injury, and wasted energy (Bernstein, 2007; Bernstein and Gordon, 1974; Roscoe, 2007).

In summary, research shows that *restrained, nonlethal* aggression, in contrast to more risky escalated combat, has evolved as the predominant pattern of intraspecific competition in many species (Alcock, 2005; Archer and Huntingford, 1994; Bernstein, 2007; Bernstein and Gordon, 1974; Fry et al., 2010; Fry and Szala, 2013; Hinde, 1974, p. 269; Kokko, 2008, p. 49; Riechert, 1998, p. 65). Natural selection favors nonlethality among conspecifics. "If aggression is elicited, then it must be limited, controlled, and regulated in such a way that it terminates with minimal risk of injuries," explains Bernstein (2008, p. 59). The prevalence in the animal kingdom of displays instead of contact aggression and ritualized tournaments instead of "total war" suggests that restraint is a more successful evolutionary strategy than engaging in unbridled intraspecific aggression. Alcock (2005, p. 309) sums up the evolutionary reasoning: "The 'fight no matter what' types would eventually encounter a superior opponent who would administer a serious thrashing. The 'fight only when the odds are good' types would be far less likely to suffer an injurious defeat at the hands of an overwhelmingly superior opponent." We would expect the same evolutionary logic to apply to humans.

Display and Tournaments in Nomadic Forager Societies

Examples of noncontact displays can be found in the literature on nomadic foragers (Fry et al., 2010). For example, Tonkinson (1978, p. 124) explains that fights among the Australian Mardu take place "in an atmosphere of great public drama and menace, so that honor is satisfied, but with a minimum of physical violence." Individuals may deliver harangues to express grievances, for instance, as they sit by their campfires at night (Silberbauer, 1972; Tonkinson, 1978, p. 123). Some Inuit societies engage in noncontact contests wherein rivals deride each other verbally in song (Balikci, 1970).

The typical pattern of tournament contests in nomadic forager societies involves wrestling. Contests vary in intensity from one nomadic forager society to the next, and not all foragers engage in contests. The first generalization is that disputes, whether dealt with through contests or by other means, tend to be interpersonal in nature (Fry, 2005, 2011; Fry and Söderberg, 2013). The next is that the winner of a contest gains status and sometimes a concrete reward such as a wife. Hence tournament contests, like displays, are serious business. Third, the curtailed aggression evident in tournament contests in nomadic forager societies parallels the ritualized fighting of animal species. As among animals, the restrained aggression that typifies such contests allows for the establishment of dominance or for access to resources with substantially less risk than would result from all-out fighting. Thus contests in forager band societies may be over serious matters, but nonetheless, as a limited form of competition, they are less risky to the participants than uninhibited fighting (Fry, 2005; Fry et al., 2010; Fry and Szala, 2013).

In addition to song contests, the Netsilik Inuit settle disagreements as two competitors take turns striking each other on the forehead or shoulders. Eventually, one man gives up. "After the fight, it is all over," explained an Inuit man, "it was as if they had never fought before" (Balikci, 1970, p. 186). To take another example, disputes between Siriono men may be settled through wrestling (Holmberg, 1969). Rules limit the engagement, and participants usually employ self-restraint and adhere to the rules. Holmberg (1969, p. 156) explains that, "any other type of fighting is frowned upon and is usually stopped by non-participant men and women. On one occasion Eantándu when drunk, struck an opponent with his fists. Everyone began to clamor that he was fighting unfairly, 'like a white man.' He stopped immediately." Homicide is "almost unknown" among the Siriono, indicating that aggressive rivalries rarely escalate beyond the culturally acceptable wrestling matches (Holmberg, 1969, p. 152).

The Ona foragers of South America also wrestled to resolve disputes (Gusinde, 1931). The nomadic Slave and Dogrib bands of North America had the custom of allowing a man to usurp another man's wife by out-wrestling the husband (Helm, 1956). The Ingalik practiced a similar custom (Osgood, 1958, p. 204). If a married Ingalik woman took off with another man, typically she would hide in the forest while her lover and her husband wrestled over her.

Examples of contests are easy to find in the nomadic forager literature, no doubt due in part to the absence in these egalitarian societies of judicial authorities who could handle disputes. Contests in nomadic hunter-gatherer societies can be viewed as conflict resolution mechanisms that have rules which limit aggression. Hoebel (1967, p. 92) concludes that contests in Inuit societies serve to handle conflict without the loss of life; this conclusion can be generalized on the basis of the ethnographic evidence to other nomadic band societies. As we have seen, the ritualization of aggression in many species prevents injuries among contestants (Archer and Huntingford, 1994; Fry et al., 2010; Maynard Smith and Price, 1973). Among humans also, contests with rules that limit aggression allow for the resolution of differences with less risk for injury than might occur during less restrained forms of fighting (Fry, 2005, 2006). Spectators take a role in enforcing contest rules if necessary (Goodale, 1974; Holmberg, 1969). The metacommunicative context of contests reflects the meaning that they are simultaneously *serious yet not dangerous*, or at least not as dangerous as unbridled, escalated aggression. Winning a contest by the rules enhances status, but winning through cheating—by fighting unfairly— may have the opposite effect within the small-scale social world of nomadic foragers (Fry, 2005).

Nomadic forager analogy suggests that aggression in the EEA probably carried certain social costs aside from the more obvious risks to life and limb. Values and behaviors that are uniformly appreciated in nomadic band societies include generosity, cooperation, egalitarianism, and sharing, whereas those that are not appreciated include bullying, aggressiveness, rule breaking, and stinginess (Boehm, 1999; Fry, 2006; Lee, 1979; Lips, 1947; Tonkinson, 1978). For example, the Paliyan place a special emphasis on respecting other people and behaving nonviolently (Gardner, 2004, 2013). Among the Ju/'hoansi, the ideal son-in-law should lack a reputation for fighting (Lee, 1993). Lips (1947) reports how a Montagnais-Naskapi hunter and his family starved to death in the winter after being ostracized from the band for antisocial behavior. The point is that engaging in too much or too severe aggression, or other types of antisocial behavior, probably had fitness-reducing social costs in the EEA.

Inclusive Fitness

A second selection pressure against killing and unbridled aggression involves the concept of inclusive fitness (Fry et al., 2010). Hamilton (1964, 1971) posited that the genetic relatedness among individuals affects how they treat each other. He proposed that "the social behaviour of a species evolves in such a way that in each behaviour-evoking situation the individual will seem to value his neighbours' fitness against his own according to the coefficients of relationship appropriate to that situation" (Hamilton, 1964, p. 19). Assisting relatives enhances an individual's own fitness in this inclusive sense because relatives share alleles. At the opposite extreme, natural selection would be expected to minimize aggression among genetic relatives for the same reason. The killing of relatives would be strongly selected against.

Based on demographic data on nomadic hunter-gatherer societies, it seems probable that many, social interactions in the EEA took place among related individuals (Lee, 1993; Marlowe, 2005, 2010, p. 49). Marlowe (2010) explains that most persons within a Hadza camp are related, with a group of sisters often forming the core network of relationships within a band. Marlowe (2010, p. 49) also points out that "Any Hadza can usually decipher some kin connection to any other, given that there are only about 1,000 Hadza and kin ties are so overlapping." This relative-intensive social world of nomadic foragers differs markedly from that of present day nation-states, for example, in which people regularly interact not only with nonrelatives but also with complete strangers.

When a person cooperates, shares, protects, or cares for relatives, the person is likely to enhance inclusive fitness. Killing or injuring a relative has the opposite effect on inclusive fitness and therefore should have been selected against in the EEA. As the Gilyak say, brothers should not fight brothers (Shternberg, 1999, p. 63). When Lee (1979, p. 383) examined Ju/'hoansi homicides, he found that close relatives, although interacting frequently, tended not to kill each other.

Revenge Killing Within the EEA

Based on studies of extant nomadic foragers, it can be hypothesized that another powerful selection force favoring restrained, nonlethal forms of aggression in the EEA has resulted from the tendency for the family members of a murder victim to avenge the death of their relative by killing the killer (Fry, 2006; Fry and Söderberg, 2013). Cases of revenge homicide among other animal species seem not to exist. The important implication is that by perpetrating a homicide within the nomadic forager social environment, a killer may be signing his own death warrant to be executed at the hands of his victim's kin. Given that nomadic band social organization is the social type of the EEA, this additional selective force favoring restrained aggression instead of killing may have been very significant. Thus the tendency for family members to avenge a murder of a relative may constitute a third significant evolutionary selective force against intraspecific killing in humans.

Recall that nomadic band societies are not warlike, and some such societies have extremely low rates of homicide. This obviously reflects community-wide restraint against engaging in serious aggression. However, in social situations in which homicides do periodically occur, revenge was found to be the most consistent motive for killing among a sample of 21 nomadic forager societies in the Standard Cross-Cultural Sample (Fry, 2011). Westermarck (1924) concluded that humans possess a psychological predilection to repay a good deed with a corresponding act of kindness and also to repay an abuse with a punishment. Revenge homicide can be considered a manifestation of this reciprocity principle. In nomadic band society, a recurring motif is for a homicide victim's family to try to kill the murderer. If the victim's family kills the killer, this typically ends the matter because the second killing balances the scales of justice and restores the peace (Fry, 2006, p. 230).

This reciprocity principle, as played out in the nomadic band context, is illustrated by the Micmac of North America who believed that "If thou killest, thou shalt be killed" (Le Clercq, 1910, p. 286), as well as in the observation for the Chukchee of Siberia that "a murder rarely remains unavenged" (Bogoras, 1975, p. 663). The words of a Ju/'hoansi man also reflect his awareness of the reciprocity principle of revenge: "I want to hunt eland, kudu, and gemsbok, but hunting men is what gets you killed" (Lee, 1979, p. 391). The Montagnais-Naskapi of Canada traditionally believed that the appropriate response to a homicide was the execution of the killer by a family member of the victim (Lips, 1947, p. 470), which was also the case for the Yukaghir of Siberia, whose custom validated the exaction of revenge by a brother or another close relative of a homicide victim (Jochelson, 1926). Ingalik custom held that revenge for a killing could be enacted only by the victim's father, son, brother, grandfather, grandson, or uncle, but not by more distant relatives. In violation of this rule, the friend of a recently killed man became enraged at the disrespectful behavior that his friend's killer was exhibiting and, on impulse, stabbed him to death. A couple of days later, the new victim's father, uncle, and brother came to confront the avenger, saying: "You had no business to kill that boy" (Osgood, 1958, p. 54).

"I know that," he answered, "but he talked to me without politeness and having already killed my friend, it made me mad and I killed him. You would do the same in the circumstances."

The man's assessment rang true even to these family members: "After considering the character of the one who had just been killed, they concluded that perhaps it was better he was dead" (Osgood, 1958, p. 54). This case illustrates again the generalization that overly aggressive persons and troublemakers are not socially appreciated. Perhaps also the nomadic forager sense of justice that "If thou killest, thou shalt be killed" (Le Clercq, 1910, p. 286) came into play as the relatives contemplated the situation. In any case, no further redress was sought.

If killing once is risky, then becoming a recidivist killer seals one's fate (Boehm, 1999; Fry, 2006). The execution of bullies, violent troublemakers, and especially serial killers is a theme in the ethnographic literature on nomadic band societies.

Based on his studies of the Copper Inuit, Damas (1991, p. 78) concludes that "Certain men were feared for their aggressiveness or violent tendencies, but they almost invariably met with violent ends themselves." Hoebel (1967, p. 88) observes that the recidivist killer in band society becomes a public enemy. "The single murder is a private wrong redressed by the kinsmen of the victim. Repeated murder becomes a public crime punishable by death at the hands of an agent of the community." Lee's (1979, p. 394) account of the demise of a Ju/'hoansi recidivist killer illustrates Hoebel's point: "He had killed two people already, and on the day he died he stabbed a woman and killed a man.... No one came to his aid because all those people had decided he had to die.... They all fired on him with poison arrows till he looked like a porcupine." Based on his reading of numerous nomadic forager ethnographies from Africa, Australia, North America, and the Arctic, Boehm (1999, p. 82, italics added) concludes that aggressive men are likely to be executed: "My suspicion is that the *pattern* may be generalized to nomadic foragers in general."

The recurring resort to payback killings and executions in forager society reflects Westermarck's (1924) reciprocity principle regarding tit-for-tat paybacks. Bullies, overly aggressive persons, serious troublemakers, and especially recidivist killers usually receive their just desserts in accordance with this reciprocity principle, and this tendency would seem to constitute an additional, uniquely human selection pressure favoring the restrained use of intraspecific aggression in humans. Thus it is no surprise that restraint in the use of intraspecific aggression, which as we have considered represents a widespread pattern in the animal kingdom, also constitutes a theme among nomadic hunter-gatherers. Exercising restraint during competitive interactions may well be the outcome of strong selective forces operating in the EEA (Fry, 2006, 2007).

Rough-and-Tumble Play and the Development of Restraint

Features that typify mammalian R&T (Fry, 1990, 2005) are as follows: Threats are absent or infrequent, movements are free and easy, muscle tone is relaxed, biting is inhibited, play signals such as the play face and play vocalizations are evident, roles frequently reverse, dominance relations are relaxed, individuals of different sizes are partners, and sequences of behavior vary (Aldis, 1975; Bekoff and Byers, 1981, 1985; Fagen, 1978, 1981; Pellis, 1984; Scott and Panksepp, 2003; Smith, 1982; Symons, 1978). Human R&T consists of restrained wrestling, grappling, hitting, and chasing and fleeing, usually with clear indicators of playful intent such as laughter or smiles (Blurton Jones, 1972; Fry, 1990, 2005; Smith and Lewis, 1985).

Rough-and-tumble play (R&T) almost certainly was a regular developmental feature of childhood in the EEA. This assertion is based on the observations that R&T is common in the animal kingdom, is ubiquitous among primate species, and has been reported in societies around the world (Fry, 2005). The observations that R&T is widely, probably universally, distributed across human societies and that boys tend to engage in more frequent and more vigorous R&T than do girls, along with research results on age differences in R&T, all combine to suggest that, as in other species, R&T in humans has evolved to fulfill certain adaptive functions (Boulton, 1996; Boulton and Smith, 1992; Fry, 1990, 2005; Pellegrini, 1994, 2002, 2003; Smith, 1997; Smith and Boulton, 1990).

This section of the chapter explores two ideas regarding R&T and restraint. First, it considers the proposition that R&T plays a role in the developmental learning of restrained aggression. Second and relatedly, this section focuses on how the R&T of adolescents has many interesting parallels to the contests of adults, thus suggesting a link between the learning in adolescence of aggression-limiting social skills and the contests engaged in by adults. As we have considered, the recurring pattern across many species is for intraspecific competition to be expressed short of serious fighting. How might R&T play a role in the learning of such restraint?

There are indications that the process of becoming socially competent in the use of restrained aggression depends on having opportunities to engage in R&T as juveniles. Animals and humans that lack R&T experience tend to be less competent at dealing with their peers, for example, as they misinterpret an act of play as a real attack. Pellis and Pellis (2009) thoroughly review the literature on R&T among rats and reach the conclusion that the animals that lack R&T experience when young are deficient in their social interaction ability as adults. For example, the rats that have been deprived of R&T overreacted to benign social contact in such a way as to bring on attacks by other animals.

Similar deficiencies in managing agonistic situations have been reported for male mice raised only among females (Korpela and Sandnabba, 1994). These male-deprived male mice engaged in significantly more aggressive attacks than did mice that had been raised with other males (Korpela and Sandnabba, 1994). Bernstein (2008, p. 60) notes that monkeys who have lacked the opportunity to interact with other members of their species while growing up, rather than showing the restraint that is typical under natural conditions, "launch suicidal attacks against opponents who are clearly physically superior to them or, alternatively, may mount murderous attacks on opponents who are signaling submission and attempting to withdraw from the site of a contest." In human children, engaging in R&T correlates positively with social competency (Pellegrini, 1993, 1995). Play researchers Pellis and Pellis (2009, p. 144) observe, "Whether it is employed by rats, hyenas, monkeys, or humans, play fighting offers a level of nuance in social interactions that permits differences to be sorted out without the use of extreme violence."

We now turn to a consideration of the similarity between adolescent R&T and adult contests as described among nomadic forager societies. At the same time, a cross-cultural examination of R&T reveals that stylistic variations are clearly learned during development (Fry, 1987, 2005). Human R&T provides an interesting example of how evolutionary factors *and* elements of the social environment interact over the course of development. For example, the Semai of Malaysia are an extremely peaceful people who shun war and feuding, and rarely experience homicide (Dentan, 1968). Semai parents discourage R&T. Correspondingly, Semai children engage in R&T, but compared with such behaviors in most other cultures, Semai R&T is mild, involving only minimal or no physical contact (Fry, 2005).

The preliminary evidence suggests that the practice of fighting skills and the establishment of dominance are probable evolutionary functions of R&T that shift in importance depending on age (Boulton, 1996; Boulton and Smith, 1992; Fry, 1990, 2005; Neill, 1976, 1985; Pellegrini, 1994, 2002, 2003; Smith, 1982, 1997; Smith and Boulton, 1990). Specifically, the importance of an R&T practice function in young children may be replaced by a dominance function in older children and teens (Fry, 2005; Pellegrini, 1994, 2002, 2003; Pellis and Pellis, 2009; Smith and Boulton, 1990). That is, these fighting practice and dominance hypotheses may be applicable to different degrees at different stages of development. Even at the same age, these two functional explanations need not be viewed as mutually exclusive (see Neill, 1985). For example, assessing a partner's strength during R&T could relate both to gaining practice in a generalizable skill useful in later life (Boulton, 1996; Fry, 1990) and also to establishing dominance over a particular opponent in the short or long term (Pellegrini, 2002).

Several events observed among Zapotec teenagers (who are not from a nomadic forager society) indicate that the clear distinction between R&T and fighting, apparent in the 3- to 8-year-old Zapotec children, may blur somewhat by the teenage years (Fry, 1987, 2005). Sometimes horseplay among Zapotec teenagers appears, judging from facial expressions, to become somewhat serious, but then shifts back to play again (Fry, 1987). This observation supports Neill's (1976, pp. 218, 219) proposal that the intermingling of R&T and aggression sometimes occurs among 12- to 13-year-old boys: "Once the weaker boy has registered distress the bond can be maintained by the fight taking a more playful form, but if he does not do so at the start of the fight, the stronger boy may increase the intensity of the fight until he does." Thus, by adolescence, R&T may have a dominance function, an interpretation that gains credence from observational and interview data on older children (Pellegrini, 1994, 2002, 2003; Smith, Hunter, Carvalho, and Costabile, 1992).

By adolescence, R&T participants seem to be well aware that play and aggression are not as distinct phenomena as they were at younger ages (e.g., Pellis and Pillis, 2009; Smith et al., 1992; Smith, Smees, Pellegrini, and Menesini, 2002). To evoke Bateson's (1972) concept of metacommunication, instead of the shared under-standing between older partners being "this is not real aggression"—as would seem to aptly apply to the R&T of young children—the shared understanding becomes something like "we both know this has a serious component, but we implicitly agree to pretend that it does not," or, perhaps, "we both know that our status is involved, but it is not as serious a situation as it would be if we were to stop pretending that it is not serious" (Fry, 2005). Perhaps some additional insights about the likely func-tions of R&T might arise from comparing it with both contests and adult aggres-sion (Fry, 1990, 2005).

The intermingling of play and aggression among adolescents has parallels to the contests in nomadic forager contexts. Contests, as in adolescent R&T, can involve dominance struggles while allowing for the resolution of differences with less injury than might occur during real aggression. Contests, like adolescent R&T, have features that straddle play and aggression. Contests have rules that promote restraint, and spectators take a role in enforcing the rules if necessary. Thus contests are simultaneously *serious yet not serious*, or *serious yet not as dangerous as escalated aggression*. Contests directly parallel the R&T of adolescents because both types of interaction may grade back and forth between play and aggression in the gray area of exercising restraint and simultaneously seeking to dominate an opponent. Pertaining to postpubescent children, especially boys, Pellis and Pellis (2009, p. 144) observe that "dominance can be negotiated through play fighting: this means that these animals do not have to resort to full-blown fighting to settle any problems of their relationships." We could equally well use the same sentence in reference to adult contests: "Dominance can be negotiated through *contests*" in some foraging societies, which also means the avoidance of full-blown fighting. The similarities between adolescent R&T and adult contests—as contrasted both with the R&T of younger, preadolescent children and serious aggression as sometimes seen in adults—are presented in Table 7.1. As reflected in this table, the clear link between winning a contest and increasing one's status (or, contrariwise, losing and suffering a loss in status) is reflected in the nomadic forager examples we have considered and hints at the importance of dominance striving in male humans. In contests, as in the R&T among adolescents, curtailed aggression parallels the ritualized aggression of some animal species. Restrained aggression,

TABLE 7.1 A Theoretical Formulation: R&T Play, Contests, and Adult Aggression Compared

Preadolescent R&T	Adolescent R&T and Contests	Adult Aggression
Winning is *not* important	Winning is important (There may be sporting or juridical elements to contests)	Winning is important
Friendly mood	Friendly-to-hostile mood	Hostile mood
No attempt to dominate	May include domination attempts	Attempts to dominate
No intent to injure	No intent to seriously injure	Intent to injure
Serious injury extremely rare	Serious injury possible, but rare	Serious injury possible
Much restraint	Some restraint	Minimal restraint
Resources irrelevant	Resources possibly relevant	Resources usually relevant
Others not interested	Others interested as referees and spectators	Others very interested as peace-keepers or allies

The elements suggested in this table are derived from the literature on R&T and from surveying numerous ethnographic accounts of conflict management and aggression among nomadic hunter-gatherers and in other societies (see Fry, 1987: Table 3; 2005, 2006, in 2011; Smith, 1997: Table 1; and Smith et al., 2002: Table 14.1). The table is adapted and updated from Fry (2005).

whether in adult contests or in the R&T of adolescents, allows dominance to be established with substantially less risk to the participants than would result from all-out fighting. The metacommunicative parallel between adolescent R&T and adult contests as *serious but not serious* is intriguing.

Could adolescent R&T provide practice at participating in restrained, rule-based competitive struggles, such as contests, later in life? It can be hypothesized that R&T not only contributes to the learning and practice of fighting skills but more broadly to gaining experience at handling agonistic interactions with *restraint,* such as developing an understanding about when not to fight at all, how to "fight by the rules" within a particular social context, when and how to signal submission, and how to respond with deescalation to an opponent who wants to give up (Bernstein, 2007, 2008; Einon and Potegal, 1991; Fry, 2005; Korpela and Sandnabba, 1994; Pennisi, 2000).

Summary and Conclusion

Killing is not the norm in nomadic band societies; most male–male competition takes restrained paths. Ethnographic descriptions of nomadic foragers portray men as following the rules of limited engagement as they wrestle, grapple, punch, or hit. Some nomadic forager societies have extremely low levels of physical aggression. When conflicts do occur, they involve interpersonal motives, not intergroup hostility; in other words, warfare is atypical at the nomadic band level of social organization (Fry, 2006; Fry and Söderberg, 2013).

We have considered three reasons that natural selection would seem to favor restrained use of intraspecific aggression and specifically the avoidance of lethal aggression. First, a comparison of physical aggression across species, including humans, suggests that the risks for escalated fighting that can lead to intraspecific killing are high (Fry and Szala, 2013; Maynard Smith and Price, 1973; Maynard Smith, 1974). Second, in band societies, some social interaction is among relatives on a daily basis, and thus selection pressures against killing conspecifics may have been reinforced through inclusive fitness considerations (Hamilton, 1964, 1971). The data on nomadic forager societies suggests a third selective force may have operated to favor of nonlethal aggression in humans: Killers tend to be targeted for execution by the families of their victims, and recidivist killers tend to be targeted by the whole group.

Certain common elements of human R&T are apparent in widely distributed cultures. When information exists, wrestling and grappling, restrained hitting and punching, and chasing and fleeing recur in descriptions of children's R&T. Engaging in R&T during childhood and adolescence may facilitate the developmental learning and practice of restraint. Research on R&T in children suggests that both practice and dominance functions are likely. For humans, the practice of fighting skills may be more complex than in some other species. Humans may have to practice not only fighting maneuvers but also restraint within a social world that includes rules for fighting and dispute resolution. It is interesting to contemplate how much aggression among humans is restrained, curtailed, or limited through social conventions, enforced by the participants themselves and by other members of the group. Contests are one obvious example of restrained aggression and may be similar to the R&T in adolescent boys by providing a way to resolve dominance struggles with minimal risk to the participants.

Among animals, it seems that one lesson learned during play fighting is the use of restraint (Bernstein, 2007, 2008; Einon and Potegal, 1991; Fry, 2005; Korpela and Sandnabba, 1994; Pennisi, 2000). Bernstein (2008, p. 60; see also Pellis and Pellis, 2007) points out that "monkeys reared in social isolation seem to lack the social skills required to assess the willingness of a rival to engage in escalated aggression, the ability of the rival to inflict aggressive costs, and even the meaning of signals that a rival uses when conceding access to a contested resource." In the human EEA, it seems likely that lessons learned during R&T in youth about assessing opponents, fighting with restraint, and reading signals about escalation or capitulation had survival value, especially for males, in dealing with intraspecific conflict over the course of their lives so as to minimize risks and maximize benefits (Fry, 1987, 1990, 2005).

Acknowledgments

Some of the data reported in this chapter were collected as part of a research project funded by the National Science Foundation (Grant 03-13670), whose financial support is gratefully acknowledged. I extend my thanks to Darcia Narvaez for her editorial suggestions that have improved the readability of this chapter.

References

Alcock, J. (2005). *Animal behavior: An evolutionary approach* (8th ed.). Sunderland, MA: Sinauer.

Aldis, O. (1975). *Play fighting*. New York: Academic.

Archer, J. (1988). *The behavioural biology of aggression*. Cambridge, UK: Cambridge University Press.

Archer, J., & Huntingford, F. (1994). Game theory models and escalation of animal fighting. In M. Potegal & J. Knutson (Eds.), *The dynamics of aggression: Biological and social processes in dyads and groups* (pp. 3–31). Hillsdale, NJ: Erlbaum.

Balikci, A. (1970). *The Netsilik Eskimo*. Garden City, NY: Natural History Press.

Bateson, G. (1972). A theory of play and fantasy. In G. Bateson (Ed.), *Steps to an ecology of mind* (pp. 177–193). Northvale, NJ: Jason Aronson.

Bekoff, M., & Byers, J. (1981). A critical reanalysis of the ontogeny and phylogeny of mammalian social and locomotor play: An ethological hornet's nest. In K. Immelmann, G. W. Barlow, L. Petrinivich, & M. Main (Eds.), *The Bielefeld interdisciplinary project* (pp. 296–337). Cambridge, UK: Cambridge University Press.

Bekoff, M., & Byers, J. (1985). The development of behavior from evolutionary and eco-logical perspectives in mammals and birds. In M. Hecht, et al. (Eds.), *Evolutionary biology (Vol. 19*, pp. 215–286). New York: Plenum.

Bernstein, I. (2007). Social mechanisms in the control of primate aggression. In C. Campbell, A. Fuentes, K. MacKinnon, M. Panger, & S. Bearder (Eds.), *Primates in perspective* (pp. 562–571). New York: Oxford University Press.

Bernstein, I. (2008). Animal behavioral studies: Primates. In L. Kurtz (Ed.-in-Chief), *Encyclopedia of violence, peace, and conflict (Vol. 1*, 2nd ed., pp. 56–63). New York: Academic Press.

Bernstein, I., & Gordon, T. (1974). The function of aggression in primate societies. *American Scientist, 62*, 304–311.

Bicchieri, M. (Ed.) (1972). *Hunters and gatherers today*. Prospect Heights, IL: Waveland.

Blanchard, D. C., & Blanchard, R. (1989). Experimental animal models of aggression: What do they say about human behaviour? In J. Archer & K. Browne (Eds.), *Human aggression: Naturalistic approaches* (pp. 94–121). London: Routledge.

Blurton Jones, N. (1972). Categories of child-child interaction. In N. Blurton Jones (Ed.), *Ethological studies of child behaviour* (pp. 97–127). Cambridge, UK: Cambridge University Press.

Boehm, C. (1999). *Hierarchy in the forest: The evolution of egalitarian behavior*. Cambridge, MA: Harvard University Press.

Bogoras, W. (1975). *The Chukchee*. New York: American Museum of Natural History.

Boulton, M. (1996). A comparison of 8- and 11-year-old girls' and boys' participation in specific types of rough-and-tumble play and aggressive fighting: Implications for functional hypotheses. *Aggressive Behavior, 22*, 271–287.

Boulton, M., & Smith, P. K. (1992). The social nature of playfighting and playchasing: Mechanisms and strategies underlying co-operation and compromise. In J. Barkow, L. Cosmides, & J. Tooby (Eds.), *The adapted mind* (pp. 429–444). New York: Oxford University Press.

Damas, D. (1991). Copper Eskimo. In D. Levinson (Editor-in-Chief), *Encyclopedia of world cultures*, T. O'Leary & D. Levinson (Volume Eds.), *Vol. I: North America* (pp. 76–79). Boston: G. K. Hall.

Darwin, C. (1998). *The descent of man*. New York: Prometheus Books. Originally published in 1871.

Dentan, R. (1968). *The Semai*. New York: Holt, Rinehart & Winston.

de Waal, F. (1989). *Peacemaking among primates*. Cambridge, MA: Harvard University Press.

Eibl-Eibesfeldt, I. (1961). The fighting behavior of animals. *Scientific American, 205*, 112–122.

Einon, D., & Potegal, M. (1991). Enhanced defense in adult rats deprived of playfighting experience as juveniles. *Aggressive Behavior, 17*, 27–40.

Endicott, K. (1979). *Batek Negrito religion: The world-view and rituals of a hunting and gathering people of Peninsular Malaysia*. Oxford, UK: Clarendon Press.

Endicott, K. (2013). Peaceful foragers: The significance of the Batek and Moriori for the question of innate human violence. In D. P. Fry (Ed.), *War, peace, and human nature: The convergence of evolutionary and cultural views* (pp. 243–261). New York: Oxford University Press.

Fagen, R. (1978). Evolutionary biological models of animal play behavior. In G. Burdghardt & M. Bekoff (Eds.), *The development of behavior: Comparative and evolutionary aspects* (pp. 385–404). New York: Garland STPM.

Fagen, R. (1981). *Animal play behavior*. New York: Oxford University Press.

Fry, D. P. (1987). Differences between playfighting and serious fighting among Zapotec children. *Ethology and Sociobiology, 8*, 285–306.

Fry, D. P. (1990). Play aggression among Zapotec children: Implications for the practice hypothesis. *Aggressive Behavior, 16*, 321–340.

Fry, D. P. (2000). Conflict management in cross-cultural perspective. In F. Aureli & F. de Waal (Eds.), *Natural conflict resolution* (pp. 334–351). Berkeley: University of California Press.

Fry, D. P. (2005). Rough-and-tumble social play in children. In A. Pellegrini & P. K. Smith (Eds.), *The nature of play: Great apes and humans*. New York: Guilford.

Fry, D. P. (2006). *The human potential for peace: An anthropological challenge to assumptions about war and violence*. New York: Oxford University Press.

Fry, D. P. (2007). *Beyond war: The human potential for peace*. New York: Oxford University Press.

Fry, D. P. (2011). Human nature: The nomadic forager model. In R. W. Sussman & C. R. Cloninger (Eds.), *Origins of altruism and cooperation* (pp. 227–247). New York: Springer.

Fry, D. P., Schober, G., & Björkqvist, K. (2010). Nonkilling as an evolutionary adaptation. In J. Evans Pim (Ed.), *Nonkilling societies* (pp. 101–128). Honolulu: Center for Global Nonkilling.

Fry, D. P. & Söderberg, P. (2013). Lethal aggression in mobile forager bands and implications for the origins of war. *Science, 341*, 270–273.

Fry, D. P. & Szala, A. (2013). The evolution of agonism: The triumph of restraint in nonhuman and human primates. In D. P. Fry (Ed.), *War, peace, and human nature: The convergence of evolutionary and cultural views* (pp. 451–474). New York: Oxford University Press.

Gardner, P. (2004). Respect for all: The Paliyans of South India. In G. Kemp & D. Fry (Eds.), *Keeping the peace: Conflict resolution and peaceful societies around the world* (pp. 53–71). New York: Routledge.

Gardner, P. (2013). South Indian foragers' conflict management in comparative perspective. In D. P. Fry (Ed.), *War, peace, and human nature: The convergence of evolutionary and cultural views* (pp. 297–314). New York: Oxford University Press.

Goodale, J. (1974). *Tiwi wives: A study of the women of Melville Island, North Australia*. Seattle: University of Washington Press.

Gusinde, M. (1931). *The Fireland Indians, Volume 1: The Selk'nam, on the life and thought of a hunting people of the Great Island of Tierra del Fuego. In the electronic Human Relations Area Files, Ona, Doc. 1*. New Haven, CT: HRAF, 1996, computer file.

Hamilton, W. (1964). The genetical evolution of social behaviour, II. *Journal of Theoretical Biology, 7*, 17–52.

Hamilton, W. (1971). Selection of selfish and altruistic behavior in some extreme models. In J. Eisenberg & W. Dillon (Eds.), *Man and beast: Comparative social behavior* (pp. 57–91). Washington, DC: Smithsonian Press.

Helm, J. (1956). Leadership among the Northeastern Athabascans. *Anthropologica, 2*, 131–163.

Hinde, R. (1974). *Biological bases of human social behaviour*. New York: McGraw-Hill.

Hoebel, E. A. (1967). *The law of primitive man: A study in comparative legal dynamics*. Cambridge, MA: Harvard University Press.

Holmberg, A. (1969). *Nomads of the Long Bow: The Siriono of Eastern Bolivia*. New York: American Museum of Natural History.

Hrdy, S. B. (1977). *The langurs of Abu*. Cambridge, MA: Harvard University Press.

Huntingford, F., & Turner, A. (1987). *Animal conflict*. London: Chapman & Hall.

Jochelson, W. (1926). *The Yukaghir and the Yukaghirized Tungus*. The Jesup North Pacific Expedition Memoir of the American Museum of Natural History, Volume IX. New York: G. E. Stechert.

Kelly, R. (1995). *The foraging spectrum: Diversity in hunter-gatherer lifeways*. Washington, DC: Smithsonian Institution Press.

Kokko, H. (2008). Animal behavioral studies: Non-primates. In L. Kurtz (Ed.-in-Chief), *Encyclopedia of violence, peace, and conflict (Vol. 1*, 2nd ed., pp. 47–56). New York: Elsevier/Academic Press.

Korpela, S., & Sandnabba, K. (1994). Gender-specific social experiences and the development of aggressive and sexual behavior in male mice. *Aggressive Behavior, 20*, 123–134.

Le Boeuf, B. (1971). The aggression of the breeding bulls. *Natural History, 80*, 83–94.

Le Clercq, C. (1910). New relation of Gaspesia. In W. Ganong (Trans. & Ed.), *Publications of the Champlain Society (Vol. 5*, pp. 1–452). Toronto: The Champlain Society.

Lee, R. (1979). *The !Kung San: Men, women, and work in a foraging community*. Cambridge, UK: Cambridge University Press.

Lee, R. (1993). *The Dobe Jul'hoansi*. Fort Worth: Harcourt Brace College.

Lips, J. (1947). *Naskapi law*. Philadelphia: American Philosophical Society.

Marlowe, F. (2005). Hunter-gatherers and human evolution. *Evolutionary Anthropology, 14*, 54–67.

Marlowe, F. (2010). *The Hadza*. Berkeley: University of California Press.

Maynard Smith, J. (1974). The theory of games and the evolution of animal conflicts. *Journal of Theoretical Biology, 47*, 209–221.

Maynard Smith, J., & Price, G. (1973). The logic of animal conflict. *Nature, 246*, 15–18.

Neill, S. (1976). Aggressive and non-aggressive fighting in twelve-to-thirteen year old preadolescent boys. *Journal of Child Psychology and Psychiatry, 17*, 213–220.

Neill, S. (1985). Rough-and tumble and aggression in schoolchildren: Serious play? *Animal Behaviour, 33*, 1380–1382.

Osgood, C. (1958). *Ingalik social culture*. New Haven: Yale University Publications in Anthropology, number 53.

Pellegrini, A. (1993). Boys' rough-and-tumble play, social competence and group composition. *British Journal of Developmental Psychology, 11*, 237–248.

Pellegrini, A. (1994). The rough play of adolescent boys of differing sociometric status. *International Journal of Behavioral Development, 17*, 525–540.

Pellegrini, A. (1995). Boys' rough-and-tumble play and social competence: Contemporary and longitudinal relations. In A. Pellegrini (Ed.), *The future of play theory: A multidisciplinary inquiry into the contributions of Brian Sutton-Smith* (pp. 107–126). Albany: State University of New York Press.

Pellegrini, A. (2002). Rough-and-tumble play from childhood through adolescence: Development and possible functions. In P. K. Smith & C. Hart (Eds.), *Handbook of childhood social development* (pp. 438–453). Oxford, UK: Blackwell.

Pellegrini, A. (2003). Perceptions and functions of play and real fighting in early adolescence. *Child Development, 74*, 1522–1533.

Pellis, S. (1984). Two aspects of play-fighting in a captive group of Oriental small-clawed otters Amblonyx cinerea. *Zeitschrift für Tierpsychologie, 65*, 77–83.

Pellis, S., & Pellis, V. (2007). Rough-and-tumble play and the development of the social brain. *Current Directions in Psychological Science, 16*, 95–98.

Pellis, S., & Pellis, V. (2009). *The playful brain: Venturing to the limits of neuroscience.* Oxford, UK: Oneworld.

Pennisi, E. (2000). The snarls and sneers that keep violence at bay. *Science, 289*, 576–577.

Reyna, S. (1994). A mode of domination approach to organized violence. In S. Reyna & R. Downs (Eds.), *Studying war: Anthropological perspectives* (pp. 29–65). The Netherlands: Gordon & Breach.

Roscoe, P. (2007). Intelligence, coalitional killing, and the antecedents of war. *American Anthropologist, 109*, 485–495.

Scott, E., & Panksepp, J. (2003). Rough-and-tumble play in human children. *Aggressive Behavior, 29*, 539–551.

Riechert, E. (1998). Game theory and animal contests. In L. Dugatkin & H. Reeve (Eds.), *Game theory and animal behavior* (pp. 64–93). New York: Oxford University Press.

Schaller, G. (1972). *The Serengeti lion.* Chicago: University of Chicago.

Service, E. (1966). *The hunters.* Englewood Cliffs, NJ: Prentice-Hall.

Shternberg, L. (1999). *The social organization of the Gilyak.* Edited by B. Grant. Anthropological Papers of the American Museum of Natural History, number 82. Seattle: University of Washington Press.

Smith, P. K. (1982). Does play matter? Functional and evolutionary aspects of animal and human play. *Behavioral and Brain Sciences, 5*, 139–184.

Smith, P. K. (1997). Play fighting and real fighting: Perspectives on their relationship. In A. Schmitt, K. Atswanger, K. Grammer, & K. Schafer (Eds.), *New aspects of human ethology* (pp. 47–64). New York: Plenum.

Smith, P. K., & Boulton, M. (1990). Rough-and-tumble play, aggression and dominance: Perception and behaviour in children's encounters. *Human Development, 33*, 271–282.

Smith, P. K., Hunter, T., Carvalho, A., & Costabile, A. (1992). Children's perceptions of playfighting, playchasing and real fighting: A cross-national interview study. *Social Development, 1*, 211–229.

Smith, P. K., & Lewis, K. (1985). Rough-and-tumble play, fighting, and chasing in nursery school children. *Ethology and Sociobiology, 6*, 175–181.

Smith, P. K., Smees, R., Pellegrini, A., & Menesini, E. (2002). In J. Roopnarine (Ed.), *Conceptual, social-cognitive, and contextual issues in the fields of play* (pp. 235–245). Westport, CT: Ablex.

Steward, J. (1968). Causal factors and processes in the evolution of pre-farming societies. In R. Lee & I. DeVore (Eds.), *Man the hunter* (pp. 321–334). Chicago: Aldine.

Symons, D. (1978). *Play and aggression: A study of rhesus monkeys.* New York: Columbia University Press.

Tonkinson, R. (1978). *The Mardudjara Aborigines: Living the dream in Australia's desert.* New York: Holt, Rinehart, & Winston.

Westermarck, Edward (1924). *The origin and development of the moral ideas.* London: Macmillan.

Wilson, E. (1975). *Sociobiology: The new synthesis.* Cambridge, MA: Harvard University Press.

Wilson, M., & Wrangham, R. (2003). Intergroup relations in chimpanzees. *Annual Review of Anthropology, 32*, 363–392.

Wolf, E. (2001). Cycles of violence: The anthropology of war and peace. In D. Barash (Ed.), *Understanding violence* (pp. 192–199). Boston: Allyn & Bacon.

{ Commentary }

Evolutionary Adaptation and Violent Aggression
FROM MYTHS TO REALITIES
Riane Eisler

Douglas P. Fry (2006) presented an excellent survey of the literature on ritualized nonlethal aggression in both nonhuman species and human nomadic foragers. His thesis is that over the course of evolution, restraint of aggression was adaptive for most species, including ours. Fry's paper makes important points, showing that ideas such as "killer apes" and other myths about primate and human nature are not borne out by the data (e.g., de Waal, 2009). For example, Fry notes that habitual or repeated killers do not gain status in foraging groups, as has been stated or implied in some sociobiological writings and other works. On the contrary, they are often killed or expelled from the group.

Fry also debunks the notion that the only way to prevent anarchy and maintain social cohesion and order is through strict top-down control. Fry notes: "Lacking authoritative leadership, nomadic band societies nonetheless manage to deal with much conflict through avoidance, discussion, group meetings, contests, ostracism, and other nonviolent or aggression-limiting ways" (p. 168). These important points, are not highlighted in the present chapter, although he discusses them thoroughly elsewhere (Fry, 2006, 2007).

Fry (2006) notes that foraging cultures vary in the degree that homicide is present, indicating that this is a function of cultural norms. This issue is of more than academic interest: it is one of the critical questions for our species—and one that, in contrast to our genetic heritage, we *can* affect through human agency (Eisler, 2013; Eisler and Levine, 2002).

One area I would particularly have wanted to see explained more is the issue of learning, especially through early childhood experiences, and the connection of learning with the acceptance and use of violence. For example, in describing the Semai, a culture noted for nonviolence, the author quotes R. K. Dentan as writing that "even if a child wanted to become violent, it would have no very clear idea of how to proceed," since in a cultural environment that values nurturance and affiliation, the young have little opportunity to learn aggressive behavior by observation and imitation (Dentan, 1978).

This matter of learning merits much more academic attention. For example, some studies suggest that many U.S. soldiers have to be taught to kill (Grossman and Degaetano, 1999)—a suggestion that would support Fry's point about restraint of aggression developing as an evolutionary adaptation. But most contemporary world cultures have idealized killing as heroic for men through epics passed on from generation to generation (Eisler, 1987, 1995). And today we even have video games that graphically teach boys to kill as an entertaining and "manly" accomplishment, not to speak of the environment in Muslim fundamentalist cultures where children are taught that killing Westerners is blessed and rewarded by Allah, and that killing girls or women suspected of sexual independence is honorable and necessary—as the measure of a man's status is the degree to which he controls others, starting with the women in his family (e.g., Abu-Lughod, 1986).

This leads to an area of violent behavior that is extremely important, and that varies enormously from culture to culture: violence against women and children. Fry does not discuss this violence at all, even though there are strong indications of a cross-cultural correlation between the acceptance of violence against women and children and intertribal raids, warfare, and terrorism (Eisler, 1987, 1995). If we are discussing the development of human nature from early experience, then these matters are critical (Eisler, 2007; Eisler and Levine, 2002).

This said, Fry makes an important contribution by countering notions that are still propagated by some evolutionary theorists that warfare and rape are "evolutionary adaptations" (e.g., Pinker, 2002). And precisely because these ideas have so much traction in popular culture, it is important to highlight studies such as those presented by Fry as forcefully disproving these kinds of assertions.

Still, I would have liked in this article to see more specific discussion of these two critical points:

1. Evidence showing that restraint of aggressive violence—rather than aggressive violence—was an evolutionary adaptation, with specific references to the works of sociobiologists and evolutionary psychologist that propagate a contrary view.
2. Data on the interaction of genes and cultures, with particular attention to what cultural norms at all levels—from intimate relations to international relations—must be understood and changed so there is less violence in human relations across the board. I suggest this because I believe that the crux of the matter is not our genetic or evolutionary heritage but rather gene expression—which is always a matter of the interaction of genes and experiences as molded by cultures.

References

Abu-Lughod, L. (1986). *Veiled sentiments*. Berkeley: University of California Press.

de Waal, F. (2009). *The age of empathy: Nature's lessons for a kinder society.* New York: Harmony.

Dentan, R. K. (1978). Notes on childhood in a nonviolent context: The Semai case. In A. Montagu (Ed.), *Learning non-aggression*. Oxford, UK: Oxford University Press.

Eisler, R. (1987). *The chalice and the blade: Our history, our future.* New York: Harper & Row.

Eisler, R. (1995). *Sacred pleasure: Sex, myth, and the politics of the body*, New York: Harper Collins.

Eisler, R. (2007). *The real wealth of nations: Creating a caring economics*. San Francisco: Berrett-Koehler.

Eisler, R. (2013). Protecting the majority of humanity: Toward an integrated approach to crimes against present and future generations. In M. Cordonier Segger and S. Jodoin (Eds.), *Securing the rights of future generations: Sustainable development and the Rome Statute of the International Criminal Court*. Cambridge, UK: Cambridge University Press.

Eisler, R., & Levine, D. S. (2002). Nurture, nature, and caring: We are not prisoners of our genes. *Brain and Mind, 3*, 9–52.

Fry, D. (2006). *The human potential for peace: An anthropological challenge to assumptions about war and violence*. New York: Oxford University Press.

Fry, D. (2007). *Beyond war: The human potential for peace*. New York: Oxford University Press.

Grossman, D., & Degaetano, G. (1999). *Stop teaching our kids to kill: A call to action against TV, movie and video game violence*. New York: Crown Publishers.

Pinker, S. (2002). *The blank slate: The modern denial of human nature*. New York: Viking.

8

Play Theory of Hunter-Gatherer Egalitarianism

Peter Gray

Here's the puzzle. Almost everywhere we look, human beings, especially men, organize themselves into hierarchical social structures. We see hierarchical organization
in prestate tribes headed by chiefs or "big men." We see it in the governments of all
states and nations, with their top-down structures of power. We see it in businesses,
where bosses tell employees what to do. We see it in schools, where principals tell
teachers what to do and teachers tell students what to do. We see it in gangs and
in many sorts of male gatherings, where boys or men jockey, sometimes violently,
for status or dominance. We also see that most other species of primates live in
hierarchically organized groups, with alpha individuals (generally males) at the top
and frequent squabbling for status. And yet, there is one very significant cultural
category of human beings where we don't see hierarchical organization. We don't
see it in band hunter-gatherers (as defined in chapter 1).

In all band hunter-gatherer societies that have been studied, the dominant cultural ethos is one of individual autonomy, nonviolence, sharing, cooperation, and
consensual decision making (Ingold, 1999). Their core value, which underlies all of
the rest, is that of the equality of individuals. They do not have chiefs or other leaders of the type who tell others what to do; they make all group decisions through
discussions aimed at consensus. If it is true that strivings for status and dominance
are intrinsic to human nature, then hunter-gatherers somehow overcome that aspect
of their nature and apparently have been doing so for a long, long time. How do
they it?

The writings of anthropologists make it clear that hunter-gatherers are not
passively egalitarian; they are actively so. Indeed, in the words of anthropologist
Richard Lee (1988, p. 264), they are "fiercely egalitarian." They do not tolerate
anyone's hoarding food or other goods, boasting, putting on airs, or trying to lord
it over others. On the basis of such observations, Christopher Boehm (1993, 1999)
developed what he calls the *reverse dominance theory* of hunter-gatherer egalitarianism. His theory is that hunter-gatherers everywhere have learned to turn the
dominance hierarchy upside down, so that the band as a whole acts in concert to

suppress any individuals who attempt to dominate them. They use ridicule, shunning, and threats of ostracism to counteract any budding alpha male behavior. At the extreme, they might banish a domineering person from the band. On the very rare occasions when even banishment doesn't work, where the offender continues to hang around and use violence to dominate others, they might, if it's the only solution, stop the perpetrator with capital punishment or the threat of it. They have, of course, no prisons, so they have no other way to stop someone who cannot be dissuaded from violence. Boehm presents a powerful case for this theory, and I have no doubt that he is correct. But, as a supplement to his theory, I have previously suggested what I call the *play theory* of hunter-gatherer egalitarianism (Gray, 2009a, 2012a), which I develop further and more explicitly in the present chapter.

In brief, the play theory is that hunter-gatherers have learned, over their long history, to foster the playful side of their human nature as a way to promote good will and egalitarian behavior within and across bands. In all mammals, social play is a form of behavior that requires cooperation, fairness, and the setting aside of dominance. Hunter-gatherers, I suggest, combat the tendency toward dominance by imbuing nearly all of their social life with a spirit of play. To develop the theory, I'll first discuss the role of play in promoting egalitarian behavior in nonhuman animals and then some of the many ways that hunter-gatherers seem to use play to maintain peace and equality (the latter part draws from and expands on my previous article on play as a foundation for hunter-gatherer social life—Gray, 2009a).

Play and Egalitarian Behavior in Nonhuman Mammals

WHY SOCIAL PLAY IS NECESSARILY COOPERATIVE AND EGALITARIAN

The young of nearly all mammals play with one another, most commonly by engaging in mock fighting and chasing. A play fight is in many ways the opposite of a real fight. It may include movements and postures resembling a real fight, but the goal is opposite.

While the goal of a real fight is to end the fight as quickly as possible by winning and driving off or asserting dominance over the other, the goal of a play fight is to keep the interaction going for the pleasure and, perhaps, the practice it provides. To keep it going, each animal must avoid hurting or threatening the other, that is, avoid winning or even appearing as if it wants to win. Play always requires the voluntary participation of both (or all) partners, so play is always an exercise in restraint and in retaining the other's good will. If one player fails at that, the other will quit and the play will end. Play very often involves animals that differ considerably in age, size, and strength. To keep the play going, the larger, stronger, or otherwise more dominant animal must continuously self-handicap, so as not to intimidate the other. Thus, play is always an egalitarian, cooperative activity.

Extensive research on play fighting in rats reveals that, for this species at least, the preferred positions generally are the more vulnerable defensive ones, such as the belly-up position (Pellis, 2002; Pellis and Pellis, 1998). Apparently, one evolutionary function of such play is to practice getting out of such positions. The animals more or less take turns at this. The stronger one must not exert full strength against the weaker one when on top because only when the weaker one breaks out of a pin can the stronger one get a turn at being in the vulnerable position. This, too, makes a play fight opposite to a real fight. In a real fight, of course, the preferred position is the dominant, attack position, and no rat in a real fight would voluntarily relinquish that position unless the other signaled defeat. Voluntary acceptance or choice of the vulnerable position distinguishes play fighting from real fighting in other species as well (Bekoff, 2004).

Similarly, in playful chasing, the preferred position for at least many species of animals is that of being chased rather than that of chasing, just as it is in human games of tag. Again, the preferred position is the more vulnerable one, the one that would normally be that of the subordinate or loser (in a fight) or the prey (in a predatory encounter), not that of the dominant animal. So, play reverses the preferences of serious life; in play it is better to be subordinate and vulnerable than to be dominant and invulnerable. (An exception to this occurs in the chasing play of some predatory animals, including wolves and dogs, that run down their prey. For them, chasing play appears to serve as practice in predation, and the position of pursuer appears to be at least as valued as that of being pursued.)

Marc Bekoff (2001, 2004) has pointed out that, in play, animals exhibit behaviors that are considered to be core elements of morality when they occur in humans. These include making a deal (a social contract), trusting, behaving fairly, apologizing, and forgiving. The play starts with some sort of signal, given by one and returned by the other, which essentially says, "Let's not fight, mate, or ignore one another right now; let's play." For dogs, wolves, and other canids, the common signal for play is the play bow, in which each animal crouches down on forelimbs and elevates on hindlimbs. For primates, it is the relaxed open-mouth display, or play face, which is homologous to playful laughing and smiling in humans. That's how the deal is initiated and sealed. Then, during the play, each animal must play fairly, which means abiding by the rules of not hurting or threatening the other while going through the motions of fighting or chasing in ways that at least partly resemble patterns of real fighting and chasing. If one animal accidently hurts another, perhaps by nipping too hard in a moment of excitement, an apology is due. The apology may take the form of backing off and again manifesting the play signal, perhaps repeatedly. Forgiveness is manifested if the nipped animal accepts the apology and rejoins the play.

According to Bekoff (2004), who has spent a long career studying play in canids, animals rarely cheat in play, which would occur if they sealed the contract to play and then broke it by seriously attacking when the other was in a vulnerable position. Those few who do cheat—as Bekoff observed very rarely in young coyotes—tend to become social isolates and have shortened lives because others avoid them. One function of play in animals might be to test one another's willingness and capacity to stick to a social agreement.

It is important to distinguish play fighting from ritualized aggression. Many species of animals engage in nonviolent ritualized contests as means of establishing dominance without risking injury (Natarajan and Caramaschi, 2010). Depending on the species, they may puff themselves up while facing one another, paw the ground, butt horns, pound their chests, screech, hiss, or show their teeth or other weapons in postures of mutual threat until one or the other backs off or until the confrontation escalates into violence. These are competitive, not cooperative interactions. They are closely related to real fighting, not to play. Some of the intense competitive games played by humans in our culture, where winning has real-world consequences, might be regarded as blends of play and ritualized aggression (Gray, 2009b), but there is little if any evidence that such blends occur in other species.

In all mammals, play is more common in the young than in adults. That is part of the evidence that a major evolutionary function of play is to provide practice in skills that the young must develop for their long-term survival. The skills that appear to be practiced include physical skills, such as those needed for fighting, preying, and fleeing; social skills, such as restraint, cooperation, and sensitivity to other's signals; and emotional skills, such as the ability to regulate or minimize fear and anger in close encounters with conspecifics (e.g., LaFreniere, 2011; Pellis and Pellis, 2011; Pellis, Pellis, and Bell, 2010).

Play among adults is rare or nonexistent in many species but is relatively common in others. Some research with primates suggests that adult play is more common for species that live in relatively loosely structured groups, where individuals are not regularly in close contact, than for those that live in more tightly structured groups (Pellis and Iwaniuk, 2000). In these cases, play may be a way of reasserting affiliation upon contact and testing one another's willingness to get along without fighting. A good portion of the adult–adult play in such species is cross sex, and in that case it is often a prelude to mating. Other research suggests that adult–adult play is also relatively common in pack-hunting animals such as wolves, which, like human hunters, must cooperate in killing large game (Cordoni, 2009). Still other research (described next) suggests that primates that live in relatively egalitarian social groups engage in more adult play, and play differently as juveniles, compared with primates that live in steeply hierarchical groups.

PLAY RELATED TO EGALITARIAN SOCIAL ORGANIZATION IN MACAQUES

All species of macaque monkeys live in multi-male, multi-female social colonies. For some species, most notably Japanese macaques (*Macaca fuscata*), these colonies are steeply hierarchical, characterized by sharp power differences between dominants and subordinates, frequent unidirectional attacks, prominent submissive signals, and relative lack of friendly interactions among non-kin. At the other extreme, Tonkean macaques (*Macaca tonkeana*) and crested macaques (*Macaca nigra*) live in relatively egalitarian colonies, where individuals are relatively unconcerned with rank, rarely attack one another, do not have formal signals of submission, and engage often in friendly interactions with non-kin as well as with kin (Ciani, Dall'Olio, Stanyon, and Palagi, 2012; Matsumura, 1999; Thierry, 2000). These differences apply to relationships among females as well as among males, and to relations between females and males.

In observations of captive colonies living in semi-natural conditions, Ciani and colleagues (2012) found much more play, both among juveniles and among adults, in the egalitarian Tonkean macaques than in the more despotic Japanese macaques. The difference in adult play, however, was accounted for entirely by differences in play among females. Female Tonkeans played extensively with one another, whereas female Japanese did not play at all with one another. There was no difference between the two species in amount of play observed among adult males. The researchers suggest that adult play may serve different functions for male and female macaques. Males must leave their natal colony and join a new one when they reach adulthood, so play for them may be a way of establishing new relationships, a function that may be as important in steeply hierarchical species as in egalitarian ones. For females, who stay in their native colony, adult play may be primarily a means of maintaining egalitarian relationships among long-term friends, which is crucial to the Tonkean macaque way of life but not to the Japanese macaque way of life.

Other research indicates that the manner of play for the more egalitarian species differs from that for Japanese macaques (Petit, Bertrand, and Thierry, 2008; Reinhart et al., 2010). Young Tonkean and crested macaques commonly wrestle while lying on their sides or backs, in a manner that bears little resemblance to real fighting, and often engage in group play, with multiple partners, in which they cluster into "writhing masses of bodies." In contrast, young Japanese macaques play-fight almost entirely in dyads, in which they adopt defensive postures and play-bite in ways that mimic the postures and attacks of real fighting. These observations suggest that the young of the egalitarian species are practicing different sets of skills in their play than are the young of the hierarchical species. The former appear to be practicing social skills that enable close contact without fighting or fleeing, whereas the latter appear to be practicing fighting and may also be gaining information about one another's strengths and weaknesses for use in dominance struggles to come.

PLAY RELATED TO EGALITARIAN BEHAVIOR IN BONOBOS

Bonobos and chimpanzees are our two closest animal relatives. We are equally related to the two species; the branch of ape ancestry that led to both chimpanzees and bonobos split off from that which led to us approximately 6 million years ago

(Corballis, 1999). Bonobos and chimps look quite similar to one another and in some ways have similar social structures, but bonobos are much more egalitarian than are chimpanzees or any of the other apes. Bonobos are also the most playful of all apes, especially in adulthood (Palagi, 2008).

Male bonobos do form dominance hierarchies, but their hierarchies are subtler and involve less fighting than is the case for chimpanzee male hierarchies (Surbeck, Deschner, Schubert, Weltring, and Hohmann, 2012). The most striking social difference between the two species, however, is that female bonobos are generally dominant over males (Parish and de Waal, 2000), whereas chimpanzees show the more typical primate pattern of male dominance over females, which is sometimes quite violent (Muller, Kahlenberg, and Wrangham, 2009).

Female bonobos are dominant over males even though they are smaller and weaker than them. They achieve dominance because they form close social bonds with one another and come to one another's aid in aggressive encounters with males (Parish and de Waal, 2000). Male bonobos, in contrast, do not help one another in encounters with females. As part and parcel of their capacity to cooperate, female bonobos maintain highly egalitarian, friendly relationships with one another (Palagi, 2011). Their capacity to form and maintain such relationships is all the more striking given that bonobos (like chimpanzees, but opposite from macaques) practice female exogamy—the females, not the males, leave their natal group and join a new one upon reaching adulthood. Thus, the bonds formed among female adult bonobos are generally among individuals that are not close relatives and were not raised together. The females apparently build and maintain these relationships at least partly through play (Palagi, 2011).

In one study, Palagi (2006) compared the social behaviors of a captive group of bonobos with those of a captive group of chimpanzees, both housed in semi-natural conditions. As expected, she observed far more egalitarian behavior in the bonobos than in the chimps. The bonobos showed fewer one-way attacks and fewer bared-teeth displays and other signals of fear or submission than did the chimps. She observed equivalent amounts of play among immature animals for the two species, but far more adult–adult play among bonobos than among chimps. Adult chimps often played with immature chimps, but almost never with one another. Among the adult bonobos, females played with other females more often than with males and far more often than males played with one another. In further research focused just on adult bonobos, Palagi and Paoli (2007) found that rough-and-tumble contact play (as opposed to noncontact forms of play such as pirouetting) was much more common in female–female dyads than in female–male dyads and was completely absent in male–male dyads. That study also revealed a significant correlation between play and other signs of affiliation. Females that played frequently together also often groomed one another and sat in physical contact with one another.

Palagi and her colleagues also found evidence that adult bonobos use play to prevent or reduce agonistic encounters in stressful situations. In one study, play was most frequent during the prefeeding period, a time when tension in the group is especially high because of anticipated competition for food (Palagi, Paoli, and Tarli, 2006). In another study, play signals and noncontact forms of play among adults increased significantly when the animals were temporarily restricted to relatively crowded indoor quarters (Tacconi and Palagi, 2009).

How Hunter-Gatherers Use Play to Promote Peace and Equality

The research just described suggests that play may help animals to establish and maintain friendships, reduce aggression, and cooperate. Humans, when free to do so, play more than any other primate, and the capacity for play extends into adulthood for humans even more than for bonobos. Moreover, for humans, unlike bonobos, adult play is at least as common among males as it is among females.

My thesis here is that a major evolutionary reason for the extension of human play into adulthood—that is, a major reason for the natural selection of adult playfulness in humans—was that it enabled the high degree of cooperation and sharing essential to the hunter-gatherer way of life. Bands of humans that played together were more likely to stick together, cooperate, and share—and thereby to survive—than bands that did not play together. This is a group selection explanation, but I also suggest an individual-selection explanation. If hunter-gatherer groups expelled domineering, aggressive people (as implied by Boehm's reverse dominance theory) or in other ways reduced their participation in the gene pool, this would have contributed to genetic selection for playfulness, if playfulness reduces the tendency toward aggression and dominance. Sexual selection might also have played a role. The more fully a culture shunned aggressive men, the greater would be the likelihood that women would shun them as mating partners. So, we have here the possibility of a conjoining of cultural and biological evolution. The more a culture promoted play as a value and devalued aggression, the more selection there would be for the genetic capacity for adult play. In turn, more genetic capacity for adult play would allow hunter-gatherers to add ever-greater degrees of playfulness to their cultural practices.

The rest of this chapter is primarily about the playfulness of hunter-gatherer cultural practices and the apparent roles of play in promoting the egalitarian values of these cultures. But first, a few words about the general nature of human play.

THE NATURE OF HUMAN PLAY AND PLAYFULNESS

Play, both in animals and in humans, is generally characterized by researchers as behavior that is (1) *self-chosen* (voluntary) and (2) *intrinsically motivated* (conducted apparently for its own sake, for pleasure, rather than for some end outside of itself)

(Bekoff and Byers, 1981; Burghardt, 2011; Gray, 2012b). As is often acknowledged by play researchers, characteristic 2 presents a challenge from an evolutionary perspective because the ubiquity of play suggests that it must serve some useful, survival purpose or purposes. A route around this seeming contradiction is to elaborate on the meaning of "intrinsically motivated" so that it refers to behavior that is not motivated by a drive state other than a hypothesized play drive and is not oriented toward some end that naturally terminates the behavior. The behavior may resemble fighting, predation, fleeing, or mating (or any or all of these mixed together) in some ways, but is not motivated by hostility, hunger, fear, or sexual drive and does not result in the consummatory ends that those drives are oriented toward. Unlike behaviors motivated by other drives, play has no apparent goal, if goal is defined as some specific consequence that naturally terminates the behavior.

Researchers who focus on human play commonly add further characteristics, beyond the two just mentioned, to their full definition of play—characteristics that would be difficult to apply in observations of animals. Elsewhere, I have elaborated on a five-characteristic definition of human play, derived from combining the definitions of many play scholars (Gray, 2012b). By this definition, play is activity that is (1) *self-chosen and self-directed*; (2) *intrinsically motivated* (not motivated by a drive other than a hypothesized play drive and not oriented toward ends that terminate it); (3) *guided by mental rules* (which give structure to the activity, but which also permit creativity within that structure); (4) *imaginative* (in some way separate, in the players' minds, from real-world, serious activity); and (5) *conducted in an active, alert, but relatively nonstressed frame of mind*. People who study animal play tend to see play as categorical, all or none, perhaps because it generally is all-or-none in animals, or perhaps because it is difficult to identify gradations of play in animals' behavior. But people who study human play see it as existing in all possible gradations. An activity is seen as more or less playful to the degree that it has all five of the characteristics just listed.

In their writings about hunter-gatherers, anthropologists and other observers often refer to the "good nature," "cheerfulness," and "humor" of the people they observed, but do not often use the specific terms "play" or "playful" in describing their activities. One researcher, in response to my question about that, suggested that anthropologists may avoid these terms at least partly because they could be interpreted as derogatory—a way of suggesting that the people are "childish" or irresponsible. From my perspective, play ranks among the supreme human activities, so I have no hesitation in using "play" and "playful" to describe admirable activities and qualities of a cultural group. In fact, elsewhere I have suggested that the play drive is equivalent to what humanistic psychologists refer to as the self-actualization drive, which lies at the top of Maslow's hierarchy of human motives (Gray, 2011, p. 579). In my examination of anthropologists' writings on hunter-gatherers, I have used the five-part definition, above, to identify activities as playful, regardless of whether the writer specifically referred to them as "play" or "playful" (Gray, 2009a). What follows is a summary of the results of that examination.

GAMES AS COOPERATIVE, BONDING ACTIVITIES

One of the most surprising discoveries about hunter-gatherers—especially to those indoctrinated in the Hobbesian view that life in prestate societies is "solitary, poor, nasty, brutish, and short"—is that they have a lot of free time, and they use much of that time for activities that most of us would call play. Indeed, one researcher (Sahlins, 1972) famously referred to hunter-gatherer cultures in general as "the original affluent society"—affluent not because they have so much, but because they want so little. They can satisfy those wants with relatively little work, and, as a result, they have a lot of free time. One study of the Ju/'hoansi revealed that on average men spend about 2.7 hours per day and women about 2.1 hours per day at food-getting (hunting and gathering), and about 3 hours more on subsistence-related tasks around camp, such as food preparation, cooking, and making tools (Lee, 1984). In the words of another researcher who studied the Ju/'hoansi (Shostak, 1981, p. 10), the people spend the rest of their waking time at such activities as "singing and composing songs, playing musical instruments, sewing intricate bead designs, telling stories, playing games, visiting, or just lying around and resting." Observations of other hunter-gatherer groups have produced similar conclusions (Rowley-Conway, 2001; Sahlins, 1972).

A striking aspect of the games that hunter-gatherers play is that they are rarely if ever competitive. In a cross-cultural analysis conducted many years ago, Roberts and colleagues concluded that the only societies that regularly lack competitive games are hunter-gatherer societies (see Sutton-Smith and Roberts, 1970). In a survey of 10 anthropologists who had observed play in seven different hunter-gatherer cultures, which Ogas and I conducted some years ago, only two said they had seen competitive play, and they said they had seen it rarely (Gray, 2009a). Even when hunter-gatherers play games such as soccer, which they learn from outsiders and are played competitively by outsiders, they find ways to play noncompetitively. Consistent with their egalitarian ethos, hunter-gatherers choose to avoid any assertion of superiority over others, in games as in any other activities. As a result, their games are more clearly and fully play than are our games, which are confounded by the motive to win. Their group games generally involve a high degree of coordination and cooperation among the players, and many are dancelike.

The most extensive account of games for any hunter-gatherer group is that provided by Lorna Marshall (1976) concerning the Ju/'hoansi. One game she describes is a line game, played by women and girls, in which the players toss a melon (or a ball if they have one) over their heads, to the person behind them, so that it keeps moving from one to another in a fluid motion, in time to music as the players sing and dance in unison. Many different songs are used in this game, and mothers often play with babies on their backs.

Another game, played by men and boys, is called (for unknown reasons) the porcupine game. This game is superficially competitive, but, according to Marshall, nobody keeps score or cares, beyond a moment or two, who "wins" a given bout. The players form two lines (teams), and on each bout one player from each team steps forth and challenges one from the other. In response to a cue from the chanting of the whole group, each one thrusts out either of his two hands toward the other—one of which holds an imaginary axe and the other of which holds an imaginary assegai. The game is a bit like rock, paper, and scissors. If both thrust out the same arm, the challenger wins, otherwise he loses. According to Marshall, the winner pantomimes great joy, and the loser sorrow, but in reality nobody cares who wins or loses, and no cumulative score is kept. The other players in the lines chant or sing the whole time, and musical instruments may be played to accompany the actions. The fun lies in the drama they create.

Although some games, such as the above two, are played just by one sex or the other, many others are played by both together. In general, the games involve as many players as wish to participate and often include children and adults together. The games seem to focus on rhythm, coordination, and joining together as if they were a single entity. Whether intentionally or not, they clearly seem to be activities that help to unite the band.

In his writings about the Mbuti, Turnbull (1982, pp. 142–143) described how these people play ceremonial games of tug-of-war that seem to mock the idea of competition. Men and boys take one side of a vine rope, women and girls take the other, and they sing in antiphony as they pull. In Turnbull's words:

"[When the men and boys start to win], one of them will abandon his side and join the women, pulling up his bark-cloth and adjusting it in the fashion of women, shouting encouragement to them in a falsetto, ridiculing womanhood by the very exaggeration of his mime.... [Then, when the women and girls start to win], one of them adjusts her bark clothing, letting it down, and strides over to the men's side and joins their shouting in a deep bass voice, similarly gently mocking manhood.... Each person crossing over tries to outdo the ridicule of the last, causing more and more laughter, until when the contestants are laughing so hard they cannot sing or pull any more, they let go of the vine rope and fall to the ground in near hysteria. Although both youth and adults cross sides, it is primarily the youth who really enact the ridicule.... The ridicule is performed without hostility, rather with a sense of at least partial identification and empathy. It is in this way that the violence and aggressivity of either sex 'winning' is avoided, and the stupidity of competitiveness is demonstrated."

THE PLAYFUL, EGALITARIAN NATURE OF HUNTER-GATHERER RELIGIONS

The idea that religion is an extension of play is not new. For example, Miller (1970, p. 168), in his *Gods and Games: Toward a Theology of Play*, contends that faith arises from "being gripped by a story, a ritual (game). It is being seized...by a pattern of meaning that affects one's life pattern, that becomes a paradigm for the way one sees the world.... Faith is make-believe. It is playing as if it were true." Faith, by anyone's definition, is belief that does not require empirical proof; it is belief that people choose to accept. That, logically, is make-believe. The idea that religions, in all their diversity, originated and evolved culturally because they helped to promote the cohesion and survival of the groups that practice them is also not new; it is, for example, a theme of Wilson's (2002), *Darwin's Cathedral: Evolution, Religion, and the Nature of Society*.

Combining the idea of religion as play with the idea that religions promote group survival, I suggest that religions help groups survive partly because they provide a life narrative, a story that enables individuals to regulate their own behavior in group-promoting rather than egoistic ways. By entering into the story and living it out, people turn all of life into something of a group game, wherein all are playing by the same broad set of rules. The story gives meaning and purpose to the norms, rules, and values of the social group, and in doing so it also gives meaning and purpose to each person's life. From this point of view it makes sense that religions that arise at any given time and place reflect—and thereby help guide—the predominant modes of human life at that time and place.

It makes sense that Judaism, Christianity, and Islam—which arose in hierarchical societies and reached their apogees in feudal times—all posit a steeply hierarchical spiritual cosmos. When most people are slaves, servants, or serfs, a religion espousing the virtues of servitude to lords and masters—and ultimately to an all-powerful god, who is king of kings—gives meaning to a life of servitude and helps maintain the earthly hierarchies. Similarly, in hunter-gatherer societies, where group cohesion and survival depend on cooperation and sharing among equals, a religion in which the spirit world consists of many gods or spirits who are all relatively equal to one another and must find ways to get along makes sense. It also makes sense that hunter-gatherer religions would be more obviously playful than the hierarchical religions that followed them because play and hierarchy are incongruous.

Hunter-gatherer religions are playful beyond the ways that all religions are in the sense that they (1) are nondogmatic, (2) involve gods and spirits who are playful, and (3) involve ceremonies that are carried out in a spirit of play and creativity rather than one of somber worship or repetitive ritual. Here I'll summarize evidence for these three claims, one at a time.

Researchers who write about hunter-gatherer religions commonly emphasize their nondogmatic nature (e.g., Endicott, 1979; Guenther, 199; Kent, 1996; Tsuru, 1998). In part because they have no writing to solidify the stories and no authorities to enforce doctrine, the stories and ceremonies vary from band to band within any given hunter-gatherer culture and from time to time within any given band. In some cases the variations contradict one another, but nobody is bothered by the contradictions. When children reach adulthood and marry into another band, where they adopt different religious beliefs and practices, parents are unfazed. The people move freely from one set of religious beliefs to a somewhat different set just as you and I might move freely from one game to another that is played by a somewhat different set of rules.

Although hunter-gatherers find meaning in their religious stories and beliefs, they apparently do not confound them with empirical reality. Thomas (2006) reports that when the Ju/'hoansi she observed used religious stories to explain natural phenomena, they did so in a light-hearted manner. For example, in a religious context, a man explained, in story-telling mode, that the stars disappear during the daytime because they are ant lions, who come out at night and crawl back into their sandy pits at dawn. But later, when the same man was asked the same question in a nonreligious context, he responded, matter-of-factly, that the stars remain in the sky all day but can't be seen because the sun is too bright.

Researchers also report that hunter-gatherers are generally practical people, who ground their decisions in experience, not in magic or superstition. For example, according to Kirk Endicott (1979, p. 22), "[The Batek] go about their daily lives with few of the signs of those 'irrational' behaviors that cry out 'religion' to the anthropologist.... They seem to believe that they can succeed at such projects [as hunting and fishing] if they just do them correctly and take proper care." Similarly, Thomas (1959, p. 152) describes how the/Gwi people (hunter-gatherer neighbors to the Ju/'hoansi) have a rain dance, not to bring on rain, but to rejoice when they can see from the sky that rain is coming. Living in the desert, where water is the limiting factor for life, they would certainly dance to bring on rain if they thought it would work, but they do not believe they have such power. They can, however, dance to lift their own spirits and prepare for the rain and the bounty to follow. Gould (1969, p. 128) makes the same point regarding the Yiwara, of the Australian Desert, stating: "[They] do not seek to control the environment in either their daily or sacred lives. Rituals of the sacred may be seen as efforts of man to combine with his environment, to become 'at one' with it." From the perspective of this chapter, it is a small step to suggest that in such ceremonies hunter-gatherers turn natural phenomena into playmates, thereby uniting with nature as they unite among themselves.

Researchers also often contrast the playful, whimsical gods and spirits of hunter-gatherers with the more fearsome gods and spirits of nearby farmers. According to Endicott (1979), for example, the hunter-gather Batek do not generally believe, as the agricultural Malays do, that the environment is populated with evil spirits, which must be continuously avoided, combated, or propitiated. Likewise, Turnbull (1968) contrasts the playful religious practices of the Mbuti with the more severe and often fearful practices of the nearby villagers.

A common character in hunter-gather religions is that which mythologists call the "trickster," a morally ambivalent deity or semi-deity who often interferes with the best laid plans of others (Guenther, 1999). Accounts of hunter-gatherer religions suggest that the trickster might be best thought of, not as a single individual, but rather as a character trait of many if not most hunter-gatherer deities. The gods are whimsical and are not particularly concerned with human morality. They may hurt or help a person just because they feel like it, not because they are dishing out justice or trying to make people more moral. Consistent with their egalitarian world-view, hunter-gatherers don't see morality as something that is imposed top-down; they see it as something that they have to take care of themselves. The gods, like the weather and other natural phenomena that they may represent, have their own agendas.

Nearly all hunter-gatherer religions include shamanic ceremonies as a foundation. Shamanism involves techniques for attaining an altered state of consciousness, or trance, for the purpose of interacting with the spirit world. What appear to be shamanic practices are depicted in Upper Paleolithic cave art (Rossano, 2006). According to one possible scenario (hinted at by Rossano, 2006), the pre–Upper Paleolithic precursors to hunter-gatherer religions may have involved ecstatic ceremonies of drumming, singing, and dancing that induced trance states and hallucinations, some of which may have involved encounters with otherworldly spirits. Eventually stories about these spirits would develop, which could be recounted even in nontrance states, to complement the trance experiences. The stories would be shaped to fit the daily experiences and needs of the group. Among modern hunter-gatherers, the most common immediate purpose of shamanic ceremonies is healing, but the ceremonies also enable band members to interact personally, in all sorts of ways, with the spirit world.

Those who enter into trance states (the shamans) assume the properties of and/ or communicate with specific deities. In the words of Mathias Guenther (1999, pp. 427–428):

> "Often the shaman is a showman who employs rich poetic imagery and histrionics. He may sing and dance, trembling and shrieking, and speak in strange languages. He may also employ prestidigitation and ventriloquism.... Shamanic séances are very much performance events, not infrequently with audience feedback. They involve the shaman in role playing, engaging in dialogue with various spirits, each of whose counter-roles he plays himself."

Each shamanic event is a new creation. In the séances, the people interact with spirits much as they interact with one another—joking, arguing, singing, dancing, sharing, and asking for help and advice (Bird-David, 1999).

Some hunter-gatherer researchers have commented that, in general, the religious ceremonies of the group they studied are indistinguishable from play (see Tsuru, 1998). The ceremonies typically involve the kinds of self-determined, imaginative, joyful, yet rule-guided actions that fit the definition of play. While other games bind hunter-gathers to one another as equals, religious ceremonies bind them also to spiritual and natural entities outside of themselves, again as equals.

THE PLAYFUL NATURE OF HUNTER-GATHERER "WORK"

In our culture we commonly think of "work" and "play" as opposites; one is what we have to do, the other is what we want to do. By all accounts, hunter-gatherers don't make that distinction. Many hunter-gatherer groups don't even have a word for work as toil (unpleasant activity that one must do), or, if they do, it applies to what non–hunter-gatherers do (Gould, 1969; Gowdy, 1999). Lee (1993, p. 39) noted that the group he observed sang a song that went, "Those who work for a living, that's their problem." Clearly, hunter-gatherers must hunt, gather, process foods, cook, make tools, build huts, care for infants, and so on in order to survive and maintain their way of life, but they don't think of those activities as burdensome. They think of them as voluntary and fun, not different from play. For the rest of this discussion, to avoid confusion, I'll use the term *work* to refer to sustenance activities, whether pleasant or unpleasant, and *toil* to refer to activities that are undesired. With these definitions, toil cannot be play, but work can be play.

What is it about hunter-gatherers' approach to work that makes it play to them rather than toil? My reading of the accounts of hunter-gatherer sustenance activities suggests several factors. First, as I said before, hunter-gatherers don't spend long hours working, and certainly don't spend long hours at any given task, so the tasks do not become tedious.

Second, most hunter-gatherer sustenance activities require a high degree of skill, knowledge, and intelligence. To hunt successfully, hunters must be extraordinarily skilled not just at making and using the tools of hunting, such as bows and arrows or blowpipes and darts, but also at tracking (Kaplan, Hill, Lancaster, and Hurado, 2000; Liebenberg, 1990). As they track, hunters continuously develop and test hypotheses about such matters as the size, sex, physical condition, speed of movement, and time of passage of the animal they are tracking, based on the subtlest of clues—tiny dents in the sand, or a few bent blades of grass. Successful gathering likewise requires much knowledge and skill. Gatherers must know which of the countless varieties of roots, tubers, nuts, seeds, fruits, and greens in their area are edible and nutritious, when and where to find them, how to dig them (in the case of roots and tubers), how to extract the edible portions efficiently (in the case of grains, nuts, and certain plant fibers), and in some cases how to process them to make them edible or more nutritious than they otherwise would be. These abilities include physical skills, honed by years of practice, as well as the capacity to remember, use, add to, and modify an enormous store of culturally shared verbal knowledge (Bock, 2005; Kaplan et al., 2000). In our culture and everywhere, people who make their living through work that requires knowledge, skill, intelligence, and continuous learning are much more likely to enjoy their work and call it "play" than are those who make a living at repetitive, mind-numbing or back-breaking tasks (Kohn, 1980).

A third reason that hunter-gatherer work is play is that it is almost always highly social. Men usually hunt in ways that require teamwork, and women usually forage in groups. Regarding the latter, one researcher (Wannenburgh, 1979, p. 30) wrote, "In our experience all of the gathering expeditions were jolly events. With the [Ju/'hoansi's] gift of converting chores into social occasions, they often had something of the atmosphere of a picnic outing with children." We humans everywhere are social beings, inclined to enjoy activities we do with others, especially those we do with our friends.

The fourth reason, and I think ultimately the main reason why hunter-gatherer work is play, is that it is voluntary and self-directed. Hunter-gatherers have developed, to what in our culture may seem to be a radical extreme, an ethic of personal autonomy. They deliberately avoid telling one another how to behave, in work as in other contexts. It is up to each person to decide what he or she wants to do. On any given day a person might choose to hunt, or gather, or hang around camp, or begin a journey to visit a neighboring band. Endicott (1979, p. 16) has described how decisions are made on a typical day: "Three women agree to dig tubers together..... Two of the men decide to go hunting.... Four young men and two adolescent girls decide to go after Malacca cane.... They may be entirely different groups from the previous day, for the Batek like variety both in their work and their companions." Because food is shared, there is no direct relationship, as far as the individual is concerned, between productive effort and reward. This, of course, violates a basic principle of Economics 101 in our culture. The man who stays in his hammock will get the same food at the end of the day as the ones who go out hunting. From the individual's perspective, you don't hunt for food; you hunt because you want to. An advantage of this is that nobody goes out hunting or gathering begrudgingly, which would hold others back and dampen everyone's spirits.

Hunter-gatherers don't seem to be concerned, as we Westerners automatically are, about the free-rider problem. In one recorded case, a single man acquired nearly 80% of the meat for the entire camp for a month while four other men did no hunting at all, yet those four were apparently not excluded or criticized (Hawkes, 1993). In the system of hunter-gatherer ethics there is great social pressure to share, but not to produce. The genius of this is that it keeps the activities of production within the realm of play by disassociating them from extrinsic rewards. Ultimately, of course, hunting and gathering are crucial to the band's survival. Everyone knows that, and that no doubt influences people's choices of what to do. My guess is that if the hunter who brought in 80% of the meat one month had been less successful, others would have gone out and picked up the slack. But for the most part, on any given day, the decision of what to do is each person's choice, freely made, with no pressure.

THE USES OF HUMOR TO MAINTAIN PEACE
AND PROMOTE EQUALITY

Anthropologists regularly describe the hunter-gatherers they study as good-natured people who laugh and joke frequently as they go about their daily activities. The kind of humor I'll focus on now, however, is that which in our culture is labeled as teasing, or making fun of, or, in the extreme, ridiculing—humor that is not always completely friendly.

Teasing, by definition, entails some sort of humorous pointing out of a flaw or non-normative behavior or attribute of the target of the tease (Keltner, Horberg, and Oveis, 2006). Teasing among friends can be a good-natured way of demonstrating that they are well aware of one another's flaws and quirks, but that they accept one another anyway and may even find the flaws and quirks endearing. By all accounts, hunter-gatherers engage in a great deal of that kind of teasing, which no doubt helps to bind them emotionally together.

But teasing can also be serious criticism in the guise of humor, and hunter-gatherers apparently use it quite regularly for that purpose. For example, Turnbull (1968, p. 114) wrote: "[The Mbuti] are good-natured people with an irresistible sense of humor; they are always making jokes about one another, even about themselves, but their humor can be turned into an instrument of punishment when they choose." Thomas (2006) makes the same point concerning the Ju/'hoansi, and illustrates it with an example involving two women who argued loudly with one another, disturbing the whole band, until others made up a song about them and sang it when they began arguing. The song made them feel ashamed, and they stopped arguing.

Hunter-gatherers do not criticize one another directly because that violates their principle that people should not tell others what to do or act in any way suggesting that one is superior to the other. But they do criticize indirectly through humor. Such humor seems to be a way of criticizing without raising oneself up on a moral plane above the other. It is both play and not play at the same time. The playful element implies equality, even as the critical element implies a request for behavioral change. Moreover, teasing of this sort may be more effective than direct criticism, even for us Westerners. Direct criticism tends to provoke argument and defensiveness. In contrast, teasing acts at an emotional level that bypasses verbal defensiveness, and it gives targets a choice of how to respond. They can laugh along with the teasers, thereby acknowledging the ridiculousness of what they have done, which appears to be the most common hunter-gatherer way of responding. This keeps the entire interaction within the realm of play, even as the targets implicitly indicate their intent to change. Or they can feel and express shame, likewise expressing the intent to change. Or they can stew for a while in resentment, but then eventually come around. Or, in the very rare case in which it is a serious matter and the targets have no intention to change and the ridicule becomes extreme, they might leave and join another band or start a new one of their own.

Teasing of all sorts is also a means of promoting humility, and that may be its most crucial function in hunter-gatherer bands. Even the friendliest teasing promotes humility because it reminds people of their flaws. Beyond friendly teasing, hunter-gatherers deliberately use ridicule to deflate the ego of anyone who, even in an incipient way, seems to express superiority over others in the band. They recognize that the human tendency toward arrogance is a threat to their means of existence, and they are constantly on guard to nip it in the bud. They are particularly vigilant about arrogance in young men.

For example, hunter-gatherers often engage in a practice that anthropologists refer to as "insulting the meat" (Lee, 1988). When a hunter brings a fat antelope or other prize kill back to the band, for everyone to share, he must act humbly about it. He must say that the animal is skinny, hardly worth bothering with. He must say that he killed it through sheer luck, or because of the fine arrow that someone else had made and lent him, or because it was sickly and an easy mark, or all of these things. If he acts even the slightest bit arrogant about his hunting, others will mock both him and the meat he has brought them. The men and women alike, especially the grandmothers, will complain that the antelope is nothing but a bag of bones and hardly worth cooking. They might make up a song about the man's flaws and about how he thinks he is such a "great hunter" but is really a weakling. They might mockingly call him "chief" or "big man." In a culture that doesn't have chiefs or big men and values equality, this is one of the greatest insults that can be hurled.

The man who is insulted in this way knows what is happening, but the insults nevertheless work. He knows that he has crossed a line that hunter-gatherers must not cross, and he must immediately make amends by expressing great humility about the meat and himself. He must join the others now in taunting himself. If he doesn't, he knows that the taunting will escalate and could, in the extreme, even lead to ostracism or banishment from the band. Such taunting is a form of teasing. It has all the elements of teasing, including humor. But it is teasing with a very serious and deliberate purpose. When Lee (2003, p. 53) asked a wise healer in the hunter-gatherer group he was studying to explain this practice of insulting the meat, the healer replied: "When a young man kills much meat, he comes to think of himself as a big man, and he thinks of the rest of us as his inferiors. We can't accept this. We refuse one who boasts, for someday his pride will make him kill somebody. So we always speak of his meat as worthless. In this way we cool his heart and make him gentle."

THE PLAY-FILLED CHILDHOODS OF HUNTER-GATHERERS

I'll be brief in this section because I discussed the play life of hunter-gatherer children extensively in the previous book in this series (Gray, 2012a) and in a recent trade book (Gray, 2013). Children in hunter-gatherer cultures are generally free to play from dawn to dusk, every day, from early childhood on into the teenage years. In their play they practice the activities they observe in the social world around them, such as hunting, gathering, tool making, dancing, and singing, and in that way become skilled at the sustenance and artistic activities essential to successful hunter-gatherer adulthood (see also Hewlett, Fouts, Boyette, and Hewlett, 2011; Hewlett and Lamb, 2005). More central to the point of this chapter, however, they also, in their play, necessarily practice the values and social skills essential to successful hunter-gatherer adulthood. That is because those values and skills are the same as those required for social play—autonomy, equality, cooperation, sharing, resolving disputes, reaching consensus. Without these, players quit, and the game ends.

Hunter-gatherer adults treat children in essentially the same way that they treat other adults. They trust children to run their own lives and make their own decisions, just as they trust adults to do so. Because it is hard for Western readers to believe that children anywhere would be so trusted, I feel compelled to insert quotations from observers who have seen it first hand. Here are three, from different researchers concerning different hunter-gatherer societies (on three different continents):

- "Hunter-gatherers do not give orders to their children; for example, no adult announces bedtime. At night, children remain around adults until they feel tired and fall asleep....Parakana adults do not interfere with their children's lives. They never beat, scold, or behave aggressively with them, physically or verbally, nor do they offer praise or keep track of their development." (Gosso, Otta, de Lima, Ribeiro, and Bussab, 2005, p. 218.)
- "Infants and young children [among Inuit hunter-gatherers of the Hudson Bay area] are allowed to explore their environments to the limits of their physical capabilities and with minimal interference from adults. Thus if a child picks up a hazardous object, parents generally leave it to explore the dangers on its own. The child is presumed to know what it is doing." (Guemple, 1988, p. 137.)
- "Foragers value autonomy and egalitarianism, so parents, older children or other adults are not likely to think and feel that they know what is best or better for the child and are generally unlikely to initiate, direct, or intervene in a child's social learning." (Hewlett et al., 2011, p. 1173, regarding the Aka, but also regarding hunter-gatherers in general.)

In this trustful environment, children play with one another independently of adult direction and practice the values and skills of play, which are the values and skills of their culture, as they learn to get along with one another as equals. It is worth noting also that just as the games of adults (and those of adults and children together) are noncompetitive, so are the games of hunter-gatherer children (Gray, 2009a; Marshall, 1976). Children play in ways that allow them to build their own skills and harmonize their behavior with others, not in ways designed to show off or defeat others.

THE HUNTER-GATHERER BAND VIEWED AS A PLAYGROUP

Sometimes hunter-gatherer bands are characterized as kinship groups, but they are not really that. People move from band to band, so those in a band are not all close relatives, and any given person may have more relatives in other bands than in his or her own. It may be more useful to think of hunter-gatherer bands as playgroups—if not literally, then at least by analogy. The band is a group of individuals who have come together voluntarily to play out their lives with one another, at least for a period of time.

The most basic individual right in social play is the right to quit. If you can't quit, your participation is not voluntary, and it's not play. That right provides the foundation for the egalitarian, cooperative nature of play. Every player knows that the others can quit at any time and will quit if they are bullied or if their needs and desires aren't taken into account. Therefore, every player knows that they must treat the others respectfully, share, make rules by discussion and consensus rather than fiat, find ways to resolve arguments, and take care not to lord it over others if they want to keep the game going with the present group.

As many hunter-gatherer researchers have pointed out, freedom to leave the band—to join another band or to start a new one—is the ultimate foundation for hunter-gatherer egalitarianism. If people feel oppressed, they leave. Because hunter-gatherers have few possessions, do not own land, and do not live in permanent dwellings, they can leave the band at a moment's notice, just as someone in a pickup game of baseball who feels put upon can quit at any moment. In the words of Woodburn (1982, p. 435), "Individuals are not bound to fixed areas, to fixed assets, or to fixed revenues. They are able to move away without difficulty and at a moment's notice from constraint which others may seek to impose on them and such possibility of movement is a powerful leveling mechanism, positively valued like other leveling mechanisms in these societies." Regarding the group he studied, Endicott (1988, p. 122) wrote, "There is nothing to constrain Batek from moving to another camp if someone tries to force them to do something they do not want to do, and movement to avoid potential or real conflict is common." And, in Turnbull's (1968, p. 137) always-poetic words, regarding the Mbuti, "It is plain in each case the process of fission and fusion [splitting up and reformation of bands] follows lines of dissent rather than descent, and the major function is conflict resolution." To ensure that they can leave at any time, hunter-gatherers frequently visit friends and relatives in other bands to maintain their welcome there.

Although hunter-gatherers treasure their freedom to move from one band to another, they also no doubt find value in a stable band—a band of friends who know one another intimately and have had much experience cooperating together. Therefore, they are motivated to treat one another well, to keep the playgroup together.

Conclusion and Implications for Modern Societies

Human beings are endowed with all sorts of conflicting drives and tendencies. People differ across cultures because cultures differentially nurture some of these drives and tendencies and not others. The focus of this chapter has been on the opposition between our natural drive toward dominance and our natural drive to play with one another.

Social play requires that individuals set aside their concern for dominance. In primates, natural selection has apparently enlarged the drive and capacity to play and extended it into adulthood in species—such as bonobos and the "egalitarian" species of macaques—that have evolved a relatively egalitarian mode of social existence. Human cultures differ greatly in the degree to which they are hierarchically structured or egalitarian. Hunter-gatherer cultures are the most egalitarian of all. They are egalitarian not because hunter-gatherers are genetically different from other people, but because they have developed cultural practices that promote egalitarian behavior. The thesis here is that these egalitarian-promoting practices are suffused with play. Hunter-gatherer games, dances, religious practices, and work are highly playful. Even their means of criticizing one another for the purpose of altering behavior are playful. The young educate themselves through play; they grow up in the spirit of play. By maintaining a playful mood, I contend, hunter-gatherers more or less continuously suppress the urge to dominate one another. Of course, it works the other way, too: by suppressing dominance, they promote play.

Many of our modern Western cultural practices, in contrast, seem deliberately designed to suppress play and promote competition and struggles for dominance. We suppress children's natural playful ways of learning by requiring them to "work" in school, believing that this is for their own good. We put children into competitions with one another beginning at a young age, in our schools, where they vie for grades and status, and in games and sporting events, which we call "play" but which are not fully play because of the focus on winning. We reward people with praise and higher pay for climbing the hierarchy in our hierarchically organized workplaces. Our religious institutions contain hierarchies carried over from feudal times, and our stories of the heavens emphasize hierarchy and top-down control and judgment. Even our use of the word "equality," in describing our democratic principles, has connotations of competition. We think of equality as equality of opportunity, which means fair competition; we don't so often think of it as sharing. This is not the place to argue one way or the other whether we would be better off if we became more egalitarian; but it is interesting to contrast our relatively nonplayful, competitive, nonegalitarian cultural practices with the highly playful, noncompetitive, egalitarian practices of hunter-gatherers.

References

Bekoff, M. (2001). Social play behavior: Cooperation, fairness, trust, and the evolution of morality. *Journal of Consciousness Studies, 8*, 81–90.

Bekoff, M. (2004). Wild Justice and fair play: Cooperation, forgiveness, and morality in animals. *Biology and Philosophy, 19*, 489–520.

Bekoff, M., & Byers, J. A. (1981). A critical reanalysis of the ontogeny of mammalian social and locomotor play: An ethological hornet's nest. In K. Immelmann, G. W. Barlow, L. Petrivoch, & M. Main (Eds.), *Behavioral development: The Bielefeld interdisciplinary project* (pp. 296–337). New York: Cambridge University Press.

Bird-David, N. (1999). "Animism" revisited: Personhood, environment, and relational epistemology. *Current Anthropology, 40*, S67–S91.

Bock, J. (2005). What makes a competent adult forager?" In B. S. Hewlett & M. E. Lamb (Eds.), *Hunter-gatherer childhoods: Evolutionary, developmental, and cultural perspectives* (pp. 109–128). New Brunswick, NJ: Transaction.

Boehm, C. (1993). Egalitarian behavior and reverse dominance hierarchy. *Current Anthropology, 34*, 227–254.

Boehm, C. (1999). *Hierarchy in the forest: The evolution of egalitarian behavior*. Cambridge, MA: Harvard University Press.

Burghardt, G. M. (2011). Defining and recognizing play. In A. D. Pellegrini (Ed.), *The Oxford handbook of the development of play* (pp. 9–18). Oxford, UK: Oxford University Press.

Ciani, F., Dall'Olio, S., Stanyon, R., & Palagi, E. (2012). Social tolerance and adult play in macaque societies: A comparison with different human cultures. *Animal Behaviour, 84*, 1313–1322.

Corballis, M. C. (1999). Phylogeny from apes to humans. In M. C. Corballis & S. E. G. Lea (Eds.), *The descent of mind: Psychological perspectives on hominid evolution*. Oxford, UK: Oxford University Press.

Cordoni, G. (2009). Social play in captive wolves (*Canis lupus*): Not only an immature affair. *Behaviour, 146*, 1363–1385.

Endicott, K. (1979). *Batek Negrito religion: The world-view and rituals of a hunting and gathering people of Peninsular Malaysia*. Oxford, UK: Clarendon Press.

Endicott, K. (1988). Property, power, and conflict among the Batek of Malaysia. In T. Ingold, D. Riches, & J. Woodburn (Eds.), *Hunters and gatherers 2: Property, power, and ideology*. Oxford, UK: Berg.

Gosso, Y., Otta, E., de Lima, M., Ribeiro, F. J. L., & Bussab, V. S. R. (2005). Play in hunter-gatherer societies. In A. D. Pellegrini & P. K. Smith (Eds.), *The nature of play: Great apes and humans* (pp. 213–253). New York: Guilford.

Gould, R. A. (1969). *Yiwara: Foragers of the Australian desert*. New York: Charles Scribner.

Gowdy, J. (1999). Hunter-gatherers and the mythology of the market. In R. B. Lee & R. Daly (Eds.), *The Cambridge encyclopedia of hunters and gatherers*. New York: Cambridge University Press.

Gray, P. (2009a). Play as a foundation for hunter-gatherer social existence. *American Journal of Play, 1*, 476–522.

Gray, P. (2009b). The biological distinction between play and contest, and their merging in modern games. Blog at Psychology Today: Freedom to Learn, Nov. 4, 2009, online at http://www.psychologytoday.com/blog/freedom-learn/200911/the-biological-distinction-between-play-and-contest-and-their-merging-in-m.

Gray (2011). *Psychology (6th ed.)* New York: Worth.

Gray, P. (2012a). The value of a play-filled childhood in development of the hunter-gatherer individual. In D. Narvaez, J. Panksepp, A. Schore, & T. Gleason (Eds.), *Evolution, early experience and human development: From research to practice and policy* (pp. 352–370). New York: Oxford University Press.

Gray, P. (2012b). Definition of play. In *Encyclopedia of play science*, online at http://www. scholarpedia.org/article/Encyclopedia_of_Play_Science.

Gray, P. (2013). *Free to learn: Why unleashing the instinct to play will make our children happier, more self-reliant, and better students for life*. New York: Basic Books.

Guemple, L. (1988). Teaching social relations to Inuit children. In T. Ingold, D. Riches, & J. Woodburn (Eds.), *Hunters and gatherers 2: Property, power, and ideology* (pp. 130–149). Oxford, UK: Berg.

Guenther, M. (1999). From totemism to shamanism: Hunter-gatherer contributions to world mythology and spirituality. In R. B. Lee & R. Daly (Eds.), *The Cambridge encyclopedia of hunters and gathers* (pp. 426–433). Cambridge, UK: Cambridge University Press.

Hawkes, K. (1993) Why hunter-gatherers work: An ancient version of public goods. *Current Anthropology, 34*, 341–361.

Hewlett. B. S., Fouts, H. N., Boyette, A., & Hewlett, B. L. (2011). Social learning among Congo Basin hunter-gatherers. *Philosophical Transactions of the Royal Society B, 366*, 1168–1178.

Hewlett, B. S., & Lamb, M. B. (Eds.) (2005). *Hunter-gatherer childhoods: Evolutionary, developmental, and cultural perspectives*. New Brunswick, NJ: Transaction.

Ingold, T. (1999). On the social relations of the hunter-gatherer band. In R. B. Lee & R. H. Daly (Eds.), *The Cambridge encyclopedia of hunters and gatherers* (pp. 399–410). Cambridge, UK: Cambridge University Press.

Kaplan, H., Hill, K., Lancaster, J., & Hurado, A. M. (2000). A theory of life history evolution: Diet, intelligence, and longevity. *Evolutionary Anthropology, 9*, 156–185.

Keltner, D., Horberg, E. J., & Oveis, C. (2006). Emotional intuitions and moral play. *Social Justice Research, 19*, 208–217.

Kent, S. (1996). Cultural diversity among African foragers: Causes and implications. In S. Kent (Ed.), *Cultural diversity among twentieth-century foragers: An African perspective* (pp. 1–18). New York: Cambridge University Press.

Kohn, M. L. (1980). Job complexity and adult personality. In N. J. Smelser & E. H. Erikson (Eds.), *Theories of work and love in adulthood (pp. 193–210)*. Cambridge, MA: Harvard University Press.

LaFreniere, P. (2011). Evolutionary functions of social play: Life histories, sex differences and emotion regulation. *American Journal of Play, 3*, 464–488.

Lee, R. B. (1984). *The Dobe !Kung*. New York: Holt, Rinehart & Winston.

Lee, R. B. (1988). Reflections on primitive communism. In T. Ingold, D. Riches & J. Woodburn (Eds.), *Hunters and gatherers 1 (pp. 252–268)*. Oxford, UK: Berg.

Lee, R. B. (1993). *The Dobe Jul'hoansi*. Orlando, FL: Harcourt Brace.

Lee, R. B. (2003). *The Dobe Jul'hoansi (3rd ed.)* Belmont, CA: Wadsworth.

Liebenberg, L. (1990). *The art of tracking: The origin of science*. Clairmont, South Africa: David Philip.

Marshall, L. (1976). *The !Kung of Nyae Nyae*. Cambridge, MA: Harvard University Press.

Matsumura, S. (1999). The evolution of "egalitarian" and "despotic" social systems among macaques. *Primates, 40*, 23–31.

Miller, D. L. (1970). *Gods and games: Toward a theology of play*. New York: World Publishing.

Muller, M. N., Kahlenberg S. M., & Wrangham, R. W. (2009). Male aggression against females and sexual coercion in chimpanzees. In M. N. Muller & R. W. Wrangham

(Eds.), *Sexual coercion in primates and humans* (pp. 184–217). London: Harvard University Press.

Natarajan, D., & Caramaschi, D. (2010). Animal violence demystified. *Frontiers in Behavioral Neuroscience, 4*. Online at http://www.frontiersin.org/Behavioral_Neuroscience/10.3389/fnbeh.2010.00009/full.

Palagi, E. (2006). Social play in bonobos (*Pan paniscus*) and chimpanzees (*Pan troglodytes*): Implications for natural social systems and interindividual relationships. *American Journal of Physical Anthropology, 129*, 415–426.

Palagi, E. (2008). Sharing the motivation to play: The use of signals in adult bonobos. *Animal Behaviour, 75*, 887–896.

Palagi, E. (2011). Playing at every age: Modalities and potential functions in non-human primates. In A. D. Pellegrini (Ed.), *The Oxford handbook of the development of play* (pp. 70–82). Oxford, UK: Oxford University Press.

Palagi, E., & Paoli, T. (2007). Play in adult bonobos (*Pan paniscus*): Modality and potential meaning. *American Journal of Physical Anthropology, 134*, 219–225.

Palagi, E., Paoli, T., & Tarli, S. B. (2006). Short-term benefits of play behavior and conflict prevention in *Pan paniscus*. *International Journal of Primatology, 27*, 1257–1269.

Parish, A. R., & de Waal, F. B. (2000). The other "closest living relative": How bonobos (*Pan paniscus*) challenge traditional assumptions about females, dominance, intra- and intersexual interactions, and hominid evolution. *Annals of the New York Academy of Sciences, 907*, 96–113.

Pellis, S. M. (2002). Keeping in touch: Play fighting and social knowledge. In M. Bekoff, C. Allen, & & G. M. Burghardt (Eds.), *The cognitive animal: Empirical and theoretical perspectives on animal cognition* (pp. 421–427). Cambridge, MA: MIT Press.

Pellis, S. M., & Iwaniuk, A. N. (2000). Adult-adult play in primates: Comparative analysis of its origin, distribution and evolution. *Ethology, 106*, 1083–11104.

Pellis, S. M., & Pellis, V. C. (1998). The structure-function interface in the analysis of play fighting. In M. Bekoff & J. A. Byers (Eds.), *Animal play: evolutionary, comparative, and ecological perspectives (pp. 432–441)*. Cambridge, UK: Cambridge University Press.

Pellis, S. M., Pellis, V. C. (2011). Rough and tumble play: Training and using the social brain. In A. D. Pellegrini (Ed.), *The Oxford handbook of the development of play* (pp. 245–259). Oxford, UK: Oxford University Press.

Pellis, S. M., Pellis, V. C., & Bell, H. C. (2010), The functions of play in the development of the social brain. *American Journal of Play, 2*, 278–296.

Petit, O., Bertrand, F., & Thierry, B. (2008). Social play in crested and Japanese macaques: Testing the covariation hypothesis. *Developmental Psychobiology, 50*, 399–407.

Reinhart, C. J., Pellis, V. C., Thierry, B., Gauthier, C-A., VanderLaan, D. P., Vasey, P. L., & Pellis, S. M. (2010). Targets and tactics of play fighting: Competitive versus cooperative styles of play in Japanese and Tonkean Macaques. *International Journal of Comparative Psychology, 23*, 166–200.

Rossano, M. J. (2006), The religious mind and the evolution of religion. *Review of General Psychology. 10*, 346–364

Rowley-Conwy, P. (2001). Time, change and the archaeology of hunter-gatherers: How original is the "Original Affluent Society"? In C. Panter-Brick, R. H. Layton, &

P. Rowley-Conwy (Eds.), *Hunter-gatherers: An interdisciplinary perspective* (pp. 39–72). Cambridge, UK: Cambridge University Press.

Sahlins, M. (1972). *Stone age economics*. Chicago: Aldine-Atherton.

Shostak, M. (1981) *Nisa: The life and words of a !Kung woman*. Cambridge, MA: Harvard University Press.

Surbeck, M., Deschner, T., Schubert, G., Weltring, A., & Hohmann, G. (2012). Mate competition, testosterone and intersexual relationships in bonobos, *Pan paniscus*. *Animal Behaviour, 83*, 659–669.

Sutton-Smith, B., & Roberts, J. M. (1970). The cross-cultural and psychological study of games. In G. Lüschen (Ed.), *The cross-cultural analysis of sport and games* (pp. 100–108). Champaign, IL: Stipes.

Tacconi, G., & Palagi, E. (2009). Play behavioural tactics under space reduction: Social challenges in bonobos, *Pan paniscus*. *Animal Behaviour, 78*, 469–476.

Thierry, B. (2000). Covariation and conflict management patterns across macaque species. In F. Aureli & F. B. M. de Waal (Eds.), *Natural conflict resolution* (pp. 106–128). Berkeley, CA: University of California Press.

Thomas, E. M. (1959). *The harmless people*. New York: Knopf.

Thomas, E. M. (2006). *The old way*. New York: Farrar, Straus & Giroux.

Tsuru, D. (1998). Diversity of ritual spirit performances among the Baka Pygmies in southeastern Cameroon. *African Study Monographs, Suppl. 25*, 47–83.

Turnbull, C. M. (1968). *The forest people*. New York: Simon & Schuster.

Turnbull, C. M. (1982). The ritualization of potential conflict between the sexes among the Mbuti. In E. G. Leacock & R. B. Lee (Eds.), *Politics and history in band societies* (pp. 133–155). Cambridge, UK: Cambridge University Press.

Wannenburgh, A. (1979). *The bushmen*. New York: Mayflower Books.

Wilson, D. S. (2002). *Darwin's cathedral: Evolution, religion, and the nature of society*. Chicago: University of Chicago Press.

Woodburn, J. (1982). Egalitarian societies. *Man, 17*, 431–451.

Comparative Studies of Social Play, Fairness, and Fitness

WHAT WE KNOW AND WHERE WE SHOULD BE HEADING

Marc Bekoff

Peter Gray's fascinating chapter on the relationship between hunter-gatherer egalitarianism and patterns of social play (hereafter, play) rang many familiar chords for me. For decades, I have conducted many comparative analyses of social play in canids, members of the dog family. Dr. Gray's essay reflects much current thinking about the evolution of social play and highlights just how important detailed observations across diverse species are to generating "grand theories" of social behavior.

Dr. Gray begins: "My thesis here is that a major evolutionary reason for the extension of human play into adulthood—that is, a major reason for the natural selection of adult playfulness in humans—was that it enabled the high degree of cooperation and sharing essential to the hunter-gatherer way of life. Bands of humans that played together were more likely to stick together, cooperate, and share—and thereby to survive—than bands that did not play together. This is a group selection explanation, but I also suggest an individual-selection explanation." Dr. Gray writes about viewing the hunter-gatherer band as a playgroup.

Along these lines I have also argued, "a family that plays together stays together," and that group selection and individual selection are both important in the evolution of cooperation and fairness. People who years ago eschewed group selection, such as the renowned zoologist Edward O. Wilson, now embrace it enthusiastically, as they should (Wilson, 2012).

Nobel laureate, Niko Tinbergen, stressed that studies of behavior should focus on four major areas: evolution, adaptation, causation, and development. Psychologist Gordon Burghardt suggested that we add a fifth category of inquiry to Tinbergen's scheme, namely, subjective experience. Applied to play, we can ask, Why did play evolve? How does it allow individuals to adapt to various situations? What causes play? How does it develop? and What does it feels like to engage in play? Detailed research has shown that animals enjoy playing (Bekoff, 2007).

For many years some researchers claimed that play was a "garbage pail" category of behavior. When people could not figure out what animals were doing, they called it play. However, they were dead wrong because the kaleidoscopic nature of play simply meant that people would actually have to study it in detail and analyze what individuals do when they play (Bekoff, 1972, 1974, 1995; Bekoff and Pierce, 2009; Pierce and Bekoff, 2012). Play research would have been doomed to a premature death if people listened to the skeptics, and I'm thrilled I did not. And, the critical importance of play would have been lost, at least for a while.

Play is a model example of how details about what animals do when they do something can lead to the development of very interesting, challenging, and testable hypotheses and some wide-ranging thinking, and Peter Gray's essay touches on a number of very important topics. These include comparing how play emerges and how individuals play in different cultures, the need for youngsters to engage in what I call "wild play" (http://www.psychologytoday.com/blog/animal-emotions/201202/the-need-wild-play-let-children-be-the-animals-they-need-be), letting human youngsters be the animals (mammals) who they are, and the relationship between play and egalitarian behavior. Some of these ideas are also explored in Douglas Fry's essay in this book.

In my own work I've studied the nitty-gritty details of what young canids do when they play, how there are marked species differences in the development of play strategies, how play signals are honest signals or signs of trust, how play is almost exclusively fair, and how fair play seems to be related to individual reproductive fitness (Bekoff, 1974, 1995, 2004). We really need a lot more data on possible relationships between play and fitness, but this information is extremely difficult to collect under field conditions. We were very lucky to be able to collect some data on wild coyotes.

Ask First, Be Honest, Follow the Rules, and Admit You're Wrong

I fold fair play and how it is related to learning what is "right" and what is "wrong" into the notion of "wild justice" (Bekoff and Pierce, 2009; Pierce and Bekoff, 2012; see also Dugatkin and Bekoff, 2003). Canids and individuals of many other species have evolved mechanisms for keeping play safe and honest, including the use of specific signals to initiate and to maintain the play mood, self-handicapping, and role reversing. Play is a voluntary activity, and as Dr. Gray puts it, individuals have the right to quit.

Play also serves a number of different functions that may vary across species. These include the importance of play in social development, physical development, cognitive development, and training for the unexpected (Bekoff and Byers, 1981; Spinka, Newberry, and Bekoff, 2001). Dr. Gray's stimulating essay made me think about how play as training for the unexpected might enable individuals to learn not to be stressed by, and become competitive when, their expectations about the outcome of a social interaction are not met. During play, they don't "freak out" and try to subdue another individual but rather understand that there are rules of social engagement to which they need to adhere. When these rules are violated, there are ways to get back to play. Across diverse species, the four basic aspects of fair play in animals are as follows: ask first, be honest, follow the rules, and admit you're wrong. When the rules of play are violated, and when fairness breaks down, so does play.

Although play is fun, it's also serious business. Play can take some work, in that it takes some effort to keep it under control. When animals play, they are constantly working to understand and follow the rules and to communicate their intentions to play fairly. They fine-tune their behavior on the run, carefully monitoring the behavior of their play partners and paying close attention to infractions of the agreed-on rules (Pierce and Bekoff, 2009).

"Better a Broken Bone Than a Broken Spirit."

Dr. Gray also writes about how young hunter-gatherers grow up in the spirit of play, and this made me recall the slogan of the group called Play Wales—"Better a broken bone than a broken spirit." (http://www.playwales.org.uk/login/uploaded/documents/Shop/lady%20allen%20of%20hurtwood.pdf)

We can learn a lot about the nature of social play by studying nonhuman and human animals and by comparing what we learn in species that live in various types of social groups with different patterns of social interaction. Play is not a garbage pail at all, but rather is one of the most important types of behavior in which an individual engages.

It is wonderful and so important for future studies of play to have researchers cross disciplines and species. It is the best way to gain a better grasp on theories focusing on the evolution of various categories and patterns of social behavior and for the development of extremely important "grand theories."

References

Bekoff, M. (1972). The development of social interaction, play, and metacommunication in mammals: An ethological perspective. *Quarterly Review of Biology, 47*, 412–434.

Bekoff, M. (1974). Social play and play-soliciting by infant canids. *American Zoologist, 14*, 323–340.

Bekoff, M. (1995). Play signals as punctuation: The structure of social play in canids. *Behaviour, 132*, 419–429.

Bekoff, M. (2004). Wild justice and fair play: Cooperation, forgiveness, and morality in animals. *Biology & Philosophy, 19*, 489–520.

Bekoff, M. (2007). *The emotional lives of animals*. Novato, CA: New World Library.

Bekoff, M., & Byers, J. A. (1981). A critical reanalysis of the ontogeny and phylogeny of mammalian social and locomotor play: An ethological hornet's nest. In K. Immelmann, G. Barlow, M. Main, & L. Petrinovich (Eds.), *Behavioral development: The Bielefeld interdisciplinary project* (pp. 296–337). Cambridge, UK: Cambridge University Press.

Bekoff, M., & Pierce, J. (2009). *Wild justice: The moral lives of animals.* Chicago: University of Chicago Press.

Dugatkin, L. A., & Bekoff, M. (2003). Play and the evolution of fairness: A game theory model. *Behavioural Processes, 60,* 209–214.

Pierce, J., & Bekoff, M. (2009). Moral in tooth and claw. *Chronicle of Higher Education.* Retrieved September 11, 2013, from http://chronicle.com/article/Moral-in-ToothClaw/48800/.

Pierce, J., & Bekoff, M. (2012). Wild justice redux: What we know about social justice in animals and why it matters. *Social Justice Research* (special issue edited by Sarah Brosnan), *25,* 122–139.

Spinka, M., Newberry, R. C., & Bekoff, M. (2001). Mammalian play: Training for the unexpected. *Quarterly Review of Biology, 76,* 141–168.

Wilson, E. O. (2012). *The social conquest of earth.* New York: Liveright.

9

Incentives in the Family I

THE FAMILY FIRM, AN EVOLUTIONARY/ECONOMIC THEORY FOR PARENT–OFFSPRING RELATIONS

Joan Roughgarden and Zhiyuan Song

Introduction

The organizers of this and the previous volume on early childrearing experience have called attention to a declining competency of childrearing in America (Narvaez, Panksepp, Schore & Gleason, 2013). This decline is marked by epidemics of anxiety, depression, aggression, and attention deficit hyperactivity disorder among the young, delinquency and increasing expulsion rates of prekindergarten children for psychosocial problems, increasing use of psychotropic medications on children, and a burgeoning prison population. Narvaez and colleagues argue that this decline in childrearing competency is caused by an American culture that increasingly deviates from social practices in our ancestral *environment of evolutionary adaptedness* (EEA) as exemplified by the childrearing practices in foraging (hunter-gatherer) human communities that allow more affiliative physical bonds to develop. They claim, moreover, that mammals generally require nurturing caregiving for optimal postnatal development. Finally, Narvaez and colleagues (Narvaez et al., 2013) lament that scientific theory and policy recommendations do not match up with the findings from psychologists and anthropologists about the harmful effects of popular childrearing practices on brain development.

Our contribution to this discussion is to review, criticize, and extend the evolutionary theory for parent–offspring relations in biology, with particular reference to an avian parent with one nestling. The symposium organizers argue that present-day scientific theory does not do justice to the empirical findings about family dynamics in humans, and we observe that existing theory also does not do justice to empirical findings about parent–offspring relations elsewhere in the animal kingdom. We develop a way to rethink the evolutionary theory of parent–offspring relations in biology based on the perspective of "social selection" (Roughgarden, 2009). In this perspective, the parent–offspring relation is modeled as a behavioral rather than as an evolutionary-genetic process.

Volume contributors point out that abundant research now shows that affiliative physical bonds between parent and offspring are crucial to successful parenting. Why, then, have practices that restrict a close physical bond between offspring and parent, practices like the common use of infant formula, the isolation of infants in their own rooms, the belief that responding to a baby is spoiling it, the placing of infants in day care, and so forth, been normalized and not widely discouraged by pediatricians? One answer perhaps lies, at least partly, in the premedical biology education. The perspective of biologists, particularly those with an evolutionary background, is that the family is a locus of conflict. Genuine love and affiliative or empathetic emotions have no place in the evolutionary-biology picture of family life, and instead the expression of behavior that might be labeled as affiliative or empathetic is construed as Machiavellian manipulation.

The perspective of present-day evolutionary theory concerning the family is illustrated by the following quotation (Parker, 2006a): "The family is now perceived as a cauldron of conflict, with each of the players having different interests...sexual conflict, parent-offspring conflict, and sib-competition simultaneously." The theme of conflict is also applied to the parent–parent interaction, so that offspring are condemned to witness their parents in continual conflict (Tregenza, Wedell, and Chapman, 2006): "There has been a dramatic shift in the prevailing view of matings as being essentially 'a good thing' for both participants, to one in which they are regarded as 'bad' for females." Previous views are "mistakenly viewing male-female interactions as more benign than they actually are."

Indeed, sexual conflict is asserted to underlie the evolutionary origin of the distinction between male and female, wherein large and small gametes, eggs and sperm, respectively, differentiated from a primitive single size of gamete (Parker, 2006b): "[A] primitive form of sexual conflict may have occurred during the early evolution of anisogamy." Thus, sexual conflict is supposedly ubiquitous throughout nature. Where did this present-day emphasis on conflict originate?

The parent–offspring relationship in animal families has been theorized since the early 1970s in terms of conflict, as diagrammed in Figure 9.1. Trivers (1972, 1974) argued that offspring extracted more investment from the parent than was in the parent's best interest, leading to the idea that "parent–offspring conflict" is universal in animal families. Trivers' examples tended to focus on discord at the time of weaning in mammals, and on the possibility of offspring being able to psychologically manipulate their parents. The Trivers perspective was given a more mathematical treatment by Parker and Macnair (1978, 1979) and Macnair and Parker (1978, 1979).

Today, the universality of parent–offspring conflict is taken as axiomatic in evolutionary psychology, as the following quotation (Salmon, 2005, p. 514) from the *Handbook of Evolutionary Psychology* illustrates: "Parent-offspring conflict can arise because some actions that advance the fitness of an offspring can potentially reduce the lifetime success of the parent just as some actions that benefit parental fitness can reduce the lifetime fitness of a particular offspring...we might expect each offspring to want to extract more than its own share of parental investment."

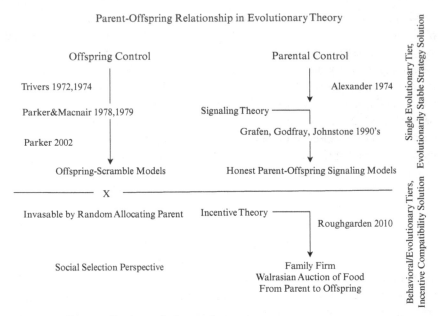

FIGURE 9.1 *Parent–offspring evolutionary theory.*

Also in the early 1970s, Alexander (1974) argued instead that offspring are completely controlled by their parents, and cited instances of natural infanticide as extreme examples of parents deciding the fate of their offspring by sacrificing some of them to reduce the brood size into accord with low resource availability. In Trivers' view, agency is assigned primarily to the offspring, and in Alexander's view, agency is assigned primarily to the parent. Either way, the focus is on family conflict.

However, a still different theoretical tradition, also from the 1970s, arose that emphasized the possibility of honest communication between offspring and parent, based on an equilibrium analysis of the genetic conditions for honest signaling. This approach aligns with Alexander's in allowing the parent, rather than the offspring, to control the allocation of parental resources, but differs in focusing on conflict resolution achieved through honest signaling rather than on the continuation of manifest conflict. Zahavi's idea (1977) for the "handicap principle" was developed by Grafen (1990) to show that in the context of mate choice, the "handicap" could be viewed as the cost of signaling in a way that underwrites honesty. In 1991, Godfray (1991) in turn applied the costly signaling theory of Grafen to parent–offspring signaling to show that chicks could honestly communicate their needs to the parent. According to honest signaling theory, parent–offspring conflict is "resolved" in the sense that the offspring do not psychologically manipulate their parents, but instead honestly convey their needs. This approach has been still further developed by Johnstone and Grafen (1992, 1993) and Godfray and Johnstone (2000) to treat the relationship between siblings.

Today, the distinction between the Trivers/Parker perspective of offspring control and the Alexander/Grafen/Godfray/Johnstone perspective of parental control is expressed in terms of a contrast between so-called scramble and honest-signaling models. As Parker, Royle, and Harley write (2002):

"The critical distinction between scramble and honest signalling models relates to the mechanism of food allocation by the parent. From each offspring's point of view, however, the different feeding mechanisms will affect the way in which they attempt to obtain food from the parent. With scramble, parents simply feed passively to the chick presenting the greatest stimulus. With honest signalling, parents actively choose between competing signals. Consequently, scramble competition is likely to apply when offspring control food allocation, and honest signalling when parents have control."

Despite the continued existence of two evolutionary perspectives about parent–offspring conflict, the honest signaling perspective appears to be largely ignored by workers in evolutionary psychology, primatology, and anthropology, who continue to adhere solely to the original claims in Trivers 1972, as exemplified by Maestripieri (2002, 2004) with nonhuman primates and Fouts, Hewlett, and Lamb (2005) with human societies in Africa.

It is unclear, however, whether the Trivers/Parker scramble version of parent–offspring conflict is theoretically tenable. A scramble system of parent–offspring communication is costly to the chicks and thereby indirectly to the parent. Hence a gene for scramble signaling is always subject to invasion by a gene causing a parent to allocate to offspring randomly, thereby removing any benefit to scrambling. In contrast, a gene for honest parent–offspring communication is stable against invasion by a gene for random allocation provided the cost of signaling is low enough because the signaling allows a more efficient allocation of food (Meirowitz, Fearon, Akçay, and Roughgarden, 2012). And indeed, the energetic cost of begging is apparently low, with numbers like 0.02% to 0.25% of the energy budget being typical (Moreno-Rueda, 2007).

Turning to the empirical evidence of parent–offspring conflict, the data suggest caution. A review (Mock and Forbes, 1992) states that the theory of parent–offspring conflict "has been modelled extensively, but its predictions for phenotypes are murky and have been subjected to scant empirical testing." Another review (Bateson, 1994) concludes, "the process of weaning in mammals is not happily explained in terms of conflicts of interest that inevitably lead to squabbling. From an evolutionary perspective, the findings encourage a re-thinking of the original ideas about conflict of interest." And a still more recent review of parent offspring conflict in birds (Kilner and Drummond, 2007) concludes as follows:

"Anyone who spends time watching parent birds tend their young will be struck by the squabbles that go on in the nest, as offspring jostle, shove or fight violently to reach close to the feeding parent, and by the exuberance of the begging displays that offspring perform to secure feeds. Although squabbling and squawking can each fuel sibling rivalry for parental care, neither has yet been shown to give offspring the edge in evolutionary conflicts of interest with their parents."

The continuing empirical uncertainty about whether the Trivers/Parker theory of family conflict is true invites an alternative approach. Moreover, the reliance of Grafen/Godfray/Johnstone honest signaling theory on an evolutionary-genetic analysis, even though the phenotype is behavioral, suggests that an approach located in the behavioral "tier" may be timely. Indeed, the empirical review of Mock and Forbes (1992) calls explicitly for "creating *phenotypic* models that generate testable, quantitative predictions" (our emphasis), and Batson (1994) points out that "From a behavioural standpoint, the interplay between parent and offspring is much more dynamic than was originally conceived."

Furthermore, an evolutionary-genetic analysis for behavioral traits, including use of the *evolutionarily stable strategy* (Maynard Smith, 1982) as the solution criterion for the evolutionary analysis, invites an ambiguous use of the word *conflict*. If the genetic interests of any two individuals are not identical (as is automatically true if they are not clones), they are said to have a genetic conflict of interest. Yet such a conflict is resolvable through behaviors such as bargaining and side payments that lead to compromise. Focus on the genetic basis for a conflict easily slips into a claim about behavioral conflict. Although genetic conflict of interest may be ubiquitous between individuals, a behavioral conflict is not necessarily ubiquitous or even common.

Nonetheless, Arnqvist and Rowe (2005, p. 218) write, "Conflict exists because there are two sexes, and therefore will be present in all anisogamous species, and has neither an evolutionary starting point nor an end." They continue, "The term 'resolution,' or 'resolved,' is often used in context of sexual conflict.... It is important to note that resolution does not in any real sense make sexual conflict disappear or even fade. There is no solution to sexual conflict that somehow causes the evolutionary interests of individuals of the two sexes to coincide." It is trivial that a genetic conflict of interest exists between individuals who mate, yet this fact says nothing about the behavioral interaction between the mates. The biological family conflict literature fails to give behavior enough credit—much of behavior might be understood as offering a technique for resolving genetic conflicts of interest.

In light of this picture painted by biologists of family life in nature, it is hardly surprising that medical advice fails to support familial love and empathy. Indeed, if behavioral conflict really were the norm in families, then separating family members from one another would be a reasonable recommendation.

According to the perspective that we are pursuing, called *social selection* (Roughgarden, 2009), behavior and evolution should be modeled in separate and distinct "tiers." Behavior is an aspect of an organism's phenotype that continually develops during its life span. Throughout life, an animal accumulates fitness, and at each instant in behavioral time, an animal is assumed to act so as to increase its fitness accumulation rate at that instant, *ex anti*. The dynamics in the behavioral tier rely on both cooperative and competitive game theory (*sensu* Roughgarden, Oishi, and Akçay, 2006). At the end of its life, an animal has accumulated some lifetime fitness, and this number is used in the evolutionary tier, whose dynamics may consist of conventional population-genetic models, or may come from evolutionary game theory, in which case the overall two-tier framing consists of nested games. The two-tier formulation is *not* group selection, or so-called multilevel selection, in which selection favors, say, selfishness at one level (individual) and altruism at the higher level (group), because the two-tier formulation does not have a selection process at two levels. Instead, the dynamics at the lower level are developmental, whereas only the higher level is a selection process.

According to the social selection perspective, a family, or any reproductive social group, should be viewed as a team or "firm" whose product is offspring. Accordingly, it is appropriate to turn to management science and the economic theory of the firm to see how a family might be organized to maximize its offspring production. We sketch here an approach motivated by Groves (1973) that considers the problem of optimal incentives in a kind of firm called a *conglomerate*. A conglomerate consists of a parent corporation and divisions. The profit for the conglomerate accrues from the earnings of its divisions, and similarly, the profit in fitness earned by a family comes accrues from the fitness of the offspring it produces.

Our approach confirms Grafen, Godfray, and Johnstone's results predicting that offspring should signal honestly to their parent, but offers a different derivation, and shows that if the parent implements optimal "incentive policies," the parent and chicks work honestly together as a team to maximize the fitness produced by the nest. Unlike genetic approaches, the optimal incentive approach in the behavioral tier can be extended to predict the time of weaning or fledging—this amounts to the time for "spinning off" divisions from the parent corporation.

Like Grafen, Godfray, and Johnstone, our approach agrees with Alexander's perspective that emphasizes parental control. However, in contrast to Alexander, who visualized continuing parent offspring conflict dominated by the parent, according to our theory, the parent resolves conflict by how it allocates resources to the offspring. Our theory fundamentally disagrees with the Trivers/Parker perspective, which features unresolved and continuing parent–offspring conflict as well as dishonesty in parent–offspring signaling whereby offspring continually psychologically manipulate their parents, especially at the time of weaning or fledging.

The Family Firm

Our "biological conglomerate" consists of a parent as "manager," and one, or potentially two or more chicks, as the "divisions" within the conglomerate, literally, a "parent corporation with offspring divisions" (herein dubbed the PCOD game). The following analysis concentrates on a family with one chick, as diagrammed in Figure 9.2. The chick is assumed to possess private knowledge about its state that

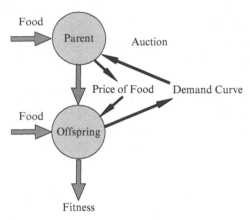

FIGURE 9.2 *Diagram of family firm.*

must somehow be communicated to the parent. As we will see later, the state to be communicated consists of its "demand function" for food. The demand function will change as the chick grows and also surely depends on various random environmental fluctuations such as temperature. Low-temperature days, for example, would require the chick to have more food on that day to sustain a higher metabolic rate to maintain its body temperature than a hot-temperature day would. In any case, the parent is assumed not to know the chick's demand function for food at any given time and needs to have the chick honestly communicate its state so that it may act accordingly at that time.

The dynamics take place in the "behavioral tier" of the two-tier system for the evolution of social behavior envisioned according to the social selection program. In our approach, the offspring and the parent are each fitness-maximizing agents. However, the parent does control the food and is in a position to set up an incentive mechanism whereby the interests of the offspring are made to coincide with its own interest. Although the chick and parent participate in a common enterprise, their play is still noncooperative in the sense that the enterprise's success relies on a coincidence of individual interests.

During the growing season, the parent feeds the chick each day, and the chick grows accordingly. The fitness a chick earns depends on the size it attains when fledged. The fitness of a parent equals the fitness of its chick, perhaps discounted by the hazard it has encountered while foraging to provide for the chick. The task is for the parent to structure its payout of food to the chick such that its own fitness is maximized, as is the fitness of its chick as well.

How should the parent structure its payout of resources? Groves discusses incentive mechanisms whereby the conglomerate's manager communicates with the divisions, and *vice versa*. Among the incentive structures Groves discusses is a scheme that amounts to setting up an internal market for the goods supplied by the manager to the divisions. He shows that if the manager requires the divisions to participate in a kind of auction for the resources they need, then the resulting distribution of resources from the manager to the divisions is optimum in the sense that the production from the corporation is maximized, as is the production from each of the divisions, and the information being conveyed by the divisions to the manager is accurate. This "internal market" incentive mechanism motivates thinking of food begging by chicks as an auction whereby the parent distributes food to the chicks optimally.

The theoretical development that follows is crafted in two stages, the first without allowing for the chick to forage by itself, and the second with allowing the chick to increasingly collect food on its own as it grows, which leads to weaning or fledging.

A CHICK'S "LABOR"

A chick's size is labeled as s, where size here means *weight*. When a chick accepts food, it grows, and its growth is considered the "labor" it carries out. By growing, a chick produces fitness for itself and for its parent. Here, a chick is assumed potentially to be able to grow in size, s, from its hatchling size up until a terminal size of s_m, according to

$$\Delta s = g(sm - s)$$

where g is a coefficient that depends on the amount of food. In particular, with a constant food supply so that g remains constant across time steps, the chicks start out growing by an increment of $g(s_m - s_0)$ where s_0 is the hatchling size, and they level off at s_m.

Ricklefs (1968) has reviewed patterns of growth in birds and has investigated sigmoid curves including the logistic Gompertz and Van Bertalanffy equations that describe sigmoid growth. The growth rule used here is slightly simpler than a sigmoid curve—the growth curve here levels off at an asymptote as in a sigmoid curve, but the inflection in a sigmoid curve is not represented. According to the data presented by Ricklefs (1968), the inflection is not especially conspicuous, and the data would often seem satisfactorily represented by the simple formula used here. In any case, the growth curve above is used only for the numerical illustrations, and not for the derivations, which are based on a general growth curve.

The fitness a chick earns is proportional to its size, s, at the time when it stops growing, according to

$$W = as$$

where a is a coefficient converting units of size into fitness. Hence the chick's fitness production per time interval from its labor is

$$\Delta W = a(\Delta s) = ag(s_m - s)$$

A PARENT'S "INVESTMENT"

The growth rate coefficient at any one time, g, depends on how much food the chick is receiving from the parent at that time. Let K be the amount of food given to the chick. K might vary in time should the parent vary the amount of food it gives the chick. K is the capital investment by the parent into the chick, that is, the owner's investment into the conglomerate's division.

Let the growth coefficient be

$$g = bK^c$$

where b is a coefficient converting units of food into units of growth rate, and c is a coefficient between 0 and 1 to indicate a diminishing marginal rate of return in growth rate from increasing the chick's food supply.

Let $L(s)$ denote the expression $a(s_m - s)$, which can be thought of as the work, or labor, that will be done by the chick per unit resource allocated to it through the act of growing. Thus, the production of fitness during the time step resulting from the parent's investment into chick's growth is

$$bK^c L(s)$$

The use of the symbols K for the parent's food contribution and L for the chick's growth, together with a power-law expression involving these variables, invites comparison with the Cobb-Douglas production function in economics.

THE FOOD MARKET

The parent is interested in maximizing its own fitness production rate (i.e., fitness accumulation per time step). It would like the chick to request the amount of food it wants to give it, neither more nor less. To do this, the parent can set up a mechanism whereby it charges for the food it dispenses to the chicks. It can view each unit of time spent begging as purchasing a certain amount of food from it. Now, for any given price, there is a certain amount of food the chick will want to buy, its "optimal demand" for the given price. By setting the price accordingly, the parent can lead the chick to want to purchase exactly the amount of food it wants to give.

This market can be thought of as a form of auction, albeit with just one bidder because there is only one chick. A *Walrasian auction,* defined in Wikipedia, is "a simultaneous auction where each agent calculates its demand for the good at every possible price and submits this to an auctioneer. The price is then set so that the total demand across all agents equals the total amount of the good. Thus, a Walrasian auction perfectly matches the supply with the demand." In our case, because the parent can set the price, the chick will want to buy exactly what the parent has to give it. This perfect match of demand with supply leads to "market clearing," whereby no food is left on the table, so to speak. Using this auction to dispense resources from the manager to the divisions is shown by Groves (1973) to be an optimal incentive system in the sense that both parties, the parent and chick, find the outcome to be optimum. The Walrasian auction is not the only type of auction consistent with an optimal incentive system. Akçay (2012) explores another auction setup called the *Vickrey-Clark-Groves mechanism,* in which each successful bidder winds up bidding enough to compensate the collective for its impact on the collective's welfare, as though each chick bid enough to compensate the remaining chicks for the food it consumed.

THE CHICK'S PERSPECTIVE—WHAT IT WANTS TO GET

How, then, do we find what the chick wants to buy for any give price set by the parent? Let P be the price of food, that is, the time spent begging per unit of resources given to the chick. Then the time spent begging to acquire K resources is PK.

Let the loss of growth resulting from the time spent begging for K resources be dPK where d is a coefficient converting units of begging time to units of growth. Therefore, the cost to the fitness accumulation rate from the begging for food is $adPK$. (Recall that the coefficient, a, converts units of size into units of fitness.) Let's introduce the parameter p defined as ad to simplify the notation somewhat. Hence the cost for begging is

$$pPK$$

So, combining the term for fitness production earned by the chick's growth with the debit to its fitness accumulation resulting from its begging for food leads to a fitness production function for the chick:

$$f(K, L(s)) = bK^cL(s) - pPK$$

For any given price, there is an "optimal demand", that is, a demand that maximizes the chick's fitness. If the price of food is low, the chick's optimal demand is high—the chick wants a lot of food because begging for it is cheap.

For any given price for food, P, the amount of food the chick wants, that is, its "*optimal* demand curve" is found from setting

$$\frac{\partial f(K,L(s))}{\partial K} = 0$$

and then solving for K. The result, denoted as $\hat{K}(P)$, is

$$\hat{K}(P) = \left(\frac{pP}{bcL(s)} \right)^{\frac{1}{c-1}}$$

This, then, is the chick's optimal demand curve for food K, as a function of the price of begging, P. Figure 9.3 illustrates the optimal demand curve for three sizes

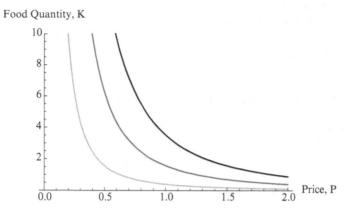

FIGURE 9.3 *Optimal demand curves for chick. Small chick is s → 0.25, medium chick is s → 0.5, Large chick is s → 0.75. Other coefficients are a → 0.5, b → 0.5, c → 0.5, d → 0.1, s_m → 1.*

of chick. As the chick ages, its demand curve shifts on the graph to the left, indicating that for any given price, the optimal demand for a small chick is higher than for a large chick—a small chick optimally "wants" more food for a given price than a large chick.

The chick, then, must somehow communicate this curve to the parent. Groves describes an iterative process (called *tâtonnement*) in which the auctioneer displays a trial price and the bidders indicate what they will buy at that price. Then the auctioneer adjusts the price up or down until a price is found at which all the material for sale would be allocated. There is continuing research in economics and operations research about how a monopolist (i.e., the parent) can learn the demand function of its customers (i.e., the chicks; Aghion, Bolton, Harris, and Jullien, 1991; Balvers and Cosimano, 1990; Lin, 2006) that might be adapted to give insight into how a parent can interpret a chick's begging as revealing its food demand function.

We should be clear that a possible limitation of our approach is whether it is plausible to think a parent can somehow elicit such information from a chick. A bird tending a nest might present various quantities of prey to its nestling to see how much begging each quantity evokes. If a bird could do this somehow, it would learn what the chick's demand curve is. According to our theory, whether communication between parent and chick does convey the demand curve is an important issue to examine empirically. Our theory would be falsified if it proves impossible for a chick to communicate its demand curve to the parent.

The Parent's Perspective—What It Wants To Give

Next we turn to the parent's perspective, and determine the best price for it to charge. We form the expression for the parent's fitness as distinct from the chick's fitness. The fitness production function for the parent might include considerations not present in the chick's fitness production function. The chick's fitness production function, however, remains the same as before.

We might hypothesize that the fitness the parent accumulates during the time interval equals the fitness earned through investing in the chick's growth discounted by a measure of the probability of surviving through the time interval during which the food has been gathered. And for a given degree of inherent danger in the environment (e.g., few vs. many predators, exposure to abiotic hazards), the more food the parent must collect, the lower the probability of survival. Let's hypothesize that the probability of the parent's surviving the interval is

$$e^{-hK}$$

where h is a coefficient measuring the amount of hazard incurred per unit of resource collected, and K is the amount of resource collected.

Therefore, a possible expression for the parent's fitness production function, f_o, is

$$f_0(K, L(s)) = fe^{-hK} = (bK^c L(s) - pPK)e^{-hK}$$

At this point, the parent must choose the price of food, P, to maximize its fitness production. To do this, the chick must first communicate its optimal demand curve to the parent, who then takes this information into account and forms its own fitness production function by substituting $\hat{K}(P)$ for K, yielding, symbolically,

$$f_0(\hat{K}(P), L(s)) = (b\hat{K}(P)^c L(s) - pP\hat{K}(P))e^{-h\hat{K}(P)}$$

This f_0 is a function of P. Figure 9.4 illustrates this f_0 for three sizes of chick. Maximizing this f_0 with respect to P, given the chick's size s, yields the optimal price, $\hat{P}$, the parent should charge to a chick of size, s. Based on this price, the chick bids to buy $\hat{K}(\hat{P})$, and the parent should forage for this amount of food to satisfy the bid while, as a result, experiencing a probability of survival during the interval of $e^{-h\hat{K}(\hat{P})}$.

Chick Self-Feeding—Weaning and Fledging

Now we add to the model the ability of a chick to collect some food by itself. This ability improves as the chick ages and grows in size, until a point is reached at which it is advantageous for both parent and chick to discontinue the parental feeding. This point is when "weaning" or "fledging" occurs, and is analogous to the "spin-off" of a division by a parent company. Here is how the point of weaning can be determined according to the optimal incentives approach.

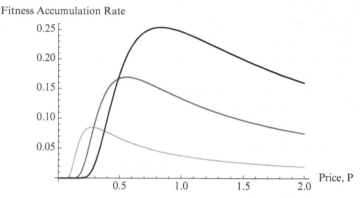

FIGURE 9.4 *Fitness production function for parent. Fitness accumulated per time interval by the parent as a result of the chick's growth during the period, as a function of how much the parent is charging the chick for food, and taking into account its own hazard while foraging. Coefficients for the chicks are same as in Figure 9.3, and the parental foraging hazard coefficient, h is 0.1.*

The chick's fitness production function is now modified to include self-feeding. The food supplied by the chick is K_c and by the parent is K_p. The chick grows according to the sum of its own food and the food supplied by the parent, $bL(K_c+K_p)^c$. The cost of begging is only assessed on the food supplied by the parent, $K_p pP$, where, as before, p is short for the product, ad. When collecting its own food, the chick is assumed to incur hazard, just as the parent does when it collects food. Therefore, the fitness production from its growth, less its cost of begging, is discounted by its foraging hazard in the same way as the parent's fitness production is discounted by its foraging effort. These considerations lead to a new chick fitness production function, f_c, of

$$f_c = (bL(K_c + K_p)^c - K_p pP)e^{-hK_c}$$

The peak of the chick fitness production function indicates the optimal demand for parental food as a function of its price, P, and taking into account the amount of self-feeding it is doing, K_c.

$$\hat{K}_p(P) = \left(\frac{pP}{bcL(s)} \right)^{\frac{1}{c-1}} - K_c$$

The formula for the optimal demand for parental food is the same as previously given without self-feeding, except here the optimal demand is decremented by the amount of food the chick can supply on its own.

Because the demand for parental food is decremented by K_c, there is a price for food at which the demand for parental food is zero.

The parent's fitness production function is the same as the chick's fitness production function, discounted, as before, by the amount of hazard it incurs during its own foraging.

$$f_{0c} = f_c e^{-hK_p} = \left(\left(b \left(K_c + K_p \right)^c L - K_p p P \right) e^{-hK_c} \right) e^{-hK_p}$$

To determine the optimal price the parent should charge, the chick's optimal demand function, $\hat{K}_p(P)$, is substituted in place of K_p, yielding an expression for the parent's fitness accumulation rate as a function of the price it charges for its share of the chick's food.

$$f_{0c}(\hat{K}_p(P), L(s), K_c) = f_{0c} \mid_{\hat{K}_p = K_p(P)}$$

Figures 9.5 to 9.7 illustrate the parental fitness production functions for three levels of self-feeding by the chick; these should be compared with Figure 9.4, wherein no self-feeding was assumed. The sequence of figures shows the parental fitness production function for an increasing degree of self-feeding. The curves terminate at the maximal price the parent can charge and still have the chick solicit food.

CRITERION FOR WEANING

For a low degree of self-feeding (see Fig. 9.5), the curves reveal a local maximum that indicates an optimal price involving some degree of parental support for the chick. In contrast, when the self-feeding yields a lot of food, the parent's highest fitness is attained by pricing the food so high that no food is solicited by the chick—in Figure 9.7, the curves are monotonically increasing with P, and the peak fitness is toward the right where the curves terminate.

Figure 9.6 illustrates the transition degree of self-feeding that marks the break between parental feeding and no parental feeding. For the parameters in the illustration, the transition from parental feeding to no feeding occurs when the chick obtains 0.857864 units of food per time interval from its own foraging efforts. Self-feeding that yields more food than this implies that the parent does not find it advantageous to continue feeding the chick, and self-feeding that yields less than this amount implies that the parent finds it optimum to continue feeding the chick.

We define the criterion for *weaning* to be the self-feeding level at which the parental fitness production function changes from having a local maximum to becoming monotonic. In practice, as the chick grows, its foraging capacity also grows, and when the chick reaches an age or size at which it passes the weaning level of self-feeding, the parent should price the food it delivers so high that the chick no longer solicits parental food. At this point, the parent has "spun off" the chick to

Parental Fitness Production Function,
Chick Size: Red=Large, Dark Green=Medium, Blue=Small
Self Feeding: Chick Supply, Kc = 0.5

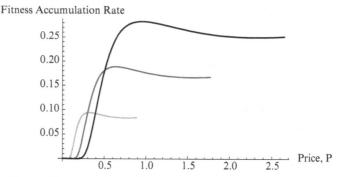

FIGURE 9.5 *Parental fitness production function with chick self-feeding. The self-feeding here yields little food, and the optimal price, located at the local maximum, is low enough to induce the chick to solicit parental food.*

Parental Fitness Production Function,
Chick Size: Red=Large, Dark Green=Medium, Blue=Small
Self Feeding: Chick Supply, Kc=0.8578639984130859

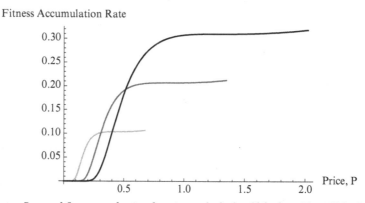

FIGURE 9.6 *Parental fitness production function with chick self-feeding. The self-feeding here yields exactly the amount that marks the transition from parental feeding to no parental feeding. This threshold degree self-feeding yield is the point of weaning.*

forage on its own. The parent continues to accrue fitness gains as the chick grows under its own power and without further parental investment.

The optimal quantity of food delivered by the parent to the chick declines, but remains positive, as the amount of self-feeding increases up until the weaning threshold is passed. Once the weaning threshold is passed, however, the optimal quantity drops abruptly to zero. Thus, weaning is not a gradual loss of the chick's dependence on the parent, but rather is a sudden onset of full independence.

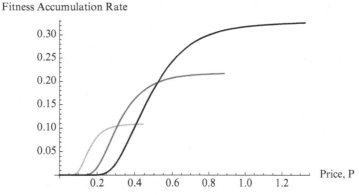

Parental Fitness Production Function,
Chick Size: Red=Large, Dark Green=Medium, Blue=Small
Self Feeding: Chick Supply, Kc=2

FIGURE 9.7 *Parental fitness production function with chick self-feeding. The self-feeding here yields ample food so that the optimal price, which is located at the right end of the curves, is so high that the chick will not solicit parental food.*

Discussion

This paper begins by observing that the theory of family in present-day evolutionary biology revolves around conflict—a theory of family at war with itself, a theory that often refers to any network of family interactions as a "battlefield." This focus on conflict exaggerates the genetic conflict of interest that automatically exists between organisms who are not genetically identical. The existence of a genetic conflict of interest is then all too easily projected into the behavioral realm, where behavioral conflict is uncritically assumed to mirror genetic conflicts of interest. If this biological picture were correct, there would be few grounds for assuming that the EEA, in which early human childrearing practices were presumably evolved, was characterized by an emphasis on empathetic, or loving, family relationships.

However, the program in psychology of recovering childrearing practices that rely on physical affiliative bonds need not stumble on present-day evolutionary biology's picture of family life. Instead, it is present-day evolutionary biology that may be mistaken and, in any case, that needs to pass empirical tests when juxtaposed with alternative hypotheses.

This paper develops an alternative biological picture of family life to that emphasizing genetic conflict. In our social selection perspective, behavior exists, in part, to resolve genetic conflicts of interest by fashioning bargains and incentives that may lead to social harmony, as diagrammed in Figure 9.8.

In previous publications, we have discussed the social selection perspective on the relationship between parents. We envision that potential parent–parent genetic conflict is resolved behaviorally through reciprocal pleasure-producing physical (or vocal) intimacy. Through frequent mutual grooming, preening, sexual contact, and interlocking synchronized calls, animals can stay in touch with one another and ensure coordinated action. Because of the reciprocal pleasure, each can physically enjoy the other's welfare. This process, which we have called *team play*, is hypothesized to produce coordinated action directed to a team goal that is greater than the sum of the payoffs to each individual, approaching even the product of the payoffs (Akçay, Van Cleve, Feldman, and Roughgarden, 2009; Akçay and Roughgarden, 2009; Roughgarden, 2009; Roughgarden et al., 2006). Thus, the parents are assumed to be socially bonded through physical intimacy and working together toward a common goal, which is maximizing a team fitness function that exceeds the sum of their individual fitnesses. According to this perspective, discord that arises between socially bonded mates represents a difference of "opinion" about how best to achieve their common goal of maximizing their team fitness function, and does not represent conflict in the sense of an attempt to subvert their joint effort by making the other partner shoulder more of the burden than is optimum for their common success. We've termed a family with differences of opinion about tactics, but not objectives, an *almost-perfect family*.

In this paper we move on to develop our social selection perspective on the relationship between parents and offspring. We envision that potential parent–offspring genetic conflict is resolved behaviorally by the parents controlling the allocation of resources in response to offspring begging. The parents can carry out what amounts to an auction for the food they have to dispense, and the quantity of begging an offspring is prepared to offer for food amounts to a bid. If an offspring communicates, or the parent otherwise learns, the schedule of the offspring's demand for food as a function of how much begging is required per unit food, the parent can then set the amount of begging needed per unit food so as to satisfy its objectives. The amount of begging needed per unit food is, in effect, the price for food, which the parent can control. This scheme provides an incentive for the offspring to honestly communicate their needs because in so doing they maximize their own fitness, given the price the parent has established, which in turn the parent has set to maximize its own fitness. This scheme of optimal incentives ensures a coincidence of self-interests and results in a group with maximal production of fitness.

As the offspring grow, the parent can continually adjust the price of food as their need changes. As the offspring become increasingly able to get food on their own, a threshold is passed at which the parent should set the price so high that the offspring no longer wish to beg for any. At this point, the offspring are weaned or fledged.

The mathematical modeling presented in this paper is developed explicitly for a parent with one offspring. The approach is extensible to two or more offspring, and this extension will be the subject of a later paper.

It is not clear whether pro-hominid families in the EAA match the description offered here. The degree of physical contact and intimacy believed to occur in human childrearing suggests that the type of bonds social selection theory envisions

Parent-Parent Relation:
Team-Play, Coordinated Action Toward Team Goal,
Physical Intimacy as Mechanism Producing
Nash Bargaining Solution Resolve Genetic Conflict

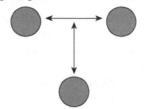

Parent-Offspring Relation:
Auction of Resources to Offspring
as Mechanism Producing Incentives
to Resolve Genetic Conflict

FIGURE 9.8 *Social selection perspective on family dynamics.*

as occurring only between parents *also* occur between parents and their offspring. If so, a theory for family dynamics specifically tailored for pro-hominid societies, and perhaps mammals more generally, would include ingredients of the team play from previous papers now extended to apply to both parent–parent relationships and to parent–offspring relationships. Moreover, this extended family-wide team play may also be mixed in with the optimal incentives approach of this paper.

Acknowledgments

For help and insight, we especially thank Erol Akçay, Jim Fearon, Adam Meirowitz, Lou Gross, Angela Potochnik, Joel Brown, Priya Iyer, and others associated with the Function and Evolution Working Group of the National Institute for Mathematical and Biological Synthesis, an Institute sponsored by the National Science Foundation, the U.S. Department of Homeland Security, and the U.S. Department of Agriculture through NSF Award #EF-0832858, with additional support from the University of Tennessee, Knoxville.

References

Aghion, P., Bolton, P., Harris, C., & Jullien, B. (1991). Optimal learning by experimentation. *Review of Economic Studies, 58,* 621–654.

Akçay, E. (2012). Incentives in the family II: Behavioural dynamics and the evolution of non-costly signaling. *Journal of Theoretical Biology, 294,* 9–18.

Akçay, E., & Roughgarden, J. (2009). The perfect family: Biparental care in animals. *PLoS One, 4,* e7345.

Akçay E., Van Cleve, J., Feldman, M., & Roughgarden, J. (2009). A theory for the evolution of other-regard integrating proximate and ultimate perspectives. *Proceedings of the National Academy of Sciences USA, 106,* 19061–19066.

Alexander, R. D. (1974). The evolution of social behaviour. *Annual Review of Ecology and Systematics, 5,* 325–383.

Arnqvist, G., & Rowe, L. (2005). *Sexual conflict* (pp. 219–220). Princeton, NJ: Princeton University Press.

Balvers, R. & Cosimano, T. (1990). Actively learning about demand and the dynamics of price adjustment. *The Economic Journal, 100,* 882–898.

Bateson, P. (1994). The dynamics of parent-offspring relationships in mammals. *Trends in Ecology and Evolution, 9,* 399–403.

Fouts, H., Hewlett, B., & Lamb, M. (2005). Parent-offspring conflicts among the Bofi farmers and foragers of Central Africa. *Current Anthropology, 46,* 29–50.

Godfray, H. (1991). Signaling of need by offspring to their parents. *Nature, 352,* 328–330.

Godfray, H., & Johnstone, R. (2000). Begging and bleating: The evolution of parent-offspring signalling. *Philosophical Transactions of the Royal Society of London Series B, 355,* 1581–1591.

Grafen, A. (1990). Biological signals as handicaps. *Journal of Theoretical Biology, 144,* 517–546.

Groves, T. (1973). Incentives in teams. *Econometrica, 41,* 617–631.

Johnstone, R., & Grafen, A. (1992). The continuous Sir Philip Sidney Game: A simple model of biological signalling. *Journal of Theoretical Biology, 156,* 215–234.

Johnstone, R., & Grafen, A. (1993). Dishonesty and the handicap principle. *Animal Behaviour, 46,* 759–764.

Kilner, R., & Drummond, H. (2007). Parent-offspring conflict in avian families. *Journal of Ornithology, 148*(Suppl. 2), S241–S246.

Lin, K. (2006). Dynamic pricing with real-time demand learning. *European Journal of Operational Research, 174,* 522–538.

Macnair, M. R., & Parker, G. A. (1978). Models of parent–off-spring conflict. II. Promiscuity. *Animal Behaviour, 26,* 111–122.

Macnair, M. R., & Parker, G. A. (1979). Models of parent–off-spring conflict. III. Intra-brood conflict. *Animal Behaviour, 27,* 1202–1209.

Maestripieri, D. (2002). Parent-offspring conflict in primates. *International Journal of Primatology, 23,* 923–951.

Maestripieri, D. (2004). Genetic aspects of mother-offspring conflict in rhesus macaques. *Behavioral Ecology and Sociobiology, 55,* 381–387.

Maynard Smith, J. (1982). *Evolution and the theory of games.* Cambridge, UK: Cambridge University Press.

Meirowitz, A., Fearon, J., Akçay, E., & Roughgarden, J. (2014). Incentives in the family III: Evolutionary mechanism design. In preparation.

Mock, D., & Forbes, L. (1992). Parent-offspring conflict: A case of arrested development. *Trends in Ecology and Evolution, 7,* 409–413.

Moreno-Rueda, G. (2007). Is there empirical evidence for the cost of begging? *Journal of Ethology, 25,* 215–222.

Parker, G. A. (2006a). Behavioural ecology: The science of natural history. In J. R. Lucas and L. W. Simmons (Eds.), *Essays on animal behaviour: Celebrating 50 years of animal behaviour* (pp. 23–56). Amsterdam: Elsevier.

Parker, G. A. (2006b). Sexual conflict over mating and fertilization: An overview. *Philosophical Transactions of the Royal Society of London Series B, 361,* 235–259.

Parker, G. A., & Macnair, M. R. (1978). Models of parent-off-spring conflict. I. Monogamy. *Animal Behaviour, 26*, 97–110.

Parker, G. A., & Macnair, M. R. (1979). Models of parent–off-spring conflict. IV. Suppression: Evolutionary retaliation by the parent. *Animal Behaviour, 27*, 1210–1235.

Parker, G., Royle, N., & Harley, I. (2002). Begging scrambles with unequal chicks: Interactions between need and competitive ability. *Ecology Letters, 5*, 206–215.

Ricklefs, R. (1968). Patterns of growth in birds. *The Ibis, 110*, 419–451.

Roughgarden, J. (2009). *The genial gene: Deconstructing Darwinian selfishness.* Berkeley, CA: University of California Press.

Roughgarden, J., Oishi, M., & Akçay, E. (2006). Reproductive social behavior: Cooperative games to replace sexual selection. *Science, 311*, 965–970.

Salmon, C. (2005). Parental investment and parent-offspring conflict. In Buss, D. *The handbook of evolutionary psychology* (pp. 506–527). New York: Wiley.

Tregenza, T., Wedell, N., & Chapman, T. (2006). Introduction. Sexual conflict: A new paradigm? *Philosophical Transactions of the Royal Society of London Series B, 361*, 229–234.

Trivers, R. L. (1972). Parental investment and sexual selection. In B. Campbell (Ed.), *Sexual selection and the descent of man, 1871–1971* (pp. 136–179). Chicago: Aldine Atherton.

Trivers, R. L. (1974). Parent-offspring conflict. *American Zoologist, 14*, 249–264.

Zahavi, A. (1977). The cost of honesty (Further remarks on the handicap principle). *Journal of Theoretical Biology, 67*, 603–605.

10

Preliminary Steps Toward Addressing the Role of Nonadult Individuals in Human Evolution

Agustín Fuentes

Children are often absent from our reconstructions of human behavioral evolution. When they are present, it is usually as infants or youngsters placing a reproductive or energetic burden on the mother or both parents. The one place where infants and young have played a distinct role is in the theories of attachment and bonding (Bowlby, 1969), and more recently *affect hunger* (Goldschmidt, 2006). Although there is much theorizing about the core roles of children–caretaker interactions as they relate to the development of healthy humans, there has been less attention to the possibility that nonadult humans played (play) important roles in creating the human niche and are participants in the ongoing process of human behavioral evolution (however, see Konner, 2011).

Basic neo-Darwinian theory prioritizes the action of natural selection and sexual selection as the prime factors in evolutionary change and the emergence of adaptations. Natural selection results in certain phenotypes (morphology and behavior) that effectively reproduce themselves (and their genetic basis or genotype) in a given environment becoming more frequent in their population across generations. Sexual selection is the overrepresentation of specific phenotypes across generations as a result of mate choice or intrasexual competition. Traits that lead to the success of phenotypes and become the predominant traits in subsequent generations are termed adaptations. These traits and those individuals having them are then said to be more "fit" (better at reproducing themselves into subsequent generations) than other individuals in the same population with less successful traits. The basal neo-Darwinian paradigm holds that most systems will strive for optimality, such that those best "fit" phenotypes and their associated genotypes will rise to a majority status within the population over evolutionary time. The traditional assumptions associated within the *environment of evolutionary adaptedness* hold that we can look at this period (circum-Pleistocene) and find the environment of natural selection for modern human phenotypes (behavioral and otherwise). Emergent complexity in evolutionary theory and a firm grasp of the fossil record and modern human evolutionary pathways argues otherwise. Rather than imagining a filter in the past that set up a specific pattern of optimal human behavior, one can better envision human evolution as ongoing, with a dynamic and entangled relationship both temporally and behaviorally with our environments (Fuentes, 2009a, 2009b).

Current concepts regarding complexity and diversity in evolutionary theory are forcing changes in basic assumptions about evolutionary processes (Pigliucci, 2009). It is evident that there is an important role for behavioral modification of social and ecological spaces and their inheritance (Laland, Odling-Smee, J., and Myles, 2010). Recent work acknowledges that patterns and contexts of natural selection are affected by social, epigenetic, and developmental interactors (Jablonka and Lamb, 2005; Odling-Smee, Laland, and Feldman, 2003). We also are increasingly realizing that social and experiential contexts shape bodies and behavior, affecting trajectories in more substantial manners than previously envisioned (Fuentes, 2009b, 2013a, 2012b; Laland et al., 2010). Here I suggest that applying the concepts of niche construction and other emerging perspectives in evolutionary theory in the context of what we know about the fossil record enables us to hypotheses that social cooperation involving significant contributions by nonadult individuals plays a major role in shaping human behavioral patterns, past and present.

Complexity in Evolutionary Theory Helps Us Think About Human Evolution

To begin this discussion we need to review the major emerging perspectives in evolutionary theory.

PLASTICITY AS NORMATIVE

Mary Jane West-Eberhard (2003) suggests that plasticity is one of the key factors for understanding adaptive evolution. She argues that reducing the processes of development and evolutionary change to genomic levels is not always possible or preferable. Her analyses demonstrate that evolved plasticity in development enables the evolution of variant, but adaptive, phenotypes without substantial, or significant, genetic change. This phenotypic plasticity and its relation to ecologies and evolutionary patterns is of core interest in evolutionary theory and thus to our understanding of human evolution.

Phenotypic plasticity is defined as "the production of multiple phenotypes from a single genotype, depending on environmental conditions" (Miner, Sultan, Morgan, Padilla, and Relyea, 2005). There is evidence that a range of organisms express phenotypic plasticity through changes in behavior, physiology, morphology, growth, life history, and demography and that this plasticity can occur both individually and in intergenerational contexts (Miner et al., 2005; Pigliucci, 2001). Research into modeling this plasticity, its potential adaptive value and contexts, and its ecological impact all suggest that phenotypic plasticity is a significant factor for many organisms' evolutionary histories and current behavior and morphology. For humans, variable behavioral patterns are a very important component of our phenotype and thus might be reflective of a specific adaptation enabling a broad range of potential behavioral expression. Piersma and Drent (2003, p. 28) suggest that "when environments change over shorter timescales than a lifetime, individuals that can show continuous, but reversible, transformations in behavior, physiology or morphology, might incur a selective advantage." This might be exactly the kind of inherent plasticity in behavioral systems that is important in thinking about human evolution (see Malone, Fuentes, and White, 2012).

FOUR DIMENSIONS OF INHERITANCE

The biologists Eva Jablonka and Marion Lamb (2005) argue for a "new" new synthesis in how we model evolution. They recognize evolution in four dimensions rather than a focus on just one. Their main point is that traditional neo-Darwinian approaches focus only on the genetic system of inheritance in models of evolutionary patterns and change. Because of this, the majority of hypotheses proposed for scenarios regarding the selection and adaptation of human behavior rely on, or are derived from, perspectives with explanations of ultimate causal factors residing at the genic level or some proxy for genic effect.

Jablonka and Lamb add a perspective wherein three other inheritance systems can also have causal roles in evolutionary change. These other systems are the epigenetic, behavioral, and symbolic inheritance systems. Epigenetic inheritance is found in all organisms, behavioral inheritance in most, and symbolic inheritance is found only in humans. "Information is transferred from one generation to the next by many interacting inheritance systems.... Variation is also *constructed*, in the sense that, whatever their origin, which variants are inherited and what final form they assume depend on various 'filtering' and 'editing' processes that occur before and during transmission." (Jablonka and Lamb, 2005). Many organisms transmit information through behavior and acquisition of patterns that confer evolutionary benefits can occur through socially mediated learning by observation and the reproduction of behavioral patterns and cues. Especially significant for humans is the fact that symbolic inheritance comes with language (or even proto-language) and the ability to engage in information transfer that can be temporally and spatially complex and contain a high density of information. This enables humans (and our ancestors) to construct, acquire, and reproduce a variety of potentially evolutionarily beneficial elements that have no genetic basis or linkage. In terms of human evolution, this perspective forces a concern with the way in which behavioral and symbolic systems construct and interact with social and ecological niches and how, in turn, these systems interact with epigenetic and genetic systems.

Developmental Systems Theory

Developmental systems theory (DST) is proposed as an alternative to what Susan Oyama (2000) calls "developmental dualism." The dualistic approach has led to the proposal of two selective systems, one to carry culture and one biology, with the two mirroring one another in their mode of change (selection), mutually coevolving, occasionally affecting one another (gene–culture coevolution; Richerson and Boyd, 2005; Laland et al., 2010). This approach casts "culture" as a unit or end product of selection with the justification that "Culture is adaptive because it can do things that genes cannot do for themselves" (Richerson and Boyd, 2005). As an expansion to this approach, DST discards discrete channels for synthetically interacting systems whose processes give rise to successive generations.

Oyama, Griffiths, and Gray (2001) lay out a set of main theses of DST, and others (Fuentes, 2009a, 2009b) have attempted to connect them to the modeling of human evolutionary pathways. *Joint determination by multiple causes* suggests that explanations assuming the primacy of "genes," their competition for propagation, and their interactions with an environment are not the only venues for inquiry into the evolution of human behavior. *Context sensitivity and contingency* mandates that the assessment of the evolution of human traits and patterns must take into account various developmental, experiential, and social contexts. Single aspects of human behavior or morphology cannot be seen as independent in an evolutionary sense from any others. *Extended inheritance* is especially characteristic of humans and includes the memory and experience of group members, the previous manipulation of the area in which the group lives, and the patterns of cultural interaction extant in that population. *Development as construction* posits that *traits are made—reconstructed—in development.* Human development is equally affected by the body and by social and ecological factors interacting with one another during the course of constructing the adult human (see also Herrmann, Call, Hernandez-Lloreda, Hare, and Tomasello, 2007). *Distributed control* suggests that a focus on natural selection and genic inheritance while ignoring other dimensions of inheritance is unlikely to effectively explain the full range of human behavior and evolution (see Jabonka and Lamb, 2005). *Evolution as construction* is the concept that *evolution is not a matter of organisms or populations being molded by their environments but of organism-environment systems changing over time.* Human evolutionary patterns are constantly constructing—and being constructed by—constituent elements of demography, social interactions, cultural variations, complex information transfer, and manipulation of the environment in intragroup and intergroup contexts, in addition to the developmental biological and ecological factors throughout the course of life history (Fuentes, 2009a).

Niche Construction

Odling-Smee, Laland, and Feldman (2003) argue that niche construction is a significant evolutionary force. Niche construction is the building and destroying of niches by organisms and the synergistic interactions between organisms and environments. Niche construction creates feedback within the evolutionary dynamic, such that organisms engaged in niche construction significantly modify the evolutionary pressures acting on them, on their descendants, and on unrelated populations sharing the same space (Odling-Smee et al., 2003). Niche construction affects/ alters energy flows in ecosystems through ecosystem engineering creating an ecological inheritance and, like natural selection, contributes to changes over time in the dynamic relationship between organisms and environments (niches).

In regard to humans, Odling-Smee et al. (2003) explicitly state that ecological inheritance, through material culture, and niche construction in general can occur by cultural means. They state that humans are the "ultimate niche constructors" and that adding niche construction to attempts to understand human systems makes such attempts more complicated (bypassing more simplistic neo-Darwinian adaptationist accounts). They see cultural processes as providing a particularly robust vehicle for niche construction. Odling-Smee et al. (2003) propose a specific model for human genetic and cultural evolution that they call a tri-inheritance vision model (TIV). Under TIV, human behavior results from information-acquiring processes at three levels: population genetic processes, ontogenetic processes, and cultural processes. Niche construction in humans emerges from all three of these processes, each of which can affect patterns, contexts, and structure of natural selection. They state, "Much of human niche construction is guided by socially learned knowledge and cultural inheritance, but the transmission of this knowledge is itself dependent on preexisting information acquired through genetic evolution, complex ontogenetic processes, or prior social learning" (Odling-Smee et al., 2003, pp. 260–261).

Biocultural Evolution

Biocultural approaches involve studies of human populations with the assumptions that the "environment" is more than the external physical conditions surrounding a human population (Dufour, 2006). Recent substantial advances in the understanding of the relationship and interfaces between social structures, cultural behavioral contexts, and human physiology and health act to link evolutionary approaches and sociocultural approaches with medical anthropology (Dufour, 2006; Panter-Brick and Fuentes, 2008). The common ground of "biocultural" is advocated by researchers undertaking systematic ways of understanding the co-relationship of social contexts and physiological patterns (Dressler, 2005; Goodman and Leatherman, 1998). This process is similar to the symbolic dimension of Jablonka and Lamb's (2005) approach, the first three premises of DST, and the TIV perspective of Odling-Smee et al. (2003). The concept of phenotypic plasticity, and its relation to adaptability, plays a core role here.

The biocultural approach can provide a powerful tool for studies of human behavior, and for our efforts to model the evolution of human behavior. The explicit recognition of mutual engagement between human biology and behavior and a major role of "culture" is central to most of the emerging themes in evolutionary theory as applied to humans.

Integrating These Perspectives Into Questions About Human Behavior

Humans are biocultural organisms, making social and biological evolutionary processes intertwined. Given the outline above, I would like to propose a framework as to how we might resituate our approaches to the creation of models and hypotheses for the evolution of human behavior (from Fuentes, 2009a, 2013b).

1. *Human behavioral evolution must be primarily seen as a system evolving rather than as a set of independent or moderately connected traits evolving.* While we might create hypotheses to explain specific behavioral patterns, they must be explicitly connected to broader themes and contexts. Human behavior itself is not a set of individual actions, but rather is a consortium of action, experience, and innovation.
2. *Niche construction is a core factor in human behavioral evolution.* The ability of humans to modify their surroundings is central to any explanation of human behavior. These surroundings include the social, the material, and the ecological. Understanding human evolution requires assessing the interactive and mutually mutable relationship humans have with their social and structural ecologies. We must accept the possibility that evolutionary pressures can be modified as they are occurring and that human response to such challenges need not always fit the standard ecological/evolutionary or constructivist models.
3. *Ecological and social inheritance are core to human behavior.* Humans almost always exist in a place where there have been humans before them. Social and ecological parameters are affected by the previous generations, and individuals in subsequent human generations inherit a much larger amount of information than do any other organisms. This provides humans with a broader ability to respond to challenges, though with a more diverse array of means than other organisms.
4. *Enhanced communication and information transfer is core to modeling and understanding human behavior.* Humans use their extensive ability to convey information to respond to the basic ecological and social challenges that they face; thus models should include a role for a type of communication not possible in other organisms.
5. *Feedback, rather than linear models, is central in human behavioral evolution.* This is probably true for most evolutionary models in complex organisms; however, it should be explicit in hypotheses and models for humans (it already is in many). Feedback in a system implies that, rather than moving from A to B, the system may modify (*construct*) itself

during the processes of acting. If feedback is a component of a system, outcomes are not necessarily based on the initial behavioral pattern within the systems.

6. *We should consider the potential impacts of diverse biological and social-cultural processes that shuffle variation in evolutionary change and the possibility that natural selection can occur at multiple levels.* Most hypotheses for the evolution of human behavior rely strictly on natural selection. However, we should also include impacts from the diverse array of cultural, social, and symbolic practices that alter human demography, residence, movement, and interaction patterns as having roles in genetic, phenotypic, and behavioral responses and changes.

7. *Our models must include a specific role for plasticity in behavioral response as a baseline as opposed to assumptions of optimality striving or single trait maximization.* It is most likely that the majority of human behavioral changes over time are not optimal, even if they do result in adaptation. It is likely that the majority of successful human responses reflect a pattern of behavioral plasticity as opposed to specific selection for a particular behavioral adaptation in response to a single selective pressure. This suggests that explanations that focus on the link of a particular behavior to a specific adaptive outcome are likely poor models for human behavioral evolutionary processes.

In human populations, patterns of genetic change are largely influenced by symbolic and other cultural processes that affect behavior as well as genotypic factors. That is, marriage and migration patterns are often the results of political, historical, and religious processes, not necessarily ecologically or functionally driven patterns. It is also important to note that not all behavior is functional in an evolutionary sense. Natural selection need not always, or even frequently, be invoked to explain the innovation and spread of behavior. Behavior can change over time through forces akin to drift or even in response to a wide array of processes that are not related to reproductive output or other measures of selection. When selection is invoked as a pressure affecting behavioral systems, we should also be prepared to include models that accept selection as acting on levels beyond a selfish gene or selfish individual focus and be ready to focus on group-level social contexts as the central arena of interest (as highlighted by Odling-Smee et al., 2003; Oyama, 2000; Oyama et al., 2001; Sober and Wilson, 1998; Tomasello, 1999; Wilson and Wilson, 2007). Using the above structural guidelines as a framework, we can attempt to examine potentially significant broad elements in human evolutionary history (cooperation and the potential roles for immatures, in this case) as facets of the human niche and attempt to model patterns of evolutionary change using modern human behavior, primate and hominoid-wide trends, and the fossil record as testing grounds.

Some Preliminary Thoughts on Cooperation
and Intergenerational Relationships in the
Context of Human Evolution

Humans almost always exist in a place where there have been humans before them. Social and ecological parameters are affected by the previous generations, and individuals in subsequent generations inherit a much larger amount of information than do any other organisms (at least since the advent of rudimentary language and tool use). Even when moving into new territories, humans carry some portion of the knowledge of past members of their group with them. This provides humans with a broad ability to respond to challenges. Humans may come upon multiple effective responses to the same challenges and potentially share them across individuals and possibly even groups. Humans use this extensive ability to convey information to respond to the basic ecological challenges that they face.

One startling question that we must address in reconstructing patterns of human evolution is, Of all the species and genera of hominins extant during the Pleistocene, why did *Homo sapiens* succeed and the rest go extinct? I suggest that answering this question involves taking a more careful look at intragroup behavior, including an active role for nonadult individuals (see also Hrdy, 2009; Konnor, 2011).

Mainstream approaches in the inquiry into human evolution frequently look for "big moments" in our evolutionary history as core markers for understating humanity (e.g., bipedalism, passing the 1000-cc brain size). These monumental shifts are then argued to have arisen through specific selection events or responses that catapult a lineage from one stage to the next. Is it possible that in this approach to examining human evolution we overlook some core aspects critical to niche construction, behavioral and even symbolic inheritance? More specifically, I suggest that we have ignored some important possibilities in within- and between-group behavior that might provide not only additional information about human evolutionary trends but also new explanatory models and even insight into modern human behavior (Fuentes, 2013b).

Recent renewed interest in the human heterosexual pair bond (i.e., Chapais, 2009; Lovejoy, 2010) can obfuscate the possibility that this unit is not the basal unit of human social organization. A broad array of evidence has been previously compiled to argue that early humans lived in multi-adult groups with a range of bonds between adults and across age cohorts (Fuentes, 2009a; Goldschmidt, 2008; Pederson et al., 2003). We have to move away from these notions that the basal unit of analyses for human behavior is the pair or the male–female unit, or even the mother–infant unit—we do not live in dyads, nor have dyads been the main unit of interaction for humans for millions of years. Expanding outside this pair focus might enable us to get a better grasp on why we do what we do, from an evolutionary sense. I suggest that we need to envision the social group, and all of its members, as the nexus and context for the modeling of human evolution.

During the past decade or so, a number of researchers have reintroduced a focus on intergenerational interactions (more than just mother–infant interactions) as core focal points for evolutionary questions and investigations (Hill, Barton, and Hurtado, 2009; Konnor, 2011). For example, cooperative breeding is becoming a central point for explanations of human social systems (Hrdy, 2009; Van Schaik and Burkhart, 2009). The concept that multiple caretakers interact with infants within a group suggests that human social and physiological systems are evolving in the context of a particular social ecology. That is, the bonding and social negotiations that characterize a cooperatively breeding group are going to involve group members of different age categories. If caretakers include adults of both sexes and nonadult individuals, then the social landscape for interactions and information transfer involves immatures as active participants. This system of cooperative care of the very young can itself act as a form of ecological inheritance in which the arena of social interactions, from an evolutionary standpoint, is not the dyad or the mother–infant pair, but rather is the group of multi-generational social actors.

This perspective has been supported recently by the suggestion that males were more heavily involved in caretaking of young during a range of activities (see Gettler, 2010) and that this behavioral patterning emerges relatively early in hominin evolution (possibly as early as 3 million years ago) because of the relatively large size of infants at birth combined with a lack of body hair and/or extensive infant grasping a capabilities (DaSilva, 2011). DaSilva suggests that carrying such large infants may have limited arboreality in hominin females and may have selected for alloparenting behavior earlier than previously thought, and Gettler notes that the energetic benefits (to mothers) of males (and possibly juveniles) carrying infants are substantial. This, combined with extensive evidence for alloparenting and male participation in infant care in modern humans, supports the concept that when attempting to reconstruct human evolutionary trajectories in regard to infant care, all group members are fair game as potentially significant actors.

A central role of alloparenting resonates well with the increased recent attention to the myriad ways in which extensive and substantial cooperation has been positioned as central to human evolution. Cooperation is basically when a human behaves, possibly along with others, in a manner that incurs some cost for the individual to benefit one or more other individuals (potentially including themselves). Following the work of many others, I have argued in numerous publications (Fuentes, 2004, 2013b; Oka and Fuentes, 2010) that given humans' neurologic complexity, individual biobehavioral diversity, and ability to convey extremely large and temporally disparate amounts of information behaviorally, it appears that cooperation and shared information exchange, combined with socially negotiated distribution of labor, effectively coordinates large groups of people: simply put, cooperation is what we do best and what makes us such a successful species.

Hart and Sussman (2008; see also Fuentes et al., 2010) make a robust argument for the specific evolution of hypercooperation as a core facet of the human niche. They argue that intense and focused predation pressure on *Australopithecus*, and later hominins, created a context of selection that favored intragroup coop-eration and information sharing at a very high level. The downstream effects of this, when one considers behavioral and ecological inheritance in addition to basic patterns and effects of natural selection, is a picture wherein cooperative interindi-vidual interactions form the core of human behavioral adaptation. This point is not new, but has been reiterated, researched, supported, and repeatedly demonstrated since the time of Darwin. In short, there is substantial research demonstrating that humans are unique relative to other forms of life on this planet in the extent and complexity of their cooperative patterns.

This level of cooperation can be best envisioned as emerging as part of our dynamic evolutionary histories and trajectories, not simply as an adaptive response to particular pressures at one point (or points) in our past. Primates are character-ized by a specific type of "social intelligence" (Dunbar and Shultz, 2007), such that "distinctive aspects of primate cognition evolved mainly in response to the especially challenging demands of a complex social life of constant competition and coopera-tion with others in the social group" (Herrmann et al., 2007; Silk, 2007), in addition to the external ecological pressures. There could therefore be a ratcheting up of this social complexity in anthropoids, which is increased in the apes (hominoids) and exponentially enhanced in the hominins. One could envision a scenario wherein the basal complex sociality of mammals in enhanced in primates, and then primates use their social networks and contexts as a tool to meet and modify the demands of the environment (the selective landscape; MacKinnon and Fuentes, 2011). As the local environments are being modified, selection pressures alter, changing the selective landscapes for the primate populations (i.e., niche construction). Increased cognitive complexity in the hominoids (apes) facilitates a faster or more intensive use of the social bonds and relationships as tools to meet ecological challenges. This system can be envisioned as substantially augmented in the human lineage.

This increased cooperation and reciprocity become central components of pri-mates, hominoid, and eventually human behavioral repertoires. Humans are con-stantly engaging the social and biotic ecologies in feedback scenarios resulting in niche construction and concomitant shifting or modification of selective landscapes. As broad and complex social behavioral complexes (reliant on extensive coopera-tion) become commonplace in the hominins, extensive and adaptive cooperation arises as an emergent property of the system. Because of the extensive cooperation and the generally intensive reciprocity in the human lineage, multiple instances of seemingly altruistic behavior can be experienced across the lifetimes of individuals without effectively negative fitness costs. Here cooperative action is central to the physiologic and behavioral patterns required to effectively negotiate high-level and complex social networks where coalitions, multi-party social negotiations, and reci-procity are the primary avenues for social and reproductive success (Figure 10.1). If we view this system through the lens of niche construction, multi-systems of inheri-tance and a broader developmental systems approach, it emerges as a dynamic pro-cess not a simple adaptive response (Fuentes, 2013a).

The case for cooperation as central to human success has been made for human ancestors, modern humans in simple foraging societies, agriculturalists, and modern nation states (Fry, 2013). There is copious fossil and material evidence that early on in our evolutionary history, increasing the ways in which we worked together as opposed to selfish and individually based behavior enabled humans to spread far and wide across the planet. There is also a large body of evidence that demonstrates that agriculture, village and city structures, large-scale religious interactions and political systems, and trade and market economies all rely on a substantial infrastructure of human cooperation for their success (Enfield and Levinson, 2006; Henrich, Boyd, Bowles, Camerer, Ferh, and Gintis, 2004; Hill et al., 2009). This does not mean that competition and conflict are not also extremely common, just that these are not the basis for our success. Aggression can emerge out of cooperation, or the breakdown of cooperation, but nearly every study conducted on human social behavior indicates higher frequencies and greater emphasis on cooperation than any other single behavioral pattern.

This does not mean that humans are all egalitarian, or that we are selfless. It simply reflects the reality that human societies are based on extremely complex systems of cooperation and mutual interreliance by individuals within a group, such that a consistent selfish behavioral strategy will not be sustainable in human groups. This prevalence of cooperation does not negate aggression or violence and, in fact, probably enables the kind of intense and extreme violence that is characteristic of modern warfare and civil conflicts. To create and maintain armies, you need extremely complex cooperation, engagement in wide-scale warfare coordination, and a nearly complete suppression of selfish behavior. One might even argue that war is possible directly because of humans' unique abilities to have large-scale and intensive cooperation.

Specifically what type of niche construction might be happening in populations of the genus *Homo* in the Pleistocene to lay the context for the inclusion of non-adult actors as a factor in human evolution? The period of 2 to 1 million years ago is characterized by the following patterns (Anton and Snodgrass, 2012; Fuentes, 2013b):

- An increasing brain size and an extended period of, and effort in, child care in the genus *Homo* ~1.5 million years ago led to:
- More cooperative interactions between group members, across generations
- An associated increase in communicative complexity
- Increased effectiveness at avoiding predation
- An expansion of the types and patterns of habitat exploited
- As *Homo* became more costly, predators shifted emphasis to easier prey, reducing the overall selective pressure of predation.
- *Homo* experienced increased opportunity for social interactions, range exploration, and testing a variety of novel foraging opportunities, all of which demanded—and fed back into—an emerging higher cognitive functioning.

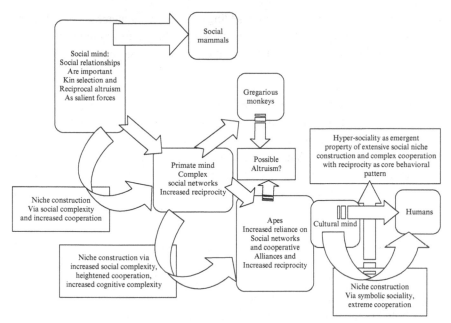

FIGURE 10.1 *The patterns and processes in primate and human evolution related to extreme cooperation and niche constructions.* (Reprinted from *Origins of Altruism and Cooperation. Developments in Primatology: Progress and Prospects,* Volume 36, Part 2, 2011, 121–143, *Primates, Niche Construction, and Social Complexity: The Roles of Social Cooperation and Altruism,* MacKinnon, K.C and Fuentes, A., with kind permission from Springer Science and Business Media.)

This leads to a suite of heritable components (biologically, ecologically, and behaviorally) resulting in human social and ecological niche construction, including complex tool manufacture and use, possibly the creation and use of fire (see Wrangham, 2009), increased infant survivorship, and enhanced information transference through increasingly complex communication patterns. These, in turn, are all involved in the feedback loops and social-ecological contexts that create the patterns and possibilities for an evolving hominin cognition, which in turn facilitates success in a suite of dynamic environments (Sterelny, 2012; Whiten and Erdal, 2012).

This model of integrated cooperation as a component of the human niche also involves nonadults as central players (Figure 10.2). If we accept that humans are cooperative breeders and function as complex cooperating groups, then we need envision to the role of nonadult individuals in the behaviors surrounding the care of the very young. It has been argued that alloparents (ranging from grandmothers to aunts and uncles, plus fathers and unrelated males) bring down the maternal costs and increase the overall payoffs in terms of increased infant survivorship (see Gettler, 2010; Hawkes, O'Connell, and Blurton-Jones, 2003; Hrdy, 2009). Thinking of immatures as part of the group in the sense of active niche construction and behavioral cooperation enables one to note that, in combination with extended allocare and extended development, come very high time and effort costs. If immatures participate extensively in allocare (as siblings or simply as members of a broadly cooperative breeding group), their contribution can be significant in terms of energetic benefits for the mothers and social (and possibly physiologic) benefits for the acting immatures.

In this system, we could also see that some level of foraging by immatures would contribute to overall foraging and food processing success rates and potentially create individual benefits to group members. This is not a simple group selection argument wherein groups with more "helpers" do better than those that have fewer. Rather, it assumes that multiple members of a human group acting in concert can alter or maintain specific patterns of niche creation and ecological exploitation that set a particularly beneficial ecological and social stage relative to other hominin species, who may not be able to cognitively or behaviorally reach this level of collaborative behavior. Thus we can see a diverse array of selective forces acting at the individual and group levels and the responses by early humans affecting the local ecologies such that the selection pressures shift or are reduced over time. This can also be seen in antipredator behavior, whereby nonadult individuals can participate as sentries, scouts, or transmitters of information over distance to contribute to the group being able to utilize a broader range while simultaneously practicing antipredator strategies that enhance the members' individual outcomes relative to other hominins where immatures are not playing such roles.

Immatures contribute to social niche through participation in, and co-creation of, the social network that is a central aspect of human behavioral ecology (e.g., Konnor, 2011). Nonadults can participate, at some level, in the process of materials collection and transport for tool construction, and may even be involved in aspects of the actual tool-making process. By extended learning opportunities (including active teaching) and enhanced modes of communication (proto-language), immatures may be participating in group symbolic communication and the creation and propagation of symbolic aspects of local cultures (and thus symbolic inheritance and group identity). All of this presents the possibility that immatures are actors alongside adults in at least some facets of the social and ecological inheritance systems that enable behavioral flexibility and extended adaptation, both factors in the long-term success of the genus *Homo*. It is very likely that unlike other hominins and most primates, immature members of the genus *Homo* were involved at some level in alloparenting, ecological and social construction, and the broad-scale cooperation that enabled our genus to outcompete all other hominins.

Although this chapter can be best seen as a speculative foray into the possibilities of nonadults as important actors in human evolution, it remains an area that has little robust fossil evidence to truly assess it. However, one cannot negate the strong possibility that children play an integral part in human evolution. Beyond seeing them as passive or minor actors in mother–infant or caretaker–immature interactions, we can posit that nonadults have effects on the local ecologies and the social and structural relationships within groups and between groups and their environments (Konnor, 2011). This means we need to think about past and present

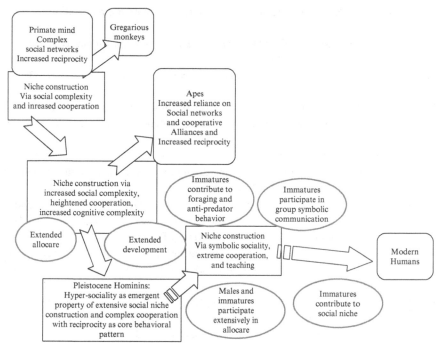

FIGURE 10.2 *Starting with a hominoid (ape) level of social complexity we can see the areas where contributions from non-adult individuals may have affected the trajectory of niche construction in human evolution.* (Adapted from *Origins of Altruism and Cooperation. Developments in Primatology: Progress and Prospects,* Volume 36, Part 2, 2011, 121–143, *Primates, Niche Construction, and Social Complexity: The Roles of Social Cooperation and Altruism,* MacKinnon, K.C and Fuentes, A., with kind permission from Springer Science and Business Media.)

intergenerational relationships as part of the human evolutionary trajectory and consider children as core agents when modeling what it means to be human.

References

Anton, S. C., & Snodgrass, J. (2012). Origin and evolution of genus Homo. *New Perspectives in Current Anthropology, 53*(6), 479–496.

Bowlby, J. (1969). *Attachment.* New York: Basic Books.

Chapais, B. (2009). *Primeval kinship: How pair-bonding gave birth to human society.* Cambridge, MA: Harvard University Press.

DaSilva, J. M. (2011). A shift toward birthing relatively large infants early in human evolution. *Proceedings of the National Academy of Sciences USA, 108*(3), 1022–1027.

Dressler, W. W. (2005). What's cultural about biocultural research? *Ethos, 33,* 20–45.

Dufour, D. L. (2006). The 23rd annual Raymond Pearl Memorial Lecture. Biocultural approaches in human biology. *American Journal of Human Biology, 18*(1), 1–9.

Dunbar, R. I. M., & Shultz, S. (2007). Understanding primate brain evolution. *Science*, 317, 1344–1347.

Enfield, N. J., & Levinson, S. (Eds.) (2006). *Roots of human sociality: Culture, cognition, and interaction*. New York: Berg Press.

Fry, D. (Ed.) (2013). *War, peace, and human nature* (pp.78–94). Oxford, UK: Oxford University Press.

Fuentes, A. (2004). It's not all sex and violence: Integrated anthropology and the role of cooperation and social complexity in human evolution. *American Anthropologist, 106*(4), 710–718.

Fuentes, A. (2009a). *Evolution of human behavior*. New York: Oxford University Press.

Fuentes, A. (2009b). Re-situating anthropological approaches to the evolution of human behavior. *Anthropology Today, 25*(3), 12–17.

Fuentes, A. (2013a). Blurring the biological and social in human becomings. In T. Ingold & G. Paalson (Eds.), *Biosocial becomings: Integrating social and biological anthropology* (pp. 42–58). Cambridge, UK: Cambridge University Press.

Fuentes, A. (2013b). Cooperation, conflict, and niche construction in the genus Homo. In D. Fry (Ed.), *War, peace, and human nature* (pp. 78–94). Oxford, UK: Oxford University Press.

Fuentes, A., Wyczalkowski, M., & MacKinnon, K. C. (2010). Niche construction through cooperation: A nonlinear dynamics contribution to modeling facets of the evolutionary history in the genus Homo. *Current Anthropology, 51*(3), 435–444.

Gettler, L. (2010). Direct male care and hominin evolution: Why male–child interaction is more than a nice social idea. *American Anthropologist, 112*(1). 7–21

Goldschmidt, W. (2006). *The bridge to humanity: How affect hunger trumps the selfish gene*. Oxford, UK: Oxford University Press

Goodman, A. H., & Leatherman, T. L. (Eds.) (1998). *Building a new biocultural synthesis*. Ann Arbor, MI: University of Michigan.

Hart, D. L., & Sussman, R. W. (2008). *Man the hunted: Primates, predators, and human evolution*. New York: Basic Books.

Hawkes, K., O'Connell, J. F., & Blurton-Jones, N. G. (2003). Human life histories: Primate trade-offs, grandmothering socioecology, and the fossil record. In P. M. Kappeler & M. E. Pereira (Eds.), *Primate life histories and socioecology* (pp. 204–227). Chicago: University of Chicago Press.

Henrich, J., Boyd, R., Bowles, S., Camerer, C., Ferh, E., & Gintis, H. (Eds.) (2004). *Foundations of human sociality: Economic experiments and ethnographic evidence form fifteen small-scale societies*. Oxford, UK: Oxford University Press.

Herrmann, E., Call, J., Hernandez-Lloreda, M. V., Hare, B., & Tomasello, M. (2007). Humans have evolved specialized skills of social cognition: The cultural intelligence hypothesis. *Science, 317*, 1360–1366.

Hill, K., Barton, M., & Hurtado, M. (2009). The emergence of human uniqueness: Characters underlying behavioral modernity. *Evolutionary Anthropology, 18*, 187–120.

Hrdy, S. B. (2009). *Mothers and others: The evolutionary origins of mutual understanding*. Cambridge, MA: Harvard University Press.

Jablonka, E., & Lamb, M. (2005). *Evolution in four dimensions: Genetic, epigenetic, behavioral, and symbolic variation in the history of life*. Cambridge, MA: MIT Press.

Konner, M. (2011). *The evolution of childhood: Relationships, emotion, mind.* Cambridge, MA: Harvard University Press.

Laland, K. N., Odling-Smee, J., & Myles, S. (2010). How culture shaped the human genome: Bringing genetics and the human sciences together. *Nature Reviews Genetics, 11*, 137–148.

Lovejoy, O. (2010). Reexamining human origins in light of Ardipithecus ramidus. *Science, 326*, 74e1–e8.

MacKinnon, K. C., & Fuentes, A. (2011). Primates, niche construction, and social complexity: The roles of social cooperation and altruism. In R. W. Sussman & R. C. Cloninger (Eds.), *Origins of altruism and cooperation. Developments in primatology: Progress and prospects* (Vol. 36, Pt. 2, pp. 121–143). New York: Springer.

Malone, N. M., Fuentes, A., & White, F. J. (2012). Variation in the social systems of extant hominoids: Comparative insight into the social behaviour of early hominins. *International Journal of Primatology, 33*(6), 1251–1277.

Miner, B. G., Sultan, S. E, Morgan, S. G., Padilla, D. K., & Relyea, R. A. (2005). Ecological consequences of phenotypic plasticity. *Trends in Ecology and Evolution, 20*(12):685–692.

Odling-Smee, F., Laland, J., Kevein, N., & Feldman, M. W. (2003). *Niche construction: The neglected process in evolution.* Princeton, NJ: Princeton University Press.

Oka, R., & Fuentes, A. (2010). From reciprocity to trade: How cooperative infrastructures form the basis of human socioeconomic evolution. In R. C. Marshal (Ed.), *Cooperation in social and economic life* (pp. 3–28). Lanham, MD: Altamira Press.

Oyama, S. (2000). *Evolution's eye: A systems view of the biology-culture divide.* Durham, NC: Duke University Press.

Oyama, S., Griffiths, P. E., & Gray, R. D. (2001). Introduction: What is developmental systems theory? In S. Oyama, P. E. Griffiths, & R. D. Gray (Eds.), *Cycles of contingency: Developmental systems and evolution* (pp. 1–12). Cambridge, MA: MIT Press.

Panter-Brick, C., & Fuentes, A. (Eds.) (2008). *Health, risk and adversity.* New York: Berghahn Books.

Pederson, C. A., Ahnert, L., Anzenberger, G., Belsky, J., Draper, P., Fleing, A. S., et al. (2003). Group report. Beyond infant attachment: The origins of bonding later in life. In C. S. Carter, L. Ahnert, K. E. Grossmann, et al. (Eds.), *Attachment and bonding: A new synthesis* (pp. 385–428). Cambridge, MA: MIT Press.

Piersma, T., & Drent, J. (2003). Phenotypic flexibility and the evolution of organismal design. *Trends in Ecology and Evolution, 18*, 228–233.

Pigliucci, M. (2001). *Phenotypic plasticity: Beyond nature and nurture.* Baltimore: Johns Hopkins University Press.

Pigliucci, M. (2009). An extended synthesis for evolutionary biology: The year in evolutionary biology. *Annals of the New York Academy of Sciences, 1168*, 218–228.

Richerson, P. J., & Boyd, R. (2005). *Not by genes alone: How culture transformed human evolution.* Chicago: University of Chicago Press.

Silk, J. B. (2007). Social components of fitness in primate groups. *Science, 317*(5843), 1347–1351.

Sober, E., & Wilson, D. S. (1998). *Do unto others: The evolution and psychology of unselfish behavior.* Cambridge, MA: Harvard University Press.

Sterelny, K. (2012). *The evolved apprentice: How evolution made humans unique.* Cambridge, MA: MIT Press.

Tomasello, M. (1999). The human adaptation for culture. *Annual Review of Anthropology,* *28*, 509–529.

van Schaik, C. P., & Burkart, J. M. (2009). *Mind the gap: Cooperative breeding and the evolution of our unique features.* In P. M. Kappeler & J. Silk J (Eds.), *Mind the gap: Tracing the origins of human universals* (pp. 477–496). Berlin: Springer.

West-Eberhard, M. J. (2003). *Developmental plasticity and evolution.* New York: Oxford University Press.

Whiten, A., & Erdal, D. (2012). The human socio-cognitive niche and its evolutionary origins. *Philosophical Transactions of the Royal Society of London Series B, 367,* 2119–2129.

Wilson, D. S., & Wilson, E. O. (2007). Rethinking the theoretical foundation of sociobiology. *Quarterly Review of Biology, 82*(4), 327–348.

Wrangham, R. (2009). *Catching fire: How cooking made us human.* New York: Basic Books.

{ Commentary }

Conflict and Evolution
Melvin Konner

Roughgarden and Song (chapter 9) make a sophisticated contribution to the ongoing debate about parent–offspring conflict, initiated by Robert Trivers (1974). According to this initial theory, conflict between parent and offspring is not incidental noise in what should be a smoothly functioning system, still less a departure from naturally harmonious family relations. On the contrary, it is intrinsic because the offspring is at least twice as related to itself as it is to any sibling (including unborn ones), whereas the parent is equally related to all its offspring, past, present, and future. Thus any one offspring should be expected to demand more than its parent wants to give, especially at certain junctures when the welfare of the parent's other offspring or potential offspring might be compromised. Weaning conflict in mammals is a classic example.

This model was important, among other reasons, because many ideas about human family functioning, and even schools of family therapy, were premised on the belief that a family is like an organism, tending toward homeostasis and equilibrium unless severely disturbed in some way. The goal in that case would be to use the intrinsic righting mechanisms of the family to restore its natural harmony. As Roughgarden and Song point out, the idea of intrinsic parent–offspring conflict is tied to sexual reproduction, and also to a claimed intrinsic conflict between the sexes. So if the parent–offspring conflict model were right, there would be multiple sources of intrinsic conflict in a multi-person family. This would make the intrinsic harmony view of the family implausible.

As Roughgarden and Song note, Trivers' view has been extended and widely applied, but it has also been challenged. Their contribution is to apply a modified version of a mathematical model borrowed from Walrasian (neoclassical) economics. This model looks at conglomerates in which the corporation must ensure its own success by maintaining cooperation among the different entities that make it up. The entity is a "biological conglomerate" or "family firm" in which the parent-as-manager resembles a parent corporation with divisions corresponding to offspring—say, a clutch of chicks begging for food.

Using mathematics plausibly derived from the economic analog, Roughgarden and Song argue that the begging of each chick is an honest signal of its need, and the energy it puts into begging is the price it is willing to pay for its next bit of food. Viewing the multi-chick begging situation as a "Walrasian auction," they go on to quote Wikipedia: "a Walrasian auction perfectly matches supply with demand." So (in neoclassical economic terms) the market clears—the internal market within the family firm leaves no need for conflict.

It is interesting that these authors choose a model from Walrasian economics, since the original models of family conflict drew on neoclassical economic models as well. But the competition is muted in this one because all are members of one firm. It is important to note, though, that Walrasian models have come under intense and often unfavorable scrutiny in recent decades from the new field of behavioral economics (Bowles, 2006). These critics argue that the psychological and behavioral assumptions of neoclassical theory (e.g., equality of information among buyers and sellers) are often quite implausible, and that in many real-world cases, supply and demand do not match, and markets do not clear.

In plain words, someone may be taking unfair advantage, and honesty does not always win the day. This behavioral economics view of markets would seem to be compatible with the idea of intrinsic family conflict. But even to use Roughgarden and Song's ingenious analogy, we can ask questions. What happens when a firm decides to spin off or sell one of its components before it can be assured of succeeding, believing that the greater good of the remaining firm will be served? Are there not situations when two or more directors of divisions want to succeed the CEO? Can they really be relied on to signal their needs honestly? Can the CEO always manage the allocation of resources accurately and fairly? If so, why do some CEOs fail?

All these fanciful-sounding analogies on the down side of family life have actually been seriously considered and tested, as shown for birds and other vertebrates in the work of Stephen Emlen (1995). Emlen has applied concepts derived from family dynamics in birds to human family therapy; in both kinds of families, both cooperation and conflict occur, and at predictable times. The posited and observed kinds of intrafamily conflict studied since Trivers' original model in no way preclude harmony, teamwork, and love in other circumstances. This of course includes the human environments of evolutionary adaptedness, in which exceptional care of infants and children can be observed, but also infanticide, severe sibling rivalry, and other expressions of interests in conflict, as in many species of frogs, birds, and other vertebrates (Mock, 2004). Conflict and teamwork are not mutually exclusive; they are alternative strategies for different adaptive circumstances.

Agustín Fuentes (chapter 10) presents a cogent theoretical discussion of the role of juveniles in evolution, in the light of much new information about the central role of plasticity. He notes the great contribution of plasticity to the process of evolution itself, as shown in Mary Jane West-Eberhard's (2003) magnum opus, and he also praises Eva Jablonski and Marion Lamb's (2005) view of evolution as consisting of four separate processes: genetic, epigenetic, behavioral, and symbolic. Three of the four are of course not new, and it remains to be seen how significant epigenetic processes are in evolution. For now it is clear that some epigenetic change (e.g., some DNA methylation) during an individual's lifetime can be passed on to offspring in the germ line with measurable phenotypic consequences in the next generation. This could in time provide evidence for a kind of Lamarckian evolution. Fuentes goes on to offer cogent discussions of cultural evolution and gene–culture coevolution with niche construction, although he does not cite the most careful analysis of this process, that of William Durham (1991).

Fuentes raises the possibility, which I have also discussed (Konner, 2010), that children may have become pioneers of a sort in human evolution at a certain point, owing to their high degree of plasticity and the high level of cooperation among adults that is needed for their care (e.g., postweaning provisioning) as well as for information transfer. I would add the uniquely human behaviors of teaching and collaborative learning (Tomasello, Kruger, and Ratner, 1993) to the complex of adaptations that may have made the greatest difference in the process of hominization. In this perspective, children may have been major contributors to the emergence of human culture.

In another direction, Douglas P. Fry (see chapter 7) has spent decades studying rough-and-tumble (R&T) play, showing that it is a universal feature of childhood in human cultures, as well as in other primates. Boys always do more of it than girls, but girls do it too, and for both sexes the childhood version bears little resemblance to real fighting. This resemblance becomes a bit closer in adolescence, but there are still important distinctions, and throughout development R&T play is not intended to harm; if it does so, it is almost always by accident. So what is its function?

Fry addresses this question by surveying the published literature on aggression in hunter-gatherer societies, and concludes that it is almost always characterized by restraint. Some groups, like the Netsilik Inuit (Eskimo), have ritualized contests to settle disputes, in which two men take turns striking each other on the shoulders or forehead until one gives up, whereupon they are reconciled. These contests resemble the great majority of combative episodes in caribou, giraffes, and many other species, in which little or no harm results from stereotyped, ritualized exchanges of blows between rival males. Indeed, the preponderance of aggressive episodes between adult males in the same species in the animal world are of this sort, whereas the "aggressive" episodes in childhood fall in the category of R&T play. Either way, harm is rare.

Fry reasons that a main purpose of R&T in any species is for juveniles to learn and practice restraint. In fact, it is remarkable that so many young mammals know instinctively how to hold back and avoid hurting each other in this kind of play, which could easily be dangerous. By the time they are grown, they should be thoroughly accustomed to "fighting" while avoiding harm. Such play has the added function of establishing dominance relationships among individuals who will be in contact for many years, teaching the weaker ones to avoid useless fights. This restraint is no less true of human hunter-gatherers, and as Fry shows, the groups studied by ethnologists did not have war, and most of them had ideologies of peaceful coexistence despite their thorough familiarity with weapons, which they daily used to kill prey of other species.

However, they did have violence, and as Fry points out, they had executions of men who were repeat offenders in fatal assaults. This of course shows that such men and such killings existed, and suggests that there was tolerance for the occasional homicide by a man who did not repeat the offense. In fact we know that the Jun/twa or !Kung San (Bushmen) had a homicide rate in the mid-20th century resembling that of U.S. cities, but that several men joined together deliberately to execute a man who had killed three people (Lee, 1979). The Semai of Malaysia, known for their pacific natures and intensely anti-aggressive childrearing, became by their own admission bloodthirsty killers when recruited to counter-insurgency by the British in the 1950s (Dentan, 1968). This shows that context matters, of course, but it also shows that generations of pacific childrearing and other traditions is no protection against certain changes of context.

It used to be said by leading naturalists that only humans among animals killed their own kind, but with the homicide rate of U.S. cities—of the order of magnitude of 1 in 10,000 per year—you would have to watch a population of 500 hunter-gatherers for 20 years before seeing one such crime. For groups of non-human primates, usually smaller in number, the needed duration would be much longer. So it should not have been surprising when, with sufficient time of scientific observation, many species and at least some hunter-gatherers were found to kill their own kind. Indeed, some archeologists have begun to speak of "retrospective pacifications" in describing past archeological excavations that ignored the evidence of violence, mainly in the post–hunter-gatherer era (LeBlanc and Register, 2003; Keeley, 1996). Historical and other evidence suggests that hunter-gatherer populations did have group violence, although it was more on the order of raiding and ambushes than all-out war. If they did not have organized violence, it was more because they were not organized than because they were not violent.

At a minimum, the absence of serious violence in hunter-gatherer societies has once again become controversial. Nevertheless, Fry's observation that in the hunter-gatherer as well as the nonhuman world, juvenile fighting is mainly play and adult fighting is often ritualistic and rarely harmful remains true, provided that we do not say that serious violence did not occur.

References

Bowles, S. (2006). *Microeconomics: Behavior, institutions, and evolution.* Princeton, NJ: Princeton University Press.

Dentan, R. K. (1968). *The Semai: A nonviolent people of Malaysia.* New York: Holt, Rinehart and Winston.

Durham, W. H. (1991). *Coevolution: Genes, culture, and human diversity.* Stanford, CA: Stanford University Press.

Emlen, S. T. (1995). An evolutionary theory of the family. *Proceedings of the National Academy of Sciences U S A, 92*(18), 8092–8099.

Jablonska, E., & Lamb, M. J. (2005). *Evolution in four dimensions: Genetic, epigenetic, behavioral, and symbolic variation in the history of life.* Cambridge, MA: MIT Press.

Keeley, L. H. (1996). *War before civilization: The myth of the peaceful savage.* New York: Oxford University Press.

Konner, M. (2006). Human nature, ethnic violence, and war. In M. Fitzduff & C. E. Stout (Eds.), *The psychology of resolving global conflicts: From war to peace* (Vol. 1). Westport, CT: Praeger Security International.

Konner, M. (2010). *The evolution of childhood: Relationships, emotion, mind.* Cambridge, MA: Harvard University Press.

Konner, M. J. (1972). Aspects of the developmental ethology of a foraging people. In N. G. B. Jones (Ed.), *Ethological studies of child behavior* (pp. 285–304). Cambridge, UK: Cambridge University Press.

Konner, M. J. (1975). Relations among infants and juveniles in comparative perspective. In M. Lewis & L. Rosenblum (Eds.), *Friendship and peer relations.* New York: John Wiley and Sons.

LeBlanc, S., & Register, K. E. (2003). *Constant battles: The myth of the peaceful, noble savage.* New York: St. Martin's Press.

Lee, R. B. (1979). *The !Kung San: Men, women and work in a foraging society.* Cambridge, UK: Cambridge University Press.

Mock, D. W. (2004). *More than kin and less than kind: The evolution of family conflict.* Cambridge, MA: Harvard University Press.

Shostak, M. (1981). *Nisa: The life and words of a !Kung woman.* Cambridge, MA: Harvard University Press.

Tomasello, M., Kruger, A. C., & Ratner, H. H. (1993). Cultural learning. *Behavioral and Brain Sciences, 16,* 495–452.

Trivers, R. L. (1974). Parent-offspring conflict. *American Zoologist, 14,* 249–264.

West-Eberhard, M. J. (2003). *Developmental plasticity and evolution.* New York: Oxford University Press.

Contexts Gone Awry

{ 11 }

Child Maltreatment and Early Mother–Child Interactions

Kristin Valentino, Michelle Comas, and Amy K. Nuttall

Child maltreatment represents an extreme failure of the early caregiving environment to provide average expected experiences and is destructive to child development in multiple developmental domains (Cicchetti and Valentino, 2006). Moreover, child maltreatment is a serious public health concern. In 2011, more than 3.7 million children were subject to child protective services investigations. The current child victimization rate is 9.1 per 1,000 children in the U.S. population. Alarmingly, approximately 80% of these children were maltreated by a parent, which underscores the pivotal role parents play in risk for child abuse and neglect (U.S. Department of Health and Human Services, Administration on Children, Youth and Families, 2012).

In addition to being a prevalent societal concern, the study of child maltreatment provides valuable information regarding the role of caregiving in child developmental outcomes. From a developmental psychopathology perspective (Cicchetti, 1984; Cicchetti and Valentino, 2006; Cummings, Davies, and Campbell, 2000; Cummings and Valentino, in press), the study of both typical and atypical developmental processes is mutually informative. Thus, because child maltreatment represents an extreme deviation from the average expected early caregiving environment (Cicchetti and Valentino, 2006), the comparison of maltreating and nonmaltreating families, as an "experiment of nature" (Cicchetti, 2003), allows us to evaluate the contribution of early caregiving to young children's development. In this chapter, we review research on mother–child interactions among maltreating and nonmaltreating families from infancy through toddlerhood to address how a maltreating family environment affects developmental outcomes. We focus on mothers in the current review because although we recognize the importance of fathers, extant research with maltreating families indicates that fathers tend to have a peripheral role in caregiving and mothers are the individuals who are most likely identified as perpetrators of maltreatment (Howes and Cicchetti, 1993; U.S. DHHS, 2010). Additionally, we discuss the clinical implications of this research and provide examples of translational research interventions for maltreated children that have been informed by basic research on mother–child interactions during early childhood.

Child Maltreatment: Definition and Measurement

Generally, child maltreatment refers to one of four experiences: physical abuse, sexual abuse, physical neglect, or emotional maltreatment. Physical abuse refers to the infliction of bodily injury on a child by nonaccidental means. Sexual abuse includes sexual contact or attempted sexual contact between a child and adult for the purposes of the adult's sexual gratification or financial gain. Physical neglect refers to both lack of adequate supervision and failure to provide minimum standards of care (i.e., food, shelter, clothing). Emotional maltreatment involves persistent and extreme thwarting of children's basic emotional needs (see Barnett, Manly, and Cicchetti, 1993, for detailed explanations).

There are several methods for measuring or quantifying child maltreatment, including parental report, adult retrospective report, and use of legal child welfare documentation, each of which has strengths and limitations. In attempting to operationalize maltreatment for the purposes of research, it is important to acknowledge that child maltreatment is a legal issue generally defined by state-level child welfare systems. As such, each state has its own criteria for what constitutes child maltreatment. Further complicating definitional issues is that corporal punishment is condoned and accepted as a legal parenting practice in our culture. Despite clear associations between spanking, for example, and negative child outcomes (Gershoff, Lansford, Sexton, Davis-Kean, and Sameroff, 2012), corporal punishment remains legal, and there is little agreement about how or where to draw the line between "acceptable" parental discipline and child maltreatment (Cicchetti and Toth, 2005). For the purposes of this chapter, we focus most of our review on research that has used multiple methods to corroborate child maltreatment information, especially those that involve the independent coding of child protective records with specific operational criteria, such as those laid out by the Maltreatment Classification System (Barnett et al., 1993).

Maltreatment and Parent–Child Interactions

Beyond isolated instances of maltreatment, maltreating families also fail to provide many of the typical caregiving experiences that facilitate competent child development. As noted by Cicchetti and Toth (2005, p. 414):

> "[C]hild maltreatment exemplifies a pathogenic relational environment that poses substantial risk for undermining biological and psychological development across a broad spectrum of domains of functioning…the social, biological, and psychological conditions that are associated with maltreatment set in motion a probabilistic path of epigenesis for maltreated children that is characterized by an increased likelihood of failure and disruption in the successful resolution of major stage-salient issues of development, resulting in grave implications for functioning across the life span."

As such, it is critical to identify specific parent–child interaction behaviors among maltreating families that may increase or decrease the probability of the emergence of psychopathology among maltreated children.

ATTACHMENT

The formation of attachment relationships is a central stage-salient developmental task during the first 2 years of life. Although overt attachment patterns are generally first observed at about 12 months of age, parent–child interactions throughout the first year shape children's emerging affect and physiologic regulation abilities, as well as their biobehavioral patterns of response (Gunnar and Vazquez, 2006; Sroufe, 1979), from which the capacity for attachment emerges. Infants rely on their primary caregivers to derive a sense of security, and they use this relationship as a base from which to explore the environment (Cummings and Davies, 1996; Sroufe, 1979, 1990). Caregiver sensitivity, responsiveness, and reliability are critical for the development of secure attachment representations because infants rely on these regularities to develop internal models and to create expectations for the future. Infants who have secure attachment relationships with their primary caregivers feel loved, view the world as a safe place to explore, and feel confident that they can rely on their caregivers to respond to their needs. In the absence of contingent responsivity, however, the development of a secure attachment relationship is often impeded, and attachment insecurity results (Sroufe and Waters, 1977). Traditionally, attachment insecurity has been characterized by two profiles of behavior: insecure avoidant or insecure anxious/resistant. Children who develop insecure avoidant attachment relationships generally expect that their caregiver will not provide comfort or responsive care, likely as a result of parental rejection or hostility. Thus even when distressed, they often do not show behavioral signs of distress, and they "avoid" or do not seek out their caregiver. In contrast, children with insecure anxious attachments display their distress behaviorally and seek out their caregiver for comfort, but are not soothed by their caregiver's presence. Often resulting from inconsistent or neglectful caregiving, these children tend to be clingy or preoccupied with their caregiver's availability (Ainsworth, Blehar, Waters, and Wall, 1978). Because inconsistent care, neglect, and hostility are hallmarks of maltreating families (Cicchetti and Valentino, 2006), it is not surprising that attachment insecurity is the norm rather than the exception among infant–parent dyads from maltreating families.

A large body of literature coheres to demonstrate high rates of attachment insecurity among maltreated infants and their caregivers (i.e., Cicchetti, Rogosch, and Toth, 2006; Crittenden, 1988; Cyr, Euser, Bakermans-Kranenburg, and van IJzenddorn, 2010; Egeland and Sroufe, 1981). Studies of attachment using the *Strange Situation procedure* (Ainsworth and Wittig, 1969) have consistently found that maltreated children are much more likely to develop insecure attachments with their caregivers than are nonmaltreated children (see

Cicchetti and Valentino, 2006, for review). When traditional classifications schemes for attachment relationships are used, in which children may be classified as *insecure-avoidant* (type A), *secure* (type B), or *insecure-resistant* (type C), approximately two-thirds of maltreated children displayed insecure patterns of attachment, whereas the reverse was true among demographically matched comparison families (i.e., Schneider-Rosen, Braunwald, Carlson, and Cicchetti, 1985; Youngblade and Belsky, 1989). In these early studies, however, the attachment behaviors of maltreated children were often described as odd and difficult to fit within the traditional classification scheme. For example, maltreated children frequently displayed inconsistent strategies for dealing with separations and reunions during the Strange Situation, as well as other bizarre behaviors, such as freezing. As such, an additional category of attachment insecurity, labeled *disorganized attachment*, was created to characterize children who demonstrate an absence or breakdown of an organized attachment strategy for seeking proximity to their caregiver when distressed (Main and Solomon, 1990).

Using revised attachment schemes, many studies report attachment insecurity up to 80% to 90% for maltreated children (i.e., Barnett, Ganiban, and Cicchetti, 1999; Cyr et al., 2010; Lyons-Ruth, Connell, and Zoll, 1989; Lyons-Ruth, Connell, Zoll, and Stahl, 1987). In particular, up to 80% of maltreated infants display disorganized attachment patterns, compared with rates of approximately 20% of attachment disorganization among demographically comparable nonmaltreated children (Carlson, Cicchetti, Barnett, and Braunwald, 1989). Meta-analytic results indicate rates of approximately 15% attachment disorganization in normative middle-class families, whereas rates among maltreated families are substantially higher (van Ijzendoorn, Schuengel, and Bakermans-Kranenburg, 1999). Moreover, the developmental outcomes associated with disorganized attachment are often more pathological and maladaptive than are those associated with other forms of attachment insecurity (Lyons-Ruth, Easterbrooks, and Cibelli, 1997; Lyons-Ruth and Jacobvitz, 2008; Moss, Cyr, Bureau, Tarabulsy, and Dubois-Comtois, 2005; van Ijzendoorn et al., 1999). Given the negative developmental sequelae associated with disruptions in the attachment relationship, research focused on identifying specific early parenting behaviors associated with maltreating families and with the development of insecure (especially disorganized) attachments have become critical research priorities, particularly with regard to how this basic research can then be translated into interventions (Cicchetti et al., 2006).

PARENT SENSITIVITY

Caregiver sensitivity has long been identified as one of the central predictors of child attachment security (Ainsworth et al., 1978). Caregiver sensitivity includes the ability to recognize children's emotional signals and to respond in an appropriate and contingent manner to the child's needs. In contrast, extreme insensitivity, which may include frightened/frightening parental behavior, is associated with the development of disorganized attachment (Lyons-Ruth, Bronfman, and Parsons, 1999; Madigan, Bakermans-Kranenburg, van Ijzendoorn, 2006; Schuengel, Bakermans-Kranenburg, and van Ijzendoorn, 1999). For example, among maltreated children, it is extremely difficult to develop an organized attachment strategy when the very caregivers on whom they would like to rely for comfort are also, at times, the source of the distress. In addition to the extreme insensitivity associated with specific incidents of abuse or neglect, maltreating parents have been rated as significantly less sensitive than nonmaltreating parents during observations of typical parent–child interactions (i.e., Cicchetti et al., 2006; Moss, Dubois-Comtois, Cyr, Tarabulsy, St. Laurent, and Bernier, 2011). Moreover, rather than being contingently responsive and sensitive to their children's cues, maltreating parents tend to be more controlling during interactions with their children, and to not encourage the development of autonomy in their children (Azar, 2002; Rogosch, Cicchetti, Shields, and Toth, 1995).

Beyond attachment relationships, research identifying specific parenting behaviors that are characteristic of maltreating families has important implications both for our understanding of child development and for informing prevention and intervention efforts. Similarly, analysis of emerging child behaviors among maltreated children provides critical information regarding how a maltreating family environment may impede normative developmental processes. In particular, observations of parent–child interactions in more naturalistic contexts (in contrast to the highly structured Strange Situation paradigm) may provide more ecologically valid insights into parent–child processes within maltreating families. The analysis of parent–child interactions in the context of free play, for example, is a rich context to observe parent behavior as well as children's emerging developmental competencies.

PARENT–CHILD PLAY

During the first years of life, parents are children's primary partners for play. Parents have a direct influence on children's play development, as well as on their developing social and communicative behaviors (Emde, 1989; Slade, 1987a, 1987b; Tamis-LeMonda, Shannon, Cabrera, and Lamb, 2004). For example, parents' availability and active engagement during play positively influence the maturity and enthusiasm of their children's play (Rubin, Fein, and Vandenberg, 1983; Slade, 1987a). Additionally, during play, children learn how to gain control over and focus their attention as parents direct their children's attention to objects and events in the environment. This skill is essential for initiating and maintaining self-directed exploration during play (Vygotsky, 1978).

Research from studies of maltreating mothers demonstrates deficits in these attention-directing behaviors (Alessandri, 1992), especially with regard to verbal attention-directing behaviors (Valentino, Cicchetti, Toth, and Rogosch, 2006). Similarly, maltreating parents tend to engage in fewer playful exchanges with less verbal input than do nonmaltreating families (i.e., Burgess and Conger, 1978;

Crittenden, 1981). These maladaptive parent–child interactional patterns are likely to have adverse effects on maltreated children's play and social development.

Regarding the cognitive complexity of children's play, observations of infants and toddlers from maltreating families has indicated no differences among children from abusing, neglecting, and nonmaltreating families (Valentino et al., 2006; Valentino, Cicchetti, Toth, and Rogosch, 2011). Although differences in children's play complexity did not emerge as a function of maltreatment, it is striking to note that only 51% of toddlers engaged in any pretend play (Valentino et al., 2011); whereas prior cross-sectional research with typically developing children from low-risk (middle-class) families indicated that, by 21 months, most, if not all, toddlers displayed pretend play (Belsky and Most, 1981).

In contrast to findings regarding play structure, significant and persistent differences in the social behaviors of maltreated infants and toddlers during mother–child play have been observed (Valentino et al., 2006, 2011). Specifically, controlling for maternal social behavior and child cognitive performance, infants from abusing families engage in less independent play than do infants from nonmaltreating families and from neglecting families. Additionally, infants from abusing families engage in more imitation than do infants from nonmaltreating families. Considering the developmental emergence of social behavior from attending, to imitating, to directing the attention of others (Carpenter et al., 1998, 2002), the differences noted among the infants from abusing families compared with nonmaltreating families suggests a delay in emerging social behavior. Moreover, although imitation is an important developmental skill, protracted reliance on imitation may become maladaptive over time, especially at the expense of learning how to explore the world in autonomous ways and initiating social interactions.

Furthermore, during toddlerhood, this pattern of behavior was sustained among children from abusing families as they continued to engage in less child-initiated play than children from neglecting or nonmaltreating families (Valentino et al., 2011). Child initiations during play have been identified as important markers of social competence in prior research (i.e., Landry, Smith, Miller-Loncar, and Swank, 1998). As such, these findings highlight that children from abusing families engage in less socially competent behavior. Moreover, the persistent deficits in social initiation and autonomous behavior observed among the children from abusing families compared with children from neglecting and nonmaltreating families underscores the disruption in normative social development associated with an abusive family context. In an abusive family environment, one could imagine how it might be adaptive for young children to engage in less autonomous behavior, and to initiate in fewer social interactions with an unpredictable caregiver who may respond to her child's social bid in a dangerous manner. As such, this reduction in child-initiated play could be conceptualized as an experience-dependent adaptation to avoid further abuse experiences. This experience-dependent hypothesis is supported by the lack of differences in child-initiated play among children from neglecting families compared with children from nonmaltreating families. Whereas children from neglecting families have lacked sufficient caregiving to meet their basic physical and emotional needs, they have not experienced the commission of abuse, or the accompanying fear, that may have motivated children from abusing families to refrain from social initiation. Although reduced social initiation and autonomous behavior during infancy and toddlerhood may be adaptive for young children from abusing families during mother–child play, such an approach to social interaction may impede the development of relationships when applied to other contexts, such as in play with peers. Indeed, research among maltreated preschool-aged children has demonstrated that children from maltreating families have a greater number of problem behaviors and less skill in initiating interactions with peers (Darwish, Esquivel, Houtz, and Alfonso, 2001), as well as reductions in the initiation of social interactions with an interviewer (Landry and Swank, 2004).

Translational Research

Research on early parent–child interactions and maltreatment has significant implications for informing intervention and prevention efforts aimed at improving the developmental trajectories of young maltreated children. For example, evidence of increased attachment disorganization, decreased maternal sensitivity, and decreased maternal verbal interactions among maltreating mothers with their children has provided several potential targets for preventive and intervention efforts (i.e., Cicchetti et al., 2006; Moss et al., 2011; Valentino, Comas, Nuttall, and Thomas, 2013). In the following section, we discuss three approaches to prevention and intervention with maltreating families, all of which have been developed as translations of the aforementioned basic research findings.

Given considerable risk for the development of insecure disorganized attachment among maltreated children, in addition to the risk posed by disorganized attachment for subsequent development, the facilitation of secure attachment among infants from maltreating families has been a primary target of preventive intervention. For example, Cicchetti and colleagues (2006) randomized infant–mother dyads from maltreating families into one of three conditions: a community standard control condition, an infant–parent psychotherapy (IPP) intervention, or a psychoeducational parenting intervention (PPI). IPP is an attachment-based, nondirective approach that encourages maternal sensitivity by helping parents to increase positive representations of themselves and the parent–child relationship. Based on the work of Fraiberg and colleagues (1975) as well as by the intervention work of Lieberman (1991, 1992), the guiding principle of IPP is that the problems maltreating mothers have in responding sensitively to their infants is a result of insecure internal representational models that developed from the mother's own experiences in childhood. As such, IPP focuses on the development of a strong therapeutic relationship between mother and therapist, through which the mother may then reflect on past relationships, differentiate current and past relationships, and develop more positive internal representations of herself and others.

PPI, in contrast, is a didactic intervention that teaches parenting skills in addition to relaxation techniques and behaviors designed to help promote social support. This intervention model was based on the nurse-home visiting program of Olds and colleagues (1997, 1998), which included a home-based education program on infant development and parenting and provided enhanced social support. PPI was additionally supplemented with several cognitive and behavioral techniques to address parenting skill deficits and limited social support. Both interventions were long term and delivered in the home for approximately 1 hour each week over the course of a year. Additionally, a nonmaltreatment comparison group was included in the study.

In the study by Cicchetti and colleagues (Cicchetti et al., 2006), at baseline infants (approximately 12 months of age) from the maltreating groups had significantly higher rates of attachment insecurity than did the nonmaltreating group. Specifically, rates of disorganized attachment were 87.5% in the IPP group, 83.3% in the PPI group, and 92.6% in the community standard (CS) condition, compared with 42.3% in the nonmaltreatment group. At postintervention, however, both IPP and PPI significantly improved attachment security and decreased disorganized attachment, whereas attachment insecurity (particularly disorganized attachment) was stable in the CS condition (Cicchetti et al., 2006). Specifically, from preintervention to postintervention, rates of attachment disorganization dropped from 87.5% to 32.1% in the IPP group and from 83.3% to 45.5% in the PPI group, whereas disorganization in the CS group did not change significantly. Moreover, analysis of children's physiological regulation indicated that whereas children in the two maltreatment groups remained indistinguishable from the nonmaltreated children across time, the children in the CS (comparison) condition demonstrated progressively lower levels of morning cortisol (Cicchetti, Rogosch, Toth, and Sturge-Apple, 2011). Thus, both early psychosocial interventions for child maltreatment were effective in improving attachment security and in normalizing biological regulatory processes among young maltreated children.

Although long-term treatment options such as infant–parent psychotherapy have been shown to be effective in improving developmental outcomes for children from maltreating families (Cicchetti et al., 2006), there is increasing interest in the development of more brief, focused interventions for this population. In particular, meta-analytic evidence has suggested that brief (5 to 16 weeks), dyadic interventions focused on parent interactive behavior and sensitivity are more effective and less costly than longer term (20 to 52 weeks) parenting programs (Bakermans-Kranenburg, van Ijzendoorn, and Juffer, 2003). Furthermore, likely because of budgetary constraints, case management, or didactic (classroom) group, parent education classes continue to be the predominant services mandated by child protective services, as opposed to other empirically supported, although often long-term, alternatives (i.e., Parent-Child Interaction Therapy, Chaffin et al., 2004; Nurse Home-Visiting Program, Olds et al., 1997, 1998).

In response to the need for effective, brief interventions for young maltreated children, Moss and colleagues (2011) tested a brief attachment-based intervention geared toward improving maternal sensitivity in order to improve child attachment security. Mother–child dyads with children 1 to 5 years of age from maltreating families were randomized into an intervention or a control condition. The intervention itself was based on the sensitivity-training work of Bakermans-Kranenburg, Juffer, van IJzendoorn (1998), Dozier et al. (2006), and Moran, Pederson, and Krupka (2005). Emphasis was placed on increasing maternal sensitivity, including responding appropriately to child signals of distress with comfort, and promoting and supporting active child exploration when the child is not distressed. The intervention phases consisted of 8 home-based visits of approximately 90 minutes each. All sessions involved discussion of attachment-related themes, live parent–child interactions, and therapist-positive reinforcement of parental sensitive behavior during parent–child interactions. Parent–child interactions were videotaped in each session and then viewed with the parent to highlight positive moments of sensitivity.

Results revealed that although there were no differences between intervention and control groups at baseline, parents in the intervention group demonstrated significantly greater sensitivity than did the parents in the control group. Additionally, the intervention was successful in facilitating greater attachment security because a greater proportion of insecure children in the intervention group became secure (42.9%) compared with the control group (15.6%). Similarly, a greater proportion of children with disorganized attachment in the intervention group became organized (37.1%) compared with the control group (15.6%). As such, Moss and colleagues' intervention represents the first attachment-based intervention tested with random assignment for young maltreated children and is quite promising in its ability to alter children's attachment security through a brief training model.

Given the potential advantage of brief parenting interventions in early childhood, as well as limitations on funds for maltreatment intervention services, we have recently developed a brief, dyadic training program for maltreating parents and their preschool-aged children. There are few empirically validated treatments for the preschool age period, and even fewer that involve both the maltreating parent and the child in the intervention (Cicchetti and Valentino, 2006; MacMillan, Wathen, Barlow, Fergusson, Leventhal, and Taussig, 2009). This intervention, called *reminiscing and emotion training* (RET), builds on our prior findings regarding the role of maternal verbal interactions in child development and focuses on facilitating elaborative and emotion-rich parent–child communication (Valentino et al., 2013). Elaborative and emotionally supportive parent–child reminiscing is an important component of the parent–child relationship, which has been extensively supported in the developmental literature for improving parenting and child functioning in multiple domains (Nelson and Fivush, 2004), and can be taught effectively through brief training (i.e., Salmon, Dadds, Allen, and Hawes, 2009).

Whereas maternal sensitivity is central to children's adaptive development during infancy, as children's verbal skills develop, parents' ability to co-construct open, elaborative, and emotionally supportive narratives about children's emotional experiences becomes critical in shaping children's representational models and in supporting children's cognitive and socioemotional development (Fivush, Haden, and Reese, 2006; Thompson, 2006). There are clear individual differences in parental reminiscing style. Mothers who are able to talk in rich, detailed ways with their children about past events (high elaborative reminiscing style) have children who are able to discuss the past more elaboratively during parent–child conversations than children of parents who use a low elaborative or repetitive style (Fivush and Fromhoff, 1988; McCabe and Peterson, 1991; Reese, Haden, and Fivush, 1993). Elaborative maternal reminiscing benefits preschool-aged children's autobiographical memory, language, and literacy development (Nelson and Fivush, 2004; Peterson, Jesso, and McCabe, 1999; Reese et al., 1993), and has been positively associated with children's self-understanding, coping skills, and reduced internalizing and externalizing symptoms over time (Nelson and Fivush, 2004; Peterson and McCabe, 1992, 1994; Wareham and Salmon, 2006). Moreover, experimental research demonstrates that an elaborative reminiscing style can be taught to parents of middle and low socioeconomic statuses and of diverse backgrounds (Boland, Haden, and Ornstein, 2003; Peterson, et al., 1999; Reese and Newcombe, 2007; Salmon, et al., 2009; Van Bergen, Salmon, Dadds, and Allen, 2009) following brief (approximately 4 weeks) training.

A reminiscing-based intervention strategy is particularly relevant for maltreating families because mothers from abusing families engage in fewer verbal interactions with their children throughout infancy (Valentino et al., 2006) and the preschool years (Alessandri, 1992). When reminiscing, maltreating mothers are less likely to discuss causes and consequences of emotion with their children, which is associated with poor emotion understanding (Shipman and Zeman, 1999) and poor emotion regulation (Shipman, Schneider, Fitzgerald, Sims, Swisher, and Edwards, 2007) in their children.

In our pilot study (Valentino et al., 2013), we randomized parent–child dyads into a 4- week reminiscing intervention (RET) or wait-list control condition. Based on the interventions of Salmon et al. (2009) and Van Bergen et al. (2009), the RET condition included four, weekly, in-home training sessions on elaborative parent–child reminiscing and emotion understanding for 1 hour each. Specific target behaviors included training parents to (1) ask more open-ended questions (e.g., "What happened next?"), (2) use detailed descriptions that describe the event and build on the children's descriptions, (3) make causal connections between children's experiences and their children's emotions (e.g., "I could tell you felt scared because…"), and (4) talk about resolutions for children's *negative* emotions (e.g., "how did you get over feeling sad?" or "I gave you a hug, and you felt better"). These conversations focused on every-day past events, and did not target traumatic events, although mothers were encouraged to engage in discussion of children's negative emotions.

Analyses indicated that parents in the reminiscing group demonstrated significantly more elaborative and emotionally supportive reminiscing compared with the control group at the postassessment, while controlling for child language and maternal pretest reminiscing. Specifically, parents in the reminiscing group used more elaborative utterances, made significantly more attributions of children's negative emotions, and provided more causes or explanations of children's emotions than did those in the control group at the postassessment.

Furthermore, analyses of child performance during parent–child reminiscing, controlling for child preassessment reminiscing performance, child language, and age, indicated that cognitive and emotional aspects of children's reminiscing in the reminiscing group were significantly better than in the control group. Univariate tests revealed that children in the reminiscing group made significantly more unique memory contributions and made more frequent references to their own emotions during reminiscing than children in the control group.

Demonstrating improvements in maltreating parents' elaborative and emotionally supportive reminiscing is important because aspects of mother–child communication generally (Valentino et al., 2006), and emotion-reminiscing specifically (Shipman et al., 2007), have been found to be deficient among maltreating parents. Given the strong foundation of research in the developmental literature, which documents the positive benefits of elaborative and emotionally supportive reminiscing for child cognitive and emotional development, as well as for parenting (see Fivush et al., 2006, for review), reminiscing-based parent training may be useful to foster the healthy development of maltreated children in multiple developmental domains. It will be important for future research to examine the long-term effects of training maltreating parents and children in elaborative and emotion-rich reminiscing in a large randomized controlled design, including the identification of the mechanisms underlying beneficial treatment outcomes.

Conclusion

Overall, the research reviewed in this chapter underscores the pivotal role of parents in children's early development. Often, when multiple ecological and developmental systems are functioning adequately, it is difficult to ascertain the influence of any one variable on child developmental outcomes. Because child maltreatment represents a severe deviation in caregiving behavior, however, research comparing maltreating and nonmaltreating families provides an opportunity to evaluate the role of early caregiving on child development. Moreover, child maltreatment serves as an extreme example of failure to provide children with the evolved and expected environmental conditions to promote child development (Cicchetti and Valentino, 2006). Toward the goal of understanding the *environment of evolutionary adaptedness* (EEA)and its significance in facilitating optimal child development (Narvaez, Panksepp, Schore, and Gleason, 2013), research detailing the developmental out comes associated with gross violations in the EEA provides essential complementary information.

A review of the early parent–child interaction literature among maltreating families indicates significant elevations in attachment insecurity, particularly disorganized attachment, and decreases in maternal sensitivity and attention-directing behaviors. Regarding child behavior, persistent deviations in the social development of children from abusing families compared with nonmaltreating families have been noted, including decreased child-initiated social interactions. Although we may conceptualize these deviations in the social behaviors of children from abusing families as experience-dependent adaptations to a potentially threatening environment, reduced child initiation and autonomy may have significant maladaptive consequences in other contexts and interfere with children's ability to achieve subsequent stage-salient developmental tasks.

More broadly, a wealth of empirical work documents the adverse developmental sequelae associated with child maltreatment, including impairments in cognitive, emotional, and social domains. As such, the development of evidence-based interventions for young maltreated children that target early parent–child interactions are needed. We have presented three promising approaches to interventions with maltreating families, all of which aim to improve the parenting behavior of maltreating mothers, and to facilitate more positive developmental trajectories among young maltreated children. The next steps for these intervention efforts will be to focus on evaluating children's developmental outcomes over the long term, and to improve dissemination efforts to communities nationally.

References

Ainsworth, M. D. S., Blehar, M. C., Waters, E., & Wall, S. (1978). *Patterns of attachment: A psychological study of the strange situation*. Hillsdale, NJ: Erlbaum.

Ainsworth, M. D. S., & Wittig, B. A. (1969). Attachment and the exploratory behaviour of one-year-olds in a strange situation. In B. M. Foss (Ed.), *Determinants of infant behaviour* (Vol. 4, pp. 113–136), London: Methuen.

Alessandri, S. M. (1992). Mother-child interactions correlates of maltreated and nonmaltreated children's play behavior. *Development and Psychopathology, 4*, 257–270.

Azar, S. T. (2002). Parenting and child maltreatment. In M. H. Bornstein (Ed.), *Handbook of parenting: Vol. 4: Social conditions and applied parenting* (pp. 361–388). Mahwah, NJ: Erlbaum.

Bakermans-Kranenburg, M. J., Juffer, F., & van IJzendoorn, M. H. (1998). Interventions with video feedback and attachment discussions: Does type of maternal insecurity make a difference? *Infant Mental Health Journal, 19*, 202–219

Bakermans-Kranenburg, M., Van Ijzendoorn, M., & Juffer, F. (2003). Less is more: Meta-analyses of sensitivity and attachment interventions in early childhood. *Psychological Bulletin, 129*, 195–215.

Barnett, D., Manly, J. T., & Cicchetti, D. (1993). Defining child maltreatment: The interface between policy and research. In D. Cicchetti, & S. Toth (Eds.), *Child abuse, child development and social policy* (pp. 7–73). Norwood, NJ: Ablex.

Barnett, D., Ganiban, J., & Cicchetti, D. (1999). Maltreatment, negative expressivity, and the development of type D attachments from 12-24 months of age. *Monographs of the Society for Research in Child Development, Vol.64* (3), 97–118. Wiley.

Belsky, J., & Most, R. K. (1981). From exploration to play: A cross sectional study of infant free play behavior. *Developmental Psychology, 17*(5), 630–639.

Boland, A. M., Haden, C. A., & Ornstein, P. A. (2003). Boosting children's memory by training mothers in the use of an elaborative conversational style as an event unfolds. *Journal of Cognition and Development, 4*, 39–65.

Burgess, R. L., & Conger, R. D. (1978). Family interaction in abusive, neglectful, and normal families. *Child Development, 49*, 1163–1173.

Carlson, V., Cicchetti, D., Barnett, D., & Braunwald, K. (1989). Disorganized/disoriented attachment relationships in maltreated infants. *Developmental Psychology, 25*, 525–531.

Carpenter, M., Nagell, K., & Tomasello, M. (1998). Social cognition, joint attention, and communicative competence from 9 to 15 months of age. *Monographs of the Society for Research in Child Development, 63*(4), V– 143.

Carpenter, M., Pennington, B. F., & Rogers, S. J. (2002). Interrelations among social-cognitive skills in young children with autism. *Journal of Autism and Developmental Disorders, 32*, 91–106.

Chaffin, M., Silovsky, J., Funderburk, B., Valle, L. A., Brestan, E. V., Balachova, T., et al. (2004). Parent–child interaction therapy with physically abusive parents: Efficacy for reducing future abuse reports. *Journal of Consulting and Clinical Psychology, 72*, 491–499.

Cicchetti, D. (1984). The emergence of developmental psychopathology. *Child Development, 55*, 1–7.

Cicchetti, D. (2003). Editorial. Experiments of nature: Contributions to developmental theory. *Development and Psychopathology, 15*(4), 833–835.

Cicchetti, D., Rogosch, F. A., & Toth, S. L. (2006). Fostering secure attachment in infants in maltreating families through preventive interventions. *Development and Psychopathology, 18*, 623–649.

Cicchetti, D., Rogosch, F. A., Toth, S. L., & Sturge-Apple, M. (2011). Normalizing the development of cortisol regulation in maltreated infants through preventive interventions. *Development and Psychopathology, 23*(3), 789–800.

Cicchetti, D., & Toth, S. L. (2005). Child maltreatment. *Annual Review of Clinical Psychology, 1*, 409–438.

Cicchetti, D., & Valentino, K. (2006). An ecological transactional perspective on child maltreatment: Failure of the average expectable environment and its influence upon child development. In D. Cicchetti & D. J. Cohen (Eds.), *Developmental psychopathology: Risk, disorder, and adaptation* (Vol. 3, 2nd ed., pp. 129–201). New York: Wiley.

Crittenden, P. M. (1981). Abusing, neglecting, problematic and adequate dyads: Differentiation by patterns of interaction. *Merrill-Palmer Quarterly, 27*, 2–1–208.

Crittenden, P. M. (1988). Relationships at risk. In J. Belsky & T. Nezworski (Eds.), *Clinical implications of attachment theory* (pp. 136–174). Hillsdale, NJ: Erlbaum.

Cummings, E. M., & Davies, P. T. (1996). Emotional security as a regulatory process in normal development and the development of psychopathology. *Development and Psychopathology, 8*, 123–139.

Cummings, E. M., Davies, P. T., & Campbell, S. B. (2000). *Developmental psychopathology and family process: Theory, research, and clinical implications*. New York: Guilford.

Cummings, E. M., & Valentino, K. (in press). Developmental Psychopathology. In W. C. Overton, P. C. Molenaar, & R. Lerner (Eds.), *Handbook of child psychology. Vol. 1: Relational, Developmental Systems Theories and Methods* (7th ed.). New York: Wiley.

Cyr, C., Euser, E. M., Bakermans-Kranenburg, M. J., et al. (2010). Attachment security and disorganization in maltreating and high risk families: A series of meta-analyses. *Development and Psychopathology, 22*(1), 87–108.

Darwish, D., Esquivel, G. B., Houtz, J. C., & Alfonso, V. C. (2001). Play and social skills in maltreated and nonmaltreated preschoolers during peer interactions. *Child Abuse and Neglect, 25*(1), 13–31.

Dozier, M., Peloso, E., Lindhiem, O., Gordon, M. K., Manni, M., Sepulveda, S., et al. (2006). Developing evidence-based interventions for foster children: An example of a randomized clinical trial with infants and toddlers. *Journal of Social Issues, 62,* 767–785.

Egeland, B., & Sroufe, L. A. (1981). Developmental sequelae of maltreatment in infancy. *New Directions for Child Development, 11,* 77–92.

Emde, R. N. (1989). The infant's relationship experience: Developmental and affective aspects. In A. Sameroff & R. N. Emde (Eds.), *Relationship disturbances in early childhood: A developmental approach* (pp. 33–51). New York: Basic Books.

Fivush, R., & Fromhoff, F. (1988). Style and structure in mother child conversations about the past. *Discourse Processes, 11*(3), 337–355.

Fivush, R., Haden, C., & Reese, E. (2006). Elaborating on elaborations: Role of maternal reminiscing style in cognitive and socioemotional development. *Child Development, 77,* 1568–1588.

Fraiberg, S., Adelson, E., & Shapiro, V. (1975). Ghosts in the nursery: A psychoanalytic approach to impaired infant–mother relationships. *Journal of the American Academy of Child Psychiatry, 14,* 387–421.

Gershoff, E. T., Lansford, J. E., Sexton, H. R., Davis-Kean, P. & Sameroff, A. J. (2012). Longitudinal links between spanking and children's externalizing behaviors in a national sample of white, black, Hispanic, and Asian American families. *Child Development, 83*(3), 838–843.

Gunnar, M., & Vazquez, D. (2006). Stress neurobiology and developmental psychopathology. In D. Cicchetti, & D. Cohen (Eds.), *Developmental psychopathology* (2nd ed., pp. 533–577). Hoboken, NJ: John Wiley & Sons.

Howes, P. W., & Cicchetti, D. (1993). A family/relational perspective on maltreating families: Parallel processes across systems and social policy implications. In D. Cicchetti & S. L. Toth (Eds.), *Child abuse, child development, and social policy* (pp. 249–300). Norwood, NJ: Ablex.

Landry, S., Smith, K., Miller-Loncar, C., & Swank, P. (1998). The relation of change in maternal interactive styles to the developing social competence of full-term and preterm children. *Child Development, 69*(1), 105.

Landry, S. H., & Swank, P. (2004). Social competence in young children with inflicted traumatic Brain injury. *Developmental Neuropsychology, 26*(3), 707–733.

Lieberman, A. F. (1991). Attachment theory and infant–parent psychotherapy: Some conceptual, clinical, and research considerations. In D. Cicchetti & S. L. Toth (Eds.), *Rochester Symposium on Developmental Psychopathology: Models and integrations* (Vol. 3, pp. 261–287). Rochester, NY: University of Rochester Press.

Lieberman, A. F. (1992). Infant–parent psychotherapy with toddlers. *Development and Psychopathology, 4,* 559–574.

Lyons-Ruth, K., Bronfman, E., & Parsons, E. (1999). Maternal frightened, frightening, or atypical behavior and disorganized infant attachment patterns. *Monographs of the Society for Research in Child Development, 64*(3), 67–96.

Lyons-Ruth, K., Connell, D., & Zoll, D. (1989). Patters of maternal behavior among infants at risk for abuse: Relations with infant attachment behavior and infant development at 12 months of age. In D. Cicchetti & V. Carlson (Eds.), *Child maltreatment: Theory and research on the causes and consequences of child abuse and neglect* (pp. 464–493). New York: Cambridge University Press.

Lyons-Ruth, K., Connell, D., Zoll, D., & Stahl, J. (1987). Infants at social risk: Relationships among infant maltreatment, maternal behavior, and infant attachment behavior. *Developmental Psychology, 23,* 223–232.

Lyons-Ruth, K., Easterbrooks, M. A., & Cibelli, C. D. (1997). Infant attachment strategies, infant mental lag, and maternal depressive symptoms: Predictors of internalizing and externalizing problems at age 7. *Developmental Psychology, 33,* 681–692.

Lyons-Ruth, K., & Jacobvitz, D. (2008). Attachment disorganization: Genetic factors, parenting contexts, and developmental transformation from infancy to adulthood. In Cassidy, J. & Shaver, P. R. (Eds.), *Handbook of attachment second edition: Theory, research, and clinical applications* (pp. 666–697). New York: Guilford Press.

MacMillan, H., Wathen, C., Barlow, J., Fergusson, D., Leventhal, J., & Taussig, H. (2009). Child maltreatment 3: Interventions to prevent child maltreatment and associated impairment. *Lancet: British Edition, 373,* 250–266.

Madigan, S., Bakermans-Kranenburg, M. J., van Ijzendoorn, M. H., et al. (2006). Unresolved states of mind, anomalous parental behavior, and disorganized attachment: A review and meta-analysis of a transmission gap. *Attachment and Human Development, 8,* 89–111.

Main, M., & Solomon, J. (1990). Procedures for identifying infants as disorganized/disoriented during the Ainsworth Strange Situation. In Greenberg, M. T., Cicchetti, D., & Cummings, M. (Eds.), *Attachment in the preschool years: Theory, research, and intervention* (pp. 121–160). Chicago: University of Chicago Press

McCabe, A., & Peterson, C. (1991). Getting the story: A longitudinal story of parental styles eliciting narratives and developing narrative skill. In A. McCabe, & C. Peterson (Eds.), *Developing narrative structure* (pp. 217–253). Hillsdale, NJ: Erlbaum.

Moran, G., Pederson, D. R., & Krupka, A. (2005). Maternal unresolved attachment status impedes the effectiveness of interventions with adolescent mothers. *Infant Mental Health Journal, 26,* 231–249.

Moss, E., Cyr, C., Bureau, J.-F., Tarabulsy, G. M., & Dubois-Comtois, K. (2005). Stability of attachment during the preschool period. *Developmental Psychology, 41,* 773–783.

Moss, E., Dubois-Comtois, K., Cyr, C., Tarabulsy, G., St Laurent, D., & Bernier, A. (2011). Efficacy of a home-visiting intervention aimed at improving maternal sensitivity, child attachment, and behavioral outcomes for maltreated children: A randomized control trial. *Development and Psychopathology, 23,* 195–210.

Narvaez, D., Panksepp, J., Schore, A., & Gleason, T. (2013). The value of using an evolutionary framework for gauging children's wellbeing. In Narvaez, D., Panksepp,

J., Schore, A., & Gleason, T. (Eds.), *Evolution, early experience and human development: From research to practice and policy*. New York: Oxford University Press.

Nelson, K., & Fivush, R. (2004). The emergence of autobiographical memory: A social cultural developmental theory. *Psychological Review, 111*, 486.

Olds, D., Eckenrode, J., Henderson, C., Kitzman, H., Powers, J., Cole, R., et al. (1997). Long-term effects of home visitation on maternal life course and child abuse and neglect. *Journal of the American Medical Association, 278*, 637–643.

Olds, D., Henderson, C., Cole, R., Eckenrode, J., Kitzman, H., Luckey, et al. (1998). Long-term effects of home visitation on children's criminal and antisocial behaviour. *Journal of the American Medical Association, 280*, 1238–1244.

Peterson, C., Jesso, B., & McCabe, A. (1999). Encouraging narratives in preschoolers: An intervention study. *Journal of Child Language, 26*(1), 49.

Peterson, C., & McCabe, A. (1992). Parental styles of narrative elicitation: Effect on children's narrative structure and content. *First Language, 12*(36), 299–321.

Peterson, C., & McCabe, A. (1994). A social interactionist account of developing decontextualized narrative skill. *Developmental Psychology, 30*(6), 937–948.

Reese, E., Haden, C., & Fivush, R. (1993). Mother-child conversations about the past—relationships of style and memory over time. *Cognitive Development, 8*(4), 403–430.

Reese, E., & Newcombe, R. (2007). Training mothers in elaborative reminiscing enhances children's autobiographical memory and narrative. *Child Development, 78*, 1153–1170.

Rogosch, F. A., Cicchetti, D., Shields, A., & Toth, S. (1995). Parenting dysfunction in child maltreatment. In M. H. Bornstein (Ed.), *Handbook of parenting* (Vol. 4, pp. 127–159), Hillsdale, NJ: Erlbaum.

Rubin, K. H., Fein, G. G., & Vandenberg, B. (1983). Play. In P. H. Mussen (Series Ed.) & E. M. Hetherington (Vol. Ed.), *Handbook of child psychology: Vol. 4, Socialization, personality and social development* (4th ed., pp. 693–774). New York: Wiley.

Salmon, K., Dadds, M., Allen, J., & Hawes, D. (2009). Can emotional language skills be taught during parent training for conduct problem children? *Child Psychiatry and Human Development, 40*, 485–498.

Schneider-Rosen, K., Braunwald, K., Carlson, V., & Cicchetti, D. (1985). Current perspectives in attachment theory: Illustrations from the study of maltreated infants. *Monographs of the Society for Research in Child Development, 50*, 194–210.

Schuengel, C., Bakermans-Kranenburg, M. J., & van Ijzendoorn, M. H. (1999). Frightening maternal behavior linking unresolved loss and disorganized infant attachment. *Journal of Consulting and Clinical Psychology, 67*, 54–63.

Shipman, K. L., Schneider, R., Fitzgerald, M. M., Sims, C., Swisher, L., & Edwards, A. (2007). Maternal emotion socialization in maltreating and non-maltreating families: Implications for children's emotion regulation. *Social Development, 16*, 268–285.

Shipman, K., & Zeman, J. (1999). Emotional understanding: A comparison of physically maltreating and nonmaltreating mother-child dyads. *Journal of Clinical Child Psychology, 28*, 407–417.

Slade, A. (1987a). A longitudinal-study of maternal involvement and symbolic play during the toddler period. *Child Development, 58*(2), 367.

Slade A. (1987b). Quality of attachment and early symbolic play. *Developmental Psychology, 23*(1), 78.

Sroufe, L. A. (1979). The coherence of individual development: Early care, attachment, and subsequent developmental issues. *American Psychologist, 34,* 834–841.

Sroufe, L. A., & Waters, E. (1977). Attachment as an organizational construct. *Child Development,* 48, 1184–1199.

Tamis-LeMonda, C., Shannon, J., Cabrera, N., & Lamb, M. (2004). Fathers and mothers at play with their 2-and 3-year-olds: Contributions to language and cognitive development. *Child Development, 75*(6), 1806–1820.

Thompson, R. (2006). Conversation and developing understanding: Introduction to the special issue. *Merrill-Palmer Quarterly, 52,* 1–16.

U.S. Department of Health and Human Services, Administration for Children and Families, Administration on Children, Youth and Families. (2012). *Child maltreatment 2011.* Available from http://www.acf.hhs.gov/sites/default/files/cb/cm11.pdf.

Valentino, K., Cicchetti, D., Toth, S., & Rogosch, F. (2006). Mother-child play and emerging social behaviors among infants from maltreating families. *Developmental Psychology, 42*(3), 474–485.

Valentino, K., Cicchetti, D., Toth, S., & Rogosch, F. (2011). Mother-child play and maltreatment: A longitudinal analysis of emerging social behavior from infancy to toddlerhood. *Developmental Psychology, 47*(5), 1280–1294.

Valentino, K., Comas, M., Nuttall, A. K., Thomas, T. (2013). Training maltreating parents in elaborative and emotion-rich reminiscing with their preschool-aged children. *Child Abuse and Neglect, 7*(8), 585–595.

Van Bergen, P., Salmon, K., Dadds, M., & Allen, J. (2009). Training mothers in emotion-rich elaborative reminiscing: Facilitating children's autobiographical memory and emotion knowledge. *Journal of Cognition and Development, 10,* 162–187.

Van IJzendoorn, M. H., Schuengel, C., & Bakermans-Kranenburg, M. J. (1999). Disorganized attachment in early childhood: Meta-analysis of precursors, concomitants, and sequelae. *Development and Psychopathology, 11,* 225–249.

Vygotsky, L. S. (1978). *Mind in society: The development of higher mental processes* (Original works published 1930, 1933, and 1935 ed.). Cambridge, MA: Harvard University.

Wareham, P., & Salmon, K. (2006). Mother-child reminiscing about everyday experiences: Implications for psychological interventions in the preschool years. *Clinical Psychology Review, 26,* 535–554.

Youngblade, L. M., & Belsky, J. (1989). Child maltreatment, infant-parent attachment security, and dysfunctional peer relationships in toddlerhood. *Topics in Early Childhood Special Education, 9,* 1–15.

{ Commentary }

Ancestral Attachment

HOW THE EVOLUTIONARY FOUNDATION OF
ATTACHMENT INFORMS OUR UNDERSTANDING OF
CHILD MALTREATMENT INTERVENTIONS

Alyssa N. Crittenden

In the chapter, *Child Maltreatment and Early Mother–Child Interactions*, Valentino, Comas, and Nuttall explore how a maltreating family environment significantly affects a child's biological and psychological developmental outcomes. The authors argue that child maltreatment, which signifies a collapse of the early caregiving environment, can best be studied by focusing on the mother–child dyad. After a thoughtful review of the literature, the authors examine several interventions that successfully improve both the parenting behavior of maltreating mothers and the developmental trajectories of maltreated children.

The authors highlight two pathways in which children from maltreating families exhibit a disruption in "normative" social development: attachment and autonomy. Higher levels of insecure and disorganized attachment are seen among maltreated infants, suggesting that maltreating parents are deficient in sensitivity—the ability to recognize emotional cues and respond appropriately. Maltreating parents are also shown to negatively affect a child's self-directed exploration, which is critical to development, by discouraging autonomy. Valentino et al. assert that brief interventions encouraging emotionally supportive parenting have proved to be incredibly effective in improving both parent and child outcomes across multiple social and psychological domains. The authors, who preferentially emphasize the mother–child dyad, highlight selected approaches that have produced promising results in terms of increased maternal sensitivity. They conclude with a detailed discussion of reminiscing-based parent training as a means to significantly improve mother–child communication and maternal responsiveness to emotional cues.

These data have intriguing implications for the evolution of children's cognitive and socioemotional development, including attachment and autonomy. To more fully situate this chapter in an evolutionary framework, a discussion of the evolutionary significance of attachment theory is outlined below.

Attachment, as initially proposed by Bowlby and later expanded by Ainsworth, is the process by which infants develop strong psychological and emotional bonds with their caregivers as an evolutionary adaptation for ensuring infant survival (Ainsworth, 1967, 1973; Bowlby, 1969). The Bowlby-Ainsworth model of attachment, which is by far the most widely cited and operationalized model, is mother centered and has, historically, largely measured attachment in laboratory settings among Western populations. Recent work in psychology and anthropology, however, suggests that a less monotropic and mother-centered approach might better inform our understanding of cross-cultural variation and highlight the evolutionary implications of the attachment process (Crittenden and Marlowe, 2013; Keller and Harwood, 2009; Meehan and Hawkes, 2013; Weisner, 2005). Explicitly evolutionary in its initial introduction by Bowlby, attachment lays the foundation for an evolutionary theory of human development by attempting to examine the selection pressures on attachment in the *environment of evolutionary adaptedness* (EEA; Bowlby, 1969). By exploring the evolutionary underpinnings of attachment, we can better understand the significance of children's cognitive and social development.

Increasingly, cross-cultural research is showing that secure attachment relationships routinely exist outside of the mother–infant dyad (Gottlieb, 2004; Howes and Spieker, 2008; Lamb and Lewis, 2010; Morelli and Rothbaum, 2007). While mother often remains the primary caregiver (Konner, 2005), cooperative child care characterizes the majority of cultures around the world and may have been a key characteristic of our evolutionary past (Crittenden and Marlowe, 2008, 2013). Evolutionary interpretations of attachment stress the importance of an adaptive flexible reproductive strategy in which a hominin mother would have relied on various forms of social support to assist her with child care and provisioning. This reliance on allomaternal assistance is considered to be a derived characteristic of the genus *Homo* and critical to survival in the Pleistocene. If humans evolved as cooperative breeders, infants would have needed to elicit care, thus monitoring intentions and emotional responses from a range of caregivers (Hrdy, 2009). Human infants, with our species-typical ability to empathize and cooperate with others, are uniquely suited to this task. Attachment theory, although grounded in the EEA, must simultaneously acknowledge these evolutionary underpinnings while contextualizing the attachment process in contemporary settings.

The contribution of Valentino, Comas, and Nuttall allows us to explore attachment and children's psychosocial development keeping this evolutionary framework in mind. The authors, although focusing almost exclusively on the mother–child dyad, provide direct evidence supporting the critical role that parental sensitivity plays in the attachment process. Caregiver sensitivity, whether mother or allomother, shapes children's cognitive, social, and emotional development, thus fostering their ability to empathize and cooperate with others—the species-specific traits outlined above. Further encouraging autonomy and individuation improves the developmental trajectories of children.

Increasingly, we are moving further away from the EEA and the "ancestral environment" of our hominin forebears. Children are spending increasing amounts of time interfacing with electronic screens—spending more time watching television than in school (Zimmerman and Christakis, 2005). With the explosion of social media, coupled with the rise of cell phone and Internet use, the average American is now exposed to 350% more information outside of the workplace when compared with 30 years ago (Bohn and Short, 2009). This escalation in the use of personal technology and media exposure has been linked with increases in narcissism and declines in empathetic behavior (Konrath, O'Brien, and Hsing, 2011). Children's interaction with technology might be aiding one type of collapse in the early caregiving environment. Valentino and colleagues outline a very different type of collapse, that of child maltreatment, but the interventions that they propose are salient to attachment processes writ large. The intervention of emotion-rich reminiscing reinforces the significance of attachment and highlights how critical it is to foster emotional sensitivity and empathy in our children during development. The face of attachment is changing, but the emotional and social underpinnings remain part of our ancestral environment.

References

Ainsworth, M. D. (1967). *Infancy in Uganda*. Baltimore: Johns Hopkins University Press.

Ainsworth, M. D. (1973). The development of infant-mother attachment. In. B. M. Caldwell & H. N Ricciuti (Eds.), *Review of child development research* (pp. 1–94). Chicago: University of Chicago Press.

Bohn, R., & Short, J. (2009). How much information? Report on American consumers. Retrieved September 15, 2013, from http://hmi.ucsd.edu/pdf/HMI_2009_ConsumerReport_Dec9_2009.pdf.

Bowlby, J. (1969). *Attachment and loss*. New York: Basic Books.

Crittenden, A. N., & Marlowe, F. (2008). Allomaternal care among the Hadza of Tanzania. *Human Nature: An Interdisciplinary Biosocial Perspective, 19*(3), 249–262.

Crittenden, A.N. & Marlowe, F. (2013). Cooperative childcare among the Hadza: Situating multiple attachment in an evolutionary context. In J.M. Mageo and N. Quinn (Eds.), *Attachment Reconsidered: Cultural Perspectives on a Western Theory* (pp. 67–84). New York: Palgrave Macmillan.

Gottlieb, A. (2004). *The afterlife is where WE come from: The culture of infancy in West Africa*. Chicago: University of Chicago Press.

Howes, C., & Spieker, S. (2008). Attachment relationships in the context of multiple caregivers. In J. Cassidy & P. Shaver (Eds.), *The handbook of attachment: Theory, research, and clinical applications* (pp. 317–332). New York: Guilford.

Hrdy, S. B. (2009). *Mothers and others: The evolutionary origins of mutual understanding*. Cambridge, MA: Harvard University Press.

Keller, H., & Harwood, R. (2009). Culture and development pathways of relationship formation. In S. Beckman & A. Aksu-Koc (Eds.), *Pathways on human development, family, and culture,* (pp. 157–177). Cambridge, UK: Cambridge University Press.

Konner, M. (2005). Hunter-gatherer infancy and childhood. In B. S. Hewlett & M. E. Lamb (Eds.), *Hunter-gatherer childhoods: Evolutionary, developmental and cultural perspectives,* (pp. 19–64). New Brunswick: Transaction Publishers.

Konrath, S. H., O'Brien, E. H., & Hsing, C. (2011). Changes in dispositional empathy in American college students over time: A meta-analysis. *Personality and Social Psychology Review, 15*(2), 180–198.

Lamb, M. E., & Lewis, C. (2010). The development and significance of father-child relationships in two-parent families. In M. E. Lamb (Ed.), *The role of the father in child development,* (pp. 94–153). Hoboken, NJ: Wiley and Sons.

Meehan, C. & Hawkes, S. (2013). Cooperative breeding and foraging among Aka foragers. In J.M. Mageo and N. Quinn (Eds.), *Attachment Reconsidered: Cultural Perspectives on a Western Theory* (pp. 85–114). New York: Palgrave Macmillan.

Morelli, G., & Rothbaum, F. (2007). Situating the child in context: Attachment relationships and self-regulation in different cultures. In S. Kitayama & D. Cohen (Eds.), *Handbook of cultural psychology* (pp. 500–527). New York: Guilford Press.

Weisner, T. S. (2005). Attachment as a cultural and ecological problem with pluralistic solutions. *Human Development, 48,* 89–94.

Zimmerman, Frederick J., & Dimitri, A., Christakis. "Children's television viewing and cognitive outcomes: a longitudinal analysis of national data." *Archives of Pediatrics & Adolescent Medicine* **159**, no. 7 (2005): 619.

12

Importance of the Developmental Perspective in Evolutionary Discussions of Post-traumatic Stress Disorder

Robyn Bluhm and Ruth A. Lanius

Post-traumatic stress disorder (PTSD) has been closely associated with early life trauma. Individuals who have experienced abuse and neglect by caregivers are more likely to develop PTSD, and the disorder in this population may be particularly complex, from a clinical perspective. Furthermore, there is evidence that early child maltreatment directly affects neural development, and several key symptoms observed in patients with PTSD subsequent to early childhood trauma can be understood through these alterations to neural development and functioning. In this chapter, we argue that the literature on evolution and mental disorders, particularly PTSD, has failed to consider the neurodevelopmental context of early life trauma; we focus on Wakefield's influential account of mental disorders as "harmful dysfunctions" of evolved mechanisms and on Cantor's recent evolutionary model of PTSD. We argue that the etiology of PTSD cannot be fully understood without including a neurodevelopmental perspective.

Mental Disorders as "Harmful Dysfunctions"

Determining what should count as a disease or disorder is a problem for both philosophy of medicine and medicine itself. While it would take us too far afield to survey this literature here, there are two main questions that all accounts of disease/disorder deal with to at least some extent (though some emphasize one question over another). These are how to understand (1) the biological aspects of disease/disorder and (2) their effects on the individuals who suffer from them. In psychiatry, of course, relatively little is known about the biology of specific conditions, and there is disagreement even about whether an adequate account of mental disorder must address biology at all.

Wakefield has developed an account of mental disorder as "harmful dysfunction." He defines a dysfunction as "a condition in which some internal mechanism is not functioning in the way it is naturally designed to function" (Wakefield,

1992b, p. 233). He argues that reference to dysfunction "is necessary to distinguish disorders from many other types of negative conditions that are part of normal functioning, such as ignorance, grief, and normal reactions to stressful environments" (Wakefield, 1992b). He also points out that the (then current) third, revised edition of the *Diagnostic and Statistical Manual of Mental Disorders* (DSM-III-R) reference to "statistically unexpectable distress or disability" is not sufficient to establish that a mental problem is a disorder because there are a number of undesirable characteristics that are statistically unacceptable but clearly not mental disorders. He gives a number of examples to illustrate this point, including laziness, gullibility, selfishness, and insensitivity (Wakefield, 1992b, p. 238).

What does Wakefield mean by dysfunction? He turns here to evolutionary biology for clarification. The concept of dysfunction implies that there must (of course) be a mechanism that has a normal function. Wakefield views the concept of a normal function in evolutionary terms. "Certain mechanisms are naturally selected because of the beneficial effects that the mechanisms have on the organism's fitness, and those beneficial effects are the natural function of those mechanisms" (Wakefield, 1992b, p. 236). Mental mechanisms that have such a natural function are associated with "[p]erception, language, learning, action, belief, emotion, thought, drive" and other psychological abilities (Wakefield, 1992b p. 236).

The other aspect of Wakefield's concept specifies that the dysfunction must be harmful. "Harmful" is a value term based on social norms (Wakefield, 1992a). Although Wakefield says less about this aspect of his concept, he notes that it is only because a dysfunction is harmful that it is of interest to mental health professionals.

Although Wakefield is concerned in these papers with giving a general account of the concept of mental disorder, rather than in determining whether a specific mental disorder does or does not meet the definition, he does mention PTSD in the course of drawing out some of the implications of his harmful dysfunction account. He points out that PTSD (or, perhaps more accurately, some of its symptoms) is an expectable response to extreme trauma. But it becomes pathological when "the reaction to those circumstances involves a breakdown in the natural functioning of internal reparative and coping mechanisms" (Wakefield, 1992a, p. 239), so that the person continues to suffer from the symptoms after the danger is long gone. For Wakefield, this prolongation of response indicates that the mechanisms that respond appropriately to trauma have become dysfunctional, in that they continue to elicit trauma-relevant responses in the absence of environmental cues.

Post-traumatic Stress Disorder

Childhood maltreatment has not only been associated with a significantly higher risk for developing a number of psychiatric disorders, including PTSD, dissociative disorders, other anxiety disorders, depression, substance abuse, somatization disorders, and personality disorders (Caspi et al., 2002; Dube, Anda, Felitti, Chapman, Williamson, and Giles, 2001; Duncan, Saunders, Kilpatrick, Hanson, and Resnick, 1996; Felitti et al., 1998; Kessler, Sonnega, Bromet, Hughes, and Nelson, 1995; Krupnick, Green, Stockton, Goodman, Corcoran, and Petty, 2004; MacMillan et al., 2001; McCauley et al., 1997; M. B. Stein et al., 1996; C. P. Widom, 1999; C. S. Widom, Marmorstein, and White, 2006) but also with cardiovascular, endocrinological/metabolic, gastrointestinal, and immunological illnesses (Cromer and Sachs-Ericsson, 2006; Felitti et al., 1998; Heim and Nemeroff, 2001; Lanius, Vermetten, and Pain, 2010). With respect to PTSD in particular, Herman has proposed a variant of the disorder, *complex PTSD* (Herman, 1992; Van der Kolk et al., 2005) that describes multifaceted adaptations to repeated traumatization during crucial developmental periods. The latter had not been adequately represented in the general PTSD diagnosis which focused predominantly on psychiatric symptoms that arose in response to traumatic events experienced in adulthood. Symptoms of *complex PTSD* include dysfunction in seven domains: (1) affect regulation (e.g., dysregulated anger, risk taking, impulsivity); (2) attention and consciousness (e.g., dissociation); (3) self-perception (e.g., believing that one is broken or damaged); (4) interpersonal functioning (e.g., inability to trust others or revictimization of oneself or others); (6) meaning making (e.g., learned helplessness); and (7) somatization (e.g., expression of psychological distress through somatic symptoms).

In recognition of the complex adaptations to repeated traumatization, including childhood maltreatment, the fifth edition of the *Diagnostic and Statistical Manual of Mental Disorders* (DSM-5; APA, 2013) has revised the PTSD diagnosis to extend its focus from solely concentrating on fear and anxiety symptoms to more broadly incorporating a wide range of emotional and self-regulatory dysfunction, as described in the complex PTSD diagnosis above. Specifically, the PTSD DSM-5 diagnosis as originally outlined by Friedman and colleagues now includes the experience of a persistent negative emotional state, including fear, horror, anger, guilt, or shame; difficulties experiencing positive emotions such as happiness or loving feelings; reckless and self-destructive behavior; and negative beliefs about oneself, others, and the world (APA, 2013; Friedman, Resick, Bryant, and Brewin, 2011). In addition, a dissociative subtype focusing on symptoms of depersonalization and derealization has been added. This subtype has been associated with repeated traumatization and early adverse experience, increased comorbidity, increased functional impairment, increased suicidality (including suicidal ideation, plans, and attempts), and greater engagement in psychiatric treatment (D. J. Stein et al., 2013; Lanius, Brand, Vermetten, Frewen, and Spiegel, 2012; Lanius, Vermetten, Loewenstein, et al., 2010; Wolf, Miller, Reardon, Ryabchenko, Castillo, and Freund, 2012). Moreover, a subtype of PTSD describing PTSD in children 6 years and younger, including dissociative reactions and a variety of negative emotional states, has been included in the most recent version of the DSM. The revision of the PTSD diagnosis in the DSM-5 therefore now captures the array of emotion dysfunction experienced by chronically traumatized individuals to a greater extent, which is particularly relevant to the population suffering from PTSD related to childhood abuse.

All of these changes make the diagnosis of PTSD more clinically relevant, but they are purely descriptive and therefore do not answer questions about the evolution or the etiology of the disorder. In the next section, we introduce two accounts of the evolution of PTSD: Wakefield briefly discusses PTSD in his influential account of mental disorders as harmful dysfunctions, whereas Cantor focuses specifically on PTSD. We will conclude that these accounts do not adequately address the important role of early childhood experience on brain development and that they are therefore not sufficient for understanding PTSD, particularly PTSD related to childhood trauma. In the second half of the chapter, we illustrate several ways in which neuroimaging research has supported the idea that the pathophysiology of PTSD related to childhood trauma is influenced by early childhood experience.

We challenge the claim that mental disorders involve a harmful dysfunction that can be understood in terms of the malfunctioning of some evolutionarily conserved mechanism. Bolton has pointed out that, because Wakefield emphasizes that the functions that are impaired in mental disorders are "selected for" by evolution, his harmful dysfunction account of mental disorders "rests on the now doubtful assumption that there is a clear (enough) division between psychological functioning that is natural (evolved and innate), as opposed to social (cultivated)" (Bolton, 2008, p. 124). Understanding complex PTSD, in particular, requires recognizing the extent to which the development of brain structures that underlie the psychological functions relevant to PTSD means taking seriously the social influences on this neural development. To do this, we will first discuss in some detail a proposed evolutionary explanation for PTSD, by Cantor, that meets Wakefield's "harmful dysfunction" criterion and that fails to take into account the effects of early childhood experience on brain development, and therefore on the pathophysiology of PTSD. At the same time, Cantor's account is a useful starting point because it attempts to provide an account of the evolution of PTSD that integrates a number of relevant theories.

Cantor's Evolutionary Model of Post-traumatic Stress Disorder

Although he does not discuss Wakefield's theory, Cantor's model of PTSD as a disorder of heightened defense can profitably be analyzed using Wakefield's idea of harmful dysfunction. At its core, Cantor's argument is that the responses characteristic of PTSD are adaptive—they are evolutionarily conserved natural functions that respond to threat. Like Wakefield, he says that the problem arises when these mechanisms are activated in situations in which they are not warranted. Cantor views his model as "integrating existing behavioral, information processing, and neuroscientific theories" (Cantor, 2009, p. 1039). He identifies a number of defense strategies that are highly evolutionarily conserved: "avoidance, attentive immobility, withdrawal, aggressive defense, appeasement, and tonic immobility" (Cantor, 2009, p. 1040).

A number of these mechanisms are linked to MacLean's triune model of the brain (MacLean, 1973), which divides the brain into three parts based on the age and the anatomical features characterizing each. The brainstem is the oldest area; it mediates primarily basic survival functions. The limbic system is the second oldest; it first occurs in reptiles. Finally, the neocortex, which occurs in mammals but is by far most developed in human beings, was the most recent area to evolve. Cantor emphasizes that some of the defense strategies observed in human beings with PTSD can also be found in other animals. For example, avoidance is described as the dominant form of defense available to reptiles and is linked to evolutionarily older parts of the brain, specifically the basal ganglia and the extrapyramidal motor systems (Cantor, 2009, p. 1042). Attentive immobility is a characteristic defense of lower mammals, such as rats, and is "mediated by the lateral projections of the central gray that also mediate stress-induced analgesia" (Cantor, 2009, p. 1042, citing Davis and Whalen, 2001). Appeasement, because it is a response to threats from conspecifics rather than predators, "suggests a more recent triune brain heritage than defenses evolving from predation" (Cantor, 2009, p. 1043). Because appeasement involves "traumatic defeat plus an inescapable relationship with a dominant oppressor" (Cantor, 2009, p. 1043), PTSD that involves this sort of defense mechanisms may be importantly different than PTSD associated primarily with other symptoms. Cantor and Price (2007) have further suggested that these reactions are the foundation of complex PTSD.

As noted above, Cantor cites MacLean's triune brain theory to support his claim that defense reactions can be classified on an evolutionary basis. Yet MacLean's three brain regions, on his own account, function largely independently of each other, suggesting that coordination among the defense mechanisms is minimal. Maclean claims that "[i]t cannot be overemphasized that these three basic brains show great differences in structure and chemistry.... The wonder is that nature was able to hook them up and establish any kind of communication between them" (MacLean, 1973, p. 7). This theory thus implies that defense mechanisms mediated by "lower" parts of the brain, ones that are shared widely across species, are unchanged in humans from their first evolutionary appearance. Cantor seems willing to accept this implication. He acknowledges that there are important cultural aspects to human behavior, but says that "[n]evertheless, biosocial factors underlie much of our culture, especially when it comes to survival behaviors" (Cantor, 2005, p. 107).

Why Evolutionary Accounts Require Development

To return to Wakefield's characterization of mental disorder, Cantor views PTSD in terms of the elicitation of evolutionarily conserved defense-related functions, in situations in which these defense mechanisms are not warranted. The evolutionary accounts given by Wakefield and by Cantor go some way toward explaining why it is that human beings in general *can* develop PTSD; however, they do not address the question of why some people do develop the disorder, whereas most do not. To address this second point, we emphasize the importance of the social shaping of neural development, particularly in early childhood.

Recent discussions of mental disorder have emphasized that they have an important developmental aspect. Although it is clear that the etiology of mental disorders is complex and multifactorial, developmental changes are increasingly seen as key. The peak age of onset for mental disorder is 14 years (Kessler, Berglund, Demler, Jin, Merikangas, and Walters, 2005), and Pavaluri and Sweeney link this to "alterations in the developmental trajectory of functional brain systems" (Pavaluri and Sweeney, 2008, p. 1274). In particular, connections between the basal ganglia and the prefrontal cortex tend to develop over time, and myelination tends to occur later in the prefrontal cortex than in sensory and motor areas (Giedd, 2004). White matter increases also occur in a posterior-to-anterior pattern (Durston, Pol, Casey, Giedd, Buitelaar, and van Engeland, 2001), suggesting that the prefrontal cortex is among the last brain areas to achieve its adult state. These findings belie MacLean's belief that the "three brains" are not integrated. They also leave open the possibility that "normal" integration depends on the care and treatment an individual receives during early life. It is to this that we turn in the next section.

Post-traumatic Stress Disorder Related to Childhood Abuse as a Neurodevelopmental Disorder

As described above, the brain undergoes a great deal of postnatal sculpting that ensures that the prefrontal cortex is closely linked, both structurally and functionally, to subcortical and limbic structures. This means, however, that early life environment is important in this period of postnatal development. Parenting makes a difference to the way the brain is wired. Schore has drawn on work in developmental psychology and neurobiology to describe the importance of early life attachment. By the age of 2 months, and peaking at approximately 9 or 10 months, an infant is able to study her mother's (and other caregivers') facial expressions. The mother modulates the infant's response to her facial expressions, teaching the infant to tolerate increasingly intense positive emotions and, ultimately, to modulate her own emotional responses. As Schore phrases it, "the mother ... is directly influencing the infant's learning of 'how to feel,' 'how much to feel' and 'whether to feel' about particular objects in the environment" (Schore, 1994, p. 108). Yet this is not a process that is understood purely in psychological terms; the process also promotes the maturation of neural circuits that will eventually underlie the adult ability to understand and modulate complex emotions and also to maintain a robust sense of self. Schore further cites studies that indicate that this relationship promotes the maturation of specific neural circuits that are necessary both for appropriate social behavior and for a robust sense of self in the adult. In the next section, we identify specific areas of psychological and neural development that may be particularly vulnerable to the effects of early childhood trauma, including the regulation of emotions and the development of a robust sense of self, and detail how these processes are central to the pathophysiology of PTSD related to childhood abuse.

Emotional Awareness and Emotion Regulation in Patients With Chronic, Early Life Trauma

Adults with chronic PTSD subsequent to early life trauma often show profound impairments with regard to emotion recognition, emotional awareness, and emotion regulation (Cloitre, Stovall-McClough, Zorbas, and Charuvastra, 2008; Ford, Stockton, Kaltman, and Green, 2006; Moore and Zoellner, 2007). Emotional awareness involves the ability to recognize and describe one's own emotions and also others' (Fridja, 2007; Lambie and Marcel, 2002) and has been linked to having a secure attachment history with one's primary caregivers (Lane and Schwartz, 1987; Winnicott, 1960).

Emotions have evolved, in part, to signal danger in the environment and to motivate escape, but children who grow up with a chronically abusive caregiver are unable to escape, and therefore the emotional signals do not result in the behavior they promote. When this is often the case, children do not learn to recognize or to use their emotional responses appropriately. As a result, they may experience learned helplessness, or come to believe (whether implicitly or explicitly) that emotional responses are pointless. They may also come to feel disconnected from their bodily sensations and emotions, thus avoiding distressing experiences that they cannot deal with effectively through action (Lanius, Bluhm, and Frewen, 2011).

Clinical research indicates that individuals with PTSD have difficulty identifying and expressing their emotional states (Frewen, Dozois, Neufeld, and Lanius, 2008) and have lower scores on the *Levels of Emotional Awareness Scale* (Lane and Schwartz, 1987; Frewen, Lane, Neufeld, Densmore, Stevens, and Lanius, 2008), as well as higher levels of emotional numbing or a reported inability to experience emotions (Frewen et al., 2012) and higher levels of alexithymia (i.e., difficulty in identifying and expressing feelings in words) (Frewen, Dozois, Neufeld, and Lanius, 2008; Frewen, Dozois, Neufeld, and Lanius, 2012).

Advances have also been made in terms of the neural underpinnings of deficits in emotional awareness in PTSD. For example, our group has examined the relationship between trait emotional numbing symptoms and brain activation patterns during emotional imagery in a group of individuals who suffered from PTSD related to prolonged childhood abuse (Frewen et al., 2012). A patient suffering from PTSD related to childhood abuse summed up feelings of emotional numbing by stating,

"It's like a blank, I think about my kids and I feel nothing for them. I'll be sitting there feeling confused and numb, and I wonder what I'm supposed to be feeling. It's like dead space...and when that happens, I have trouble using words, finding my words, I can't talk." In the functional magnetic resonance imaging (fMRI) study, patients' emotional numbing ratings were correlated with extent of brain activation during imagery of positive (receiving others' affection or praise) and negative (rejection or criticism) scripts. Women who reported increased emotional numbing symptoms exhibited *decreased* brain activation within the dorsomedial prefrontal cortex during imagery of both positive and negative socioemotional scripts, consistent with a role for the dorsomedial prefrontal cortex in higher order self-reflective functioning.

Interestingly, within healthy women completing the same task, the more an individual exhibited the capacity to *mindfully observe,* referring to the intentional paying attention to one's inner and external stimuli and experiences (e.g., *"When I'm walking, I deliberately notice the sensations of my body moving"; "I notice changes in my body, such as whether my breathing slows down or speeds up";* [Baer, Smith, and Allen, 2004); Baer, Smith, Hopkins, Krietemeyer, and Toney, 2006), the *more* activation was observed in the dorsomedial prefrontal cortex (Frewen et al., 2010). These findings suggest that dysfunction of the dorsomedial prefrontal cortex may underlie the difficulties individuals with PTSD often have reflecting on and interpreting their emotional experience. It also points to the importance of teaching PTSD patients mindful observing of inner and external experiences in order to achieve an increased capacity for self-reflection and awareness of emotional states (Siegel, 2007). Future studies will have to examine PTSD patients after treatment focusing on increasing the capacity for self-reflection, including mindful observing, in order to assess whether the deficits in the activation of the dorsomedial prefrontal cortex can be reversed through successful psychotherapeutic intervention.

Emotion recognition and emotional awareness have also been suggested to play an important role in the regulation of emotional states. As described earlier in this chapter, emerging research has repeatedly shown that emotion dysregulation (experienced by many PTSD patients) reaches far beyond fear and includes emotional states such as anger, guilt, shame, and disgust (APA, 2013; Miller, Resick, and Keane, 2009; Resick and Miller, 2009). In this chapter, the term *emotion dysregulation* will be used to refer collectively to disturbances in a number of emotional states. In addition, this term will encompass the process by which we influence how much emotion we have and when we have it as outlined by Gross (1998). Our group has suggested two pathways to emotion dysregulation in PTSD (Lanius, Frewen, Vermetten, and Yehuda, 2010), one more pertinent to adult-onset trauma and another more relevant to early developmental trauma. The first pathway focusing on adult-onset trauma proposes that emotion dysregulation develops as a result of fear conditioning and underlying mechanisms of stress sensitization and kindling. Over time, a person who is sensitized to subtle reminders of traumatic and related memories may develop a general pattern of emotion dysregulation, including anger, grief, guilt, shame, in addition to a generalization of the fear response. The mechanism underlying this process is thought to be comparable to kindling, a process involving the development of generalized seizures in response to repeated, subthreshold electrophysiological stimulation. Similarly, in PTSD, the progressive amplification and expansion of symptoms occurring over time may be related to the neural circuitry associated with the emotional memory response becoming increasingly sensitized and expanding into neighboring neural circuits that underlie emotional responses other than fear (McFarlane, 2010; McFarlane, Yehuda, and Clark, 2002; Post, Weiss, Smith, Li, and McCann, 1997). In contrast, the second pathway highlights the importance of early childhood environment and developmental trauma (A. N. Schore, 2003a, 2003b). An impoverished early environment resulting from the unavailability of a responsive attachment figure or to childhood abuse may lead to an inappropriate development of the emotional and arousal regulatory neural systems. This results in emotion dysregulation of a number of emotional states, which in turn leads to a hampered ability to regulate physiological arousal to threatening or traumatic events. In a cycle of positive feedback, an exacerbation of emotion dysregulation develops, including the development of PTSD after exposure to traumatic events later in life.

Neural Correlates of Self-Referential Processing in Post-traumatic Stress Disorder

In addition to alterations in emotional awareness and emotion regulation, patients with chronic PTSD also experience diminished self-reflective functioning. Frewen et al., 2011 have recently examined this issue using a neuroimaging paradigm. Participants were asked to provide self-descriptiveness ratings for negatively valenced (e.g., abandoned, unlovable, despicable, broken) and positively valenced (e.g., lovable, special, adorable) trait words. They then simultaneously viewed pictures of themselves and heard the words spoken while in the scanner.

PTSD patients rated more negative and fewer positive trait adjectives as describing themselves, which supports clinical observations that individuals with PTSD often experience intense negative thoughts about themselves and even self-hatred. The neuroimaging data showed that when healthy women, but not women with PTSD, viewed their faces while listening to positive trait adjectives, they had increased activation in the perigenual anterior cingulate cortex. This region has previously been shown to be highly responsive to emotional manipulations (e.g., Kober, Barrett, Joseph, Bliss-Moreau, Lindquist, and Wager, 2008) and also has been linked to self-referential processing (e.g., Kircher et al., 2000; van der Meer et al., 2010). It is also more active during negative emotional events in healthy individuals than in individuals with PTSD (see Etkin and Wager, 2007, for review).

Compared with healthy controls, patients with PTSD exhibited increased activation in the right amygdala when exposed to their picture and positive trait words.

The extent of this activation was associated with the degree to which they either felt positive or attributed those positive attributes to themselves (Frewen, Dozois, Neufeld, Densmore, Stevens, and Lanius, 2011). Interestingly, the right amygdala has been associated with social emotion processing. This suggests that more positive and healthy self-appraisal may be related to better social functioning.

Default Mode Network

Over the past decade, there has been increasing interest in understanding patterns of connectivity in the "resting" brain; it is thought that these patterns underlie the sort of task-specific patterns of activity that have been traditionally studied by neuroimaging researchers. Functional connectivity magnetic resonance imaging (fcFMRI), or resting-state fMRI, measures low-frequency oscillations in brain activity that are correlated among particular neural circuits. Perhaps the best-studied such circuit is the so-called default mode network (DMN; Buckner, Andrews-Hanna, and Schacter, 2008), which includes the posterior cingulate cortex, anterior cingulate cortex, medial prefrontal cortex, and bilateral angular gyrus–inferior parietal cortex; according to some studies, the middle temporal gyrus has also been implicated in this network (Spreng, Mar, and Kim, 2009). Although this network has no clear cognitive functions, one hypothesis that has been proposed is that the brain maintains a "default mode" that keeps it in a state of readiness to respond to changing environmental demands (Raichle and Gusnard, 2005). The brain areas associated with the default mode have also been shown to be involved in theory of mind, autobiographical memory, and prospection (Spreng and Grady, 2010). Of key importance for its role in PTSD, the network has also been linked to self-referential processing and the stream of consciousness (Northoff, Heinzel, de Greck, M., Bermpohl, F., Dobrowolny, H., and Panksepp, 2006; Sajonz et al., 2010).

Although the DMN is observed remarkably consistently in healthy adults, it is not present in early life. For example, Fransson and colleagues (2007, 2009) examined the DMN in lightly sedated preterm infants and in sleeping full-term neonates and found that it did not resemble that of adults. Instead, connectivity was observed within local areas and in homologous areas in each hemisphere, and connections between the frontal and posterior areas was lacking. Subsequent research showed that infants as young as 2 weeks of age may have three separate components that involve regions that will become part of the adult DMN (Gao et al., 2009).

Yet integration of the areas that become the DMN appears to begin during infancy; Gao and colleagues (2009) observed that some anterior-posterior integration begins to occur in infants as young as 1 year. The network does not take its adult form for some years afterward, though. One study found DMN integration similar to that of adults in children starting at 9 years of age (Thomason, Chang, Glover, Gabrieli, Greicius, and Gotlib, 2008), although another study demonstrated that significant differences remained in the DMN in children aged 7 to 9 years (Fair et al., 2008).

Given that PTSD has been associated with deficits in self-referential process-ing, as described above, and with altered activation in areas associated with the default network (e.g., medial prefrontal cortex, anterior cingulate, posterior cingulate cortex) (Bluhm et al., 2012; Bremner, Staib, Kaloupek, Southwick, Soufer, and Charney, 1999; Bryant et al., 2008; Geuze et al., 2007; Lanius et al., 2001; Liberzon et al., 1999; Shin et al., 1999; Williams et al., 2006), our group examined the integrity of this network in PTSD related to prolonged childhood abuse. Connectivity within the DMN has been shown to be affected in patients with PTSD subsequent to early life trauma (Bluhm et al., 2009). In particular, low-frequency oscillations in both the posterior cingulate cortex and the medial prefrontal cortex show lower correlations with other areas in the DMN, compared with healthy control subjects. This pattern of DMN connectivity resembles that observed in children aged 7 to 9 years. One possible explanation for this is that stress hormone exposure interferes with the myelination of white matter tracts during the process of maturation of the DMN (Daniels, Frewen, McKinnon, and Lanius, 2011). We hypothesized that the negatively valenced self-loathing and often fragmented sense of self that are often experienced by individuals with highly dissociative PTSD will be related to the degree of anterior-posterior inte-gration of the DMN (Lanius et al., 2011). Future studies will therefore need to carefully correlate clinical symptoms of self-related dysfunction and their rela-tionship to DMN connectivity.

Conclusion

Much remains to be learned about the effects on neural development and psycho-pathology of early life experiences. We have argued in this chapter that some of the key deficits observed in patients with PTSD subsequent to early childhood trauma can be understood in terms of the effects of these experiences on neural develop-ment. In particular, childhood trauma may affect adult functioning of the DMN and may impair the ability to engage in self-referential and emotion processing. From a clinical perspective, these deficits are now beginning to be recognized as central to understanding PTSD subsequent to early childhood abuse. The DSM-5 criteria, which have been expanded to include more symptoms relevant to repeated traumatization, including childhood abuse, provide an important platform from which future research in this area can progress. From a theoretical perspective, dis-cussions of the evolution of PTSD must take into account the importance of early childhood experiences for neural development; current accounts, such as those presented by Wakefield and Cantor, do not do so. It will be important for future theoretical frameworks of PTSD to incorporate not only evolution but also early childhood experience.

References

American Psychological Association (APA). (2013). *Diagnostic and statistical manual of mental disorders (5th ed.)*. Washington, DC: APA.

Baer, R. A., Smith, G. T., & Allen, K. B. (2004). Assessment of mindfulness by self-report: The Kentucky inventory of mindfulness skills. *Assessment, 11*(3), 191–206.

Baer, R. A., Smith, G. T., Hopkins, J., Krietemeyer, J., & Toney, L. (2006). Using self-report assessment methods to explore facets of mindfulness. *Assessment, 13*(1), 27–45.

Bluhm, R. L., Frewen, P. A., Coupland, N. C., Densmore, M., Schore, A. N., Stevens, T. K., et al. (2012). Neural correlates of self-reflection in posttraumatic stress disorder. *Acta Psychiatrica Scandinavica, 125*(3), 238–246.

Bluhm, R. L., Williamson, P. C., Osuch, E. A., Frewen, P. A., Stevens, T. K., Boksman, K., et al. (2009). Alterations in default network connectivity in posttraumatic stress disorder related to early-life trauma. *Journal of Psychiatry and Neuroscience, 34*(3), 187–194.

Bolton, D. (2008). *What is mental disorder? An essay in philosophy, science, and values*. Oxford, UK: Oxford University Press.

Bremner, J. D., Staib, L. H., Kaloupek, D., Southwick, S. M., Soufer, R., & Charney, D. S. (1999). Neural correlates of exposure to traumatic pictures and sound in Vietnam combat veterans with and without posttraumatic stress disorder: A positron emission tomography study. *Biological Psychiatry, 45*, 806–816.

Bryant, R. A., Felmingham, K., Kemp, A., Das, P., Hughes, G., Peduto, A., & Williams, L. (2008). Amygdala and ventral anterior cingulate activation predicts treatment response to cognitive behaviour therapy for post-traumatic stress disorder. *Psychological Medicine, 38*(4), 555–561.

Buckner, R., Andrews-Hanna, J., & Schacter, D. (2008). The brain's default network: Anatomy, function, and relevance to disease. *Annals of the New York Academy of Sciences, 1124*, 1–38.

Cantor, C. (2005). *Evolution and Posttraumatic Stress: Disorders of Vigilance and Defense*. London: Routledge.

Cantor, C. (2009). Post-traumatic stress disorder: Evolutionary perspectives. *Australian and New Zealand Journal of Psychiatry, 43*, 1038–1048.

Caspi, A., McClay, J., Moffitt, T. E., Mill, J., Martin, J., Craig, I. W., et al. (2002). Role of genotype in the cycle of violence in maltreated children. *Science, 297*(5582), 851–854.

Cloitre, M., Stovall-McClough, C., Zorbas, P., & Charuvastra, A. (2008). Attachment organization, emotion regulation, and expectations of support in a clinical sample of women with childhood abuse histories. *Journal of Traumatic Stress, 21*(3), 282–289.

Cromer, K. R., & Sachs-Ericsson, N. (2006). The association between childhood abuse, PTSD, and the occurrence of adult health problems: Moderation via current life stress. *Journal of Traumatic Stress, 19*(6), 967–971.

Daniels, J. K., Frewen, P., McKinnon, M. C., & Lanius, R. A. (2011). Default mode alterations in posttraumatic stress disorder related to early-life trauma: A developmental perspective. *Journal of Psychiatry and Neuroscience, 36*(1), 56–59.

Davis, M., & Whalen, P. J. (2001). The amygdala: Vigilance and emotion. *Molecular Psychiatry, 6*(1), 13–34.

Dube, S. R., Anda, R. F., Felitti, V. J., Chapman, D. P., Williamson, D. F., & Giles, W. H. (2001). Childhood abuse, household dysfunction, and the risk of attempted suicide throughout the life span: findings from the Adverse Childhood Experiences Study. *Journal of the American Medical Association, 286*(24), 3089–3096.

Duncan, R. D., Saunders, B. E., Kilpatrick, D. G., Hanson, R. F., & Resnick, H. S. (1996). Childhood physical assault as a risk factor for PTSD, depression, and substance abuse: findings from a national survey. *American Journal of Orthopsychiatry, 66*(3), 437–448.

Durston, S., Pol, H. E., Casey, B. J., Giedd, J. N., Buitelaar, J. K., & van Engeland, H. (2001). Anatomical MRI of the developing human brain: What have we learned? *Journal of the American Academy of Child and Adolescent Psychiatry, 40*(9), 1012–1020.

Etkin, A., & Wager, T. D. (2007). Functional neuroimaging of anxiety: A meta-analysis of emotional processing in PTSD, social anxiety disorder, and specific phobia. *American Journal of Psychiatry, 164*(10), 1476–1488.

Fair, D. A., Cohen, A. L., Dosenbach, N. U., Church, J. A., Miezin, F. M., Barch, D. M., et al. (2008). The maturing architecture of the brain's default network. *Proceedings of the National Academy of Science U S A, 105*(10), 4028–4032.

Felitti, V. J., Anda, R. F., Nordenberg, D., Williamson, D. F., Spitz, A. M., Edwards, V., et al. (1998). Relationship of childhood abuse and household dysfunction to many of the leading causes of death in adults. The Adverse Childhood Experiences (ACE) Study. *American Journal of Preventive Medicine, 14*(4), 245–258.

Ford, J. D., Stockton, P., Kaltman, S., & Green, B. L. (2006). Disorders of extreme stress (DESNOS) symptoms are associated with type and severity of interpersonal trauma exposure in a sample of healthy young women. *Journal of Interpersonal Violence, 21*(11), 1399–1416.

Fransson, P., Skiold, B., Engstrom, M., Hallberg, B., Mosskin, M., Aden, U., et al. (2009). Spontaneous brain activity in the newborn brain during natural sleep—an fMRI study in infants born at full term. *Pediatric Research, 66*(3), 301–305.

Fransson, P., Skiold, B., Horsch, S., Nordell, A., Blennow, M., Lagercrantz, H., & Aden, U. (2007). Resting-state networks in the infant brain. *Proceedings of the National Academy of Sciences USA, 104*(39), 15531–15536.

Frewen, P. A., Dozois, D. J. A., Neufeld, R. W. J., Densmore, M., Lane, R. D., Stevens, T. C., & Lanius, R. A. (2010). Individual differences in trait mindfulness predict dorsal medial prefrontal and amygdala response during emotional imagery: An fMRI study. *Personality and Individual Differences, 49*, 479–484.

Frewen, P. A., Dozois, D. J. A., Neufeld, R. W. J., Densmore, M., Stevens, T., & Lanius, R. A. (2011). Self-referential processing in women with PTSD related to childhood abuse: affective and neural response. *Psychological Trauma: Theory, Research, Practice, and Policy, 4*, 318–328.

Frewen, P. A., Dozois, D. J. A., Neufeld, R. W. J., Lane, R. D., Densmore, M., Stevens, T. K., & Lanius, R. A. (2012). Emotional numbing in PTSD: An fMRI study. *Journal of Clinical Psychiatry, 73*(4), 431–436.

Frewen, P. A., Dozois, D. J. A., Neufeld, R. W. J., & Lanius, R. A. (2008). Meta-analysis of alexithymia in posttraumatic stress disorder. *Journal of Traumatic Stress, 21*(2), 243–246.

Frewen, P. A., Lane, R. D., Neufeld, R. W., Densmore, M., Stevens, T., & Lanius, R. (2008). Neural correlates of levels of emotional awareness during trauma script-imagery in posttraumatic stress disorder. *Psychosomatic Medicine, 70*(1), 27–31.

Fridja, N. H. (2007). *The laws of emotion*. Mahwah, NJ: Erlbaum.

Friedman, M. J., Resick, P. A., Bryant, R. A., & Brewin, C. R. (2011). Considering PTSD for DSM-5. *Depression and Anxiety, 28*(9), 750–769.

Gao, W., Zhu, H., Giovanello, K. S., Smith, J. K., Shen, D., Gilmore, J. H., & Lin, W. (2009). Evidence on the emergence of the brain's default network from 2-week-old to 2-year-old healthy pediatric subjects. *Proceedings of the National Academy of Sciences USA, 106*(16), 6790–6795.

Geuze, E., Westenberg, H. G., Jochims, A., de Kloet, C. S., Bohus, M., Vermetten, E., & Schmahl, C. (2007). Altered pain processing in veterans with posttraumatic stress disorder. *Archives of General Psychiatry, 64*(1), 76–85.

Giedd, J. N. (2004). Structural magnetic resonance imaging of the adolescent brain. *Annals of the New York Academy of Sciences, 102*, 77–85.

Gross J. J. (1998). Antecedent- and response-focused emotion regulation: divergent consequences for experience, expression, and physiology. *Journal of Personality and Social Psychology, 74*, 224–237.

Heim, C., & Nemeroff, C. B. (2001). The role of childhood trauma in the neurobiology of mood and anxiety disorders: preclinical and clinical studies. *Biological Psychiatry, 49*(12), 1023–1039.

Herman, J. (1992). *Trauma and recovery: The aftermath of violence—from domestic abuse to political terror*. New York: Basic Books.

Kessler, R. C., Berglund, P., Demler, O., Jin, R., Merikangas, K. R., & Walters, E. E. (2005). Lifetime prevalence and age-of-onset distributions of DSM-IV disorders in the National Comorbidity Survey Replication. *Archives of General Psychiatry, 62*(6), 593–602.

Kessler, R. C., Sonnega, A., Bromet, E., Hughes, M., & Nelson, C. B. (1995). Posttraumatic stress disorder in the National Comorbidity Survey. *Archives of General Psychiatry, 52*(12), 1048–1060.

Kircher, T. T. J., Senior, C., Phillips, M. L., Benson, P. J., Bullmore, E. T., Brammer, M., et al. (2000). Towards a functional neuroanatomy of self processing: Effects of faces and words. *Cognitive Brain Research, 10*, 133–144.

Kober, H., Barrett, L. F., Joseph, J., Bliss-Moreau, E., Lindquist, K., & Wager, T. D. (2008). Functional grouping and cortical-subcortical interactions in emotion: a meta-analysis of neuroimaging studies. *NeuroImage, 42*(2), 998–1031.

Krupnick, J. L., Green, B. L., Stockton, P., Goodman, L., Corcoran, C., & Petty, R. (2004). Mental health effects of adolescent trauma exposure in a female college sample: Exploring differential outcomes based on experiences of unique trauma types and dimensions. *Psychiatry, 67*(3), 264–279.

Lambie, J. A., & Marcel, A. J. (2002). Consciousness and the varieties of emotion experience: A theoretical framework. *Psychological Review, 109*, 219–259.

Lane, R. D., & Schwartz, G. E. (1987). Levels of emotional awareness: A cognitive-developmental theory and its application to psychopathology. *American Journal of Psychiatry, 144*(2), 133–143.

Lanius, R. A., Bluhm, R. L., & Frewen, P. A. (2011). How understanding the neurobiology of complex post-traumatic stress disorder can inform clinical practice: A social cognitive and affective neuroscience approach. *Acta Psychiatrica Scandinavica, 124*(5), 331–348.

Lanius, R. A., Brand, B., Vermetten, E., Frewen, P. A., & Spiegel, D. (2012). The dissociative subtype of posttraumatic stress disorder: Rationale, clinical and neurobiological evidence, and implications. *Depression and Anxiety*, *29*(8), 701–708.

Lanius, R. A., Frewen, P. A., Vermetten, E., Yehuda, R. (2010). Fear conditioning and early life vulnerabilities: Two distinct pathways of emotional dysregulation and brain dysfunction in PTSD. *European Journal of Psychotraumatology*, *1*, 5467–5477.

Lanius, R. A., Vermetten, E., Loewenstein, R. J., Brand, B., Schmahl, C., Bremner, J. D., & Spiegel, D. (2010). Emotion modulation in PTSD: Clinical and neurobiological evidence for a dissociative subtype. *American Journal of Psychiatry*, *167*(6), 640–647.

Lanius, R. A., Vermetten, E., & Pain, C. (Eds.). (2010). *The impact of early life trauma on health and disease: The hidden epidemic*. Cambridge, UK: Cambridge University Press.

Lanius, R. A., Williamson, P. C., Densmore, M., Boksman, K., Gupta, M. A., Neufeld, R. W., et al. (2001). Neural correlates of traumatic memories in posttraumatic stress disorder: A functional MRI investigation. *American Journal of Psychiatry 158*, 1920–1922.

Liberzon, I., Taylor, S. F., Amdur, R., Jung, T. D., Chamberlain, K. R., Minoshima, S., et al. (1999). Brain activation in PTSD in response to trauma-related stimuli. *Biological Psychiatry, 45*, 817–826.

MacLean, P. D. (1973). *A Triune Concept of the Brain and Behavior*. T. J. Boag & D. Campbell (Eds.), Toronto: University of Toronto Press.

MacMillan, H. L., Fleming, J. E., Streiner, D. L., Lin, E., Boyle, M. H., Jamieson, E., et al. (2001). Childhood abuse and lifetime psychopathology in a community sample. *American Journal of Psychiatry, 158*(11), 1878–1883.

McCauley, J., Kern, D. E., Kolodner, K., Dill, L., Schroeder, A. F., DeChant, H. K., et al. (1997). Clinical characteristics of women with a history of childhood abuse: unhealed wounds. *Journal of the American Medical Association, 277*(17), 1362–1368.

McFarlane, A. C. (2010). The long-term costs of traumatic stress: Intertwined physical and psychological consequences. *World Psychiatry, 9*(1), 3–10.

McFarlane, A. C., Yehuda, R., & Clark, C. R. (2002). Biologic models of traumatic memories and post-traumatic stress disorder: The role of neural networks. *Psychiatric Clinics of North American, 25*(2), 253–270.

Miller, M. W., Resick, P. A., & Keane, T. M. (2009). DSM-V: Should PTSD be in a class of its own? *British Journal of Psychiatry, 194*(1), 90.

Moore, S. A., & Zoellner, L. A. (2007). Overgeneral autobiographical memory and traumatic events: An evaluative review. *Psychological Bulletin, 133*(3), 419–437.

Northoff, G., Heinzel, A., de Greck, M., Bermpohl, F., Dobrowolny, H., & Panksepp, J. (2006). Self-referential processing in our brain: A meta-analysis of imaging studies on the self. *NeuroImage, 31*(1), 440–457.

Pavaluri, M. N., & Sweeney, J. A. (2008). Integrating functional brain neuroimaging and developmental cognitive neuroscience in child psychiatry research. *Journal of the American Academy of Child and Adolescent Psychiatry, 47*(11), 1273–1288.

Post, R. M., Weiss, S. R., Smith, M., Li, H., & McCann, U. (1997). Kindling versus quenching: Implications for the evolution and treatment of posttraumatic stress disorder. *Annals of the New York Academy of Sciences, 821*, 285–295.

Raichle, M. E., & Gusnard, D. A. (2005). Intrinsic brain activity sets the stage for expression of motivated behavior. *Journal of Comparative Neurology, 493*(1), 167–176.

Resick, P. A., & Miller, M. W. (2009). Posttraumatic stress disorder: Anxiety or traumatic stress disorder? *Journal of Traumatic Stress, 22,* 384–390.

Sajonz, B., Kahnt, T., Margulies, D. S., Park, S. Q., Wittmann, A., Stoy, M., et al. (2010). Delineating self-referential processing from episodic memory retrieval: Common and dissociable networks. *NeuroImage, 50*(4), 1606–1617.

Schore, A. N. (1994). *Affect regulation and the origin of the self: The neurobiology of emotional development.* Hillsdale, NJ: Erlbaum.

Schore, A. N. (2003a). *Affect dysregulation and disorders of the self.* New York: W. W. Norton.

Schore, A. N. (2003b). *Affect dysregulation and the repair of the self.* New York: W. W. Norton.

Shin, L. M., McNally, R. J., Kosslyn, S. M., Thompson, W. L., Rauch, S. L., Alpert, N. M., et al. (1999). Regional cerebral blood flow during script-driven imagery in childhood sexual abuse-related PTSD: a PET investigation. *American Journal of Psychiatry, 156,* 575–584.

Siegel, D. J. (2007). *The mindful brain: Reflection and attunement in the cultivation of wellbeing.* New York: W. W. Norton.

Spreng, R. N., & Grady, C. L. (2010). Patterns of brain activity supporting autobiographical memory, prospection, and theory of mind, and their relationship to the default mode network. *Journal of Cognitive Neuroscience, 22*(6), 1112–1123.

Spreng, R. N., Mar, R. A., & Kim, A. S. (2009). The common neural basis of autobiographical memory, prospection, navigation, theory of mind, and the default mode: A quantitative meta-analysis. *Journal of Cognitive Neuroscience, 21*(3), 489–510.

Stein, D. J., Koenen, K. C., Friedman, M. J., Hill, E., McLaughlin, K. A., Petukhova, M., et al. (2013). Dissociation in posttraumatic stress disorder: Evidence from the world mental health surveys. *Biological Psychiatry, 73*(4), 302–312.

Stein, M. B., Walker, J. R., Anderson, G., Hazen, A. L., Ross, C. A., Eldridge, G., & Forde, D. R. (1996). Childhood physical and sexual abuse in patients with anxiety disorders and in a community sample. *American Journal of Psychiatry, 153*(2), 275–277.

Thomason, M. E., Chang, C. E., Glover, G. H., Gabrieli, J. D., Greicius, M. D., & Gotlib, I. H. (2008). Default-mode function and task-induced deactivation have overlapping brain substrates in children. *NeuroImage, 41*(4), 1493–1503.

Van der Kolk, B. A., Roth, S., Pelcovitz, D., Sunday, S., & Spinazzola, J. (2005). Disorders of extreme stress: The empirical foundation of a complex adaptation to trauma. *Journal of Traumatic Stress, 18,* 389–399.

van der Meer, C. S., Aleman, A., & David, A. S. (2010). Self-reflection and the brain: A theoretical review and meta-analysis of neuroimaging studies with implications for schizophrenia. *Neuroscience and Biobehavioral Reviews, 34,* 935–946.

Wakefield, J. (1992a). The concept of mental disorder: On the boundary between biological facts and social values. *American Psychologist, 47,* 373–388.

Wakefield, J. (1992b). Disorder as harmful dysfunction: A conceptual critique of DSM-III-R's definition of mental disorder. *Psychological Review, 99,* 232–247.

Widom, C. P. (1999). Posttraumatic stress disorder in abused and neglected children grown up. *American Journal of Psychiatry, 156,* 1223–1229.

Widom, C. S., Marmorstein, N. R., & White, H. R. (2006). Childhood victimization and illicit drug use in middle adulthood. *Psychology of Addictive Behaviors: Journal of the Society of Psychologists in Addictive Behaviors, 20*(4), 394–403.

Williams, L. M., Kemp, A. H., Felmingham, K., Barton, M., Olivieri, G., Peduto, A., et al. (2006). Trauma modulates amygdala and medial prefrontal responses to consciously attended fear. *NeuroImage, 29*(2), 347–357.

Winnicott, D. W. (Ed.). (1960). *The maturational processes and the facilitating environment.* New York: International Universities Press.

Wolf, E. J., Miller, M. W., Reardon, A. F., Ryabchenko, K. A., Castillo, D., & Freund, R. (2012). A latent class analysis of dissociation and posttraumatic stress disorder: Evidence for a dissociative subtype. *Archives of General Psychiatry, 69*(7), 698–705.

{ Commentary }

Modeling of Complex Post-traumatic Stress Disorder Can Benefit From Careful Integration of Evolutionary and Developmental Accounts

Pierre Lienard

In their contribution, Bluhm and Lanius promote a general proximate explanation for a variant of post-traumatic stress disorder (PTSD), complex PTSD, a syndrome affecting survivors of prolonged (often interpersonal) traumatic exposure (Ball and Stein, 2012). Also, Bluhm and Lanius advance the idea that complex PTSD linked to childhood trauma is a potentially fruitful model for informing our study of disorders belonging to the PTSD spectrum. The contributors' model rests on the hypothesis that childhood trauma–related complex PTSD might be linked to a disruption of neurodevelopment induced by prolonged and repeated exposure to stressors at critical maturation phases during which occurs widespread structural and functional integration of the brain. The investigation of how childhood trauma affects neural development could provide new insights into the etiology of PTSD.

Bluhm and Lanius' contribution pertains to the debates around the definition, classification, phenomenology, and etiology of trauma and stressor-related disorders that have accompanied the production and recent release of the new fifth edition of the *Diagnostic and Statistical Manual of Mental Disorders* (*DSM-V*). A general diagnostic criterion of PTSD is the exposure to a potentially traumatic event (American Psychological Association, 2013), typically uncontrollable or unpredictable, such as torture, aggression, rape, and natural disasters (Friedman, 2009). However, a greater awareness has recently emerged about a specific subset of traumatic disorders, complex PTSDs, for which it might be harder to identify one specific main traumatic event that would constitute the sole cause of the disorder (Cougle, Kilpatrick, and Resnick, 2012). In such cases, cumulative exposure to stressors of various types, intensities, and frequencies at critical developmental stages might be the main etiologic factor behind the onset of the disorder.

Complex PTSD has a specific behavioral signature: among the most prominent are poor affect regulation (e.g., excessive impulsivity and risk taking); dissociative episodes and event-specific amnesia; feelings of guilt, shame, and low self-esteem; trust issues; and hopelessness (Ball and Stein, 2012). Bluhm and Lanius identify two main loci of disruption of the psychological development that would explain some of the main signature features of complex PTSD: (1) emotional awareness and experience, and (2) representation of the self.

Typical patients have difficulties identifying—as well as experiencing—emotional states. Brain imaging studies hint at a dysfunction affecting the dorsomedial prefrontal cortex, an area of the brain involved in the cognitive generation, regulation, and appraisal of emotional experience (Kober, Barrett, Joseph, Bliss-Moreau, Lindquist, and Wager, 2008). PTSD patients' creation of representations of—and access to information about—the self also seem to be affected. There is strong evidence that, along with the rostral anterior cingulate cortex, the medial prefrontal cortex plays an essential role in encoding and retrieving self-referent information (Beer, 2012; D'Argembeau et al., 2007; Gusnard, Akbudak, Shulman, and Raichle, 2001). In a recent study, Bluhm and colleagues (2012) found evidence of an altered function of the medial prefrontal cortex in self-referential processing associated with PTSD.

Both emotion appraisal and self-referential processing disruptions in childhood-related complex PTSD might thus be linked to faulty brain maturation. The successful development of brain functions requires both maturation of brain regions and establishment and reinforcement of pathways through axonal projections between segregated cerebral areas. An important part of that maturation involves myelination, the buildup of a myelin sheath around the axon of neurons. That sheath allows brain activation to travel efficiently along nerve cells. Sustained exposure to cortisol, the typical response to physical and psychological stress, has a direct impact on myelination, thus affecting the proper integration of brain regions during childhood maturation (see, for a general presentation, National Scientific Council on the Developing Child, 2005). Bluhm and Lanius see in that disruption the main mechanism behind the etiology of childhood-related complex PTSD.

The systematic adoption of Bluhm and Lanius' developmental model of the proximate causes that would account for the observed complex PTSD symptoms is likely to deliver new invaluable insights into the phenomenology of the disorder. However, a full account of the syndrome might benefit from the integration of developmental and evolutionary models. Indeed complex PTSD following early life trauma is an ideal area of research for investigating the interplay (and respective influences) of conditions of socialization, particular elicitations of evolutionarily conserved functions, and programmed species-typical developmental trajectory in the expression of particular phenotypes. Some of the typical features of PTSD variants seem to be too specific to support the sole claim of a domain-general disorder. At the minimum, as noted by Bluhm and Lanius in their opening presentation of PTSD, we observe gender-specific behaviors and target-specific concerns (specific phobia) in the various expressions of the disorder, specificity that an *adaptationist* account, framing the problem in terms of ultimate causations, could help inform.

Humans follow a relatively slow life history, including long periods during which juvenile agents rely on the support of more mature individuals (Hawkes, 2006). Social agents at different ages must be capable of handling the age- and gender-specific challenges that the particular developmental stage they are in typically affords. It is thus likely that each age has its specific suite of problem-solving cognitive adaptations (Lienard, 2011). Those protracted periods of dependence allow for the acquisition of a great amount of knowledge and the emergence and calibration of complex age-relevant problem-solving and precaution psychologies. As mentioned above, these developmental phases are also periods during which greater brain integration proceeds in a stepwise manner following a species-typical developmental trajectory. In an "ordinary" postnatal nurturing context (i.e., with proper care and support of more mature individuals), the necessary conditions for the proper buildup and parameters setting of refined adult problem-solving and precaution psychologies will be typically met. In situations of prolonged abused or mistreatment, proper cognitive development might be impeded for lack of adequate elicitation or proportional reinforcement of efficient and measured reactions to challenging situations. The typical disorders resulting from such long-term traumatic exposure during early developmental phases should therefore not appear as diffuse impairments generally affecting various cognitive processes, but they should come into existence as specific impairments of evolutionarily conserved functions. Such perspective, focusing on the faulty edification or calibration of evolved inference systems, might shed light on some of the typical, more domain-specific, features of PTSD, whereas other aspects of the disorder, seemingly less specific in their expression, might be traced to more general impairments. Alternatively, the complicated expression of complex PTSD might be linked to the impairment of patient-particular blends of domain-specific inference systems differentially affected during development, given the case-specific timing of onset (at particular developmental stages, when specific skills and abilities are due to mature) and duration of exposure to the trauma-inducing stressors. Bluhm and Lanius', Wakefield's, and Cantor and Price's models can and should be integrated (Wakefield, 1992; Cantor and Price, 2007).

References

American Psychiatric Association. (2013). *Diagnostic and statistical manual of mental disorders: DSM-V.* Washington, DC: American Psychiatric Association.

Ball, T. M., & Stein, M. B. (2012). Classification of posttraumatic stress disorder. In J. G. Beck, & D. Sloan (Eds.), *Oxford handbook of traumatic stress disorders* (pp. 39–53). New York, NY: Oxford University Press.

Beer, J. S. (2012). Self-evaluation and self-knowledge. In S. T. Fiske & C. N. Macrae (Eds.), *Sage handbook of social cognition* (pp. 330–349). London: Sage.

Bluhm R. L., Frewen, P. A., Coupland, N. C., Densmore, M., Schore, A. N., & Lanius, R. A. (2012). Neural correlates of self-reflection in post-traumatic stress disorder. *Acta Psychiatrica Scandinavica, 125*(3), 238–246.

Cantor, C., & Price, J. (2007). Traumatic entrapment, appeasement and complex post-traumatic stress disorder: Evolutionary perspective of hostage reactions, domestic abuse and the Stockholm syndrome. *Australian and New Zealand Journal of Psychiatry, 41*(5), 377–384.

Cougle, J. R., Kilpatrick, D., & Resnick, H. (2012). Defining traumatic events: Research findings and controversies. In J. G. Beck & D. Sloan (Eds.), *Oxford handbook of traumatic stress disorders* (pp. 11–27). New York: Oxford Library of Psychology.

D'Argembeau, A., Ruby, P., Collette, F., Degueldre, C., Balteau, E., Luxen, A., et al. (2007). Distinct regions of the medial prefrontal cortex are associated with self-referential processing and perspective taking. *Journal of Cognitive Neuroscience, 19*(6), 935–944.

Friedman, M. J. (2009). Phenomenology of posttraumatic stress disorder and acute stress disorder. In M. M. Antony & M. B. Stein (Eds.), *Oxford handbook of anxiety and related disorders* (pp. 65–72). New York: Oxford University Press.

Gusnard, D. A., Akbudak, E., Shulman, G. L., & Raichle, M. E. (2001). Medial prefrontal cortex and self-referential mental activity: Relation to a default mode of brain function. *Proceedings of the National Academy of Sciences U S A, 98*(7), 4259–4264.

Hawkes, K. (2006). Slow life histories and human evolution. In K. Hawkes & R. Pain (Eds.), *Evolution of human life history* (pp. 95–126). *Oxford, UK: SAR Press* James Currey.

Kober, H., Barrett, L. F. Joseph, J., Bliss-Moreau, E., Lindquist, K., & Wager, T. D. (2008). Functional groups and cortical-subcortical interactions in emotion: A meta-analysis of neuroimaging studies. *NeuroImage, 42*, 998–1031.

Lienard, P. (2011). Life stages and risk-avoidance: Status- and context-sensitivity in precaution systems. *Neuroscience and Biobehavioral Reviews, 35*, 1067–1074.

National Scientific Council on the Developing Child (2005). *Excessive stress disrupts the architecture of the developing brain: Working paper #3*. Retrieved September 16, 2013, from Center on the Developing Child at Harvard University, http://www.developing-child.net.

Wakefield, J. (1992). Disorder as harmful dysfunction: A conceptual critique of DSM-III-R's definition of mental disorder. *Psychological Review, 99*, 232–247.

13

From the Emergent Drama of Interpretation to Enscreenment

Eugene Halton

The Emergent Drama of Interpretation

The human body, psyche, and social relations can be understood as the result of adaptations and emergent modes of conduct in the course of evolution. John Bowlby's concept of the *environment of evolutionary adaptedness* draws attention to how natural selection hones bodily capacities, and in the human context, how "the deep human need for profuse sociality" (Narvaez, Panksepp, Schore, and Gleason, 2013) must be understood as a product of prior adaptation.

Frequently adaptation is viewed in the light of a utilitarian conception of survival, but I wish to pursue another perspective, what I call *dramatic evolution* (Halton, 2013). Dramatic evolution, though growing out of prior adaptive habits, is not reducible to adaptation. Rather, it also involves a spontaneous element, live to the enactment of the situation. It involves what philosopher Charles Peirce called "energetic projaculation," the throwing forth in spontaneous creation, or "the putting of sundry thoughts into situations in which they are free to play" (1931–1935, p. 301). Peirce's claim for "energetic projaculation," for a modality of spontaneous conduct capable of "breaking the mold," so to speak, and of bodying forth new habits through experience allows creative conduct as a real capacity of the human creature. It addresses how human culture can be real and formative, expressive and purposeful, in a Lamarckian-like way usually undervalued or denied by Darwinian accounts of human evolution.

Most common developmental experiences, such as breastfeeding, play, and rites of passage, as well as broader capacities, such as mating, dreaming, and even eating, evolved in drama-like contexts, including ritual. The banter of mother and infant, the imaginary play of young children, the infatuation of new lovers, the fantastic scenarios of REM dreaming, the stealth and tracking abilities in hunting and foraging, all involve narrative or quasi-narrative patterning. They may grow out of robust prior adaptive patterning, but they also involve the spontaneous moment of enactment as a locus of learning, wherein new habits of conduct can arise, then to be honed by experience as well as natural selection. From this perspective human development is as much a fantasia bodying forth into being as it is a survival mechanism. Indeed, they may be merely two sides of the same coin. And central to the human narrative is the emergence of the capacity for symbolic communication.

Human capacities for symbolic communication emerged through a variety of practices, all of which can be considered as dramatic. What I am calling the emergent drama of interpretation involves considering how symbolic signification, representation through convention or habit, or what I will call *symboling* to emphasize the processual nature of semiosis, or sign-action, first appeared and came to predominate the human mind. This question is clearly far more complex than can be adequately answered in a chapter. But I would simply like to explore some likely sources, all of which involve what could be called *dramatic interaction*.

After outlining some views of the development of self and symboling set in the contexts of early development and hunter-gatherer practices, I will turn to issues of media and technology as contemporary socializing agents, especially in patterns of use. I hope to show how social media and technology today, despite positive things they provide, have taken such a dominating influence in socialization that they can also be viewed as inversions of evolutionary socializing practices; how contemporary techno-consumption culture strangely mimics aspects of those practices, yet subverts what they were about.

The rise of the symbol can be viewed in the context of social practices such as mother–infant interaction, tracking and group hunting, and ritual life, all of which arise in dramatic interplay. Certain aspects of mother–infant interaction make the rise of symboling developmentally possible, whereas ritual and tracking practices shed light on some likely evolutionary developments in cooperative communication. Such dramatic interplays of individual and other, through gestural and indexical signification, helped literally to body forth the capacities of self and symbolic interpretation in the course of evolution. Hence I am viewing the dramatic as a far broader realm than theater or the ubiquitous commercial and entertainment productions that pervade contemporary everyday life.

Let me introduce a character in that drama, aka *Homo sapiens sapiens*, but given a different name by philosopher Charles Peirce, the founder of pragmatism and semiotics, in 1901. Peirce saw how "man the knower," *Homo sapiens sapiens*, might be seen under less idealized light as "but a degenerate monkey."

"One of these days, perhaps, there will come a writer of opinions less humdrum than those of Dr. (Alfred Russel) Wallace, and less in awe of the learned and official world...who will argue, like a new Bernard Mandeville, that man is but a degenerate monkey, with a paranoic talent for self-satisfaction, no matter what scrapes he may get himself into, calling them 'civilization,' and who, in place of the unerring instincts of other races, has an unhappy faculty for occupying himself with words and abstractions, and for going wrong in a hundred ways before he is driven, willy-nilly, into the right one. Dr. Wallace would condemn such an extravagant paradoxer." (1979, pp. 17–18)

Peirce meant the term "degenerate monkey" both playfully, as a creature that "monkeys around," and in the mathematical sense of "degenerate," as a falling away from pure type, in this case, primate. Most people might think humans fell away from pure primate type by getting smarter, but Peirce meant to draw attention to something else, namely, the prolonged neoteny of humans, and how the most characteristically sapient qualities of humankind derive from the newest, and in that sense most immature, portions of the brain. The fact that humans are born with roughly 25% of final brain size, compared with roughly 45% for chimpanzees and much higher rates for most other mammals, shows how our big-brain bodies get out while we can, so to speak (Iriki and Taoka, 2012).

We degenerate monkeys are born "prematurely" and engage in intense early child socialization to reach levels of brain building that other primates and mammals reach in utero (Coqueugniot et al., 2004; McKenna, Thoman, Anders, Sadeh, Schechtman, and Glotzbach, 1993). For this reason human mother–infant attachment practices are literally brain building, and in this sense more profoundly biosocial than in other primates, precisely because we are born with a less developed but late-blooming brain. This demonstrates how human social life, however diverse our human cultures and their conventional and even arbitrary norms, can also be real and natural in appropriately nurturing our unfinished brains and minds.

Human plasticity follows dramatic patterns of socializing engagement in the earliest phases of life, dramas that not only engage the caregiver's empathic attention but also engage the infant on a trajectory toward full degenerate monkeyhood, capable of symboling as well as blundering, yet capably gifted, in Peirce's view, with a special talent for guessing, for hypothesizing, for imagining: a characteristic that can be taken as one precious upside deriving from our neotenously softened distance from the "unerring instincts of other races." I take that prolonged neoteny, our relative dematurity, as requiring a more generalized and generalizing attunement to the habitat. By attuning to the intelligible signs of the wild environment, drawing its intelligence, exhibited, for example, through relatively "unerring instincts" of animals, into our dematured, blundering selves through intuitive inference, our gift for guessing, or what Peirce termed abductive inference, as well as other ways of inferencing and interpreting, the degenerate monkey finds its maturity. Apart from that learning relationship, it runs the risk of self-inflation, that "paranoic talent for self-satisfaction, no matter what scrapes he may get himself into, calling them 'civilization,'" as Peirce put it.

Development of Symbolic Interaction

Peirce's idea of the degenerate monkey provides insight into how progressive neoteny figures into human development, wherein greater plasticity allows for, and even requires, greater cooperative communication and attunement. A fellow pragmatist, George Herbert Mead, gives an account of the rise of the self as a dialogical process involving cooperative communication, and culminating in a self capable of symbolic communication. Like Peirce and fellow pragmatist John Dewey, Mead roots meaning in communicative practices, and views the self as the result of being able to communicate to oneself what one communicates to another, becoming "a social object in experience to himself" (1964, p. 243).

Earliest development involves what Mead, borrowing from Wundt, calls a "conversation of gestures," which includes vocal gestures. Mead used a "conversation" of dogs barking at each other as an example. The infant or young toddler can communicate at this gestural level, though not yet capable of symbolic communication.

The beginnings of self emerge in the next phase Mead calls "play," when the child starts to take the role of specific others through play or imaginative fantasy. But it is only with the final phase, which Mead termed "game," when the child becomes capable of internalizing the attitudes of the surrounding community, internalizing what Mead called "the generalized other," that the fully organized self appears. The process of internalizing this community is the development of the capacity for what Mead also terms the *significant symbol*: "It is just because the individual finds himself taking the attitudes of the others who are involved in his conduct that he becomes an object for himself....We appear as selves in our conduct in so far as we ourselves take the attitude that others take toward us, in these correlative activities....We take the role of what may be called the "generalized other" (1964, pp. 283–284).

Symbolic communication involves the ability to simultaneously address the other *and* self, to take the role of the generalized other in the communication. Both self and symbolic communication in this sense constitute a dialogue of the habituated attitudes of the generalized other, or what Mead also called the "me," with the spontaneity of the "I" in the living moment. Thinking is an internal version of this dialogue. The development of the self out of play and conversation of gestures through the game stage is thus framed in narrative, dramatic terms.

A significant symbol may be linguistic speech or artistic expression in paint, music, or other media, or gestural, say, as in flipping someone off with an obscene gesture. Such a gesture is a significant symbol by virtue of the attitude of the intended recipient being involved in the signifying gesture. But even linguistic speech simultaneously includes nonreflective subliminal gesturing, or conversation of gestures. Human gestural signification can move fluidly from conversation of gestures to significant symboling. One strength of Mead's theory is that it encompasses a range of communicative conduct in a developmental framework that is congruent with an account of progressively cooperative conduct as crucial to human evolution. Cooperative communication is seen as a practice progressively internalized:

"The probable beginning of human communication was in cooperation, not in imitation, where conduct differed and yet where the act of the one answered to and called out the act of the other. The conception of imitation as it has functioned in social psychology needs to be developed into a theory of social stimulation and response and of the social situations which these stimulations and responses create. Here we have the matter and the form of the social object, and here we have also the medium of communication and reflection." (1964, p. 101)

There are crucial pre- and proto-self developmental stages not dealt with explicitly in Mead's theory. One is the idea of "borderline" development in the first year, the establishment of boundaries, which, when not successfully negotiated, can result in "borderline personality disorder." Another is the varieties of mother–infant attunements that begin with birth, and that stem from genetically transmitted, physiological needs of the infant. Mead's original theory, though still valuable, requires a greater appreciation of the role of biosemiotic processes excluded from his account.

Though communicative cooperation is the starting point for Mead's model of the interactive situation, it begins even earlier than Mead imagined, stemming from the subcortical infant brain from within hours of birth, as (Meltzoff and Moore, 1977; Meltzoff, 2002) and Trevarthen (1980) have shown. Such communicative cooperation is possible in newborn and infant interaction with mothers, a dramatic dialogue without the presence of a fully organized object that can be responded to, yet an object sufficiently co-present that dialogical interaction can occur. This situation stems from genetically transmitted, physiological needs of the infant, called out through call and response gestural repartee with the mother/caretaker (Hrdy, 2009). This dialogue illustrates one of the ways in which nature *and* culture play, and how *Homo sapiens sapiens* needs to be understood not simply as *Homo competitor*, but as what Johannes Huizinga originally introduced as *Homo ludens*, man playing.

Interplay

A mother holding her baby coos to it, and the baby laughs and coos back, its face entranced with hers. In this simple example, we see how the interplay of human infant and mother is rhythmic and musical from the beginning. It has also been characterized as a kind of "dance." Kirsti Määttänen (2007), a philosopher and psychologist who developed the "Baby Dance Method" for parent–infant interaction beginning at 8 weeks, finds that through "simple movement sequences in a playful interaction with the baby," a mutual conversation of gestures is established as a basis of learning:

"Basically, Baby Dance Method (BDM) is about how to "speak" babyese. In BDM the baby is provided with a consistent opportunity to gain a sense of understanding the intentions of the adult, as they unfold in and by the sequence of jointly performed movements.... The quality of the interaction in Baby Dance is shown to display the basic formal features of ordinary polite conversation. It is shown to be a true dialogue, though not with words, but with moves." (2007)

From another angle, Dean Falk has argued that with enlarging brains pushing a shift toward females giving birth to "relatively undeveloped neonates," "pre-linguistic vocal substrates for protolanguage that had prosodic features similar to contemporary *motherese* evolved." She hypothesizes that new foraging strategies required greater "maternal silencing, reassuring, and controlling of the behaviors of physically removed infants," promoting increased prosodic and gestural communications (2004, p. 491).

Stephen Malloch and Colwyn Trevarthen (2009, p. 4) describe the complex "communicative musicality" of weeks-old infants, showing "precise formulation in terms of three parameters: *pulse, quality*, and *narrative*," which are revealed in turn-taking interactions with mothers, and charted through spectrographs and pitch plots. And this occurs at a time when the cerebral cortex is not yet fully functioning, when the bulk of its synaptic connections are yet to be formed in the period of "synaptic exuberance" and subsequent pruning.

Again, Trevarthen from 1986:

"Infants display from the beginning a spontaneous integrity of action and expression that corresponds with the *anemos* of the ancient Greeks, an invisible wind that moves, and the *anima* of Latin that became the Judeo-Christian "soul." This stirring spirit (akin to the breadth of life, *pneuma*), with insistent beat and subtle rhythmic variations, resists analysis in machine terms. All parts of the baby's body move together to express shades of feeling. The expressive flowing of an infant's emotion is highly responsive. It encourages a mother, deeply moved by the birth of her infant, to feel she is appreciated by another being who is intimately like herself. A new system of two persons— a self-sustaining relationship—is made of their behaving together." (1986, p. 186)

Hence there is something inborn manifesting in the spontaneous gesture afforded by the genetically prepared physiology in social interplay. Right at the start of human life we can say with Shakespeare, the play's the thing.

These results illustrate the dramatic interplay of human biology and culture, of robust inborn capacities in interaction with plastic socializing practices. Humans appear to be born to rhythmic, communicative interaction between what could be called *natural construction*, stemming from the infant's biological needs for sustenance and empathic touch, and social construction, stemming from the mother or caretaker's empathic responsiveness. From the proto-drama of gestation and birth, we are bodied forth into the original drama of our waking life, in which organic needs from the subcortical brain of the infant call out the mothering response in empathic interaction.

The newborn brain comes equipped to engage in precise mimetic narrative, "communicative musicality," without the benefit of what will become the narrative, symbolizing cortex. It is this drama of interaction that is the subject, not the infant; the drama of interaction of what Trevarthen calls "primal intersociality," that will body the infant toward selfhood. Trevarthen says, "a human mind is equipped with needs for dialogical, intermental engagement with other similar minds" (1999, p. 417). Through such interaction, the neocortex is developmentally called into engagement over time to the play of communicative life, eventuating in the rise of the natured–nurtured abilities to symbol, to communicate in the symbolic signs through which language, identity, and rational thought are largely comprised.

Viewing the drama of interaction rather than the infant as the subject allows a perspective in which the emergent symbol itself may initially be the center of awareness and self-awareness, both developmentally and in its evolutionary emergence. Again, the play's the thing, whether the player is aware or not. Now for Mead, the significant symbol, as he calls it, is the sign "which is addressed to the self when it is addressed to another individual, and is addressed to another, in form to all other individuals, when it is addressed to the self ... through this sympathetic placing of themselves in each other's roles, and finding thus in their own experiences the responses of the others, what would otherwise be an unintelligent gesture, acquires just the value which is connoted by signification" (1964, p. 246). Mead describes a process that involves what 75 years later would be identified with mirror neurons, but a mirroring as self-awareness. Yet I am claiming that this "addressing" oneself may initially be located in the entraining dramatic narrative constituting the symbolizing activity itself, as in drumming, dancing, or singing, and only gradually becoming self-awareness.

The capacities for symbolic interaction that mark the emergence of the self do not spring from a fixed instinct or language structure like Athena from Zeus's forehead, but from an intricate call and response dialogue of playful touch, rhythm, and empathic communion, in which the child begins to try out autonomy, gradually separating from the bonding with the mother or caretaker. Empathy is, in this sense, a neurosocial achievement, where wiring meets mothering.

And though contemporary societies may have opened up the social possibilities for how infants are fed, this potential freedom remains determined by the requirement for warm emotional communion between infant and caretaker. It is important to note that play and breastfeeding, as well as REM dreaming, are, at their peak, intense dramatic experiences of intrinsic delight and ecstasy. All three are mammal, not simply primate, capacities. And play, REM dreaming, and mother–infant bonding and separation are significant for the most sophisticated human activities.

Modern culture has thus not eradicated the biological basis for communion so much as generalized its possibilities. With milk frozen or made from formula, the mother need not be present for every feeding, and the father or other caretakers may share in the feeding experience. Yet the feeding of milk remains embedded in the needs of the infant for the tactile and empathic "milk of human kindness."

Contractions of Mind: From Dramatic
Participation to Spectatorship

What is typically viewed as progress in human development, from the advent of civilization to the rise of the modern scientific worldview, the saga of historical development, can be taken as progress in precision embedded within a regression of consciousness. History is the regression from the evolutionary conditions of human consciousness that I will call *animate mind* (Halton, 2007).

By animate mind I mean the evolved outlook and consciousness that bodied our foraging human ancestors into being, immersed in passionate, ritualizing participation with their habitat, attuned to the animate earth. Animate mind is, in this sense, the internalization and incorporation of the intelligible signs emanating from the animate earth. The domestication of plants and animals through settlement, beginning about 10,000 years ago and eventuating in cities and civilization, represented a transformation to a very different outlook, to that of *anthropocentric mind*, in which the human element became central, as I will explain later. The rise of the modern mechanical worldview represented a further transformation, beginning with the invention of the mechanical clock in about the 1270s, which I term *mechanico-centric mind*, characterized by the view that the universe is like a vast machine. I view these transformations not as progress, but as contractions of mind (Figure 13.1). Human consciousness contracts, through progressive precision, from physiologically neotenic creatures to a form of infantilization, determined by a delusional representation of the universe as a schizoid machine. A precise part of reality is taken to be the whole, excluding other real elements of the whole.

Though the evidence shows clearly evolving human foragers were smart in their practical lives, there still is widespread undervaluing or outright denial of how the development of their ritual, religious practices were not only just as smart but also of a piece with their foraging activities. The fantastic nature of those practices and beliefs grate against modern rational understandings, despite some recent works having begun to show the wisdom of those worldviews.

Primatologist Frans de Waal (Oct. 17, 2010) stated concerning religion: "Not that religion is irrelevant—I will get to this—but it is an add-on rather than the well-spring of morality." If I understand his argument correctly, de Waal assumed religion is at base about morality, neglecting that it is really only in the period of what John Stuart Stuart-Glennie termed "the moral revolution," between roughly 800 and 200 B.C.E. (later called "the axial age" by Karl Jaspers), that religion becomes

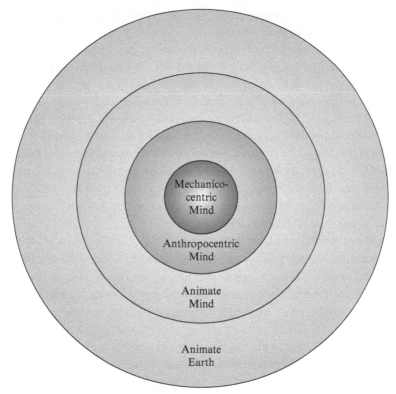

FIGURE 13.1 *Contractions of mind*

primarily concerned with morality.[1] That is very late, and though the religions of that period dominate the earth today, they seem to me to exist at a great remove from the sources of what I would call *evolutionary religion*.

Religion arose in our evolutionary past primarily as a way to connect to the intelligible and edible habitat, through ritual, dance, song, and foraging arts and sciences such as tracking. Our bodies walked out of the Pleistocene era as foragers reverentially attuning to the circumambient signs of life, on which we depended for survival. Religion in this sense is both aesthetic and practical, both sides of which are essentially dramatic. "Each animal knows way more than you do.... The physical environment is spiritual, conscious, and subject to rules of respectful behavior," says anthropologist Richard Nelson (1993, p. 222) of the Koyukan people's beliefs. Rather than reducing such views to the Darwin-matrix, showing their "survival value" as "add-ons," we would do well simply to act with the wisdom of such a view as Nelson describes, as a working hypothesis. Religious attunement to the

---

[1] I have shown how original credit for this concept needs to be given to Stuart-Glennic, not Jaspers, and why it should be termed "the moral revolution," not "the axial age" (Halton, 2014). For a broad-ranging contemporary discussion of the axial age, see Bellah, 2011.

circumambient signs of life is spiritual, aesthetic, dramatic, *and* practical, not simply practical (see also Ingold, 2007).

The business of evolutionary religion is like the business of art, as D. H. Lawrence described it: "The business of art is to reveal the relation between man and his circumambient universe, at the living moment....And this perfected relation between man and his circumambient universe is life itself, for mankind. It has the fourth-dimensional quality of eternity and perfection. Yet it is momentaneousness" (1936, p. 527).

Speaking of Bushmen trackers, Louis Liebenberg states: "Religious belief is so fundamental to the hunters' way of thinking that it cannot be separated from hunting itself. At the end of the day, if they have had no luck in tracking down an animal, !Xo hunters will say that the greater god did not 'give' them an animal that day. If, on the other hand, they have had a successful hunt, they will say that the greater god was good to them" (1990, p. 98).

A featured persistence hunter in the documentary *The Great Dance: A Hunter's Story* (2000), !Nqate Xqamxebe, a !Xo San hunter of the Kalahari Desert Bushmen, puts it this way: "When you track an animal—you must become the animal. Tracking is like dancing, because your body is happy—you can feel it in the dance and then you know that the hunting will be good. When you are doing these things you are talking with God."

More generally, the other animals were, with plants, our great teachers in an evolutionary dialogue toward humankind. By closely observing them, ruminating over them by dancing them, ritualizing them, imitating their calls, incorporating them as food and clothing and soul food, revering them for their instinctive genius in what each species does so well, we participated in what Paul Shepard called *The Sacred Game* (1998a). The sacred game was the drama-like ethos animating the evolution of humans into symboling and symbolic interaction. His term plays on game as prey, and on game as the mutual deep involvement of humans with animals, both prey and predator, as well as progressively cooperative communication practices in both practical and ritual life (see also Sterlny, 2012). For it was in the sacred game, played between predator and prey, and in the practical and play forms of mimesis and poiesis that we humans found our voice. From the attunement to the living habitat, through practices of tracking, awareness of properties of plants and animals, inferences from the living habitat to weather patterns and other significant signs, we internalized signs that over evolutionary time became the basis of the human language capacity.

Tracking alone incorporates roughly 5,000 potential signs from any given track, forming a whole language in itself. It is one whose grammar is that of a micro-landscape, where terrain features are applied to the tiny, subtle indexical indicators gravitized in the track. The tracking mind represents an internalization from engagement with the habitat, whose terrain features can be translated to the micro-world of the track, through the sacred game. Reading of gestural signs, in this case tracking, would seem a natural practice for the emergence into human varieties, transitioning from iconic and indexical sign reading capacities into symbolic sign abilities, just as the knowledge of a huge range of plants and minute reading of subtle plant indicators and other animal behaviors, such as birdsong, would be.

As Pollick and deWaal showed, chimps and bonobos exhibit fairly uniform meanings for facial gestures and vocalizations, but greater context-related flexibility in hand, finger, and arm gesturing (2007). Perhaps the signs of sign language, hand-gestured, provided some of the earliest moves toward incarnating the symbol. Kalahari San Bushmen give sign gestures at first glance resembling contemporary gang signs when tracking in groups, running down their prey in the oldest form of hunting, with only the intelligence of tracking and signing, but no required use of weapons. Some of the signs iconically resemble the prey, just as some of the earliest writing resembles represented animal forms: their hand sign for the kudu, index and ring fingers for horns, middle finger for snout, can be found in modified and inverted form today in the alpha of the alphabet, originally a sign of the ox.

Tracking can give a picture of a creature, including human, more accurate in some ways than magnetic resonance imaging. The potential 5,000 signs that can be read by a master tracker form a vocabulary almost as large as the numbers of Chinese language characters. But they are more than a vocabulary; they iconically and indexically reveal states of body and mind of animals, from the blink of an eye to, as Tom Brown Jr., puts it:

"...the condition of the small intestine, the large intestine, the bladder, and the colon. We can see the rhythm of the breathing, whether the animal is taking a breath in or out in any given track. We can read mild afflictions, such as a common cold, a slight injury, arthritic conditions, congestion, sniffling, as well as growling, grunting, and other vocal callings. Here too we can read countless other normal body functions, conditions, and internal movements. Yet here in the lobulars we are also connected to the finest outer body movements. Movements that cannot be picked up by the human eye, even as it physically watches the animal or human.

Soft external movements, they are called. Shivering, panting, degree of ear cocking, tongue position, hesitations, twitches, minute balance compensations, snarling, nose twitching, slight tail movements, and so many others are the soft external movements. But to identify, and understand, these deep internal and soft external movements, there is a price to pay. A price that is measured in countless hours of dirt time and intense, impassioned, almost obsessive experimentation." (1998, pp. 118–119)

Those large numbers of indicators give some insight into the vocabulary of aboriginal mind, fluid in the language of tracks, the language of plants, and whole other languages of the wild other. As trackers Tom Brown, Jr., and Jon Young note, it is possible to become precisely aware of movement in the surrounding couple of kilometers of habitat through precise reading of the calls of birds, which radiate out like a stone thrown in a pond (Young, 2012). Literal attunement to the audio maps provided by the community of life extended our senses and subtilized our minds, aesthetically and practically. Attending to sunrises and sunsets, when the songbird symphony wherein music was discovered sounds the transformations of the day-shift and night-shift animals, engaged us in the living moment as musical sociality, as cooperative celebratory communication; it also revealed unseen predators and prey, audibly echoed players in the symphonic habitat narrative of the animate earth.

It is out of such stuff as this that linguistic mind emerges in my view; out of its intimate relation to the living, informing habitat and its perceptible "vocabulary." Tracking and similar practices, including dancing the animal without and within, and learning the syntactic-like songs of the song birds as well as how to mimic them, may very well provide grammar-like sources that helped body human grammatical brain capacities forth. We learned to become progressively cooperatively social not only through our emergent human social groups but also through the society of animals and plants we participated in and reverentially attuned ourselves to.

But a traumatic transformation of the sacred game occurred with the rise of agriculturally based civilization, which changed everything (Halton, 2005, 2007; Shepard, 1998a, 1998b). Physically, for example, average heights dropped 4 to 6 inches because of reduced nutrition, and populations exploded, wherever civilization broke out, including North and South America. But the changes were more than simply physical. Domestication of plants and animals shifted human attunement from the wild others to the controlled, demautred domesticates that mirrored the demautred primates, us, who domesticated them. Humans changed from worldviews stressing what Levy-Bruhl characterized as "participation mystique" to those of spectators; from the drama of life as a gift to life as a sacrifice; from religious reverence combining practical and spiritual attunement to living beings in the sacred game to religions based on spectatorial gods who grew increasingly anthropomorphic over time. The human wild habitat drama that bodied us into being over tens or hundreds of millennia shifted to a new one that placed our demautred primate consciousness at the center, in new forms such as divine kingship, mass-killing organized warfare, and settled, walled-in cities. Ritual gave rise to theater and other arts, all undeniable achievements. Yet the hidden cost might have been a loss or obscuring of the original participation sense, which theater yet partly recovers, though in spectator format. Perhaps the original sacred game bleeds partially through in the Dionysian tragedy of Euripides' play, *The Bacchae*, or in Shakespeare's *Macbeth*, or in the image of the sacrificed divinity as anthropomorphized sacred prey, the master symbol of Christianity.[2]

That participation sense involved attunement to and repartee with parenting figures, playmates, and clan, but it was more than human, also involving dramatic

---

[2] In *The Birth of Tragedy* Nietzsche drew attention to the felt presence of the ancient animal relation, albeit anthropomorphized, through the chorus of satyrs in Greek tragedy: "The metaphysical comfort—with which, I am suggesting even now, every true tragedy leaves us—that life is at the bottom of things, despite all the changes of appearances, indestructibly powerful and pleasurable—this comfort appears in incarnate clarity in the chorus of the satyrs, a chorus of natural beings who live ineradicably, as it were, behind all civilization and remain eternally the same, despite the changes of generations and of the history of nations." (2000, p. 59).

attunement to and repartee with the animals and plants and elements on which we depended, and which we incorporated in mind and stomach. Animate mind has its locus in the sacred game, which involves the human "gamers," but is not limited to them. That is why what has been clumsily called animism is more than an ideology; it is both the practical and dramatic, even fantastic, sensed participation in a living, signifying, circumambient universe.

Neuroscientists who conceive of mind as solely brain, and of brain as a computer, miss how brain is involved in mind rather than the reverse, and how communicative minding typically involves a sign transaction in a habitat or environment inclusive of the object of the experience. As Mead put it: "Our contention is that mind can never find expression, and could never have come into existence at all, except in terms of a social environment.... If mind is socially constituted, then the field or locus of any given individual mind must extend as far as the social activity or apparatus of social relations extends; and hence that field cannot be bounded by the skin of the individual organism to which it belongs" (Mead, 1934, p. 223).

Far from being bottled up in brain, the human mind emerged fully engaged in and through the sacred game, a product of it, as the conversation of gestures evolved into the significant symbol of the human self. The symbol, a communicative achievement worked out to its wider possibilities in the course of human evolution, is nothing less than the full energizing into being of the realm of symbolic virtuality. We became creatures progressively determined by our symbolic lives, by new habitats of virtuality originally closely attuned to our foraging habitats. It is through those symbolic lives that humans came to dominate life on the earth thus far, albeit perhaps to our disadvantage.

We are creatures who live by the symbol and die by the symbol, and it gives many people satisfaction to think that these virtual worlds of symbolism we inhabit, such as the very words you are now reading, are proof positive of our superior status as evolved animals. What if the purposes originally released in the emergence of symbolic communication, later contracted to the mechanico-centric outlook, became transformed into something quite different: into forms of confinement, into mind-forg'd manacles, as William Blake put it?

From Wild Entrancement to Enscreenment

Being human involves being virtual, in living in and believing in symbolic constructions that go beyond the stomach and skin, not to mention the brain. Family, religious beliefs, local neighborhood and wider community, institutions, nation and globe, all are symbolic constructions. In that context consider the ever-increasing enscreening of experience through electronic devices, especially for very young children, who face not only increased quantity of enscreened experience daily (including audio enscreenment) but also increased enscreened quality of virtualized experience. How do these emerging conditions relate to the requirements and capabilities of the live interpreting human creature and its interactions?

One of the things these devices do is to displace face-to-face relationships and person-to-person tactile relationships onto machine-mediated relationships. Remember how psychologist Harry Harlow's monkeys clung to cloth-fabricated mothers, even at the loss of nutrition? Human haptic needs for touch are no less significant: untouched infants will die without touch, despite being nutritionally provided for (Montagu, 1986, pp. 97, 99). So what are the implications, when, for example, 61% of babies 1 year or younger view TV or videos every day for at least an hour on average, as a recent Kaiser Foundation study revealed? Or that 83% of children under the age of 6 years watch about 2 hours of combined screen media per day, including TV, videos/DVDs, video games, and computers? (Rideout and Hamel, 2006).

At these early ages we have biological needs as very young children to face our mothers, to face our parents, to face playmates, other people, and the living world. The face is a subtle neuromuscular organ of attunement, a key organ of perceptive, empathic development. And so what does it mean to be habitually displaced on a daily basis from live face-to-face contact to virtual interaction through a screen? A recent study showed that Botox treatments, in paralyzing facial muscles, reduce the micro-mimicry of empathic attunement to the other face in an interaction. The Botox recipient not only is impaired in exhibiting her or his own emotional facial micro-muscular movements but also is impaired in subconsciously micro-mimicking that of the other, thus reducing the embodied feel of the other's emotional-gestural state (Neal and Chartrand, 2011). This illustrates how micro-muscular mimicry of others is a communicative practice that can atrophy from disuse, resulting in impaired empathy. And it suggests another level of how socializing attunement through face-to-face interaction was likely to have been crucial in early child development as well as in the evolution of everyday communicative life.

Commercial television serves systemic alienating purposes in removing children from everyday face-to-face, tactile-friendly, empathically based interaction. A good-enough mother, in psychoanalyst D. W. Winnicott's sense of this term, is a caretaker who empathically meets a young child's developing needs. A bad mother is one who demands that the child meet her needs, in this case, to buy things. In this sense a television, and electronic screen devices more generally, can function as a bad mother, not only in being unempathic to a child's needs, but also in demanding of the child that it meet the television's "needs," through commercial advertising and the desires it instills.

The studies of media time for American children paint a bleak picture, involving a huge giving up of here-and-now social interaction as anchoring one's real life to a virtual life of virtual communications for what would be almost a full work day, 7 days a week. A Kaiser Foundation study found that children 8 to 18 years reported spending a whopping 7 hours and 38 minutes of media time per day, actually 10 hours and 45 minutes including multitasking squeezed into those 7 hours, 38 minutes. For tweens between 11 and 14 years, it is actually 8 hours 40 minutes, and even higher for African American and Hispanic children (Rideout, Foehr, and Roberts, 2009). If one sleeps for 8 hours and is involved with school for 8 hours, then virtually all remaining available time is totally enscreened time.

This represents a significant loss of face-to-face contact and tactile connection to a virtual world that is supposed to be there as a convenience, a means to self-direction, toward self-originated experience, where you are engaged in the moment, emotionally available to the moment, and capable of self-determination and unscripted spontaneous conduct. But that is not where most 8- to 18-year-olds are "at." They are undergoing what I call *The Great Brain Suck*.

A 2010 University of Michigan study found that college students today are about 40% lower in empathy than those of 20 or 30 years ago as measured by standardized tests, with the largest drop occurring after the year 2000. One of the researchers, Sarah Konrath, reported, "Compared to 30 years ago, the average American now is exposed to three times as much nonwork-related information. In terms of media content, this generation of college students grew up with video games, and a growing body of research, including work done by my colleagues at Michigan, is establishing that exposure to violent media numbs people to the pain of others" (Swanbrow, 2010). Other standardized tests show that Narcissism has gone up for this age group.

Sociologist Juliet Schor studied young teenagers in the Boston area and found that the children "more involved in consumer culture are more depressed, more anxious, have lower self-esteem, and suffer from more psychosomatic complaints.... High consumer involvement is a significant cause of depression, anxiety, low self-esteem, and psychosomatic complaints" (Schor, 2004, pp. 166–167). She had expected that higher levels of psychological problems would cause those children to be heavier users of media because of their problems, but media use was not directly related to psychological functioning. Instead, she found that "media use matters, but its effect flows through consumer involvement...(heavy users) become more involved in consumer culture. Television induces discontent with what one has, it creates an orientation to possessions and money, and it causes children to care more about brands, products, and consumer values" (2004, p. 169).

Of course we have uses of Facebook and Twitter for political activism, and even social revolution. But consider: typically these uses make of the social media a means for actual public real-time encounter, toward a public end. That is not where American 8- to 18-year-olds are spending an average of 7 hours and 38 minutes per day, 7 days a week.

Sociologist Zeynep Tufekci (2012) claims that TV is more a problem than social media, that average uses of social media are liberating, helping to bring people together, even if virtually. No one is denying that social media can do this, introducing new ways for family and friends to connect, for example. But use is not the same thing as abuse. Her argument misses the point that people, and children in particular, are being enscreened, spending vast amounts of time pushing buttons, living large parts of their waking lives from their necks up in front of a screen or with perpetual soundtracks.

Yes, this is socializing, but into norms that are heavily commercialized and that stress conformity to spend time "performing" media for longer than a full-time adult job.

Much of the enscreening content is commercial, so it appears that these little kiddies are going to market virtually all of their spare time, becoming branded in the process with logos and with endless acts of violence for boys and images of sex objects for girls. The dynamics of how kiddies get captured by pseudo-ecstatic button pushing speak not only of corporate consumerist capitalism maximizing itself but also of unbounded technological innovation as another agent of the transformation of social lives and identities, including gender. Some people actually call this progress. Jerry Mander has a different name; he calls it confinement:

> "As technology has evolved, step by step, it has placed boundaries between human beings and their connections with larger, nonhuman realities. As life acquired ever more technological wrapping, human experience and understanding were confined and altered.... Technology plays a critical role in this process because it creates standardized arbitrary forms of physical and mental confinement. Television is the ideal tool for such purposes because it both confines experience and implants simple, clear ideas.... Seen in this way, a new fact emerges. Autocracy needn't come in the form of a person at all, or even as an articulated ideology or conscious conspiracy. The autocracy can exist in the technology itself. The technology can produce its own subordinated society, as though it were alive." (1978, pp. 96–97)

But confinement can feel good. In Aldous Huxley's 1932 dystopian novel, *Brave New World*, identities are fashioned through pleasure conditioning, which are utterly dependent on conforming to the expectations of norms encoded in the social matrix. It is a termite society, where identity is only valid insofar as it serves the colony, the functionally differentiated social matrix of mechanico-centric mind. Community is conformity, is purely extrinsic identity devoted to the device, excavated from the spontaneous organic self.

Devices have increasingly become our technical surrogates for socializing; weaning us from the engagement with life, from solitude and self-originated sociality, not because virtuality is wrong, but because allowing mere means to dictate ends is destructive. Seven hours and 38 minutes per day, every day, is the kind of pleasurable slavery Huxley envisioned. The spontaneous self gives way to the compliant self, conditioned to perform media as its life, onscreen or off.

Infant Conditioning and Narco-Hypnosis

> "A life predicated on being obedient and taking orders is a very comfortable life indeed. Living in such a way reduces to a minimum one's own need to think."
>
> ——Adolf Eichmann

In his October 21, 1949 letter to his former student George Orwell, congratulating him on his new book *1984*, Aldous Huxley predicted that within the next generation pleasure conditioning would replace pain conditioning as a more efficient means of control: "Within the next generation I believe that the world's leaders will discover that infant conditioning and narco-hypnosis are more efficient, as instruments of government, than clubs and prisons, and that the lust for power can be just as completely satisfied by suggesting people into loving their servitude as by flogging them and kicking them into obedience" (2005, post script, p. 13).

During that next generation, TV spread from almost no homes in America to almost every home. Key to the advent of consumer culture and its pleasure conditioning was the diffusion of commercial television and its screens and spectators. Television functioned as the major apparatus of socializing people into the role of consumers, as a new landscape of consumption began to emerge in the 1950s with the development of franchised businesses and shopping malls. Unprecedented prosperity and technical innovation combined to create what I term *megatechnic America*, marked by heightened centralization of power and consumption, fueled by "pleasure conditioning."

And in the 60 years following Huxley's prediction, consumption became the centerpiece of a globalizing economy, relentlessly expanding until the bubble burst in 2008. Predicated on pleasure, it promised freedom. But to what degree has it been the opposite, a soft tyrannical pleasure machine bent on, in Huxley's words, "suggesting people into loving their servitude?" Servitude to what? To whom? And to what end?

Children are growing up into a world ever more literally faceless while simultaneously more virtually enfaced, a world where texting can displace talking and reading, where Facebook can displace actual faces in everyday life, where MySpace can displace my place, my here and now, localized in self-originated experience. Children and adults face an ever-enlarging culturescape of buttons, actual ones on devices and virtual ones enscreened on the devices. The droll, neo-Puritan button-pushers of the 1950s have been transformed into the ecstatic texting, gaming, net surfing button-pushers of today, in a world where both work and play have become dominated by button pushing. Consider how many thousands of buttons people push per day at their computers, cell phones, music players, and other devices, all in the service of virtualized social interaction. The palpable world of what I call *homo percussionis*, rhythmically touching, grasping, feeling, is inverted to an endless impalpable repetition of touching without feeling that which is literally touched: not talking heads, but typing heads.

Let me coin and define a term, *electro-insulation*: A device used to insulate one from actual face-to-face social interaction or self-originated experience. One example would be portable music devices. Music devices provide great conveniences, but as part of the larger array of daily device interaction, they also remove one from one's actual audiovisual experience when jogging, walking, or driving, through greater attention paid to the music and less to the circumstance.

The word ecstasy means to stand outside of oneself, and in a sense the canned music played on these devices can provide canned ecstasy, an audio utopia, even as background, to occupy consciousness independent of actual circumstance. This can be a great source of enjoyment, but when habituated as a daily practice, it can softly condition people to machine-mediated consumption rather than active music making, to the idea that living requires an ever-present "soundtrack," without which something is missing. For example, 15- to 18-year-old American children listen to portable music devices about an hour per day, and they listen to more than 3 hours of music per day from all sources (Rideout et al., 2009, p. 28). And this is part of a total average of 7 hours and 38 minutes of total media use per day. As Rideout et al. report: "The story of media in young people's lives today is primarily a story of technology facilitating increased consumption" (2009, p. 2). Yet making music is a way of being the circumstance, of creating an ecstasy that is of the here and now. It accompanied us in the evolution into anatomically modern humans, and yet today, it may risk being appropriated to an automatic culture antagonistic to self-originated experience.

The video "rhythm" games "Guitar Hero" and "Rock Band," which glowed brightly between 2005 and 2009, making billions of dollars for their owners before tanking by the end of 2009 as iPhone became a major platform for game apps, are pleasure conditioning devices predicated on imitation of ecstatic celebrity musicians and their music projected on a screen. Now imitating an other is as old as "monkey see monkey do," and even has a physical basis in the mirror neurons of the brain. It can be fun. But imitating a living or imaginary other in children's play or adult ritual is not the same as imitating automata. These devices remove one from one's time and place to the realm of pseudo-ecstatic spectacle and canned music, through conditioning the pushing of buttons that simulate guitar or percussion. Players simulate being rock celebrities minus musicianship.

But techno-consumer culture celebrates celebrities and consumer devices, as the following glowing statement from a *New York Times* article by Seth Schiesel on the 2009 Beatles version of the video game "Rock Band" illustrates:

> "Not only was the game serving to reintroduce this music, but by leading the players through a schematic version of actually creating the songs, it was also doing so in a much more engaging way than merely listening to a recording... listening to a finished song is perhaps like being served a finished recipe: you know it tastes great even if you have no sense of how it was created. By contrast, playing a music game like Rock Band is a bit closer to following a recipe yourself or watching a cooking show on television... you may have a greater appreciation for the genius who created the dish than the restaurant-goer, because you have attempted it yourself."

In Schiessel's account, the game promises to involve players in creation, unlike the mere listening to a song, which is "like being served a finished recipe." But the engaging experience is described as "a bit closer to following a recipe yourself," so that you might "have a greater appreciation for the genius who created the dish than the restaurantgoer."

The spontaneous face-to-face experience involved in making music becomes a virtualized cookie-cutter replica in the game, through players being led "through a schematic version of actually creating the songs." Celebrity spectacle, in the avatar of The Beatles, trumps spontaneous face-to-face experience, as does the consumption machine mediation of experience.

Consider Guy Debord's words on the hypnotizing yet strangely off-the-radar way that modern spectacle works:

"When the real world is transformed into mere images, mere images become real beings—dynamic figments that provide the direct motivations for a hypnotic behavior. Since the spectacle's job is to use various specialized mediations in order to *show* us a world that can no longer be directly grasped, it naturally elevates the sense of sight to the special preeminence once occupied by touch: the most abstract and easily deceived sense is the most readily adaptable to the generalized abstraction of present-day society. But the spectacle is not merely a matter of images, nor even of images plus sounds. It is whatever escapes people's activity, whatever eludes their practical reconsideration and correction. It is the opposite of dialogue." (1967)

Here the images and canned music become "dynamic figments" of Beatle spectacle, "real beings" motivating a kind of hypnotic identification with them through synchronizing to them through the hand devices. Debord noted in 1967 how the sense of sight came to predominate over touch, but in the 21st century, button-pushing touch has been reintegrated into the rituals of the society of the spectacle, though still at the service of spectacle. One of Debord's key points in describing the alienating nature of modern spectacle is that estrangement hides in plain sight ("It is whatever escapes people's activity, whatever eludes their practical reconsideration and correction."). Celebrity is a focal point of this process, where idealized figures become idolized and identified with, allowing idealized self-conceptions to colonize the spontaneous self. The idealized "guitar hero" is stamped with spectacular legitimacy, capable of providing substitute emotions to consuming believers. It's not that the game is not fun to play. Rather, the pleasurable activity of games such as "Rock Band" and "Guitar Hero" provides an audiovisual, celebritized entrancement, so that players lose contact with the reality of their schematized, button-pushing situation, ecstatically transported to the realm of the ersatz. As Debord says of this interaction: "It is the opposite of dialogue."

Though a game such as "Rock Band" involves multiple players present, it subverts the face-to-face primary relation by channeling the players to interact through the machine-mediated tertiary relation provided by the song program. The narco-hypnotic, pleasurable interaction with the automaton distracts players from the possibility of practicing a musical instrument: the video music game "Rock Band" distracts players from actually learning to play their own music in a rock band, risking both learning an instrument and learning to interact as a musical ensemble, without schematic. It "outsources" players' possibilities for rhythmic spontaneous bodily experience through providing canned ecstatic feedback, infused with celebrity consumption ideology. The Beatles game never sold well, and the adrenylation quickly wore off these games, moving on to other schemata, to the so-called "stupid games." Stupid games can be played as apps on the omnipresent cell phone, require no talent, and can be brief, repetitive, and addicting (Anderson, 2012). They are the perfect tool for conditioning the narco-hypnotized button-pusher, whether young child or adult.

In 2009 Rovio introduced "Angry Birds," a game involving pushing buttons to slingshot birds at pigs for as long as the button-pusher wants. It has been downloaded almost 2 billion times, and within months of introduction was the most popular game on the iPhone. Imagine a planet where millions of people spend hundreds of millions of minutes enscreened in this game every single day. The fantastic world of the hunter-gatherer attuned to the circumambient sacred game of life reaches its complete inversion in the enscreened consciousness of the button-pusher focused on a tiny machine device of cartoon virtual animals senselessly slaughtered: the playful, pleasurable killing machine.

Albert Borgmann has described the difference between "device paradigms" and "focal things and practices" (1992). Where focal things and practices involve the commitment of time, attention, and disciplined practice, device paradigms typically tend not to impose such "burdens." They are convenient and do not require us to understand them or how they produce what they produce. Music devices in this sense invite us to consume music passively without entering into how to make it. They are fun conveniences, to be sure. But they also pose the challenge of technology to displace spontaneous experience. They illustrate how consumerist "choice" can be too easily the way to spell relief from the burdens of everyday practices, spontaneity, and self-determination.

The sheer numbers of ear-budded people in public, narco-hypnotically attuned to their canned music, anesthetized to the people around them and to the audible situation they are in, testifies to the normative power of device paradigms in everyday life to dematerialize face-to-face interaction. Look straight into the occupied face of the next person interacting with a device you meet in public, and you will see Huxley's vision of "suggesting people into loving their servitude" realized. Yet like the story of the sorcerer's apprentice, technology should serve human goals with limits, not take on unlimited maximizing goals of its own.

The Virtue of Virtuality

How did the virtuality that transformed us into healthy humans now become the virtuality that may be virtually extinguishing our humanity? The answer is suggested by something that D. H. Lawrence once wrote: "That which is lovely to the automatic process is hateful to the spontaneous soul. The wakeful living soul fears automatism as it fears death: death being automatic."

In the dramatic evolutionary virtualizing processes that created the symbol the way we related to the other was as "wakeful living souls," alive to the moment, and to the signifying voices of wildness to which we attuned ourselves and who we revered in ritual life: animate mind bodied forth out of degenerate monkey's attunement to animate earth. But a strange thing happened in the course of human development. The symbol, created out of ecological symbiosis and dramatic interaction with forms of wildness, became domesticated into an anthropocentric self-representation as humans moved into settlement and civilization. The play of wild animals and plants in the generalized other retreated. Symbolic consciousness contracted to the human world, creating an increasing array of human-centered virtualities, increasingly removed from the ecological order through which they came into being. And in the modern era it contracted again, to the image of the machine as ultimate "other," model of the universe: the ultimate reality of the generalized other as schizoid machine.

The practical purpose of virtuality is to help bring us to live the good life. The destination of the good life may be something we strive toward, learning and improving our practices along the way. But there is another aspect of the good life important to make clear. The good life is ultimately to be found in our surroundings, in our circumstance. It is found in those closest to us, loved ones, neighbors, coworkers; in parenting, neighboring, working and playing. It can be found in cultivating wildness, not only a walk in the woods, but wildness within. Thoreau said, "It is in vain to dream of a wildness distant from ourselves."

The expression, "the best things in life are free," is true, if we but pay attention to the best things. The best things in life are the relationships we develop, relationships which must be grounded in everyday interactions, but which can also include virtual interactions enabled by technology. In this sense the meaning of long-distance contact in personal life is that it is a surrogate for face-to-face relations, not a means of displacing them.

The original Greek term *symbol* meant something thrown or joined together, and referred to an idea of two friends parting, breaking a coin and each taking half, with the hope of meeting again and throwing together, or *symboling,* the coin as sign of their relationship. The symbol, in this sense, is literally a social relationship, a virtual social relationship whose goal is a face-to-face reuniting.

The automaton has gained an ascendency that in our time has created virtualized worldviews that one could consider the complete inversion of aboriginal mind, including its absorption in face-to-face relations. This is the script being enacted worldwide now: automatization, death being automatic. The alternative then, it seems to me, is neither to create a Brave New Technology, a virtual Deus-ex-Machina that can save us from overdependence on machined enscreened existence, nor to sound a Luddite retreat from technology. Rather it is to consider how virtuality can be made to again be the servant of "wakeful living souls," of spontaneous, self-originated conduct as central to the practice of everyday life. Tactile, empathic parenting, varieties of the Paleolithic diet as model both for eating and for connecting to the earth, a sense of limits on habitat use, rhythmically engaged, full-body educational practices that allow the spontaneous child in, these are just some possibilities for institutionalization today.

We retain Pleistocene bodies, as ecological philosopher Paul Shepard put it, and deeply tempered Pleistocene needs, bodied into being over our longer 2 million–year evolution. Animate mind remains a dormant reality, capable of renewing our contracted modern civilization, if we can undo the mind forg'd manacles. The conditions through which the symbol originally arose, in progressively cooperative parenting and habitat relations, can be selectively recalled here and now, from the very bodies we inhabit.

References

Anderson, S. (2012). Just one more game…Angry birds, farmville and other hyperaddictive "stupid games." *New York Times*, April 4. Retrieved April 4, 2012, from http://www.nytimes. com/2012/04/08/magazine/angry-birds-farmville-and-other-hyperaddictive-stupid-games. html?pagewanted=all.

Bellah, R. N. (2011). *Religion in human evolution: From the paleolithic to the axial age*. Cambridge, MA: Belknap Press of Harvard University Press.

Borgmann, A. (1992). The moral significance of the material culture. *Inquiry, 35*, 291–300.

Brown, T. Jr. (1998). *The science and art of tracking*. New York: Berkley Books.

Coqueugniot, H., Hublin, J.-J., Veillon, F., Houët, F., & Jacob, T. (2004). Early brain growth in homo erectus and implications for cognitive ability. *Nature, 431*, 299–302.

Debord, G. (1967). *The society of the spectacle*. Chapter 1, paragraph 18. Retrieved August 20, 2009, from http://www.bopsecrets.org/images/sos.pdf.

de Waal, F. (2010). Morals without God? *New York Times*, October 17.

Falk, D. (2004). Prelinguistic evolution in early hominins: Whence motherese?. *Behavioral and Brain Sciences, 27*, 491–503.

Halton, E. (2005). Peircean animism and the end of civilization. *Contemporary Pragmatism, 2*(1), 135–166.

Halton, E. (2007). Eden inverted: On the wild self and the contraction of consciousness. *The Trumpeter, 23*(3), 45–77. Retrieved September 16, 2013, from http://trumpeter. athabascau.ca/index.php/trumpet/article/view/995/1387.

Halton, E. (2008). *The great brain suck: And other American epiphanies*. Chicago: University of Chicago Press.

Halton, E. (2014). *From the axial age to the moral revolution*. New York: Palgrave MacMillan.

Halton, E. (2013). Tale of the evolutionary drama of symboling: A dramaturgical digression. In C. Edgley (Ed.), *The drama of social life: A dramaturgical handbook* (pp. 27–41). Surrey, UK: Ashgate.

Hrdy, S. B. (2009). *Mothers and others: The evolutionary origins of mutual understanding*. Cambridge, MA: Belknap Press of Harvard University Press.

Huizinga, J. (1955 [1950]). *Homo ludens*. Boston: Beacon Press.

Huxley, A. (2005). *Brave new world* and *Brave new world revisited*. New York: Harper Perennial Modern Classics.

Ingold, T. (2007). *Lines: A brief history*. New York: Routledge.

Iriki, A., & Taoka, M. (2012). Triadic (ecological, neural, cognitive) niche construction: A scenario of human brain evolution extrapolating tool use and language from the control of reaching actions. *Philosophical Transactions of the Royal Society Series B: Biological Sciences, 367,* 10–23.

Lawrence, D. H. (1936). *Phoenix: The posthumous papers of D. H. Lawrence*. Edited with an introduction by Edward D. McDonald. New York: Viking Press.

Liebenberg, L. (1990). *The art of tracking: The origin of science*. Claremont, South Africa: David Philip.

Määttänen, K. (2007). *Melodies of feeling and patterns of moving: Mediating the origins of understanding in early infancy*. Paper presented at Applying Peirce: International Conference on Charles Sanders Peirce's Thought and Its Applications. Helsinki, June 11–13.

Malloch, S., & Trevarthen, C. (2009). *Communicative musicality: Exploring the basis of human companionship*. New York: Oxford University Press.

Mander, J. (1978). *Four arguments for the elimination of television*. New York: William Morrow.

McKenna, J. J., Thoman, E. G., Anders, T. F., Sadeh, A., Schechtman, V. L., & Glotzbach, S. F. (1993). Infant-parent co-sleeping in an evolutionary perspective: Implications for understanding infant sleep development and the sudden infant death syndrome. *Sleep, 16*(3), 263–282.

Mead, G. H. (1934). *Mind, self, and society*. Edited by Charles W. Morris. Chicago: University of Chicago Press.

Mead, G. H. (1964). *Mead: Selected writings*. Edited by A. J. Reck. Indianapolis: Bobbs-Merrill.

Meltzoff, A. N. (2002). Imitation as a mechanism of social cognition: Origins of empathy, theory of mind, and the representation of action. In U. Goswami (Ed.), *Blackwell handbook of childhood cognitive development (pp.* 6–25). Malden, MA: Blackwell..

Meltzoff, A. N., & Moore, M. K. (1977). Imitation of facial and manual gestures by human neonates. *Science, 198*, 75–78.

Montagu, A. (1986). *Touching: The human significance of the skin*. New York: Harper and Row.

Narvaez, D., Panksepp, J., Schore, A., & Gleason, T. (2013). The value of using an evolutionary framework for gauging children's wellbeing. In D. Narvaez, J. Panksepp, A. Schore, & T. Gleason (Eds.), *Evolution, early experience and human development: From research to practice and policy*. New York: Oxford University Press.

Neal, D. T., & Chartrand, T. L. (2011). Embodied emotion perception: Amplifying and dampening facial feedback modulates emotion perception accuracy. *Social Psychological and Personality Science, 2*, 673–678.

Nelson, R. (1993). Lost arrow: Physical and spiritual ecology in the hunter's world. In S. R. Kellert & E. O. Wilson (Eds.), *The biophilia hypothesis* (pp. 201–228). Washington, DC: Island Press.

Nietzsche, F. (2000). *Basic writings of Nietzsche*. Translated and edited by Walter Kaufman. New York: Modern Library.

Peirce, C. S. (1931–1935). *The collected papers of Charles Sanders Peirce* (Vol. 6). Edited by Charles Hartshorne and Paul Weiss. Cambridge, MA: Harvard University Press.

Peirce, C. S. (1979). *Charles Sanders Peirce: Contributions to the nation, Part Three: 1901–1908* (pp. 17–18). Edited by Kenneth Laine Ketner and James Edward Cook. Lubbock, TX: Texas Technological University Press.

Pollick, A. S., & de Waal, F. B. M. (2007). Ape gestures and language evolution. *Proceedings of the National Academy of Sciences USA, 104*(19), 8184–8189.

Rideout, V. J., Foehr, U. G., & Roberts, D. F. (2009). *Generation M2: Media in the lives of 8- to 18-year-olds.* Menlo Park, CA: The Henry J. Kaiser Foundation. Retrieved September 16, 2013, from http://www.kff.org/entmedia/upload/8010.pdf.

Rideout, V. J., & Hamel, E. (2006). *The media family: Electronic media in the lives of infants, toddlers, preschoolers and their parents.* Menlo Park, CA: The Henry J. Kaiser Foundation (May 2006). Retrieved September 16, 2013, from http://www.kff.org/entmedia/upload/7500.pdf.

Schiesel, S. (2009). All together now: Play the game, Mom. *New York Times*, September 6. Retrieved September 16, 2013, from http://www.nytimes.com/2009/09/06/arts/television/06schi.html?hp.

Shepard, P. (1998a [1973]). *The. tender carnivore and the sacred game.* Athens, GA: University of Georgia Press.

Shepard, P. (1998b [1982]). *Nature and madness.* Athens, GA: University of Georgia Press.

Schor, J. (2004). *Born to buy: The commercialized child and the new consumer culture.* New York: Scribner.

Sterlny, K. (2012). *The evolved apprentice.* Cambridge, MA: MIT Press.

Swanbrow, D. (2010). "Empathy: College students don't have as much as they used to." University of Michigan News Service, May 27. Retrieved July 8, 2013 from: http://ns.umich.edu/new/releases/7724

Trevarthen, C. (1980). The foundations of intersubjectivity: Development of interpersonal and cooperative understanding in infants. In D. Olson (Ed.), *The social foundations of language and thought: Essays in honor of J. S. Bruner* (pp. 316–342). New York: W. W. Norton.

Trevarthen, C. (1986). Brain science and human spirit. *Zygon, 21*(2), 161–200.

Trevarthen, C. (1999–2000). Musicality and the intrinsic motive pulse: Evidence from human psychobiology and infant communication. *Musicae Scientiae*, Special issue, 3(1), suppl, 155–215.

Tufekci, Z. (2012). Social media's small, positive role in human relationships. *The Atlantic*, April 25. Retrieved September 16, 2013, from http://www.theatlantic.com/technology/archive/2012/04/social-medias-small-positive-role-in-human-relationships/256346/.

Young, J. (2012). *What the Robin knows: how birds reveal the secrets of the natural world.* New York: Houghton Mifflin Harcourt.

{ Commentary }

Darwinism and Children
Jonathan Marks

Halton's provocative essay combines biology and philosophy, using Darwinism as a form of cultural critique. There are many aspects of the analysis that that I agree with, in particular the central point that symboling is a general intellectual process whose expressions can be found in diverse forms of human activity. But I want to focus on the two weakest aspects of his argument.

The first is the casual invocation of evolution. The study of human evolution is in a two-front war, against the anti-Darwinians and the hyper-Darwinians (Stephen Jay Gould called them Darwinian fundamentalists) simultaneously. One of the features of the hyper-Darwinians is their assumption that that everything must be understood as having been forged in the crucible of directional selection as an adaptation for something. The fact is, however, that it is ridiculously hard to prove that anything is an adaptation, from bipedalism, to craniofacial form, to Tay-Sachs disease; and consequently the assumption that everything must be understood that way often is taken to be an ideological red flag. Thus, whether religion indeed "arose in our evolutionary past primarily as a way to connect to the intelligible and edible habitat, through ritual, dance, song, and foraging arts and sciences" or just happens to do that well, ought probably to be posed as a question, rather than as a declaration. Likewise, whether the intellectual features attributed to hunting and tracking could not have emerged from fishing and gardening is probably better queried than axiomatized.

The second is the attitude toward modern society that the paper expresses, and I write these words with a self-conscious bias as a happy player of "Angry Birds." I have a proud identity as a grumpy old man, and there are surely a lot of things wrong with the world, but how high on the list really are teenagers and their video games? I don't mean to dispute the observation that kids sit in a cocoon and interact virtually, while they eat junk food and get no exercise. My daughter spends too much time playing "Minecraft," but I'm happy that we have indoor plumbing and that she's not going to get polio. Life is trade-offs.

What I'm trying to get at is that there is a culture history here that is at least as important as the Darwinism. It's urbanism (building cities), industrialism (going where the jobs are, in the city), neolocal residence (moving away), the segregation of the nuclear family as a domestic and legal unit, and the individual as a political unit, that all contribute to our modern ability to smoothly establish our personal space, to alienate ourselves from traditional social interactions, and to live in a bubble of "personal entertainment." The autonomous individual is a historically produced fiction, but it's what we've been groping toward for millennia. You get the Bill of Rights, and with it comes unofficially the right to listen to the exact piece of music you want, when you want to, and the right to be left the hell alone, which were as unfulfilled in the Pleistocene as the right to vote.

It seems to me that, as highly adaptable creatures, we adapt not only to our "natural" environments, which Thoreau admired, but as well to our social and technological environments, which are changing even more rapidly. This is an important aspect of human evolution, which has recently begun to be theorized under the rubric of "niche construction." Our environments are not passive or given; they are constructed historically and technologically: A stick is something to sharpen; a rock is something to extract the minerals from; a tree is something to be cut down so you can build a house; a telephone is something to talk to people with who aren't physically present. Like our ancestors, we use the things we have available, which may be stones, tree branches, animal sinew, flowers, tame animals, quill pens, televisions, or the Internet, and we incorporate them into our lives in various ways.

So when anyone tells me about "the good life" I immediately wonder whether we cannot conceive of multiple good lives. Just as there were multiple Paleolithic diets (none of which was much like "The Paleolithic Diet"), I hope future generations will be able to lead fulfilled lives, although I doubt that they will be very much like my own, much less like Benjamin Franklin's, Julius Caesar's, or Og's.

Finally, I think Halton is spot-on in observing that pleasure is a more effective way of governing than pain; might we now entwine video games, religion, and opium in the same thought?

{ SECTION V }

Child Flourishing

14

Childhood Environments and Flourishing

Tracy R. Gleason and Darcia Narvaez

Early childrearing provides a critical environmental context for development. As the authors in this book have illustrated, early life context has implications for all manner of later outcomes, including the management of aggression (see chapter 7), brain development (see chapter 2), participation in relationships (see chapter 4) and mental health (see chapter 3). In all of these chapters, the emphasis is on the nature of the early environment that best prepares the infant for healthy physiological and psychological functioning, not just for a particular physical environment, but for the social, relational world and membership in a community. Perhaps the single most significant goal of early development is this preparation for social interaction and participation in close relationships, a large component of which depends on successful sociomoral functioning.

To achieve "successful" sociomoral functioning, early communal contexts must support development of the individual in a way that emphasizes not only the happiness and goal attainment of the self but also a socially-skilled self within changing relational contexts. Healthy relationships are reciprocal and mutually responsive. Thus, raising a child who will interact and work *with* others rather than against them is a goal of development itself. A child who never learns, or is unable, to focus on the needs and feelings of others will likely have trouble with the fundamental tenets of dyadic and group dynamics, such as negotiation, cooperation, compromise, and empathy. Even if such skills are learned, the facility with which a child functions in a social context probably has a significant range, from necessary interactions that promote *survival* to myriad mutually fulfilling, long-term social relationships that promote *thriving*. In between these poles may lie our current state of parenting in the United States, in which many children—particularly those with resources—reach adulthood relatively unscathed, but the rates of depression, anxiety disorders, behavior problems, and toxic stress are at record levels, even among the middle class (American Academy of Child and Adolescent Psychiatry, 2011a, 2011b; Shonkoff and Garner, 2012; U.S. Department of Health and Human Services Substance Abuse and Mental Health Services Administration, 1999).

According to neo-Darwinian evolutionary theory, organisms have three basic aims: survival, reproduction, and dispersal (Williams, 1966), and parenting typically facilitates them. As Halton (chapter 13) points out, our prolonged neoteny as a species and consequent plasticity allow for adaptation to a wide variety of environmental conditions that promote these outcomes. A prolonged childhood gives humans a level of resilience that allows some individuals to emerge physiologically and psychologically healthy despite significant risk factors in their early environments (Masten, Best, and Garmezy, 1990; Wright and Masten, 2005; Zolkoski and Bullock, 2012). However, success in these situations is often identified, not as thriving, but as *average* functioning: showing a lack of symptoms or pathology and meeting developmentally appropriate goals. Furthermore, often in studies of resilience, competence is measured in a single domain, such as education (e.g., graduation from high school), rather than across domains (e.g., academic, behavioral, and emotional), thus providing an incomplete picture of individual wellbeing (Walsh, Dawson, and Mattingly, 2010). If, instead, success were defined as thriving or optimal functioning in many, if not all, domains, the consequences of negative early life experiences might be illustrated in sharp relief.

Certainly developmental outcomes are influenced by a host of environmental factors of which early childrearing is only one, and yet our ever-increasing understanding of the centrality of parenting contexts suggests that the goal of early childrearing should not simply be survival, or avoiding psychopathology and otherwise compromised functioning. As this volume demonstrates, our knowledge of the connections between early childrearing contexts and later outcomes is significant and continually growing, and by attending to this knowledge we have the potential to promote policies and programs that encourage not just survival, or resilience, but *flourishing.*

Flourishing

Flourishing among adults has been defined by positive psychologists as living "within an optimal range of human functioning, one that connotes goodness, generativity, growth, and resilience" (Fredrickson and Losada, 2005, p. 678). Keyes (2002) has suggested that flourishing requires a combination of three types of wellbeing: *emotional* (positive emotion and life satisfaction), *psychological* (e.g., self-acceptance, autonomy, purpose), and *social* (e.g., social acceptance, actualization, contribution, integration). For the sake of measurement, in research these factors are often conceptualized in terms of a ratio that has low levels of individual disease and psychopathology but high levels of wellbeing and happiness (Keyes, 2002).The work in this volume and the prior, related one (Narvaez, Panksepp, Schore, and Gleason, 2013) suggests that *physiological regulation* is another key aspect of flourishing that underlies the other types of wellbeing and might be heavily influenced by early social contexts.

Our concept of flourishing for *children* includes these same areas of physiological, emotional, psychological, and social health. We explicitly expand the notion of flourishing to include an emphasis on the sociomoral aspects of development, such as strengths in empathy and cooperation. In other words, flourishing is conceptualized with an emphasis on the moral domain, such that it includes considering how actions affect others, taking into account the wellbeing of others, and including the community when making decisions and selecting actions.

The emphasis on a social sense of wellbeing is an important distinction between parenting aimed at child survival, child resilience, or even adequate care, as well as the type of parenting that fosters child flourishing within a community. Most childrearing contexts stress the need to distinguish right and wrong and follow through with moral reasoning and empathic behavior (Kochanska and Murray, 2000), and certainly such an orientation is important to nurture. Parenting that fosters flourishing, however, might be conceptualized as equally focused on other aspects of morality identified by Rest (1984), such as recognizing moral issues inherent in situations (i.e., moral sensitivity), prioritizing moral values over other (e.g., personal, religious, patriotic) values (i.e., moral motivation), and the ability and ego strength to follow through on moral decisions (i.e., moral character). In essence, childrearing contexts that promote child flourishing are designed to encourage *proactive*, rather than *reactive*, forms of sociomoral behavior. The childrearing contexts that support child flourishing support a high level of autonomy, but within a strong socially connected community. Such robust functioning prepares the individual for a fulfilling social life and provides the individual with capacities to foster flourishing in others. In this way, flourishing is a communal affair (Aristotle, 1988) and is evident in some of the hunter-gatherer societies documented in the present volume (e.g., Endicott and Endicott).

Parenting that supports child flourishing is also distinguishable from other developmental contexts in terms of its conceptualization of morality as encompassing all human beings, such as the morality that characterizes individuals identified as moral exemplars. For example, individuals who hid Jews during World War II provide accounts of childhood upbringings in which care for all people was emphasized (Monroe, 2004; Oliner and Oliner, 1988). Fostering this perspective starts early and evolves with the changing capacities of the child. Initially, adults treat the infant with tender empathy, generating a similar response in the infant (Schore, 1996; Siegel, 1999; Stern, 1999). Beyond infancy, empathic parents bring to children's attention the feelings and behaviors of specific others (Zahn-Waxler and Radke-Yarrow, 1990), followed developmentally by an emphasis on how the child's behavior affects others generally (Farrant, Devine, Maybery, and Fletcher, 2012). The key here is how "others" are identified. In the somewhat isolated hunter-gatherer tribes described in this volume, relevant others might be the community that gathers into small groups with fluid boundaries (see chapter 5). In the United States, national, religious, ethnic, or geographic boundaries might define the group of moral concern. However, at an abstract level, "others" can theoretically be conceptualized as *all* humans. This idea of humanity as the backdrop for socio-moral behavior can also include consideration of the needs of future generations, as is common among indigenous peoples concerned for "the seventh generation" into the future (Martin, 1999).

Based on examination of hunter-gatherer lifestyles and attitudes, Narvaez (2014) suggests that a focus on the individual or even a set of human beings is an inadequate framing for flourishing. In this view, biodiversity and entities in the natural environment must also be taken into account. The community thus extends even beyond humanity. By this definition, small-band hunter-gatherers flourished by living sustainably, with the welfare of the natural world in mind (Gowdy, 1998; Ingold, 1999). Parenting supportive of child flourishing might therefore encourage consideration of sociomoral issues from as broad and abstract a perspective as cognitively possible at various points in development.

Contexts for Development

In recent years, research has focused on childrearing environments variously described in the literature as "average" (Baumrind, 1993), "good enough" (Hoghughi and Speight, 1998; Ryan, Martin, and Brooks-Gunn, 2006; Winnicott, 1957), and "positive" (von Suchodoletz, Trommsdorff, and Heikamp, 2011) or on the resilience of children growing up in dangerous, abusive, neglectful, or otherwise compromised environments. The latter, substandard environments are relatively easy to identify based on the presence of factors that clearly undermine, if not threaten, children's development. The features of adequate parenting are less well defined. The initial definition for "good enough" parenting provided by Winnicott (1957) centered on caregiving that was neither overtly problematic nor provided by someone with a clear psychiatric illness—rather low standards. More recent variations have somewhat higher bars, describing adequate parenting as including such components as unconditional love, clear boundaries for behavior, and facilitation of development primarily through the provision of a secure base for exploration (Hoghughi and Speight, 1998). They also may mention requirements such as a mentally healthy parent, with some knowledge of child development and a commitment to putting in the time required to care for the child (Mrazek, 2013).

In general, the outcomes associated with care described as good enough are positive in comparison with care that is less than adequate. For example, work on attachment has clearly established parental warmth, unconditional love, and the provision of a secure base as essential to a whole host of positive self-regulatory, social, and emotional outcomes and the avoidance of behavior problems (e.g., Eisenberg, Zhou, Spinrad, Valiente, Fabes, and Liew, 2005; Kochanska and Kim, 2012). Positive guidance, or developmentally appropriate limit-setting beyond infancy, has been associated with compliant behavior (Calkins, Smith, Gill, and Johnson, 1998), and of course the importance of parental mental health and supportive parenting for positive child mental health outcomes is well established (e.g., DeMulder and Radke-Yarrow, 1991; Fisher, Rahman, Cabral de Mello, Chandra, and Herrman, 2010; Ge, Best, Conger, and Simons, 1996). Above all, sensitive and responsive care, a basic requirement for adequate childrearing, is heavily implicated in the development of successful stress regulation (Liu et al., 1997), regulation of arousal (Schore, 2001), appropriate social and emotional reactivity (Porges, 2007), and the development of conscience (Kochanska, 2002).

The fact that the outcomes associated with average or adequate (good enough) parenting are positive raises two questions. How is a developmental context that promotes flourishing different from parenting characterized as "good enough"? And if they are different styles, do the developmental and cultural outcomes of these two environments differ significantly? The first question can be addressed by the fact that the characteristics of flourishing defined above are embodied in many of the hunter-gatherer groups discussed in this volume, suggesting that the parenting practices they employ may foster the kind of prosocial, moral stance associated with flourishing (Narvaez, 2013).

PROMOTING FLOURISHING

Among the hunter-gatherer groups described in this book (chapters 4, 5, 6, and, 7) and elsewhere (e.g., Hewlett and Lamb, 2005; Narvaez, Panksepp, et al., 2013), childrearing is intense and communal. For example, babies are held most of the time, and distress is mitigated quickly. Breastfeeding is infant initiated, shared among women, and lasts for several years. As they grow, children are rarely coerced but given ample time to play, and aggression is either ritualized or met with strong social consequences. Children, and infants in particular, are cared for and conceptualized as the responsibility of the whole group, meaning that parents receive extensive social support and children have many resources from which to elicit caregiving. Children are integrated into the life of the band at whatever level they are capable of participating, which, as Fuentes (chapter 10) points out, may make them integral to the evolutionary adaptations of the species. In this context, children are not "parented" or "reared" so much as supported as they actively develop as individuals within the community (Gray, 2013; see chapter 4).

In this volume, Gray, Morelli et al., and Hewlett and Roulette (chapters 4, 6, and 8) all highlight ways in which cultural values relate to parenting behaviors, such as encouraging play to promote egalitarianism, fostering sharing and cooperative exchange to create connections to others and positive interpersonal relationships, and engaging in co-sleeping to nurture interdependence and foster family bonds. In each case, the behaviors include features of good enough parenting, such as responsivity, secure attachment, mental health, and avoidance of behavior problems. But the caregiving associated with these flourishing cultures goes further to emphasize autonomy and respect for others, even infants and young children (see chapter 5).

The critical importance of interpersonal harmony, a characteristic of the social section and cooperative family theory that Roughgarden and Song (chapter 9) show to be a better model of family relations than the dominant competitive theory, centers the community in sociomoral development. In other words, success is not defined as the absence of antisocial behaviors but by the presence of prosocial, cooperative actions and contributing, active membership within the group. The distinction to be drawn is between the *absence* of the type of psychopathology well described in chapters by Valentino, Comas, and Nuttall (chapter 11), and Bluhm and Lanius (chapter 12), a characteristic of good enough parenting, and the *presence* of optimality or wellbeing, characteristic of a developmental context that fosters flourishing. After all, a caregiving environment that is not characterized by disadvantage is not the same as one that is characterized by thriving (Baumrind, 1993).

OPTIMIZING DEVELOPMENTAL OUTCOMES

If a distinction can be made between adequate parenting and parenting that promotes flourishing, then the question becomes whether their developmental and cultural outcomes differ significantly. Evidence is mounting that an orientation toward optimizing development with its corresponding expectations leads beyond positive outcomes to actual flourishing. Aspects of the early environment that are not usually discussed in the context of good enough or adequate parenting, such as breastfeeding, touch, alloparenting, and play, are associated with important physiological and psychological outcomes that set the stage for social group membership and flourishing (Narvaez, Panksepp et al., 2013). In particular, the social context of the neonatal period is emerging as a critical time for psychological and physiological development that leads to flourishing or otherwise (Shonkoff and Garner, 2012; Shonkoff and Phillips, 2000). Significant changes to and regulation of social functioning in adulthood have been documented in relation to early brain and central nervous system development as a function of neuropeptides, steroids, and hormones (Cushing and Kramer, 2005). These physiological changes might mean the difference between adult behavior that is, for example, reactive rather than proactive with regard to sociomoral demands. Furthermore, parenting practices like breastfeeding and touch have been associated with physiological regulatory functions (Carter and Porges, 2013), suggesting they might be relevant in fostering flourishing.

Breastfeeding

Breastfeeding has multiple benefits. Although it is protective from disease and is accompanied by increases in maternal focus on the infant in comparison with bottle feeding (Lavelli and Poli, 1998; Newburg and Walker, 2007), it also has significant regulatory functions. Breastfeeding has been implicated in regulation of the sleep–wake cycle, positive emotional tone, and brain functions such as reducing depression (Goldman, Goldblum, Garza, Nichols, and Smith, 1983).

Moreover, in our own work (Narvaez, Cheng, Brooks, Wang, and Gleason, 2012; Narvaez, Gleason, Brooks, Wang, Lefever, and Cheng, 2013; Narvaez, Wang, Gleason, Cheng, Lefever, and Deng, 2013), we have found connections between breastfeeding and aspects of self-regulation (e.g., inhibitory control) and sociomoral outcomes (e.g., empathy, conscience) in maternal reports of 3-year-olds drawn from both the United States and China. Initiation of breastfeeding is also related to prosociality at 18 months and fewer behavior problems at 24 months. All of these results remained significant even after we controlled for potentially influential factors, such as income, maternal age, and responsivity. Taken together, these findings suggest that either the process of breastfeeding or its components (thousands of ingredients, including all immunoglobulins, probiotics, amino acids needed for brain growth and food for helpful bacteria)—likely both—might be directly related to children's sociomoral outcomes, or influential on factors that influence sociomoral development, such as physiological regulation.

Touch

Copious positive touch in infancy is another behavior that may promote flourishing. Field and others have provided extensive evidence of the benefits of gentle massage to the health and development of premature infants and neonates (see Field, Diego, and Hernandez-Reif, 2010, for a review), the consequences of which have been documented as long as 2 years later in the cognitive and to a lesser extent in the motor domain (Procianoy, Mendes, and Silveira, 2010). This positive impact of massage was observed even in comparison with simple skin-to-skin contact, which has also been demonstrated to be beneficial for infants' cognitive, emotional, and physiological regulation 6 months later (Feldman, Weller, Sirota, and Eidelman, 2002). This documentation of increased benefits of purposeful, positive touch over simply holding a baby suggests that further investigation of touch is warranted. Generally, touch associated with flourishing would be nearly constant in infancy, as practiced among hunter-gatherers, including carrying and co-sleeping. Both touch and co-sleeping have been associated with regulatory processes, possibly through effects on the vagal system and reduction of stress hormones (Carter and Porges, 2013; Field et al., 2010; McKenna et al., 1994). If such effects are cumulative, they are likely to mediate a distinction between adequate parenting and contexts that foster flourishing. Our work supports such a distinction, in that in two cultures (United States and China), we found that maternal reports of positive touch both in terms of behavior and attitudes were positively correlated with their reports of greater empathy and inhibitory control in their 3-year-olds (Narvaez, Wang, Cheng, and Gleason, 2013). These results remained significant even after controlling for maternal education and income, as well as the responsive care associated with good enough parenting.

Alloparenting, Social Support, and Cooperative Childrearing

The idea that alloparenting supports sociomoral development and consequent flourishing is simple: multiple responsive caregivers allow for not only shared responsivity to the child's needs but also greater support for the child's primary caregiver. Multiple caregivers are associated with a higher standard of living and more effective parenting than families with single parents, thus lowering the child's risk for cognitive, social, and emotional problems (Amato, 2005). Traumatized mothers will also have difficulty providing the responsive care their children need (see chapter 12). Such trauma indicates a breakdown in social support for the mother at some point in her life. Relatedly, mothers who perceive themselves as living within a supportive social context are more likely to have children with better social skills and fewer behavior problems than those who do not. Presence of multiple adults may well provide good opportunities for the child to engage in beneficial social interactions (Koverola, Papas, Pitts, Murtaugh, Black, and Dubowitz, 2005). Social support is directly related to parenting in that higher levels of parental social support are correlated with less parenting stress and less ineffective parenting. Social support is also negatively correlated with parents' reports of children's behavior problems (McConnell, Breitkreuz, and Savage, 2011).

Although work on adequate parenting and children's resilience under adverse circumstances often mentions the importance of nonparental adults in children's lives (e.g., Masten et al., 1990), the notion of alloparenting as a critical component of childrearing is not typically emphasized. We have found (Gleason, Narvaez, Cheng, Wang, and Brooks, 2013) that mother's attitudes toward alloparenting cohere with attitudes toward responsivity, touch, and play into a singular construct of nurturing parenting. This cohesion emphasizes the importance of positive attitudes toward alloparenting as an important component of the social environment that might predict children's sociomoral outcomes and flourishing.

Play

In contrast to breastfeeding, touch, and alloparenting, whose effects are arguably felt most distinctly if they are missing in infancy, play is central most notably in the preschool- and school-aged years (Rubin, Fein, and Vandenberg, 1983). In the context of child flourishing, play is critical for two functions: (1) the development of physiological regulation, particularly with respect to emotion in social situations; and (2) exposure to and experience in reciprocal social relationships with peers and friends—individuals who, in contrast to adults, are similar to the child in competence and power.

Play is universal and takes many forms, from solitary to fantasy based to the physical interactions typical of rough-and-tumble (R&T) play. Both fantasy and R&T play have been associated with the successful development of emotion regulation in early to middle childhood (Lillard, Lerner, Hopkins, Dore, Smith, and Palmquist, 2013; Pellegrini and Smith, 1998). These forms of play involve intricate interactions with others that require both parties to understand that the nature of the behaviors is playful. Social pretend play, particularly if involving frightening or angry themes, requires appropriate modulation of emotion and arousal (Galyer and Evans, 2001)—as does successful involvement in R&T (Peterson and Flanders, 2005). Although little research has examined the effects on children denied these forms of play over long periods, short deprivation periods are followed by longer and more intense engagement in play and are associated with compromises in attention (Pellegrini and Smith, 1998).

Fry (chapter 7) has described typical R&T play in both humans and other primates and has made the argument for consideration of this type of play as a way of learning restraint in aggressive interactions with others. Similarly, Gray (chapter 8) has discussed play generally as a way of developing and reinforcing egalitarian interactions within hunter-gatherer communities. Social pretend play has also been discussed in the developmental literature as a forum for practicing important social skills such as negotiation, compromise, and cooperation (Black, 1992; Doyle and Connolly, 1989; Howe, Petrakos, and Rinaldi, 1998). Perhaps more important, play in childhood typically involves peers, a critical context for social development, and is an important basis for friendship (Hartup, 1992). Because successful creation of close, egalitarian, social relationships is a hallmark of flourishing, provision of opportunities for play in order to develop such relationships is a critical component of the nurturing caregiving environment.

Conclusion

Social relationships are the cornerstone of human development. From the moment of existence, each individual is nested in a network of ties to others that both create and modulate a whole host of biological and behavioral systems (Reis, Collins, and Berscheid, 2000). Although survival after childhood is possible without a complex network of social relationships, both physical and psychological functioning are seriously compromised in those who are socially isolated (Berscheid and Regan, 2005). What is more, even a close connection to a single adult is typically insufficient for optimal development (Amato, 2005). For children, particularly infants, entrenchment in a social context is a critical step toward survival, but flourishing requires a community. As the chapters in this volume illustrate, the quality of the nurturing environment is key to whether children endure, adapt to, or actively benefit from it. Flourishing must therefore be defined not just in terms of the successful formation and maintenance of close ties to others, but also in terms of the child's resultant sociomoral orientation toward others and active, positive participation in the community as a child and as an adult.

Although warm, sensitive, and responsive care is the foundation of sociomoral behavior (Kochanska, 2002; Kochanska and Kim, 2012; Kochanska and Murray, 2000), consideration of other parenting and communal practices, such as breastfeeding, touch, alloparenting, and play might illustrate the difference between adaptive and optimal development. These behaviors, common to the small-band hunter-gatherers, are associated with important physiological and psychological outcomes that significantly raise the likelihood of a child interacting with others in prosocial ways. Most important, a community of individuals who receive the kind of parenting that is associated with sociomoral flourishing is more likely to create a community in which joy and wellbeing are fostered by and for all.

References

Amato, P. (2005). The impact of family formation change on the cognitive, social, and emotional wellbeing of the next generation. *The Future of Children, 15*, 75–96.

American Academy of Child and Adolescent Psychiatry. (2011a). *Stress in America*. Washington, DC: American Psychological Association.

American Academy of Child and Adolescent Psychiatry. (2011b). *Campaign for America's kids*. Retrieved January 19, 2011, from http://www.campaignforamericaskids.org.

Aristotle. (1988). *Nicomachean ethics* (W. D. Ross, Trans.). London: Oxford University Press.

Baumrind, D. (1993). The average expectable environment is not good enough: A response to Scarr. *Child Development, 64*(5), 1299–1317.

Berscheid, E., & Regan, P. (2005). *The psychology of interpersonal relationships*. Upper Saddle River, NJ: Pearson Prentice Hall.

Black, B. (1992). Negotiating social pretend play: Communication differences related to social status and sex. *Merrill-Palmer Quarterly, 38*(2), 212–232.

Calkins, S. D., Smith, C. L., Gill, K. L., & Johnson, M. C. (1998). Maternal interactive style across contexts: Relations to emotional, behavioral, and physiological regulation during toddlerhood. *Social Development, 7*(3), 350–369.

Carter, C. S., & Porges, S. W. (2013). Neurobiology and the evolution of mammalian social behavior. In D. Narvaez, J. Panksepp, A. Schore, & T. Gleason (Eds.), *Evolution, early experience and human development: From research to practice and policy* (pp. 132–151). New York: Oxford University Press.

Cushing, B. S., & Kramer, K. M. (2005). Mechanisms underlying epigenetic effects of early social experience: The role of neuropeptides and steroids. *Neuroscience and Biobehavioral Reviews, 29*(7), 1089–1105.

DeMulder, E. K., & Radke-Yarrow, M. (1991). Attachment with affectively ill and well mothers: Concurrent behavioral correlates. *Development and Psychopathology, 3*(3), 227–242.

Doyle, A.-B., & Connolly, J. (1989). Negotiation and enactment in social pretend play: Relations to social acceptance and social cognition. *Early Childhood Research Quarterly, 4*(3), 289–302.

Eisenberg, N., Zhou, Q., Spinrad, T. L., Valiente, C., Fabes, R. A., & Liew, J. (2005). Relations among positive parenting, children's effortful control, and externalizing problems: A three-wave longitudinal study. *Child Development, 76*(5), 1055–1071.

Farrant, B., Devine, T., Maybery, M., & Fletcher, J. (2012). Empathy, perspective taking and prosocial behaviour: The importance of parenting practices. *Infant and Child Development, 21*, 175–188.

Feldman, R., Weller, A., Sirota, L., & Eidelman, A. I. (2002). Skin-to-skin contact (kangaroo care) promotes self-regulation in premature infants: Sleep-wake cyclicity, arousal modulation, and sustained exploration. *Developmental Psychology, 38*(2), 194–207.

Field, T., Diego, M., & Hernandez-Reif, M. (2010). Preterm infant massage therapy research: A review. *Infant Behavior and Development, 33,* 115–124.

Fisher, J., Rahman, A., Cabral de Mello, M., Chandra, P. S., & Herrman, H. (2010). Mental health of parents and infant health and development in resource-constrained settings: Evidence gaps and implications for facilitating "good-enough parenting" in the twenty-first-century world. In S. Tyano, M. Keren, H. Herrman & J. Cox (Eds.), *Parenthood and mental health: A bridge between infant and adult psychiatry* (pp. 429–442). Chicester, UK: Wiley-Blackwell.

Fredrickson, B. L., & Losada, M. F. (2005). Positive affect and complex dynamics of human flourishing. *American Psychologist, 60,* 678–686.

Galyer, K. T., & Evans, I. M. (2001). Pretend play and the development of emotion regulation in preschool children. *Early Child Development and Care, 166,* 93–108.

Ge, X., Best, K. M., Conger, R. D., & Simons, R. L. (1996). Parenting behaviors and the occurrence and co-occurrence of adolescent depressive symptoms and conduct problems. *Developmental Psychology, 32*(4), 717–731.

Gleason, T., Narvaez, D., Cheng, Y., Wang, L., & Brooks, J. (2013). The relation of nurturing parenting attitudes to wellbeing and socio-moral development in preschoolers. Manuscript submitted for publication.

Goldman, A. S., Goldblum, R. M., Garza, C., Nichols, B. L., & Smith, E. O. (1983). Immunologic components in human milk during weaning. *Acta Paediatrica Scandinavica, 72,* 133–134.

Gowdy, J. (1998). *Limited wants, unlimited means: A reader on hunter-gatherer economics and the environment.* Washington, DC: Island Press.

Gray, P. (2013). The value of a play-filled childhood in development of the hunter-gatherer individual. In D. Narvaez, J. Panksepp, A. Schore, & T. Gleason (Eds.), *Evolution, early experience, and human development: From research to practice and policy* (pp. 352–370). New York: Oxford University Press.

Hartup, W. W. (1992). Friendships and their developmental significance. In H. McGurk (Ed.), *Childhood social development: Contemporary perspectives.* (pp. 175–205). Hillsdale, NJ: Erlbaum.

Hewlett, B. S., & Lamb, M. E. (2005). *Hunter-gatherer childhoods: Evolutionary, developmental, and cultural perspectives.* New Brunswick, NJ: Aldine.

Hoghughi, M., & Speight, A. N. P. (1998). Good enough parenting for all children—a strategy for a healthier society. *Archives of Disease in Childhood, 78*(4), 293–296.

Howe, N., Petrakos, H., & Rinaldi, C. M. (1998). "All the sheeps are dead. He murdered them": Sibling pretense, negotiation, internal state language, and relationship quality. *Child Development, 69*(1), 182–191.

Ingold, T. (1999). On the social relations of the hunter-gatherer band. In R. B. Lee & R. Daly (Eds.), *The Cambridge encyclopedia of hunters and gatherers* (pp. 399–410). New York: Cambridge University Press.

Keyes, C. L. M. (2002). The mental health continuum: From languishing to flourishing in life. *Journal of Health and Social Behavior, 43,* 207–222.

Kochanska, G. (2002). Mutually responsive orientation between mothers and their young children: A context for the early development of conscience. *Current Directions in Psychological Science, 11,* 191–195.

Kochanska, G., & Kim, S. (2012). Toward a new understanding of legacy of early attachments for future antisocial trajectories: Evidence from two longitudinal studies. *Development and Psychopathology, 24*(3), 783–806.

Kochanska, G., & Murray, K. T. (2000). Mother-child mutually responsive orientation and conscience development: From toddler to early school age. *Child Development, 71*(2), 417–431.

Koverola, C., Papas, M. A., Pitts, S., Murtaugh, C., Black, M. M., & Dubowitz, H. (2005). Longitudinal investigation of the relationship among maternal victimization, depressive symptoms, social support, and children's behavior and development. *Journal of Interpersonal Violence, 20*(12), 1523–1546.

Lavelli, M., & Poli, M. (1998). Early mother-infant interaction during breast- and bottle-feeding. *Infant Behavior and Development, 21*, 667–684.

Lillard, A. S., Lerner, M. D., Hopkins, E. J., Dore, R. A., Smith, E. D., & Palmquist, C. M. (2013). The impact of pretend play on children's development: A review of the evidence. *Psychological Bulletin, 139*(1), 1–34.

Liu, D., Diorio, J., Tannenbaum, B., Caldji, C., Farancis, D., Freedman, A., et al. (1997). Maternal care, hippocampal glucocorticoid receptors, and hypothalamic-pituitary-adrenal responses to stress. *Science, 277*, 1659–1662.

Martin, C. L. (1999). *The way of the human being*. New Haven, CT: Yale University Press.

Masten, A. S., Best, K. M., & Garmezy, N. (1990). Resilience and development: Contributions from the study of children who overcome adversity. *Development and Psychopathology, 2*(4), 425–444.

McConnell, D., Breitkreuz, R., & Savage, A. (2011). From financial hardship to child difficulties: Main and moderating effects of perceived social support. *Child: Care, Health and Development, 37*(5), 679–691.

McKenna, J., Mosko, S., Richard, C., Drummond, S., Hunt, L., Cetel, M. B., & Arpaia, J. (1994). Experimental studies of infant-parent co-sleeping: Mutual physiology and behavioral influences and their relevance to SIDS (sudden infant death syndrome). *Early Human Development, 38*(3), 187–201.

Monroe, K. (2004). *The hand of compassion: Portraits of moral choice during the holocaust*. Princeton, NJ: Princeton University Press.

Mrazek, D. A. (2013). Caregiving in early childhood. In R. C. Talley & R. J. V. Montgomery (Eds.), *Caregiving across the lifespan: Research, practice, policy* (pp. 11–20). New York: Springer Science + Business Media.

Narvaez, D. (2013). Development and socialization within an evolutionary context: Growing up to become "a good and useful human being." In D. Fry (Ed.), *War, peace, and human nature: The convergence of evolutionary and cultural views* (pp. 643–672). New York: Oxford University Press.

Narvaez, D. (2014). *The neurobiology and development of human morality: Evolution, culture and wisdom*. New York: W. W. Norton.

Narvaez, D., Cheng, Y., Brooks, J., Wang, L., & Gleason, T. (2012, October). *Does early parenting influence moral character development and flourishing?* Paper presented at the annual meeting of the Association for Moral Education, San Antonio, TX.

Narvaez, D., Gleason, T., Brooks, J., Wang, L., Lefever, J., & Cheng, Y. (2013). The evolved developmental niche: Longitudinal effects of caregiving practices on early childhood psychosocial development. *Early Childhood Research Quarterly, 28*, 759–773.

Narvaez, D., Panksepp, J., Schore, A., & Gleason, T. (Eds.). (2013). *Evolution, early experience, and human development: From research to practice and policy*. New York: Oxford University Press.

Narvaez, D., Wang, L., Cheng, Y., & Gleason, T. (2013). The importance of touch for early moral development. Manuscript in preparation.

Narvaez, D., Wang, L., Gleason, T., Cheng, Y., Lefever, J., & Deng, L. (2013). The evolved developmental niche and sociomoral outcomes in Chinese 3-year-olds. *European Journal of Developmental Psychology, 10*, 106–127.

Newburg, D. S., & Walker, W. A. (2007). Protection of the neonate by the innate immune system of developing gut and of human milk. *Pediatric Research, 61*, 2–8.

Oliner, S. P., & Oliner, P. M. (1988). *The altruistic personality: Rescuers of Jews in Nazi Europe*. New York: Free Press.

Pellegrini, A. D., & Smith, P. K. (1998). The development of play during childhood: Forms and possible functions. *Child Psychology & Psychiatry Review, 3*(2), 51–57.

Peterson, J. B., & Flanders, J. L. (Eds.). (2005). *Play and the regulation of aggression*. New York: Guilford Press.

Porges, S. W. (2007). The polyvagal perspective. *Biological Psychology, 74*(116–143).

Procianoy, R. S., Mendes, E. W., & Silveira, R. C. (2010). Massage therapy improves neurodevelopment outcome at two years corrected age for very low birth weight infants. *Early Human Development, 86*(1), 7–11.

Reis, H., Collins, W. A., & Berscheid, E. (2000). The relationship context of human behavior and development. *Psychological Bulletin, 126*, 844–872.

Rest, J. R. (1984). Research on moral development: Implications for training counseling psychologists. *The Counseling Psychologist, 12*(3–4), 19–29.

Rubin, K. H., Fein, G., & Vandenberg, B. (1983). Play. In E. M. Hetherington & P. H. Mussen (Eds.), *Handbook of child psychology. Vol. 4: Socialization, personality, and social behavior* (pp. 693–774). New York: Wiley.

Ryan, R. M., Martin, A., & Brooks-Gunn, J. (2006). Is one good parent good enough? Patterns of mother and father parenting and child cognitive outcomes at 24 and 36 months. *Parenting: Science and Practice, 6*(2-3), 211–228.

Schore, A. (1996). The experience-dependent maturation of a regulatory system in the orbital prefrontal cortex and the origin of developmental psychopathology. *Development and Psychopathology, 8*, 59–87.

Schore, A. (2001). Effects of a secure attachment relationship on right brain development, affect regulation, and infant mental health. *Infant Mental Health Journal, 22*, 7–66.

Shonkoff, J. P., & Garner, A. S. (2012). The lifelong effects of early childhood adversity and toxic stress. *Pediatrics, 129*(1), e232–e246.

Shonkoff, J. P., & Phillips, D. A. (2000). *From neurons to neighborhoods: The science of early childhood development*. Washington, DC: National Academy Press.

Siegel, D. J. (1999). *The developing mind: How relationships and the brain interact to shape who we are*. New York: Guilford Press.

Stern, D. N. (1999). Vitality contours: The temporal contour of feelings as a basic unit for constructing the infant's social experience. In P. Rochat (Ed.), *Early social cognition: Understanding others in the first months of life* (pp. 67–90). Mahwah, NJ: Erlbaum.

U.S. Department of Health and Human Services Substance Abuse and Mental Health Services Administration. (1999). *Mental health: A report of the Surgeon General*.

Rockville, MD: Center for Mental Health Services, National Institutes of Health, National Institute of Mental Health.

von Suchodoletz, A., Trommsdorff, G., & Heikamp, T. (2011). Linking maternal warmth and responsiveness to children's self-regulation. *Social Development, 20*(3), 486–503.

Walsh, W. A., Dawson, J., & Mattingly, M. J. (2010). How are we measuring resilience following childhood maltreatment? Is the research adequate and consistent? What is the impact on research, practice, and policy? *Trauma, Violence, & Abuse, 11*(1), 27–41.

Williams, G. C. (1966). *Adaptation and natural selection: A critique of some current evolutionary thought*. Princeton, NJ: Princeton University Press.

Winnicott, D. W. (1957). *The child and the family*. New York: Basic Books.

Wright, M. O. D., & Masten, A. S. (2005). Resilience processes in development: Fostering positive adaptation in the context of adversity. In S. Goldstein & R. B. Brooks (Eds.), *Handbook of resilience in children.* (pp. 17–37). New York: Kluwer Academic/Plenum Publishers.

Zahn-Waxler, C., & Radke-Yarrow, M. (1990). The origins of empathic concern. *Motivation and Emotion, 14*, 107–125.

Zolkoski, S. M., & Bullock, L. M. (2012). Resilience in children and youth: A review. *Children and Youth Services Review, 34*(12), 2295–2303.

15

Postscript

BACK TO THE FUTURE

James J. McKenna

We should acknowledge John Bowlby's ongoing contributions in helping contemporary researchers understand more fully the critical role of caregivers in shaping the developmental trajectories of young infants and children. An especially appropriate prelude in highlighting the integrative work reported in this volume is yet again offered by Bowlby himself. Using embryology as a metaphor for how mothers provide the scaffolding on which the infant's healthy development builds, he warns us:

"If growth is to proceed smoothly, the tissues must be exposed to the influence of the appropriate organizer at certain critical periods. In the same way, if mental development (of the infant) is to proceed smoothly, it would appear to be necessary for the undifferentiated psyche to be exposed during certain critical period to the influences of the psychic-organizer–the mother." (Bowlby,1951, discussed in Bretherton, 1992)

Perhaps we should not be too surprised by Bowlby's clever, spot-on attention to the importance of critical developmental windows, however more broadly primate plasticity requires us to conceptualize it. After all, he had a penchant for spending many long seminar hours building on his polymathic scholarship by familiarizing himself with Darwin's writings, and discussing human biological variability, with an array of eclectic scholars. Among them were psychologist Jean Piaget, biologists J. M. Tanner and Julian Huxley, general systems theorist Ludwig von Bertalanffy, ethologists Robert Hinde, Niko Tinbergen, and Konrad Lorenz, and anthropologist Margaret Mead. And especially relevant to the research reported here, Bowlby engaged intellectually with Harry Harlow, who was the first to initiate the long-term mother–infant research focusing on the rhesus macaque, the same species encompassed by the research of Dettmer, Suomi, and Hinde, who illustrated in chapter 3 just how far this and other lines of research have taken us. Indeed, every chapter in this volume reflects Bowlby's insistence on integration, holism, and using multidisciplinary perspectives to enrich, validate, and more fully if not critically explore the accuracy of any given set of underlying assumptions.

It is hard to know whether Bowlby's comment was intended simply as a meta-phor or as a subtle critique, perhaps, of his own work, which altogether missed the importance of breastfeeding to attachment, alloparents to infant survival, and the critical underlying *physiological* correlates associated with psychosocial (relational) processes, including with attachment itself. (Maybe we should be thankful that he left something for others to discover and to correct in the limitations of his own model.) Regardless, I am certain that he would be amazed by the diversity of disciplines repre-sented here, for which more traditional boundaries are being set aside in favor of more problem-driven, eclectic methods and theories. But that is not all. It would seem that there is a common realization similar to the one that Wilson (1998) envisioned in his perspective of the unity of knowledge—consilience, that a science of human develop-ment is not as it turns out composed of a dozen or so separate disciplines working alone but rather, of only one, involving many scientists working with vastly different backgrounds, coming together, best described as a social analogue to what is happen-ing intellectually. What is especially impressive is that although the level of analyses and the specific research collected focus on very different lines of evidence (genetic, ethnographic, experiential, cross-species, the effects of trauma and neglect, the role of symbolism, validating or promoting developmental experiences, laboratory based, field based, clinical based), the working consensus is the same: that developmental issues ultimately are best framed by evolutionary thinking requiring reference to a species phylogenetic history, while critical evolutionary questions can only be teased apart and understood by reference to how a species functions at different analytic levels that ultimately coalesce to find expression across a range of potential micro and macro habitats. Another way to state this is to say that especially during the past three decades, developmental studies have become much more evolutionary, while evolu-tionary studies have become much more developmental. Altogether, the real value of all of this unity is seen in the results, the insights gained, and recent successes in *exposing critical linkages between what look on the surface to be disparate, functionally disconnected adaptive systems and yet prove to be anything but that.*

And So Let the Next Phase Begin

All the chapters, including this summary, call attention to how a new integrative research model, comparative and holistic, evolutionary and developmental, has arrived and is poised to reveal even more "hidden" ontogenetic processes that accompany and accommodate infantile and childhood environmental experiences, all to adjust phenotypes generationally to meet the individuals' and, hence, the spe-cies' current conditions. It is extraordinary that we are on the verge of being able to understand and appreciate how biobehavioral systems evolved among various primate species to become sensitive to environmental signals in the first place. This "sensitivity" is linked into biochemical changes that adjust the *timing* as well as the form or degree of gene expression, epigenetically.

Indeed, the research investigations presented here collectively and by individual scholars from different fields serve as exemplars for identifying what primates really need for optimal growth and development and for psychological resiliency in general. Beautifully documented already are the ways primates encounter, create, experience, and most important, respond to their social and psychological environments in terms of a very flexible, learning-based, genetic system that first and foremost strives to achieve compatibility and accommodation. Certainly, much more at the molecular level will need to be clarified, such as the manner and timing by which specific alleles or allelic systems are turned on or off, and by what mechanism, in diverse social and physical habitats or circumstances. Still, on one hand, already documented here is the remarkable adaptive developmental capacities of two of the most successful primate species of all: rhesus macaques and ourselves, living as we do across so many diverse cultural and geographic topographies; but on the other hand, among primates, it is also impressive to consider just how easy it is to derail the individual's growth toward health and wellbeing. Of course, nonhuman primates, with such little control over what is done to or for them, do not have the advantages that humans do. But it would be a mistake to forget that, like nonhuman primates, human infants and children also have little or no control over their developmental settings, or who their caregivers are, or just how much access they have to more optimal familial caregiving. As Konner (2010) once said, "Its dangerous to be an infant!"

In concluding the privilege of responding to my colleagues' work, I would like all of us to remember every now and then to take some time away from our research activities to actualize, apply, and become at least momentarily a voice or advocate, a teacher outside our normal settings, to share as much of this appreciable knowledge as is possible. There will always be more to learn, of course, but there is also a lot we already know. And what we do know can be used to make a difference for infants and children by correcting or arguing in public venues and the media against damaging ideologies and recommendations that masquerade as science, recommendations like, "Never let an infant fall asleep at the breast," "Babies sleep safest alone," "Babies need to cry it out to develop their lungs," "Responding to infants in the middle of the night leads to excessive dependence," "Touching during co-sleeping sexualizes the baby," "The consolidation of infant sleep as early in life as is possible contributes critically to brain growth," and "Breastfeeding can actually poison infants, so formula is the sure bet." These are just a few of the many statements parents sent to me to respond to.

We have come a long way in understanding which primate infant care practices are more likely to be helpful than harmful and why, and I thank all my colleagues past and present for providing the critical knowledge that can be used to reject these inappropriate stereotypes. Please, wherever and whenever you can, feel free to join me, using that same remarkable spirit and intellect by which these enriching insights were collected, to improve the lives of those we love.

References

Bowlby, J. (1951). *Maternal care and mental health*. World Health Organization Monograph
   Serial Number 2.

Bretherton, I. (1992). The origins of attachment theory: John Bowlby and Mary Ainsworth.
   Developmental Psychology, *28*, 759–775.

Konner, M. (2010). *The evolution of childhood*. Cambridge, MA: Belknap Press of Harvard
   University Press.

Wilson, E. O. (1998). *Consilience: The unity of knowledge*. New York: Knopf.

{ INDEX }

The annotation of an italicized "f" or "t" indicates a reference to a figure or table on the specified page.